Resplendent Adventures with Britannia

I. *Adventures with Britannia* (1995)
II. *More Adventures with Britannia* (1998)
III. *Still More Adventures with Britannia* (2003)
IV. *Yet More Adventures with Britannia* (2005)
V. *Penultimate Adventures with Britannia* (2007)
VI. *Ultimate Adventures with Britannia* (2009)
VII. *Resurgent Adventures with Britannia* (2011)
VIII. *Irrepressible Adventures with Britannia* (2013)
IX. *Resplendent Adventures with Britannia* (2015)

and

Burnt Orange Britannia (2005)

RESPLENDENT ADVENTURES WITH

BRITANNIA
Personalities, Politics and Culture in Britain

Edited by Wm. Roger Louis

I.B.Tauris
London · New York

Harry Ransom Center
Austin

Published in 2015 by I. B. Tauris & Co Ltd
6 Salem Road, London W2 4BU
In the United States of America and Canada, distributed by
Palgrave Macmillan, a division of St. Martin's Press
175 Fifth Avenue, New York NY 10010
www.ibtauris.com

Harry Ransom Center
University of Texas at Austin
P.O. Drawer 7219
Austin, Texas 78713–7219

Copyright © 2015 by British Studies
University of Texas at Austin

All rights reserved. Except for brief quotations in a review, this book, or any part of it, may not be reproduced, stored in, or introduced into a retrieval system, or transmitted, in any form or by any means, electronic, mechanical, photocopying, recording, or otherwise, without the prior written permission of the publisher.

The paper used in this publication meets the minimum requirements of American National Standard for Information Sciences— Permanence of Paper for Printed Library Materials

ISBN 978–1-78453–472-1 hardcover
ISBN 978–1-78453–473-8 paperback

Library of Congress Control Number: 2015911539

Print production by Studio Azul, Inc., Austin, Texas

Table of Contents

	List of Authors	ix
	Introduction *Wm. Roger Louis*	1
1	Major General Charles Gordon *Richard Davenport-Hines*	21
2	The Men Who Ruled Palestine *Bernard Wasserstein*	35
3	Nancy Lambton *John Gurney*	57
4	Siegfried Sassoon *Max Egremont*	71
5	Bloomsbury's Memoir Club *Rosemary Hill*	77
6	Dylan Thomas *Kurt Heinzelman*	87
7	Philip Larkin *Joseph Epstein*	101
8	Army Life *Keith Thomas*	107
9	Gandhi *Perry Anderson*	117
10	Paul Scott *Peter Green*	131
11	*Towards Freedom* *Sucheta Mahajan*	141

12	Reflections on Early Modern Ireland *Jane Ohlmeyer*	153
13	Pleasures of the Poor *Nicholas Rogers*	163
14	The Men Who Lost America *Andrew O'Shaughnessy*	177
15	Genocide in Tasmania *Bernard Porter*	189
16	Lost Expeditions, Lost Histories *Dane Kennedy*	199
17	The Reform Club *Roger Billis*	211
18	The British Monarchy and the Tsar *Jane Ridley*	225
19	A Love Triangle: Woodrow Wilson, Colonel House, and the British *John Milton Cooper, Jr.*	239
20	Wales and the First World War *Kenneth O. Morgan*	251
21	The United Nations and Colonial Independence *Thomas Meaney*	265
22	South by Southwest: South Africa, South West Africa, and the Commonwealth *Molly McCullers*	275
23	Lost Causeways: Oxford, Experts, and the Motor Age *William Whyte*	289
24	Harold Macmillan *Ferdinand Mount*	303
25	The Last Colonial War *David Ramsbotham*	317

26	Blair and Bush *Michael Brenner*	333
27	Well Played! An Architectural View of Sports *Richard Cleary*	339
28	The Scottish Question in British Politics *Archie Brown*	355
29	British National Identity *Lawrence Goldman*	369
30	Some Notes on the Americans *A. N. Duckham*	383
31	British Studies at the University of Texas, 1975–2015	397

List of Authors

Perry Anderson, who studied modern languages at Oxford, is an historian and political essayist. He is Professor of History and Sociology at the University of California, Los Angeles. He was Editor of the *New Left Review* from 1962 to 1982 and remains a contributor. His writings also appear frequently in the *London Review of Books*. His most recent book is *American Foreign Policy and Its Thinkers* (2015).

Roger Billis studied history at Brasenose College, Oxford, and then became a commercial lawyer practicing in London, Hong Kong, and Tokyo. He was Chairman of the Reform Club in 2004–5. His publications include *Reformed Characters: The Reform Club in History and Literature* (joint compiler and editor) and two books of verse: *All Five Senses* (2013) and *Some Lasting Monuments: Fifty Oxford Sonnets* (2015).

Michael Brenner taught for many years at the University of Pittsburgh and is now a Fellow of British Studies at the University of Texas. His writings on European politics and American foreign policy include *Technocratic Politics and the Functionalist Theory of European Integration* (1969), *The Political Economy of International Monetary Reform* (1976), *NATO and Collective Security* (1998), and, most recently, *Narcissistic Public Personalities* (2009).

Archie Brown taught at Glasgow University from 1964 to 1971, when he moved to Oxford as a Fellow of St. Antony's College. From 1989 he was Professor of Politics at Oxford University. A Fellow of the British Academy since 1991, he was appointed CMG in 2005. His most recent book is on political leadership worldwide: *The Myth of the Strong Leader: Political Leadership in the Modern Age* (2014).

Richard Cleary has taught architectural history at the University of Texas since 1995. His books include *Merchant Prince and Master Builder: Edgar J. Kaufmann and Frank Lloyd Wright* (1999), on the Kaufmann family's long association with the architect; *The Place Royale and Urban Design in the Ancien Régime* (1999), on public squares in France; and *Bridges* (2007), a survey of bridge design in the United States.

John Milton Cooper, Jr., studied at Princeton and then earned his Ph.D. from Columbia University. He has taught at the University of Wisconsin–Madison for forty-three years as E. Gordon Fox Professor of American Institutions. His specialization is nineteenth- and twentieth-century American history. His recent work has focused on the wartime era 1914–18. His latest book is *Woodrow Wilson: A Biography* (2009).

Richard Davenport-Hines is a past winner of the Wolfson Prize for History and Biography. His biographical subjects include W. H. Auden, Marcel Proust, Lady Desborough, and Edward VII. He has written histories of syphilis and sexual oppression, drug taking, the Gothic Revival, the sinking of the *Titanic,* and the Profumo Affair. His most recent book is *The Universal Man: The Seven Lives of John Maynard Keynes* (2015).

Alec Narraway Duckham (1903–1988) matriculated at Clare College, Cambridge, in 1922. He served as Agricultural Attaché at the British Embassy in Washington (1945–51), traveling widely and giving lectures. He was later Professor of Agriculture at the University of Reading (1954–68), where his papers are now kept. His books include *American Agriculture: Its Background and Its Lessons* (1952) and *Farming Systems of the World* (1970).

Max Egremont, Eton and Christ Church, Oxford, is a novelist and biographer. After studying modern history at Christ Church, he worked on the staff of U.S. Senator Hugh Scott. His biographical studies include *The Cousins: The Friendship, Opinions, and Activities of Wilfrid Scawen Blunt and George Wyndham* (1977) and *Siegfried Sassoon* (2012). His most recent book is *Some Desperate Glory: The First World War the Poets Knew* (2015).

Joseph Epstein is the author of twenty-five books. Two forthcoming books of his are *Frozen in Time,* a collection of short stories, and *Wind Sprints,* a collection of his shorter essays. *Snobbery: The American Version* was published in 2002. He was the Editor of Phi Beta Kappa's *The American Scholar* magazine, 1974–98. In 2003 he won the National Humanities Medal of the National Endowment for the Humanities.

Lawrence Goldman was educated at Cambridge and taught at Oxford from 1985 to 2014. He is now Director of the Institute of Historical Research in London. He was Editor of the *Oxford Dictionary of*

National Biography, 2004–14. He has published monographs on Victorian social science and adult education. His most recent book is *The Life of R.H. Tawney: Socialism and History* (2013).

Peter Green as a student in Cambridge achieved a Double First in Classics. For many years the Dougherty Professor of Classics at the University of Texas, he is now a classical scholar at the University of Iowa. His books include *Alexander to Actium* (1990) and *The Iliad: A New Translation* (2015). During the Second World War, he met Paul Scott, who used Green as the model for Sergeant Guy Perron in the *Raj Quartet*.

John Gurney is a scholar of Persian and Persian history at Oxford. A Fellow of Wadham College, his research interests in Iranian history include the Safavid and Qajar dynasties. He is now working on a biographical study of Edward Granville Browne, the Orientalist who is remembered today, among other reasons, because of a street in Tehran still named after him despite the Iranian Revolution of 1979.

Kurt Heinzelman is the Editor of *Texas Studies in Literature and Language*. He is a former executive curator at the Harry Ransom Center and director of education at the Blanton Museum, University of Texas. An Honorary Professor at Swansea University, his books include *The Economics of the Imagination* (criticism); *Demarcations* (translations); *The Names They Found There* and *Intimacies & Other Devices* (poetry collections).

Rosemary Hill is an historian of art and ideas. Her biography of A. W. N. Pugin, *God's Architect* (2007), won the Wolfson History Prize. She is a contributing editor to the *London Review of Books*, Fellow of the Royal Society of Literature, Quondam Fellow of All Souls College, Oxford, and a member of Historic England's Blue Plaques Committee. Her current research is on antiquarianism in the Romantic period.

Dane Kennedy received his Ph.D. from the University of California, Berkeley, in 1981. He taught at the University of Nebraska before moving to Washington, D.C., to teach at George Washington University as the Elmer Louis Kayser Professor of History. His most recent books are *The Last Blank Spaces: Exploring Africa and Australia* (2013) and, as editor, *Reinterpreting Exploration: The West in the World* (2013).

Sucheta Mahajan is Professor of History in the Centre for Historical Studies at Jawaharlal Nehru University, where she teaches courses on Indian history emphasizing nationalism and decolonization. Her books include *Independence and Partition: The Erosion of Colonial Power in India* (2000). She is the Editor of the 1947 volume in the series *Towards Freedom: Documents on the Movement for Independence in India*.

Molly McCullers earned her Ph.D. in African History at Emory University in 2012 and has taught at Spelman College and Davidson College. She is now Assistant Professor of History at the University of West Georgia. She is working on a book to be entitled *South by Southwest*, which examines competing historical accounts and plans for the future of South West Africa during era of apartheid.

Thomas Meaney studied at the University of Chicago and is a Ph.D. candidate in history at Columbia University. He is writing a book about decolonization from both the American and British perspectives. His writing has appeared in the *New York Review of Books*, the *London Review of Books*, and the *Times Literary Supplement*. He is also a regular contributor to the *Nation* and an editor of *The Utopian*.

Kenneth O. Morgan has taught at The Queen's College, Oxford, and Columbia University, and is now at King's College, London. A Fellow of the British Academy and Labour member of the House of Lords, his books include the *Oxford Illustrated History of Britain* (one million copies sold) and biographies of Keir Hardie, Lloyd George, James Callaghan, and Michael Foot. His memoir, *My Histories*, appeared in September 2015.

Ferdinand Mount's novels include a six-volume sequence, *Chronicle of Modern Twilight*. (The title alludes to the sequence *A Chronicle of Ancient Sunlight* by Henry Williamson.) He was head of the Prime Minister's Policy Unit from 1982 to 1984, and Editor of the *Times Literary Supplement* from 1991 to 2002. His latest book is *The Tears of the Rajas: Mutiny, Money, and Marriage in India, 1805–1905* (2015).

Jane Ohlmeyer is Erasmus Smith Professor of History at Trinity College, Dublin. She is the author or editor of eleven books, including *Making Ireland English: The Irish Aristocracy in the Seventeenth Century* (2012). The Editor of volume 2 of the *Cambridge History of Ireland*, she is also an Investigator on the 1641 Depositions Project. She is currently working on a study of colonial Ireland and colonial India.

Andrew Jackson O'Shaughnessy is the Vice President of the Thomas Jefferson Foundation at Monticello, Virginia, and Professor of History at the University of Virginia. He is the author of *An Empire Divided: The American Revolution and the British Caribbean* (2000). His most recent book is the prize-winning *The Men Who Lost America: British Leadership, the American Revolution, and the Fate of the Empire* (2013).

Bernard Porter is Professor of History at Newcastle University. His books include *The Lion's Share: A History of British Imperialism* (1975); *The Absent Minded Imperialists: Empire, Society, and Culture in Britain* (2004); and *The Battle of the Styles: Society, Culture, and the Design of a New Foreign Office, 1855–61* (2011). He writes frequently for the *London Review of Books* and *History Today*. A collection of his essays, *Imperial Ways*, is in press.

David Ramsbotham retired from the British Army in 1993. His career then took him to United Nations peacekeeping, advising both the British government and the Under-Secretary General. He was director of international affairs of a company working on post-conflict reconstruction. From 1995 to 2001, he was Her Majesty's Chief Inspector of Prisons. In 2005 he was appointed an independent member of the House of Lords.

Jane Ridley studied at St. Hugh's College, Oxford, and Nuffield College, Oxford. She is Professor of History at Buckingham University. She won the Duff Cooper Prize in 2002 for *The Architect and His Wife*, a biography of her great-grandfather Edwin Lutyens. Her other books include *Bertie: A Life of Edward VII* (2012) and *Queen Victoria* (2014). She is working on a biography of King George V.

Nicholas Rogers is Distinguished Research Professor in the Department of History, York University, Toronto. A former editor of the *Journal of British Studies,* he is the author of five books on the eighteenth century. The last, entitled *Mayhem: Post-War Crime and Violence in Britain, 1749–53* (2012), won the John Ben Snow prize in British history, awarded by the North American Conference on British Studies.

Keith Thomas is a Distinguished Fellow of All Souls College, Oxford, a former President of Corpus Christi College, and a past President of the British Academy. His books include *Religion and the Decline of Magic* (1971), *Man and the Natural World: Changing Attitudes in*

England, 1500–1800 (1983), and *The Ends of Life: Roads to Fulfillment in Early Modern England* (2009). He edited the *Oxford Book of Work* (1999).

Bernard Wasserstein is a Visiting Professor at the Ludwig-Maximilians Universität Munich. He previously taught history at the University of Chicago. His books include *The British in Palestine: The Mandatory Government and the Arab-Jewish Conflict* (1978), *Israelis and Palestinians: Why Do They Fight? Can They Stop?* (2003), *Barbarism and Civilization* (2007), and *On the Eve: The Jews of Europe before the Second World War* (2012).

William Whyte studied at Wadham College, Oxford. A Fellow of St. John's College, Oxford, he is also Senior Dean and Professor of Social and Architectural History. His publications include *Oxford Jackson: Architecture, Education, Status, and Style* (2006) and *Redbrick: A Social and Architectural History of Britain's Civic Universities* (2015). He is currently writing a book to be entitled *The University: A Material History*.

The editor, Wm. Roger Louis, is Kerr Professor of English History and Culture and Distinguished Teaching Professor at the University of Texas at Austin, an Honorary Fellow of St. Antony's College, Oxford, and a past President of the American Historical Association. His books include *Imperialism at Bay* (1976), *The British Empire in the Middle East* (1984), and *Ends of British Imperialism* (2006). He is the Editor-in-Chief of the *Oxford History of the British Empire*. In 2013, he was awarded the Benson Medal of the Royal Society of Literature.

Introduction

WM. ROGER LOUIS

This volume begins, as have its predecessors, by endorsing G. H. Hardy's belief that the agony of having to repeat oneself is so excruciating that it is best to end the agony by offering no apology for doing so. In the spirit of the adventurous refrain—more, still more, yet more, penultimate, ultimate, resurgent, irrepressible, and now resplendent—I once again follow his example. This book consists of a representative selection of lectures given to the British Studies seminar at the University of Texas at Austin. Most of the present lectures were delivered in the years 2013–15.

Lectures are different from essays or scholarly articles. A lecture presumes an audience rather than a reader and usually has a more conversational tone. It allows greater freedom in the expression of personal or subjective views. It permits and invites greater candor. It is sometimes informally entertaining as well as anecdotally instructive. In this volume, the lecture sometimes takes the form of intellectual autobiography—an account of how the speaker has come to grips with a significant topic in the field of British Studies, which, broadly defined, means things British throughout the world as well as things that happen to be English, Irish, Scottish, or Welsh. The scope of British Studies includes all disciplines in the social sciences and humanities as well as music, architecture, and the visual arts. Most of the lectures in this collection fall within the fields of history, politics, and literature, though the dominant themes, here as previously, are literary and historical. Occasionally though rarely, the lectures have to be given in absentia. In such cases, the lectures or at least substantial parts of them are read and then critically discussed. The full sweep of the lectures will be apparent from the list at the end of the book, which is reproduced in its entirety to give a comprehensive idea of the seminar's evolution and substance.

In 2015, the British Studies seminar celebrated its fortieth year. The circumstances for its creation were favorable because of the existence of the Humanities Research Center, now the Harry Ransom Center, at the University of Texas. Harry Ransom was the founder of the HRC, a Professor of English and later Chancellor of the University, a collector of rare books, and a man of humane vision. Through the administrative and financial creativity of Ransom and subsequent directors, the HRC has developed into a superlative literary archive with substantial collections, especially in English literature. Ransom thought a weekly seminar might provide the opportunity to learn of the original research being conducted at the HRC as well as to create common bonds of intellectual interest in a congenial setting of overstuffed armchairs, Persian carpets, and generous libations of sherry. The seminar was launched in the fall semester of 1975. It has remained consistent in its dual purpose of providing a forum for visiting scholars engaged in research at the HRC and of enabling the members of the seminar to discuss their own work.

The sherry at the Friday seminar sessions symbolizes the attitude. The seminar meets to discuss whatever happens to be on the agenda, Scottish or Indian, Canadian or Jamaican, English or Australian. George Bernard Shaw once said that England and America were two great countries divided by a common language, but he understated the case by several countries. The interaction of British and other societies is an endlessly fascinating subject on which points of view do not often converge. Diverse preconceptions, which are tempered by different disciplines, help initiate and then sustain controversy, not end it. The ongoing discussions in British Studies are engaging because of the clash of different perspectives as well as the nuance of cultural interpretation. Though the printed page cannot capture the atmosphere of engaged discussion, the lectures do offer the opportunity to savor the result of wide-ranging research and reflection.

I am grateful to Philippa Levine, the Co-Director of British Studies, for help in sustaining the program. The seminar has two University sponsors, the College of Liberal Arts and the Harry Ransom Center. We are indebted to the Dean of Liberal Arts, Randy Diehl, for his support and especially for allocating resources for the program of Junior Fellows—a few assistant professors appointed each year to bring fresh blood, brash ideas, and new commitment to the program. We are equally grateful to Stephen Enniss, the Director of the HRC, for providing a home for the seminar. I wish also to thank Frances Terry, who has handled the week-by-week administrative detail from early on in the seminar's history. I am indebted to Kip Keller and Holly McCarthy for their steadfast assistance in many ways.

The seminar benefits especially from the support of the Creekmore and Adele Fath Foundation. When Creekmore Fath was an undergraduate at the University of Texas in the 1930s, he valued especially the chance to exchange ideas and become friends with faculty members. The Fath Foundation now enables the seminar to offer undergraduate and graduate scholarships and generally to advance the cause of the liberal arts. The students appointed to scholarships are known as Churchill Scholars. The Churchill Scholars, like the Junior Fellows, not only contribute to the vitality of the seminar but also extend its age range from those in their late teens to their late eighties.

For vital support we continue to thank the late Baine and Mildred Kerr of Houston, John and Susan Kerr of San Antonio, Becky Gale and the late Edwin Gale of Beaumont, Custis Wright and the late Charles Alan Wright of Austin, Tex and Charles Moncrief of Fort Worth, Althea Osborn, David Osborn, and the late Robert Osborn, and the two dozen stouthearted members of the seminar who have contributed to its endowment. We are indebted to Dean Robert D. King for his help over many years. I again extend special thanks to Sam Jamot Brown and Sherry Brown of Durango, Colorado.

THE CHAPTERS—MORE PRECISELY, THE LECTURES—are clustered together more or less chronologically and thematically. A word needs to be said about the last chapter in the book. We have never before published an archival document in the Britannia series. It is a memorandum by the agricultural attaché at the British Embassy in Washington in the five or so years after the Second World War. When I discovered it some three decades ago at the Public Record Office (as it was then called), I believed it to be an exceptionally candid assessment of the American people. So had the Ambassador in 1950, Sir Oliver Franks, who hoped that it would be read by all officials having anything to do with the affairs of the United States. I later learned from Sir Peter Ramsbotham that he had a copy in his private papers, which he had found in a file in the British Embassy when he was Ambassador in the 1970s. It has thus banged around in official circles as a document that has stood the test of time, perhaps for a variety of reasons. For all I know, it may still be mandatory reading for all British officials dealing with the United States. It carries the security classification "Guard," in other words, not for American eyes.

The first chapter deals with General Charles Gordon, known historically as Gordon of Khartoum, who died a martyr in January 1885. **Richard Davenport-Hines** challenges many long-held assumptions about a figure who has been written about extensively. He explains why Gordon's death came as a shock to the British nation, why the public hysteria matched the mourning for Princess Diana in 1997. He was an improbable national hero. Winston Churchill recorded that he was "erratic, capricious, utterly unreliable," and "frequently drunk." Yet he resembled T. E. Lawrence in his ability to conduct guerilla warfare and impose his will on his "rabble of troops." He devoted much of his leisure time to the study of the Bible. In the mid-1870s he was appointed Governor-General of Sudan. Among Arabs he acquired the reputation of a "mystical and almost divine character." After Sudan fell under the tempestuous sway of the Mahdi, Gordon was ordered to evacuate the beleaguered garrison at Khartoum. But he decided to resist the Mahdi rather than to conduct a humiliating evacuation. On 26 January 1885, Gordon was speared and beheaded on the steps of the Governor-General's palace. According to legend, his severed head was taken to the Mahdi, the one time they saw each other face to face. Gordon's martyrdom became a symbol for the civilizing mission of the British Empire. His reputation was not seriously called into question until Lytton Strachey's pen portrait in *Eminent Victorians*. The reappraisal by Davenport-Hines, a study in its own right, is in some ways an inspired continuation of Strachey's devastating depiction.

Bernard Wasserstein assesses the seven men who ruled Palestine between 1920 and 1948. They held the title of High Commissioner rather than Governor because of Palestine's status as a mandate of the League of Nations. They were in effect colonial governors holding full administrative and military authority. At the beginning of the mandate era, and as late as 1939, Zionists in England as well as politicians and officials within the British government hoped that an independent Jewish state might become a member of the British Commonwealth. But from the mid-1930s until end of the mandate, the British faced increasing hostility from Arabs and Zionists alike. Each of the High Commissioners held the responsibility to further the creation of a Jewish national home as promised by the Balfour Declaration of 1917; but each had the duty also to protect the Arab majority in Palestine. Each responded differently to the resulting "cacophony of pressures." The end of the mandate was disastrous. There was no transfer of power, simply a withdrawal. The British refused to preside over partition. But secretly they aimed at a division that would give advantage to King Hussein of Jordan. The Arab Legion of Jordan occupied the main part of Arab Palestine, thus giving, in a word used by Winston Churchill, a "thump" to further irredentism.

Anne Lambton, known to her friends as "Nancy," was the most distinguished scholar of the Persian language and history of her time. **John Gurney** traces the turning points in her life, one of which took place at the age of eighteen when she began studying Persian. In 1936 she traveled extensively in Iran, accepting the hospitality of British missionaries, rural families, and employees of the Anglo-Iranian Oil Company. She was in Tehran when war broke out in 1939. For the next six years she assisted the Ambassador, Sir Reader Bullard. She spoke Persian fluently; she made broadcasts in Persian and published articles in Persian newspapers. A myth began to develop: might she have a connection with British intelligence? We will not know the extent of the intelligence connection, if any, until MI6 records are opened, if ever. After the war she returned to scholarship and published her major work, *Landlord and Peasant in Persia* (1953). In the same year, Muhammad Musaddiq nationalized the AIOC. Officials within the British government asked her for advice, at least informally. She responded that Musaddiq could be replaced by "relatively enlightened" Iranians who would work with the British toward stable relations between the two countries. She did not take part in the actual overthrow of Musaddiq. Yet for better or worse she has been irrevocably associated with his downfall.

Max Egremont's lecture, which has been severely condensed, asks whether the digitization of Siegfried Sassoon's diaries by the Cambridge Digital Library will damage his reputation. It is a good question. A compulsive writer, Sassoon composed some of the most powerful poetry of the First World War. He won the Military Cross for brave, indeed reckless, missions across front lines, lobbing grenades in enemy trenches. His poems described the futility of war. In 1917 he denounced British war aims as "evil and unjust." Regarded as shell-shocked, he was ordered to Craiglockhart sanitarium in Scotland. Sassoon eventually returned to the battlefields of France, taking with him his red-bound set of diaries and notebooks. They reveal a courageous man who was also self-absorbed, even narcissistic. Sassoon lived until 1967, giving the impression that he had outlived his time. He continued to be an odd mixture of idealism and complacency, embittered in his belief that his style of poetry had been eclipsed by the modernism of T. S. Eliot and Ezra Pound. The diaries do not diminish his merits as a poet or his stature as the author of the great fictionalized autobiography *Memoirs of a Fox-Hunting Man* (1928). Sassoon was one of those rare men of historical as well as literary significance. The diaries express the turbulent emotions of a self-centered, awkward, and introverted personality, but in Egremont's judgment, his reputation as a poet and soldier will endure.

The Memoir Club started in 1920 as a continuation of prewar "Old Bloomsbury." **Rosemary Hill** makes the case that in its initial years, at least, it had the same intellectual energy. The dozen or so members included Virginia and Leonard Woolf, Lytton Strachey, John Maynard Keynes, and, occasionally, E. M. Forster. The requirement for membership was candor and honesty. The Bloomsberries (their own word) valued privacy and "the terrors of intimacy" as they presented papers dealing with their own pasts. The subjects were autobiographical, biographical, and sometimes historical—Strachey, the reader learns, required an historian to have a "unique" point of view. Maynard Keynes rather pompously believed that the purpose was to solidify and continue the "High Intelligence of England." Curiously enough, the memoirists seldom discussed the First World War—as Leonard Woolf put it, they seemed to be alienated from the recent past. There was thus a "historical moat" between the Memoir Club and Old Bloomsbury. The society retained its vitality and verve in the early 1920s, lapsed until 1928, and then limped to an end in the 1950s.

The year 2015 marked the hundredth anniversary of Dylan Thomas's birth. **Kurt Heinzelman** begins his inquiry into Thomas's enduring reputation by pointing out that he died at age thirty-nine and had not received much recent public attention until his centenary. Thomas as a poet seems to have disappeared from public view. There are at least two reasons. One is that he fell out of fashion with critics and academics. The other, paradoxically, is that he became popular. Thomas achieved his greatest fame while visiting the United States in the early 1950s. He read his poetry to college audiences across the country. He gave the impression, not far removed from the reality, of a young poet of scandalous behavior, as much a barroom raconteur as a distinguished university visitor. Thomas himself was not without a certain humorous sense of self-awareness, once describing himself as "a little fat man come to make a fool of himself." But fame was fleeting, and after falling out of fashion, he was nevertheless remembered as a poet with a booming delivery and a slight Welsh accent. "A Child's Christmas in Wales" became one of his most popular recordings, and so his voice became familiar to many who had never read his poetry. Despite a decline in general esteem, he may, as Kurt Heinzelman suggests, fare better in his second century.

Joseph Epstein argues in this highly compressed lecture that Philip Larkin was one of the very few poets of the last half century who wrote memorable, perhaps unforgettable poetry. Yet he seemed to be a man who belonged to another age. At St. John's College, Oxford, he became friends with Kingsley Amis. The two later conducted a notoriously scabrous, obscene correspondence. Larkin in fact was decent, witty, and convivial. His breakthrough as a poet came in 1950, when he wrote some of his best-known poems. Two decades later, while a Visiting Fellow at All Souls, he worked on the *Oxford Book of Twentieth-Century English Verse* (1973). Its reception was mixed, but he won praise from W. H. Auden and John Betjeman, both of whom he held in high esteem. During the last three decades of his life, Larkin was Librarian at the University of Hull. He built the library into one of the most efficient and resourceful ones in Britain. Toward the end of his life, he declined the Poet Laureateship on grounds that his creativity had come to an end. After his death, his reputation came under attack with the publication of his selected letters. Larkin acquired a reputation as a misogynist who made crude jokes about women and left-wing students, once referring to "Irish swine." Despite the vulgarity of his letters, his poetry continues to hold a place of its own, winning admirers in Britain and throughout the world

Many people who know, or know of, **Keith Thomas** as the Distinguished Fellow of All Souls and past President of the British Academy may be surprised at this account of his national service in Jamaica. Before his time as a student in Oxford, Thomas served in the same regiment as Robert Graves and Siegfried Sassoon; but those historic names were cold comfort in "the horrors of the barrack room," where soldiers spoke in "an unbroken stream of obscenity." Nonetheless, the rough ways of the army left little lasting impression on an eighteen-year-old who had led a sheltered life of "priggish innocence." He and his companions visited the American base at Guantanamo, where they "were amazed by the luxurious facilities." He seems not yet to have discovered his anthropological approach to history while in the Caribbean, though his experience in Jamaica at that time would certainly be a good subject to reconstruct. He was hardly aware that the purpose of the military presence in Jamaica was "to hold together the crumbling remains of the British Empire." He did acquire a liking for military bands and movies such as *Tunes of Glory*, together with a fondness for a Jamaican accent. But the immediate result was a resolve, once he got Oxford, never to leave.

Gandhi has always been a controversial personality. **Perry Anderson** emphasizes the contradictions between the spiritual icon and the political leader. He was charismatic, he could mobilize crowds, and he was an efficient manager—quick, fluent, yet often contradictory. He possessed both an impish wit and a will of iron. He gradually came to be regarded as semi-divine figure despite his autocratic temperament. He regarded himself, as he often said, as Hindu to the core. He held consistently that nonviolent resistance, or satyagraha (holding on to truth), was a religious cause in which Hindus could join with Muslims against the British. On the question of violence, Gandhi was more ambivalent than is commonly recognized. In 1942 he proclaimed that "rivers of blood" might be necessary for India to achieve freedom. Yet he did not want the British to depart if it would bring about social upheaval: "Revolution was a greater danger than the Raj." In trying to hold India together, the problem was caste. When Muslims and Sikhs insisted on separate electorates, that is to say, on being recognized as formally separate parts of Indian society, so also did the Untouchables, led by Bhimrao Ambedkar. Gandhi believed that the plight of the Untouchables was indeed abominable. But they were an integral part of Hindu society. Their autonomy would lead to the disintegration of Hinduism itself. Such was Gandhi's fundamental belief in caste as the cornerstone of Hindu India that he would fast to death rather than yield on this fundamental point. In response, "Ambedkar yielded to Gandhi's blackmail."

Peter Green and Paul Scott first met as soldiers in 1944 at a bar in Calcutta. Scott's army service in India was the turning point in his career, but it took some seven years before he began work on what became his masterpiece on the twilight of the Raj. (Though Peter Green is too modest to mention it, he became the model for the hero of the series, Sergeant Perron.) In 1964, Scott made the first of three trips to India. In Calcutta he met Neil Ghosh, who had a British public-school education and spoke neither Hindi nor Urdu; Ghosh became Hari Kumar in the *Raj Quartet*. Ronald Merrick, the malevolent police officer present in the *Quartet* from beginning to end, obliquely represents the Indian Police and the Indian Civil Service—a troubling thought to all honorable British officers who served in India. Other key figures include Colonel John and Mildred Layton (the epitome of an English bitch), and their two daughters, Sarah and Susan. The *Quartet* thus became the saga of a British military family. In Green's judgment, Scott "never put a foot wrong psychologically over either caste or gender," making the series "a tour de force virtually without rivals." He mentions that Paul Scott visited the University of Texas in 1975. He was the first speaker in the British Studies seminar, the first speaker of some 1,000 subsequent meetings every Friday afternoon.

Sucheta Mahajan explains the past and present status of the vast Indian documentary series *Towards Freedom: Documents on the Movement for Independence in India*. The historian Sarvepalli Gopal played a vital part in the early stages of the project, which was intended to be an independent historical venture, neither sponsored by the Indian government nor planned as an equivalent of the British *Transfer of Power* series. *Towards Freedom* reflects all aspects of the Indian movement for independence. The series was launched in 1988. But in 2000 the Indian government stopped its publication, under the influence of the Bharatiya Janata Party (the dominant partner in the coalition of the time). The motive for repression was to prevent the exposure of "collaboration" by the extremist Hindu party, the Mahasabha, with the British. The censorship provoked national outrage. The series was reinstated in 2004. Mahajan was asked to prepare the volume for the critical year 1947. Commenting on the volume itself, she explains that the two principal leaders of the Indian National Congress, Jawaharlal Nehru and Vallabhbhai Patel, decided that Partition was necessary in order to avoid civil war. She emphasizes also that one of their main achievements was successfully to resist the pressure to declare a Hindu state. The volume itself is only one of three parts dedicated to the year 1947. Part 1 fills 1,318 pages—in view of the subject of India's independence, perhaps symbolically as long as the statue being erected in Gujarat of Vallabhbhai Patel is high, 597 feet.

Jane Ohlmeyer reflects on the themes of her major book, *Making Ireland English*, and the useful points she received from critics. The argument can be summarized thus: the first seven decades of the seventeenth century saw the anglicization of the Irish aristocracy. Her book is a study of the acquisition and maintenance of power, the making of Irish elite society. The new aristocrats shared a corporate identity grounded in service to the monarchy. They drew their legitimacy from the English Crown. Their cultural stamp was distinctly English. They shared a sense of honor and represented styles of living that were extended to their descendants for the next two centuries. What then are the useful questions generated by the book's publication? They include thematic issues as well as points of context. What is the difference between making Ireland English and making Ireland British, a common theme in the past? Did the Irish elite play a part in the formation of the British imperial state? And what of comparisons with other states or empires, for example, the Mughal or Ottoman? Some of the answers reveal the extent to which the book has unsettled the ideas of established scholars. What of further work? She concludes that Ireland has been studied as a "laboratory for Empire." In view of the scale of migration to North America, scholarship has focused, for example, on commercial links with the West Indies and plantations in Virginia. Ohlmeyer proposes now to look eastward, especially to India.

Nicholas Rogers discusses the sudden, widespread popularity of gin in the eighteenth century, described by some historians as "the first modern drug craze." He catches the spirit of Gin Lane. In the late seventeenth century, gin began to rival beer as the most popular drink in England, but there was no control over its quality. Gin was frequently mixed with turpentine. Its consumption by the poor raised alarming questions. Those who took a cataclysmic view believed rotgut gin to be a cause of social unrest that would lead to the breakdown of society. It seemed to spawn crime, prostitution, lunacy, anarchy, and social upheaval. Unless gin drinking could be brought under control, the English would become an alcoholic race of degenerates. Even affluent alehouses, which offered not merely ale but also newspapers and tobacco, were affected. Gin disrupted such social hubs. The consequences of addiction were most easily seen in William Hogarth's famous print of Gin Lane of 1751, depicting infanticide, madness, suicide, starvation, decay, and death. By contrast, another Hogarth print portrays the inhabitants of Beer Street as healthy and happy, nourished by native English ale. The Gin Act of 1751 curbed production, which fell by nearly half within the year. Alehouses were on their way to becoming pubs; and gin became regulated. Paradoxically, making gin more respectable and more costly made it more democratic.

In an assessment of the men who lost America, **Andrew O'Shaughnessy** begins the story with George III. In the 1770s he was still physically strong and mentally robust. He proclaimed that unless America could be held, Britain would descend in rank to the lowest of the European powers. In America itself, two dates were crucial: in October 1777 at Saratoga, General John Burgoyne surrendered more than 6,500 men. Four years later to the month, Lord Cornwallis, trapped in Yorktown, was forced to surrender, effectively ceding victory to the new United States. The fundamental mistake was the assumption that most American Royalists would remain loyal. Many were ambivalent but not suicidal. What also swung the balance was that after Burgoyne's capitulation, France and Spain began to support the Patriots. A French fleet blockaded Yorktown. Toward the end, the heroic but disreputable Admiral Rodney, with malice aforethought, pillaged St. Eustatius in the Netherlands Antilles. That act of almost unbelievable greed threw off the Royal Navy's plan to support Cornwallis. It became impossible to supply the required troops and still secure Britain's home waters and the empire worldwide. In short, the overextension of the fleet was a principal reason for Britain's defeat. Yet despite losing America, the British saved Canada, the West Indies, Gibraltar, and India, thus securing the foundations of the global empire.

Bernard Porter examines the virtual extinction of the Tasmanians in the early nineteenth century. Tasmania, or Van Diemen's Land, as it was then called, was a notorious penal colony. The indigenous population at the beginning of the century was probably 5,000 to 10,000. Three-quarters of a century later, it was close to zero. The Colonial Office in London had kept a wary eye on Tasmania, but colonies of settlement were supposed to finance themselves. In 1830 the Colonial Office sanctioned the confinement of the aborigines to a small island named Flinders off the coast. The native Tasmanians were thus cut off from their homeland. They had fought to preserve the land, which they owned collectively. But within five years they agreed to resettlement, knowing that the alternative was extermination. They did not fare well in their new home, which was barren. Some fifteen years later there were only fifty survivors. Disease played a large part in the reduction of the population. The question is, was it genocide, British genocide? Porter considers the evidence ambiguous and in any event inconclusive. According to the United Nations definition, genocide requires planned intent. The white settlers in Tasmania were certainly intent on appropriating the land. They viewed the aborigines as subhuman. And the massacres certainly resembled those that marked the conquest of the American West. Yet the case for genocide, in his judgment, is weak. In 1997 the government of Tasmania extended an apology and in 2006 offered compensation of $5 million (Australian). "Genocide" was not mentioned in the apology. But it seems clear that collectively the Australians of Tasmania were attempting to come to terms with their past.

Dane Kennedy recounts the experiences of two early British expeditions to Africa, one to the lower Congo in 1816, the other in 1844 to the upper Niger. Both were failures. Nevertheless, their history reveals the state of nineteenth-century geography and the hazards of encounters with African chiefs as well as tropical diseases, poisonous plants, and ferocious animals, including lions. Commander James Tuckey of the Royal Navy led the Congo expedition. His service record included meticulous geographic surveys. The members of the expedition included a zoologist and a naturalist from Kew Gardens. They produced the first reliable survey of the mouth of the Congo; but virtually all of them died of yellow fever. The Niger expedition suffered fewer deaths; but there were problems of desertion as well as "vice and dissipation." Above all, the expeditions became dependent on Africans for porters and supplies. Kennedy concludes that African chiefs more than held their own in their encounters with the British. They drove hard bargains for logistical support. They prevented advances into territories where the British might have bartered weapons with their enemies. British survival depended on local assistance and knowledge. The realities of the two expeditions make for a much more compelling story than one seen from the hubristic point of view of eventual and inevitable Western triumph in "darkest Africa."

Roger Billis makes comprehensible the architectural, gastronomical, and literary significance, as well as the historic political importance, of the Reform Club. Founded in 1836, it served as a meeting place for those who had championed the Reform Act of 1832. The club was intended as a forum for the kinds of radical ideas and progressive thought that later became associated with the Liberal Party. The building in Pall Mall, near Piccadilly, was designed by the famous architect of the time, Charles Berry. The Reform was one of his finest Italianate buildings, notable for its palatial central Saloon with a glazed roof. Alexis Soyer became *chef de cuisine,* usually dressed in a green frock coat. His Lamb Cutlets Reform are still on the club menu. In the Victorian era, the club was renowned for spirited debate, good food and good wine, and a large library focused mainly on politics, history, and biography. With the decline of the Liberal Party, club membership began to shift to the civil service and the thin-lipped mandarins of the Treasury. Historically, the Reform had a literary reputation, counting William Thackeray Anthony Trollope, and Henry James among its members. Fictionally, Jules Verne's Phileas Fogg was playing whist in the club's game room when he made his wager to circumnavigate the world in eighty days. Winston Churchill resigned in 1913 because of one of his friends was blackballed. The blackball system of preventing membership lasted until about 1930. In 1980 there was another seismic shift: the Reform became the first club in England to admit women.

Jane Ridley raises far-reaching questions about the British monarchy and the fate of Tsar Nicholas II. He abdicated in March 1917.

George V's reaction was heartfelt. He penned a line of sympathy, but it never reached the Tsar. Later in the same month, a representative of the Tsar told the British Ambassador in Russia that it was imperative for the Tsar to leave the country. Would England offer him asylum? The King's private secretary, Lord Stamfordham, met with the Prime Minister, David Lloyd George. The answer was immediate. The British would "readily" offer asylum to the Tsar and the Empress. In the next fateful week, however, the Tsar refused to travel until his children recovered from a case of the measles. George V then changed his mind. He decided to abandon his cousin. He insisted that Lloyd George and the Foreign Secretary, A. J. Balfour, withdraw the invitation. When George V learned of the murder of the Tsar and the royal family on July 18, 1918, he showed no remorse. Who made the decision to revoke the offer of asylum? The King himself? Or Stamfordham, who persuaded the King? Or Lloyd George and Balfour? Was it perhaps the right decision, though taken for the wrong reasons? These questions have been asked for many decades. This lecture now provides the answers.

John Milton Cooper assesses Edward M. House step-by-step. A native Texan, House has always possessed the reputation of a man of mystery. He was perhaps Woodrow Wilson's closest adviser, at least until early 1919. According to House, the President regarded him as his "second personality." Deferential, and adept at reconciling divergent aims, he worked behind the scenes. He conveyed the impression that he was more Wilsonian than Wilson himself, and certainly that he had the President's ear. But at the Paris Peace Conference of 1919, the collaboration between Wilson and House began to crack. When Wilson returned briefly to the United States, House took his place in the formal rounds of negotiations. He yielded to British, French, and Italian demands that the President believed to have weakened his position. After returning to Paris, Wilson banished House to a secondary role. They never saw each other after the signing of the Treaty of Versailles. Such is the version of the story based mainly on House's own memory and diary entries. By testing the evidence, John Milton Cooper throws an entirely different light on this elusive and, until recently, enigmatic figure.

Kenneth O. Morgan reflects on the impact of the First World War on Wales. Before the war there was unmatched prosperity and a sense of optimistic pride. The Welsh language was flourishing. Welsh choirs were compared with nightingales. There was political stability. There was a recognition of Welsh identity, as was apparent in the thriving National Library and University of Wales. Wales was neither separatist nor anglophobic, in conspicuous contrast with Ireland. But things changed almost immediately with the outbreak of war in 1914. Wales was as jingoistic as the rest of Britain. Conscientious objectors were harshly treated. There were outbursts of anti-German xenophobia. Yet there was also dissent. Socialists and radicals protested against an unjust war. A surge of industrial protest grew slowly, and labor relations deteriorated. By the end of the war, it was clear that the character of the working class had become transformed. The number of Welsh speakers had dropped to roughly half the pre-war number. Welsh miners were turning away from the community values of the valleys to the class principles of the workers of the world. The new political titans included the socialist firebrand Aneurin Bevan, who began to pay careful attention to problems such as health and housing. The old confidence of the Edwardian age has never been replaced. It remains to be seen whether devolution will give Wales a new sense of an inspired destiny.

In the half century after 1945, the world of nation-states has turned out in many cases so badly that **Thomas Meaney** asks whether better alternatives might have prevented repression, violence, and despotism. In the early part of the Second World War, the Untied States had a definite anticolonial preference. One of the principal figures providing the rationale was Sumner Welles, a high-ranking State Department official who was President Roosevelt's trusted friend. Welles had experience above all with Latin American countries. He believed that in a spirit of friendship, they and other non-Western countries would cooperate with the United States in transforming the world. The plan developed, but not quite in the way Welles and others had anticipated. The non-Western representatives at the United Nations, under the leadership of Krishna Menon and others, became predominantly anticolonial. Nineteen independent countries joined the UN in 1960. To many within the British and American governments, from that point it ceased to be a useful international organization. Could things have turned out differently? Of course. But the founders of the UN were men of their time whose vision had been shaped in the interwar years. And there was another fundamental reason why the UN helped foster a world of small (even micro-) states. No one in 1945 anticipated the speed with which the colonial systems would collapse.

Molly McCullers argues that from 1945 onward there was an important but little-recognized theme in the connection between South Africa and the former German colony of South West Africa. The South Africans conquered the territory during the First World War. In 1919, it became a "C" mandate under the supervision of the League of Nations. In the unanimous view at the time, the Hottentots (Khoikhoi) and other native peoples would never be able to stand on their own. For all practical purposes, "Southwest" became an annexed territory of South Africa. At the end of the Second World War, the South Africans refused to place the mandate under the supervision of the United Nations. In the following two decades, the South African economy thrived, and the racial system known as apartheid became ever more comprehensive. South Africa left the British Commonwealth in 1961, an event usually described as a victory for such countries as India and Ghana at beginning the international anti-apartheid campaign. In fact, the Afrikaner government of Hendrik Verwoerd regarded the escape as a triumph. The Afrikaners had at last managed to sever the British connection and were now free, so it seemed, to annex Southwest as part of the South African empire. Virtually no one at the time would have guessed that three decades later apartheid would collapse and Southwest would become independent as Namibia.

William Whyte takes the reader through an acrimonious two-decade debate that touched on the very character of Oxford as a university. He discusses the plan to build a road through the meadow of Oxford's most majestic college, Christ Church. The thoroughfare, intended to alleviate Oxford's rapidly worsening traffic woes, would have ended at the entrance to St. John's College. The debate took place from 1956 to the mid-1970s. In Parliament, the question was taken up by Clement Attlee, Lord Halifax, and the Archbishop of Canterbury. According to legend, in July 1956 it appeared thus on the agenda for the Cabinet: "1. Oxford Roads; 2. Seizure of the Suez Canal." Prime Minister Anthony Eden was reminded that if he approved the proposal for the road through the meadow, he would be remembered as "among the vandals of history." At one point, a tunnel *under* the meadow was proposed as a compromise. Ultimately the debate became one of who had the greater authority: the Council of Oxford and the city planners, or the Oxford colleges. In an episode that was at once vital to the future of Oxford and yet replete with comic interludes, Christ Church meadow ultimately remained intact.

In a disillusioned but highly entertaining romp, **Ferdinand Mount** takes the reader through the major events in the career of Harold Macmillan. Macmillan was undoubtedly brave, wounded five times during the First World War. He remained memorable for his war record, his languid manner, and his drooping mustache—the very image of an old-style "Tory gent." For most of his life he kept an extensive diary, though there are critical missing passages, notably on the Suez crisis. His skill as an author reflected his involvement in the family publishing house. Macmillan was certainly one of the best-read Prime Ministers of the twentieth century. The excursion to other parts of Macmillan's career includes—the phrases are not necessarily Mount's—Oxford and "clubland" as places of conviviality; Macmillan's "vomiting" before big speeches; his wartime service in the "mausoleum" of the Colonial Office; "first in, first out" in the Suez crisis; the "Wind of Change" speech on decolonization; the development of his reputation as "Supermac"; the "night of long knives"; and his accusation that Mrs. Thatcher was "selling the family silver." Mount closely examines one especially critical episode that the reader will find original and damning: his advice in 1945 to "hand over" to the Soviets—and consign to certain death—some forty thousand Cossacks and White Russians, along with their wives and children.

David Ramsbotham provides a remarkably original history of a key episode in his career as a soldier: the "last colonial war," as it was known at the time (though in retrospect, the epithet probably belongs to the Falklands). In the late 1960s the British faced "Konfrontasi," the danger of Sukarno's Indonesia taking over and annexing islands and other territory of Malaysia. The violent conflict had its origin in the creation of Malaysia—the amalgamation of the former British colony of Malaya, Singapore, and the British dependencies of North Borneo and Sarawak. Indonesia's stratagem consisted of infiltrations into Borneo that would exploit ethnic and religious differences to split up Malaysia itself. The jungle terrain of Borneo forced Indonesian and British forces to conduct complex infantry maneuvers and air transport operations, in which the British had the advantage of better helicopters. Konfrontasi coincided with Sukarno's announcement of a "year of dangerous living" and the race riots in Singapore in 1964. British forces eventually prevailed. Peace negotiations led to the recognition of Malaysia by Indonesia in 1966. Ramsbotham's recollections and reconstruction of the specifics of jungle warfare are a major contribution to the history of the conflict—from the vantage point of a ranking officer of the time and later Commander of the British Field Army.

In a highly condensed lecture, **Michael Brenner** compares George W. Bush and Tony Blair. Bush's hero among former Presidents was Harry Truman. The Anglo-American special relationship of the Truman era has now lost most of its conceptual vitality. Even after the Second World War there were plenty of skeptics. In some areas of controversy, there was no agreement at all, notably when Truman demanded that 100,000 Jews be admitted to Palestine. Dean Acheson's subsequent remark, that Britain had lost an empire but had yet to find a role, rankled the British. But there was an element of truth in it, as if making clear Britain's decline. The Suez crisis unambiguously showed that Britain could not undertake a major initiative without American support. The war against Argentina could not have been won without the covert assistance of the U.S. Navy. Yet it is rather difficult to believe that Ronald Reagan would have uttered the greeting "Yo, Margaret!" Bush's exuberant 'Yo, Blair!' seemed to convey the true connection between the President and Prime Minister, something like a master-poodle relationship. Yet to the Bush administration, Blair served a definite function. He stated the purpose of the invasion of Iraq clearly and coherently. When he spoke before both houses of Congress in July 2003, he was interrupted thirty-five times by applause, seventeen of them standing ovations. It is inconceivable that Attlee could—or would—have done the same. The special relationship thus seems to rattle on, but Brenner's assessment of Bush and Blair suggests that its history has reached a fresh nadir.

Sports can possess an aesthetic quality related to architecture. **Richard Cleary** explains how architectural principles are often expressed on the playing field. The layout of a baseball diamond or a cricket field reflects emotional content as well as physical patterns. Golf courses subtly combine natural and man-made beauty. "Architecture on the field" can be set in motion by the dynamic interaction of soccer players, and the relation to architectural patterns can be clearly seen in the movement of the ball via triangles or squares. Golf and tennis can have properties of beauty, such as the visual appeal of a golfer as he swings his club or a tennis player as she volleys. The dynamism of team sports can give both spectators and participants a sense of pure joy similar to that felt by gazing on the play of sunlight piercing a well-placed window. The perfectly timed fencing lunge can be long remembered for its beauty within a small field measured exactly like a precise architectural design. The conclusion to this bold interpretation of the interplay of architecture and sports is that either alone or combined, they can lead to intense aesthetic involvement.

Archie Brown, speaking to the British Studies seminar in mid-November 2014, argued that the breakup of Britain was a real possibility, even though 55 percent of the people of Scotland had voted against independent statehood two months earlier. He assumed that it was clear that the Scottish National Party would, *for the first time ever,* hold a majority of the Scottish seats in the House of Commons after the May 2015 general election. He noted that the "Scottish question" had made more salient an "English question" and that the post-referendum response of Prime Minister David Cameron had shown more concern with party management than with preserving the Union. Brown has now updated his lecture to take account of the result of the 2015 election. The Scottish National Party won 56 out of 59 Scottish seats. He looks also at the longer-term factors that have facilitated or stimulated the rise of the Scottish independence movement. They include the end of empire, the demise of heavy industry in Scotland, the weakening of trade unions and the labor movement, the decline in religious observance (especially marked in Scotland), and the achievement in recent decades of independent statehood by nations with a far less extensive tradition of national consciousness than Scotland and, unlike Scotland, without any previous history of independent statehood.

Lytton Strachey once remarked that the *Dictionary of National Biography* was "one of the most useful works ever written." **Lawrence Goldman** explains how, beginning in the 1980s, the new *Oxford Dictionary of National Biography* picked up where the old one left off. It is now the longest single work in the history of the English language, yet paradoxically, the reader will search it in vain for any descriptive statement on British identity. Instead there is an implicit commitment to diversity and differences of culture based on a "Britannic" geographic principle rather than a political or historical one. Within the last few decades, the number of Welsh, Irish, and Scottish entries has greatly increased, as have the entries on women—though the last still make up less than 20 percent of the total. There are now records of personalities representing all stations of life, and not only in Britain: figures such as Mohandas Gandhi and Jomo Kenyatta are included, along with servants of empire. If there is any general change in recent decades, it is simply that the scope extends in sociological layers far beyond and below the great and the good while not neglecting the eccentric. The painstakingly accurate entries give weight to British history in its regional, national, imperial, and trans-oceanic contexts. Rather than reflecting a fixed concept of identity, the *ODNB* provides straightforward records of what individuals experienced over the course of their lifetimes. The overall tone is sober, but it can also be tangy, bracing, and witty.

The *Oxford Dictionary of National Biography* may be too reticent to define the British national character, but the memorandum by **A. N. Duckham** boldly provides the American equivalent. From 1945 to 1950, he was the agricultural attaché at the British Embassy in Washington. At the end of his posting, he wrote a memorandum on the quirks and qualities of Americans in all parts of the country. The Ambassador at the time, Sir Oliver Franks, recommended that it be printed and circulated to all British officials concerned with the United States. Duckham traveled extensively and met hundreds of Americans ("eastern Kentucky hill people," the "vigorous" entrepreneurs of East Texas), many of them farmers. He believed that their mental prowess did not match their impressive physical vigor. Americans generally shared, in a phrase he emphasized, "a basic *psychological insecurity*," which had genetic, geographic, and historical origins. For the most part, the American population consisted of "a motley and insecure peasantry." He considered Americans generous, gregarious, and usually gentle (at least when not being "bombastic" and excessively "emotional"). On the other hand, they were generally ignorant as well as intolerant. They had an "obsessional fear" of communism; and no one could speak rationally to them about the "welfare state." Duckham summed up his character sketch, devastatingly, by concluding that Americans were a nation of "industrialized kulaks."

Charles George Gordon © National Portrait Gallery, London

1

Major General Charles Gordon

RICHARD DAVENPORT-HINES

He was one of the oddest fish in the Victorian aquarium: a somber, menacing, grotesque creature who was idolized in his lifetime by English public opinion, who was a headline favorite of unscrupulous newspapermen, who was all but sanctified after his murder, and who was played by Charlton Heston in a Hollywood blockbuster. Yet most men who knew Charles Gordon—"men," because apart from his mother and one sister, he found women fearsome or repulsive—came to regard him as a dangerous, irresponsible crank. He seems one of the great cautionary figures of history. His life makes a parable for the twenty-first century: the sort of semi-socialized misfit whom journalists make into a celebrity because he has an outlandish personality; the sort of fantasist who bamboozles the gullible in their millions with his self-dramatization and insistent personal myth; the sort of creep whom one shouldn't hire as a babysitter, but who nonetheless gets to look after vulnerable children.

Charles George Gordon was born in 1833 in Woolwich, the town on the river Thames to the southeast of London that was then the location of England's military arsenal and military academy. His father was an artilleryman who reached the rank of lieutenant general. His maternal grandfather, Samuel Enderby, was the shipowner in whose bottoms the historic shipment of tea reached Boston in 1777.

The boy Charley accompanied his father on a military posting to the Mediterranean isle of Corfu, where he was taught at home by a governess. Corfu had become, following the defeat of Napoleon in 1815, the administrative capital of a now largely forgotten British protectorate called the Ionian Islands. The conservative philosopher Michael Oakeshott in 1961 listed the gifts that the British Empire bestowed on Corfu: picnics, side-whiskers, rock cakes, bookkeeping, church bazaars, and cricket: rather slighter remnants, he added, than the Romans had left in Britain.

From ages thirteen to fourteen, Charley Gordon worked hard at a military crammer near Woolwich. He was tormented by pubescent desires, henceforth wrestled with demons of guilt, and made his life a monument of sexual sublimation and its attendant ills. When he was fifty, he said that he had wished at the age of fourteen to be a eunuch. Still seething with unresolved desires, he entered the Royal Military Academy, Woolwich, at sixteen. In his frustration, he hurt younger military cadets: he was so violent a disciplinarian that he was charged with bullying after beating his juniors over their heads with a broomstick.

Gordon was commissioned into the Royal Engineers in 1852. On promotion to lieutenant in 1854, he became assistant garrison engineer at Pembroke Dock. It was at Pembroke that he began studying divinity. The sermons of Robert M'Cheyne, the fervent Church of Scotland preacher who was twice engaged to marry but exhausted himself in evangelicalism and died a bachelor at twenty-nine, were his staple reading. So, too, were the biblical commentaries of Thomas Scott, the rough-mannered, unforgiving, and querulous chaplain of London's punitive Lock Hospital for syphilitics. Scott's profuse writings accentuated Gordon's taste for constant dour scrutiny of biblical texts, for soul-searching, and for anguished concentration. Scott had limited imagination; his ardor was shallow; and his literary style was plodding, lifeless, and repetitive. He is nevertheless the writer whom Gordon said, in the age of George Eliot and Dickens and Thackeray, made contemporary novels seem drab.

Gordon's Christian faith intensified after 1862 when confinement in a sickroom with a mild case of smallpox drove him to sacred meditations. Thereafter, he saw himself as living each day in the hands of God. He came to see his life as a fight for the gospels. All his actions were ruled by his sense of God's presence: he once told Regy Brett, Viscount Esher, who lived in the smartest district of Mayfair, "As I came to your house He walked with me arm in arm up South Audley Street."[1] Gordon abominated the flesh, especially his own, as evil, and believed that all men's souls were predestined for salvation. In consequence, he came to regard death not as fearful but as the gateway to eternal life. To die and thus ascend into the gracious presence of the Lord became a passionately desirable apotheosis.

Gordon scorned rank and wealth. When he was given special postings, he insisted that his salary be reduced. Luxury he decried as effeminate. His one indulgence was cigarette smoking, which probably contributed to the onset of angina pectoris in middle life: this ailment in turn increased his fatalism about death.

Lytton Strachey's essay on Gordon in *Eminent Victorians* raised a thankless controversy whether the general was a secret inebriate, a pious toper who sat studying his Bible and prayer book while snatching glugs from a bottle of brandy. It seems that Gordon stupefied himself with occasional binges when under pressure to make hard decisions or dismayed by religious anguish, but otherwise often was abstinent. It should carry weight that Evelyn Baring, Earl of Cromer, who was honest and reliable, standing high above tittle-tattle, told Winston Churchill that Gordon in the 1880s was often drunk. When Gordon was taken to the ballet in Naples in 1880, he was scandalized by the undress of the young dancers. "You call that civilization!" he snapped. Afterward he was found at one in the morning, semi-dressed, reading the Bible with a half-empty bottle of whiskey beside him. "He was a terrible drinker of brandy," recalled his French traveling companion. "Later, in Paris, he often used to come to see me in the mornings. And after about five minutes he would ask for *cognac*."[2]

Following the outbreak of the Crimean War, Gordon landed at Balaklava in 1855 and fought as a subaltern in the siege of Sevastopol, where he afterward prepared the shafts to dynamite the dockyard. Some of his later remarks fostered the myth that he performed feats of almost theatrical courage in the hope of being killed. "I went to the Crimea hoping, without having a hand in it, to be killed," he recalled in 1883. "I survived and lived, never fearing death but not wishing to be too closely acquainted with God, nor yet to leave him."[3] This is a histrionic myth that he devised retrospectively. His letters of the period brim with ambition and brio: he found war exciting, and was pleased to be promoted and to receive decorations.

After the Treaty of Paris of 1856 settled the Crimean peace, Gordon, who was proficient in surveying territory and drawing maps, was nominated to the international commission delineating the new Danube Valley frontiers between the Russian and Ottoman Empires. He was next sent in 1857 on similar duties along the new Russo-Turkish frontier in Armenia. For his cartographical work in Armenia, he was in 1858 elected a fellow of the Royal Geographical

Society, but resigned in 1866 because he felt its members were trying to lionize him. Like T. E. Lawrence (Lawrence of Arabia), he got himself noticed by shrinking from polite attention.

Gordon disliked military life, but liked war. Military life is concerned with settled encampments, routine, drilling, office work, hierarchy, repetition: it is based on disciplined immobility. The benefits of military life are destroyed by warfare, especially by prolonged warfare, in which all stabilities are undone. War provided Gordon with opportunities for movement, improvisation, and individual initiative. He responded to war's immediacy. Supremely he enjoyed, as one sees from his military campaigns, its necessity for urgent speed. Thus Gordon thrust himself, time and again, into conflict. War was for him the only acceptable form of pleasure in life. Consequently, two years after returning from Armenia, he volunteered in 1860 to join Anglo-French forces enforcing Chinese acquiescence in the Treaty of Tientsin (Tianjin).

Although Gordon arrived too late for the fighting, he participated in the occupation of Peking (Beijing) and the plundering of its Summer Palace. In 1863, Gordon took command of a mutinous rabble of 4,000 Chinese mercenaries that was defending the international trade settlement at Shanghai from Taiping insurgents. Gordon's hatred of inaction and his social horror of fixed engagements were reflected in the tactics that he deployed against the Taipings. He contributed to their defeat by the mobility of his forces, particularly the swift maneuvering of armed steamboats along the extensive medieval canal system. His disrespect for age or position, and his supercilious indifference to his official superiors, dates from the period of his victories in China, when he had just turned thirty. In Britain, the reputation of Chinese Gordon, as he became widely known, was enhanced by the knowledge that he had spent his pay on the comfort of his troops and had declined munificent gifts from the emperor before leaving China.

Gordon was a martinet without notable success as a leader of Englishmen. In the Crimea and in China, he decried the English under his command: "grumbling, dirty, idle, helpless to a degree and without the smallest spark of *esprit de corps,* what a brute the ordinary English linesman is."[4] His powers of leadership showed best when imposing his will on destitute, ill-trained forces. In this, and in his speedy improvisations in guerrilla warfare, he resembled T. E. Lawrence. His leadership of men was helped by his piercing blue-grey eyes, which gave the misleading impression that he could penetrate men's secret thoughts: in fact, he was easily duped by impostors.

In 1865, Gordon was appointed Royal Engineer officer in command at Gravesend (a strategic port on the Thames estuary) and entrusted with erecting defensive forts. He was more frustrated than usual in this period, which saw his religious preoccupations intensify. By incessant study of the Bible and Thomas à Kempis's *Imitation of Christ*, and supported by spiritual confidences to his pious spinster sister Augusta, he strove to subdue his carnal desires and his unregenerate body to the love of God.

When not reading the Bible or pondering biblical commentaries, Gordon devoted his spare time to religious philanthropy among Gravesend's poor. He tended the sick in the workhouse infirmary and housed street urchins in his official residence, where he cleaned, fed, clothed, and taught them. His nature had been scarred forever by the tumultuous impurity of his adolescence: now he enjoyed giving baths to prepubescent boys, his "Gravesend laddies," "kings," "wangs," "doves," and "angels," as he variously called them. Many had been starved of affection, and reciprocated his tenderness. He was never caught in, and perhaps resisted, the indiscretions with boys that led to the suicide of his fellow general Sir Hector MacDonald.[5] Nevertheless, in Gordon's lifetime, Lord Cromer, Britain's consul general in Egypt, called him "a queer fellow" with "a very feminine side to his character." Eighty years ago, Hugo Wortham, one of Gordon's shrewdest biographers, characterized him as "in this matter a Platonist" who "found an outlet for the emotions [usually] generated by intercourse with the opposite sex in the company of boys and young men."[6]

In 1873, Gordon was relieved to be asked by the Khedive of Egypt to serve as Governor-General of the province of Equatoria, in the south of Egyptian-occupied Sudan. He obtained British government approval and, stipulating only that his salary should be reduced from £10,000 to £2,000, reached Khartoum in 1874. It was his ardent conviction that a governor's first duty was to the subjects he ruled, and only subordinately to the imperial power. By the end of 1876 he had suppressed slave trading in Equatoria.

In 1877, Gordon became Governor-General of the Sudan. Mindful of the terrible sickness among his previous Equatorian entourage, he resolved to face his new duties alone. He thus took solitary responsibility for an area exceeding a million square miles in which warfare, slavery, and terrible deprivation were endemic. "His chastity," suggested Sir Rivers Wilson, "which was absolutely incomprehensible to the Arab seemed to raise him to the position of a mystical and almost divine character."[7] He went with 300 men to Darfur province, where a large force of insurgent slave traders had massed. With characteristic audacity, he rode into the rebel camp in full dress as Governor-General accompanied only by an interpreter and small escort. Just as he had subdued mutinous troops in China fifteen years earlier by force of personality and histrionic power, so he cowed these rebels. Many joined his forces, others retreated, and the revolt was crushed in 1879. He thus extinguished the slave hunts from Darfur to the Red Sea littoral.

After other vicissitudes—including a hazardous overture to King John IV of Abyssinia, during which he was made captive—he left Egyptian service in December 1879, and the next month reached London, wound up to a high pitch of fatigue, exasperation, and defiance. Shortly afterward, the future imperial proconsul George Nathaniel Curzon met Gordon in Pall Mall, the street of London clubs where every gentleman should look spruce. Curzon, a stickler for correct appearance, must have flinched at seeing Gordon, as he lamented, "shabbily dressed in a seedy black frock coat, trousers that did not come down to the boots, and a very dilapidated black silk topper with a particularly narrow brim and silk mostly brushed the wrong way."[8] To dress like this in Pall Mall was inverted vanity. It made people look at Gordon: in showing his contempt for their sartorial standards, he was also asserting his sense of his own nonconformist superiority.

His attitude to British officialdom was by now willful and contemptuous. "I hate our diplomatists," he wrote. "I think with few exceptions they are arrant humbugs, and I expect they know it."[9] Diplomats reciprocated. "A long life of isolation, under circumstances well calculated to disturb coolness of head, has, I fear, told upon his reasoning powers," Sir Thomas Wade (British Minister in China, 1871–83) reported to the Foreign Office in 1880. "His nerve is perfectly unshaken, but his judgment is no longer in balance, and . . . his very devoutness is dangerous; for he has taught himself to believe, more or less, that in pursuing this course or that, he is but obeying inspiration."[10]

In 1880, the Marquess of Ripon, on his appointment by Gladstone as Viceroy of India, had the fancy of taking Gordon as his private secretary; but Gordon resigned after only a few days in Bombay. Despite official British disapproval, Gordon revisited China, where he helped avert a rebellion against the central government. During a brief visit to Peking he offended both mandarins and foreign officials. It was a sign of Gordon's deterioration that his old admirer in China, Sir Robert Hart, the inspector general of China's Imperial Maritime Customs, wrote in 1880: "Much as I like and respect him, I must say he is *'not all there'*. Whether it is religion, or vanity, or softening of the brain—I don't know; but he seems to be alternately arrogant and slavish, vain and humble, in his senses and out of them."[11]

The spiritual crisis that Gordon experienced at this time accomplished his final estrangement from countrymen of his own class. "I dwell on the joy of never seeing Great Britain again, with its horrid, wearisome *dinner* parties," he wrote in extremity in Khartoum in 1884. "At those dinner parties we are all in masks, saying what we do not believe, eating and drinking things we do not want, and then abusing one another."[12] As an escape from this bondage, he obtained in 1881 the command of the Royal Engineers in Mauritius. This enabled him to pursue elaborate investigations, as a result of which he believed that he had identified an island in the Seychelles as the site of the Garden of Eden. From January to December 1883, Gordon lived in the Holy Land, studying antiquities. His calculations and theories about the true sites of the crucifixion and burial of Jesus Christ gained currency in England and the United States.

In January 1884, at Brussels, he consented to a renewed request from King Leopold II to take command in his Congo territory. Gordon regarded this task both as an opportunity to extirpate the slave trade and also as bound to lead to his death, which he had long desired. Lord Rosmead warned Gordon that Belgian Congo had "a vile climate, that the natives were savages, that it was folly to accept." Gordon agreed: that was why he accepted, admitting that "he would have killed himself long ago if religion had allowed it—that his life was a burden and a weariness to him."[13] Gordon intended to resign his army commission and leave for the Congo in February, but other events supervened.

IN THE SUDAN, AN OBSCURE FAKIR who had proclaimed himself the Mahdi, or Expected One, had launched a holy war. His forces in December 1883 annihilated an Egyptian expedition of 10,000 men sent to repress the rebellion. Cromer, in Cairo, recommended evacuation of the beleaguered Egyptian garrison in Khartoum. In London the Foreign Secretary, Earl Granville, suggested employing Gordon to supervise this evacuation. Cromer resisted Granville's suggestion, which he correctly predicted would hinder the main policy object of avoiding being drawn into military operations in the Sudan.

On 9 January 1884 the *Pall Mall Gazette* carried a voluminous interview conducted with Gordon by its editor, the bumptiously meddlesome W. T. Stead, in which Gordon spoke with an air of high authority about the Mahdi and what might be done to pacify the Sudan. He urged that Khartoum be held as an outpost from which a counterattack could later be directed against the Mahdists, rather as Shanghai had served him when vanquishing the Taiping hordes. The newspaper also carried a leading article by Stead crying up Gordon's qualifications to solve the Sudanese impasse. This scoop incited other journalists to make feverish calls for Gordon to be sent to the Sudan. Impressionable crowds began to raise a pro-Gordon hullabaloo in the London streets. From the outset of this stunt, Stead and his press colleagues were responsible for inflating the public impression of Gordon as an infallible national savior. The object of this publicity was not displeased. Meekness was hard for a man who thought he was an instrument of divine ends.

The whigs in Gladstone's cabinet felt obliged to defer to this clamor. Despite demurrals by Gladstone and Cromer about Gordon's reliability, Granville (Foreign Secretary), Lord Hartington (Secretary of State for War), and Lord Northbrook (First Lord of the Admiralty) hoped his mesmeric influence would quell the seething rebellion of Sudan. All too hastily, Gordon was enlisted to promote governmental policy. There was, however, a flurry of confusion about his remit. Most cabinet ministers thought Gordon had been instructed to evacuate the Egyptian garrison in Khartoum and to march them back to Egypt, but there was ambiguity about this. Lord Derby, the Colonial Secretary, professed never to have known "who was responsible for the sending of Gordon to Khartoum."[14] Derby initially felt qualified optimism about Gordon's appointment: "The choice is good, for he knows the country, and has extraordinary influence over wild tribes." But he knew Gordon's disobedience was irresponsible: "A fanatic of the Puritan type, satisfied that his way in all affairs is the best . . . he has broken with his various employers successively—the Chinese government, the Khedive, the Cape authorities who wished him to settle Basutoland for them, and lastly Ripon."[15]

Similarly, Gladstone's secretary, Eddy Hamilton, expressed shrewd misgivings about Gordon's appointment: "The despatch of 'Chinese Gordon' on a mission to the Soudan has been very well received and has for the moment satisfied public opinion. But, notwithstanding all his Soudanese prestige, it is difficult to see what real good he can do. He seems to be a half cracked fatalist; and what can one expect from such a man?"[16]

The Conservative leader, Lord Salisbury, reading of this appointment by his Gladstonian opponents, exclaimed with a gesture of despair, "They must have gone quite mad."[17] But some Conservative leaders were impressed. Earl Cairns, who had been the alternative candidate to Salisbury when the Conservative leadership fell vacant on Disraeli's death, hailed Gordon as "one of our national treasures" and averred "that since the days of knight-errantry never was such an expedition undertaken."[18] Other men who had recently worked with Gordon were dismayed. "When I heard he had been appointed, I said that I knew the Govt. had chosen a man for their servant who would prove their master: and a mad one too," Lord Rosmead declared in February 1884.

"Don't be a funk," Gordon wired to the governor of Khartoum. "You are men, not women. I am coming."[19] On the march there he became increasingly excitable, volatile, and impulsive. Arriving in Khartoum on 18 February 1884, he declared, "I come without soldiers, but with God on my side, to redress the evils of the Soudan."[20] "I wish to goodness that Gordon," wrote Cromer on 11 March, "could be made to count to twenty before he writes or telegraphs."[21] Gordon had begun issuing emotive telegraphic messages and despairing dispatches that touched a chord of commiseration in many British hearts. These communications seemed a stratagem to secure a policy of conquest rather than scuttle. Trusting to his prestige at home, he asserted that he would hold out for as long as possible, trying to suppress the rebellion rather than evacuating the garrison. An agitation arose for Gordon not to be abandoned and for reinforcements to be sent. In a Cabinet discussion on 7 May, Gladstone "fired up & . . . said it was an unnatural proceeding to attempt to govern a Mahometan country."[22] The Earl of Kimberley, Secretary of State for India, noted (13 May 1884): "The London newspapers and the Tories clamour for an expedition to Khartoum, the former from ignorance, the latter because it is the best mode of embarrassing us . . . The interest of the nation is to get quit of the Soudan as soon as possible. But Gordon is a tremendous obstacle. If he cannot be got out in any other way, an expedition (a frightful undertaking) is inevitable . . . it is melancholy to think of the waste of lives and treasure which it must involve, and except the rescue of Gordon . . . no good to be attained."[23]

The publication during the summer of *General Gordon's Letters from the Crimea, the Danube and Armenia,* with a tendentious anti-Gladstone introduction by an imperial propagandist, strengthened his hold on popular sympathies. It seemed to the public that his actions resounded with self-sacrifice, although they can as easily be represented as merely self-destructive. The outcry on his behalf, together with pressure from Queen Victoria and ultimately Hartington, forced Gladstone to yield in August. An expedition to relieve Khartoum was dispatched in September, commanded by Sir Garnet Wolseley, whose instructions forbade him from extricating other Sudanese garrisons. "I own to having been very insubordinate to Her Majesty's Government and its officials, but it is my nature, and I cannot help it," Gordon recorded in his journal on 19 September. "I know if *I* was chief I would never employ myself, for I am incorrigible."[24]

Gordon withstood a siege of 317 days while supported by two white officers, his native troops wasted by famine and disease. Then, on 26 January 1885, a fall in the water level of the river Nile enabled the Mahdists to succeed in a final assault on Khartoum. Gordon was speared by dervishes in his palace, and his severed head was displayed in the Mahdists' camp. Wolseley's river steamers came in sight of Khartoum two days after Gordon's death, but then withdrew. Gordon's corpse was never found.

GORDON'S LAST YEAR WAS ACTED on a world stage, and his assassination ensured for him immediate, morbid promotion by the press into martyrdom. The first telegraphic rumors of his death reached London on 5 February. As Derby complained the next day, "great exaggeration prevails, one article saying that no such calamity has occurred since the Indian mutiny, another referring as a precedent to the destruction of the British army in Afghanistan." The Queen sent an unencrypted telegram reproaching Gladstone, Granville, and Hartington for Gordon's death. In Cabinet on 7 February, "the Premier said he believed the public cared very much about Gordon, but very little about the Soudan."[25] Gladstone's estimation was correct.

The fall of Khartoum was a military setback, but insignificant compared with the impact of Gordon's death. His death became as important a symbol in the rise of Britain's new imperialism as did the Munich accord in 1938 of the collapsed pretensions of the British to global dominance. It was construed as meaning that British interests, national honor, and imperial mission were held cheap by the Liberal Party. "England stands before the world dripping with blood and daubed with dishonour," Robert Louis Stevenson wrote on 2 March in a paroxysm of revulsion at "our ineffable shame."[26] The coercive and angry grief in England resembled the mass hysteria and compulsory mourning that followed the death of Diana, Princess of Wales in 1997. "During this stage of national hysteria," as Cromer wrote, any critic of Gordon "would have been regarded with a dislike somewhat akin to that which is felt for anyone who is heard talking flippantly in public of the truths of the Christian religion."[27] Gladstone's nickname, GOM, meaning the Grand Old Man, became inverted to MOG, Murderer of Gordon.

The journals that Gordon kept in Khartoum are opinionated,

egocentric, manipulative, and self-righteous (Gladstone's Cabinet agreed to their publication, but only in full, in order to give the public, in the words of the Home Secretary, Sir William Harcourt, "conclusive proof of Gordon's insanity").[28] He shows himself to be a sarcastic and resentful outsider in his comments on other officers and officials. The journals' insubordinate temper and air of doomed heroism have attracted rebellious or idealistic readers.

People who had not had to work with Gordon were impressed by him. "Of all the people I have met in my life, he and Darwin are the two in whom I have found something bigger than ordinary humanity—an unequalled simplicity and directness of purpose—a sublime unselfishness," wrote Thomas Huxley in 1885 after hearing "the hideous news."[29] The pioneer Edwardian gay liberationist George Ives, who believed that it was "very possible" that Gordon was "an Invert" ("it happens sometimes with zealous Christians"), thought him inspiring: it was not Gordon's way, said Ives, to "bow down before the democratic swine-trough, or grovel at courts of kings."[30]

Those who had sought Gordon's cooperation in a crisis were unforgiving. Lord Cromer remained "very bitter about him," as Winston Churchill recorded in 1899 when he had a long talk about the Sudan crisis with the Egyptian proconsul. "Cromer," wrote Churchill, "begged me not to pander to the popular belief on the subject. Of course there is no doubt that Gordon as a political figure was absolutely hopeless. He was so erratic, capricious, utterly unreliable, his mood changed so often, his temper was abominable, he was frequently drunk, and yet with all he had a tremendous sense of honour and great abilities."[31]

Gordon's posthumous reputation rose high and fell low. He became a figurehead for demotic imperialism. Sir Edward Elgar contemplated writing a symphony about him. Then, in 1918, came Lytton Strachey's *Eminent Victorians,* with its outspoken chapter on Gordon. Strachey once told Virginia Woolf that he wanted influence rather than fame: not the influence of his former lover John Maynard Keynes over ministers and economies, "but the influence of some old gentleman on whose 80th birthday people present addresses—he wants to deal little words that poison vast monsters of falsehood."[32] Grotesque and calamitous figures like Gordon are always with us. And so there is never an end to the enjoyable duty of historians to wield their pens to slay them.

Fall Semester 2014

1. James Lees-Milne, *The Enigmatic Edwardian: The Life of Reginald, Second Viscount Esher* (London, 1986), p. 56.
2. Roy Jenkins, *Sir Charles Dilke: A Victorian Tragedy* (London, 1965), p. 183.
3. Charles Chenevix-Trench, *Charley Gordon: An Eminent Victorian Reassessed* (London, 1978), p. 19.
4. Ibid., p. 25.
5. Sir Almeric FitzRoy, diary, 25 Mar. 1903, BL Add MSS 48372.
6. Evelyn Baring to Earl of Northbrook, 11 Mar. 1884, National Archives, FO 633/4; Hugo Wortham, *Gordon* (London, 1933), p. 32.
7. Sir Charles Rivers Wilson, *Chapters from My Official Life* (London, 1916), p. 199.
8. Earl of Ronaldshay, *The Life of Lord Curzon*, vol. 1 (London, 1928), p. 97.
9. Charles Gordon, *Khartoum Journal*, ed. Lord Elton (London, 1961), p. 137.
10. Pollock, *Gordon*, p. 202.
11. J. K. Fairbank, K. F. Bruner, and E. M. Matheson, eds., *The I. G. in Peking*, vol. 1 (Cambridge, Mass., 1975), p. 332.
12. Gordon, *Khartoum Journal*, p. 139.
13. Stephen Gwynn, *The Letters and Friendships of Sir Cecil Spring Rice*, vol. 1 (London, 1929), p. 34.
14. Earl of Derby, diary, 4 Sept. and 7 Dec. 1884, Liverpool Record Office.
15. John Vincent, ed., *The Diaries of Edward Henry Stanley, 15th Earl of Derby between 1878 and 1893* (Oxford, 2003), p. 627.
16. Dudley Bahlman, ed., *The Diary of Sir Edward Walter Hamilton, 1880–1885*, vol. 2 (Oxford, 1972), p. 545.
17. Lady Gwendolen Cecil, *Life of Robert, Marquis of Salisbury*, vol. 3 (London, 1931), p. 98.
18. House of Lords debates, 12 Feb. 1884, vol. 284, col. 610.
19. Marquess of Zetland, *Lord Cromer* (London, 1932), p. 110.
20. Roy Macgregor-Hastie, *Never to Be Taken Alive: A Biography of General Gordon* (London, 1985), p. 159.
21. Zetland, *Cromer*, p. 112.
22. Vincent, *Derby*, p. 660.
23. Angus Hawkins and John Powell, eds., *The Journal of John Wodehouse, First Earl of Kimberley, for 1862 to 1902* (London, 1997), p. 343.
24. Gordon, *Khartoum Journal*, pp. 56–57.
25. Vincent, *Derby*, p. 749.
26. Bradford Booth and Ernest Mehew, eds., *Letters of Robert Louis Stevenson*, vol. 5 (New Haven, Conn., 1995), pp. 80–81.
27. BL, Add MSS 44904, folio 147.
28. Vincent, *Derby*, p. 765.
29. Leonard Huxley, *Life and Letters of Thomas Henry Huxley*, vol. 2 (London, 1900), pp. 94–95.
30. George Ives, diary, 27 Jan. 1908, Humanities Research Center, University of Texas, Austin.
31. Randolph Churchill, ed., *Winston S. Churchill*, companion vol. 1, pt. 2 (London, 1967), p. 1017.
32. Anne Olivier Bell, ed., *The Diary of Virginia Woolf*, vol. 2 (London, 1978), p. 48.

General Edmund Allenby entering Jerusalem, 1917

2

The Men Who Ruled Palestine

BERNARD WASSERSTEIN

Seven men ruled Palestine as High Commissioners between 1920 and 1948 under the mandate (a form of trusteeship) granted to Britain by the League of Nations. The title of the office was "intended, no doubt, to mark the mandatory character of the territory," as the Palestine Royal Commission noted in 1937.[1] During these three decades, the Holy Land was transformed demographically, economically, and politically, leading to the establishment of Israel and the displacement of the bulk of the Palestinian Arab population.

Who were the High Commissioners? How did they see themselves, and how were they viewed by those they ruled? They were part circus masters, part occupants of ringside seats—that is, they were both historical actors and privileged observers. Since Palestine in this period never acquired any countrywide elected institutions, other than those based on ethnic or religious communities, these men wielded something close to autocratic power, at any rate on the surface. They were formally vested with full governmental authority over the country, tempered only by the supervision of the Colonial Office in London and, at a further remove, the loose oversight of the Permanent Mandates Commission of the League of Nations in Geneva. The destiny of the country during this fateful period was, as a result, in considerable measure shaped by the personalities, outlooks, and preferences of the High Commissioners.

The seven occupants of what one historian whimsically called the "seat of Pilate" had to contend with challenges of a nature that confronted the governors of no other British possession.[2] All arrived in Palestine with high hopes: all left disappointed, personally, politically, or both. Charged under the Balfour Declaration of 1917 with facilitating the development of a "Jewish National Home," they were at the same time required to protect the interests of the Arab majority population and to further British strategic objectives in the Middle East. Even in quiet times, the hope of reconciling these contradictory aims was utopian; but the quiet times did not last long, and during the crisis years of 1936 to 1948 the pressures bearing down on the rulers of Palestine became intense and, in the end, unendurable.

Four were soldiers, two were career colonial service officers, and one was a politician: that balance reflected the military exigencies that weighed heavily on Britain during much of its overlordship of Palestine. The only Jew among the seven was the first, Sir Herbert Samuel. Born to a Jewish banking family, he was educated at Balliol and entered politics as a Liberal. From the 1890s to the 1960s, he remained a staunch upholder of Liberalism even as it declined from the dominant political force in the land to little more than a picturesque parliamentary relic.

In 1909 he became the first Jew appointed to a British Cabinet, and five years later the earliest proponent of Zionism at that level of government. After leaving ministerial office in 1916, he worked closely with the Zionist Organization and formed cordial relations with Chaim Weizmann. This partnership with the dominant figure in the Zionist movement for the next two decades helped solidify the Anglo-Zionist alliance.

Samuel was the only High Commissioner who actively sought the position. His appointment gave him the opportunity to indulge his passions for Zionism and empire building. Upon arrival in Palestine, he was installed in office with pomp and circumstance. One of his first acts, in defiance of instructions from London was to annex Transjordan to Palestine. For this, some Zionists charged that he had excised Transjordan from the territory promised to the Jews in the Balfour Declaration. In fact, the declaration did not specify borders for the Jewish National Home.

Samuel alienated some by his aloofness, often misinterpreted as hostility. One British official wrote that he could be "extremely human" but "was often icily cold and almost repelled those in front of him by the isolation of his manner." At official occasions, "His Excellency afforded with meticulous care exactly five minutes to each guest after dinner in the extraordinary, bizarre drawing room" in Government House.[3] On the other hand, a young Arab official,

Fig. 2.1. Sir Herbert Samuel (1870–1963), High Commissioner, 1920–25

Wasif Jawhariyyeh, recalled appreciatively the lavish scale of the High Commissioner's parties, which he compared to "the nights of Harun al-Rashid."[4]

Although Samuel did his utmost to further the Zionist cause, many Zionists accused him of betraying them. Shocked by the Arab anti-Jewish riots of May 1921, he was confirmed in his view that Arab acquiescence in the Jewish National Home was the essential condition for the success of Zionism. He believed that this might be secured by the creation of a constitutional structure that would give the Arab majority some say in government while preserving British control of foreign affairs and security as well as Zionist rights to immigration and land purchase. But repeated attempts to create such a structure collapsed. Faute de mieux, Samuel resorted to a kind of institutional partition between quasi-autonomous institutions: the Jewish Agency and its related institutions on the one hand, and the Supreme Moslem Council, headed by the Mufti of Jerusalem, Haj Amin al-Husayni, on the other. Samuel thereby set the grooves down which the Palestine mandate trundled inexorably over the next quarter century toward civil war and territorial partition.

At the end of his term of office in 1925, Samuel left Palestine only with reluctance. He had wanted to settle in a house on Mount Carmel and write books on philosophy, but his successor vetoed the plan. It was a sign of the dimming of Samuel's hopes for Anglo-Zionist amity that the British government never again felt safe in appointing a Jew to be ruler of Palestine.

Samuel's successor, Field Marshal Lord Plumer, was educated at Eton and entered the army in 1876. He won glory in the relief of Mafeking during the Boer War. In 1917 he commanded British and Allied forces at Passchendaele on the western front, suffering a quarter of a million casualties (estimates have varied over the years) for the gain of a few miles of mud. He was rewarded with promotion to field marshal. The Colonial Secretary, Leopold Amery, hesitated before urging "a man in his sixty-eighth year to undertake one of the most difficult and thorny tasks in the field of Empire."[5] Plumer, who was suffering from painful shingles, eventually agreed to an appointment that would last three years rather than the normal five. Eschewing the grand entrance of his predecessor, he insisted on modesty in the ceremonials upon his arrival in Jerusalem with his wife and spinster daughter, Eleanor (later principal of St Anne's College, Oxford). They created a favorable initial impression in Jerusalem with their old-fashioned simplicity.

As High Commissioner in Palestine, Plumer manifested a resolution no less stolid than his firmness on the battlefield. When Zionist

Fig. 2.2. Lord Plumer (1857–1932), High Commissioner, 1925–28

representatives told him that the Jews were fighting with their backs to the wall, Plumer responded, "We will be the wall."[6] To an Arab delegation that warned that it could not be responsible for public tranquility, Plumer retorted that he did not expect it to take that responsibility—*he* would be responsible. Such responses endeared him to the Zionists. Anecdotes of this kind became part of the political lore of the country and cemented Plumer's reputation as a man of iron.

But this image belied the reality of Plumer's policy, which depended on the force of his personality to cloak the denuding of the government's military capability. The result, as the Palestine Royal Commission later commented, was to foster "a dangerous illusion of security."[7] By 1928 there were no regular troops at all stationed in Palestine. The consequence, visible shortly after Plumer's departure, was to leave the administration incapable of dealing with renewed anti-Jewish disturbances of August 1929. In retrospect, Plumer was blamed for allowing the local British forces to be wound down, almost out of existence. According to Plumer's deputy, Stewart Symes, the decision "to disband the British Gendarmerie and otherwise curtail heavy expenditure on security services . . . was his own: in matters of policy 'P' was never a 'passenger' and always made his own independent judgements. . . . He never defended his action. He wouldn't!"[8] It is true that the military reductions finally adopted were not Plumer's preferred policy; they occurred in spite of his strenuous objections, which were overruled by the Treasury, headed by the pro-Zionist Winston Churchill, as well as by the no less pro-Zionist Colonial Secretary, Amery, and, in the end, by the Cabinet.[9]

The third High Commissioner, Sir John Chancellor, attended the Royal Military Academy, Woolwich, started his career as an officer in the Royal Engineers, and then served as military secretary to the Committee of Imperial Defence. Before arriving in Palestine, he had held four colonial governorships, including that of Southern Rhodesia. But his tenure in Palestine was cut short.

The Zionists regarded Chancellor as an enemy of their cause. That was only half true. He did indeed detest them; but he soon came to hate the Arabs no less. Chancellor was severely affected by the bloody anti-Jewish riots of 1929, which erupted in Jerusalem, Hebron, and elsewhere while he was on leave. His initial reaction on returning to Palestine was one of emotional anti-Arab disgust. On the day of his arrival, he wrote to his son Christopher: "The atrocities that were committed by the Arabs were unspeakably revolting. . . . It is an awful revelation of the inate [*sic*] savagery of the Arab which has quite altered my feelings towards them."[10]

Fig. 2.3. Sir John Chancellor (1870–1952), High Commissioner, 1928–31

Upon more mature reflection, he nevertheless drew the conclusion that what was required was a drastic reversal of the government's pro-Zionist policy. He sought to apply to Palestine the principles of local self-government that had seemed to work in Southern Rhodesia. But whereas the small white-settler minority there had, uniquely in the British Empire, been granted full internal government over the country, Chancellor envisaged for Palestine elected institutions that would provide the Arab majority with the capacity to slow down or deflect the policy of the Jewish National Home.

Chancellor's proposals elicited strong and effective Jewish resistance, to which he reacted with anger and frustration. "I am so tired and so disgusted with this country and everything connected with it that I only want to leave it as soon as [I] can do so without failing in my duty," he wrote in October 1929.[11] He complained that he got nothing but abuse from both Jews and Arabs. But "the Jews are the worst because they cannot see things from any point of view but their own."[12] By February 1930, he had decided to resign: "I dislike the policy of the Balfour Declaration and consider that it is unjust to the Arabs and detrimental to the interests of the British Empire. . . . I find the Jews so antipathetic to me and so difficult to deal with that I shall be glad to sever connection with Palestine as soon as I can do so with decency."[13] He left Jerusalem in the summer of 1931, disillusioned and bitter, his policy in ruins.

Like Chancellor, the fourth High Commissioner, General Sir Arthur Wauchope, was a Scotsman. Unlike his predecessor, he was an elder of the Kirk. Wauchope had served in South Africa and India and on the western front (1914–16). In 1916 he was transferred to Mesopotamia (Iraq) in command of the Highland battalion, and took part in the doomed effort to relieve Kut. He retired from active military service in 1931. Wauchope was the longest serving and most interesting of the High Commissioners. One of his colleagues described him as "outwardly very frail; he ate very little and looked like an Egyptian mummy."[14] The Prime Minister, Ramsay Macdonald, said that in appointing Wauchope he was choosing a man "who does it with his head, not his feet."[15] Wauchope had the supreme virtue in the eyes of the historian of having very clear handwriting, but he dissipated this credit by ordering all his personal papers to be destroyed upon his death. He was an intelligent man with a passion for music and the habit, disconcerting to some, of eating his breakfast porridge in the proper Scottish manner while walking round the room. Gregarious and sociable, he entertained on a liberal scale.

Field Marshal Wavell called him "gay, gallant, and generous."[16] Some gossips drew from his delight in the company of handsome

Fig. 2.4. Sir Arthur Wauchope (1874–1947), High Commissioner, 1931–38

young men the conclusion that he was homosexual: perhaps it was as a measure of self-protection that he abruptly sent home to England one of his private secretaries who had been accused of buggery. Another private secretary, Thomas Hodgkin (later a famous historian of Africa), saw him as a liberal rather than an imperialist: "He did not believe in the nonsense of imperial missions." Hodgkin felt affection for his master, particularly when he found him in a "gay and chaffing mood."[17] But what Hodgkin found moving about Wauchope was what he considered his "very naïve" notion that "problems could be solved by personal goodwill."[18]

He had the habit of taking long walks and paying sudden, unannounced visits to Arab villages. Hodgkin, who sometimes accompanied him on these perambulations, said he was "like those medieval kings who chose to wander disguised as humble men among their peasants to get their reactions to recent pieces of legislation."[19] He would inspect the latrines, about which he was "very particular."[20] Local residents would retail their grievances. His private secretary for Arab affairs, Musa Alami, recorded that the High Commissioner's "eyes would fill with tears at some tale of woe or recital of wrongs and he would dole out bakshish, apparently under the firm impression that by giving fifty piasters he had gained a firm supporter."[21] In fact, he donated a large part of his personal fortune to the people of Palestine. But he did not gain universal respect thereby. The Arabs, whose nickname for Chancellor had been *malik* (king), called Wauchope *qabbūṭ* (grasshopper).

Wauchope compared the difficulty of dealing with the Arabs and Jews to that of a circus performer riding two horses at once. From the outset, he pursued a strongly pro-Zionist policy, perhaps recalling the words of a fellow elder of the Kirk, Robert Burns's notorious "Holy Willie":

> Lord, bless Thy chosen in this place,
> For here Thou has a chosen race!

The years 1933–35 were marked by unprecedented levels of Jewish immigration, particularly from Germany and Poland, and, as a result, by growing political tension. The Zionists regarded Wauchope as a sympathizer: David Ben Gurion, later Israel's first Prime Minister, called him "the best High Commissioner we ever had."[22] But Wauchope's renewal in 1935 of the proposal for an elected legislative council, albeit with limited powers, was rejected by Arabs and Jews as well as by Parliament.

In 1936 a three-year-long countrywide Arab revolt broke out. At first, Wauchope advocated restraint, but when clashes with the rebels intensified, he recommended resort to large-scale armed force to quell disorder. Ruthless repressive methods were employed. At the height of the revolt, no less than 40 percent of the effective field strength of the British army was mobilized in Palestine. More than two thousand Arabs were killed; many captured rebels were hanged. The Royal Commission in 1937 recommended partition of the country into Jewish and Arab states as well as a residual mandatory enclave. Despairing of an agreed solution, Wauchope backed the principle of enforced partition.[23] But under the shadow of impending war in Europe, the British government retreated from this bold policy.

Wauchope retired "on grounds of ill health" (in effect, he was compelled to retire) in February 1938, before completing his second five-year term. According to Hugh Foot, one of his subordinates, he "left Palestine broken-hearted."[24]

His successor, Sir Harold MacMichael, had distinguished himself in his youth as a classical scholar and as winner of the Public Schools Fencing Championship. Like Chancellor, he was a professional colonial administrator: he had seen twenty-nine years of service in Sudan and three as governor of the mandated territory of Tanganyika. MacMichael was the only High Commissioner who spoke the language of the country's majority population. A nephew of Lord Curzon, he shared some of his uncle's characteristics: high intelligence, cold aloofness, and trenchancy of expression. Also like Curzon, he was a "master of majestic marginalia."[25]

To MacMichael fell the duty of policing the implementation, before and during the Second World War, of the 1939 White Paper policy narrowly restricting Jewish immigration and land purchase in Palestine. He performed this task with rigor. Viewing the Zionists as akin to Nazis, he warned that young Jews in Palestine had become "infected with the gangster virus."[26] MacMichael narrowly survived an assassination attempt by Jewish extremists in 1944. In spite of his anti-Zionism, however, MacMichael moved, toward the end of his period of office, to advocacy, on grounds of *raison d'état*, of a postwar partition of Palestine and the creation of a Jewish state. The Zionists saw MacMichael as their archenemy. Yet had it not been for the assassination by Jewish terrorists in November 1944 of the British minister in the Middle East, Lord Moyne, a Jewish state might (*might*, I do not say *would*) have emerged under British auspices at the end of the war.

In April 1944, as MacMichael's term neared its end, Churchill made the extraordinary proposal that Chaim Weizmann should be appointed High Commissioner. Probably, he intended this

Fig. 2.5. Sir Harold MacMichael (1882–1969), High Commissioner, 1938–44

suggestion more as a rebuke to the Colonial Office than as a serious nomination. When the Colonial Secretary demurred, Churchill insisted that Weizmann "would be ready to work towards your partition scheme." "You can depend on Weizmann," he wrote, "I do not believe at all in Colonial Office officials or military men in this particular task so full of world politics."[27]

The eventual appointee, Field Marshal Lord Gort, had been Chief of the Imperial General Staff from 1937 to 1939 and commander of the British forces in France in 1939–40. Discredited by the withdrawal from Dunkirk, he restored his standing as governor of Malta in 1942–44, leading the island's brave resistance to Axis assault. As High Commissioner, he won admiration for his personal qualities: he had a warmer personality than his predecessor. The Zionists, in particular, liked him. In secret communication with the Colonial Office, however, he submitted a map of England with Palestine superimposed, questioning whether such a small country could be partitioned. Gort might have been the Mountbatten of Palestine, presiding, like the last Viceroy, over a dignified though chaotic British withdrawal; but he was already consumed by a mortal disease and left Palestine after only a few months.

The last of the line, Sir Alan Cunningham, served with the Royal Horse Artillery in the First World War, during which he won two medals for bravery. In the next, he led the successful campaign to conquer Italian Somaliland and to liberate Ethiopia from the Italians. But as commander of the Eighth Army in North Africa, he suffered reverses at the hands of Rommel and was dismissed by Churchill. Palestine afforded him the opportunity to redeem his reputation. When offered the post by Ernest Bevin, Cunningham was given "exactly fifteen minutes" to decide whether he wanted it.[28] No doubt the Foreign Secretary realized that he was proffering a poisoned chalice. Cunningham, like Wauchope, was a bachelor Scot. Also like Wauchope, who became a close friend, he had considerable sympathy with Zionism, though most Zionists regarded him as the public face of the British enemy.

Between 1945 and 1948, Palestine descended into a brutal three-way Zionist-Arab-British war, culminating in a savage bloodbath. The Zionists, impelled by the magnitude of the Jewish genocide in Europe, fixed on the goal of an independent state. The Palestinian Arabs, disorganized, divided, and prey to the dangerous patronage of surrounding Arab states, resisted desperately but ineffectively. The British, even with a hundred thousand armed men in Palestine, found it impossible to restore order.

Fig. 2.6. Lord Gort (1886–1946), High Commissioner, 1944–45. © National Portrait Gallery, London

Fig. 2.7. Sir Alan Cunningham (1887–1983), High Commissioner, 1945–48. © National Portrait Gallery, London

Amid the growing chaos, Cunningham wielded less effective power than any of his predecessors. Like Wauchope, he found his authority challenged by military commanders. Within a year, his relations with the Chief of the Imperial General Staff, the acerbic Field Marshal Bernard Montgomery, had reached a nadir. Never one to pull his verbal punches, Monty called him spineless and "a broken reed."[29] In March 1947, he compelled Cunningham to declare martial law, though the High Commissioner succeeded in limiting its effects and duration. When Monty visited Palestine in June of that year, he showed his contempt by not even bothering to pay a courtesy call on Cunningham.

Politically, Cunningham found that, as he later put it, "decisions on policy, when there were any decisions, had to be made outside Palestine, while we had to deal with the reactions to them inside the territory."[30] Moreover, the Colonial Office, to which he nominally reported, was itself sidelined by the Foreign Office, dominated by Bevin, who famously and unwisely told the House of Commons that he would stake his career on the solution of the Palestine problem (though he added the seldom-quoted caveat "but not in the limited sphere presented to me now").[31] The result was a catastrophe for British interests in the Middle East—though, strangely, Bevin's reputation, except among Zionists, survived more or less intact.

As terrorist attacks intensified, the British authorities retreated behind barbed wire into enclaves known as "Bevingrads." Since Cunningham had little influence on policy making and only limited control over security matters, he was left in the awkward position of responsibility without power. Fortunately, as one of his officials later recollected, he had one great pleasure in life that he carried over from his military career: he took the utmost pleasure in carrying out inspections.[32] During the final period of acute crisis, his official calendar was heavily filled with ceremonial duties such as presenting shamrocks to the Irish Guards on St. Patrick's Day and decorating the chairman of the Haifa Municipal Commission with a CBE.

One historian has commented, with wry understatement, that Cunningham "enabled the British to depart from Palestine with a modest amount of dignity and, in their own eyes, self-respect."[33] No doubt the writer intended the stress to be laid on the modifiers, because few non-British eyes saw it thus. Between Yorktown in 1781 and Hong Kong in 1997, Palestine was the only imperial possession that Britain left without handing the reins of government over to a successor administration. Unlike most of his senior officials, Cunningham privately favored partition. But he found himself obliged to administer what amounted to a policy of scuttle—"a melancholy business," as he later observed.[34] When asked what he would do with his office keys, Cunningham's deputy, Sir Henry Gurney, was said to have replied that he supposed he would leave them under the doormat. "The British were blamed," Cunningham said, "for not having handed over to anyone, whereas, in point of fact, 'there was nobody to whom to hand over.'"[35] Of course, this was a consequence of the British Government's determination not to be seen to implement partition while secretly, as Avi Shlaim has shown, seeking that very outcome.[36]

For security reasons, Cunningham left Jerusalem furtively at dawn on 14 May 1948, almost like a thief in the night. His departure led rapidly to the division of Palestine into three parts: the largest became the State of Israel; the Hashemite Kingdom of Jordan occupied what came to called the West Bank; and a small strip of Egyptian military occupation was established around Gaza.

IF WE COMPARE THE MEN WHO ruled Palestine with other British imperial rulers, it must be said that, in general, the High Commissioners did not see their role as significantly different from that of colonial governors, and that they brought similar attitudes to their task. These were the "guardians" memorably described by Philip Woodruff in his *The Men Who Ruled India* as "a corps of men specially selected, brought up in a rigour of bodily hardship to which no other people have subjected their ruling class, trained by cold baths, cricket and the history of Greece and Rome, a separate race from those they ruled, aloof, superior to bribery, discouraged from marriage until they were middle-aged, and then subjected to long separations."[37] The only exceptions among the High Commissioners to the governors from central casting were Samuel, marked out by his Zionist convictions, and Wauchope, who, alone of the seven, brought a distinctly spiritual sensibility to the Holy Land.

The power of the High Commissioners vis-à-vis their masters in London waned during the mandate. At its outset, Samuel wielded the authority of a quasi-independent satrap: he could defy even the imperious Curzon over the annexation of Transjordan, and it was he, not his nominal master, who was the real author of the policy statement of 1922, often called the Churchill White Paper. The turning point came in the final stages of the High Commissionership of Wauchope, who found his authority humiliatingly superseded by that of the General Officer Commanding Palestine, whom he nominally outranked.

The first High Commissioner had been a grand political panjandrum; the last was little more than a decorative figurehead. Cunningham's surviving papers, with their multitude of conscientiously formulated but ignored, discarded, and, in the end, historically irrelevant policy recommendations, were left blowing like chaff in the wind—they ultimately blew into the archive of the Middle East Centre of St. Antony's College, Oxford.

For most of the High Commissioners, Palestine was the graveyard of reputations. None moved on to higher positions in the empire. In moments of private vanity in the 1930s, Samuel dreamt of becoming Viceroy of India, but nothing came of that. As the first British district commissioner of Jerusalem, Sir Ronald Storrs, put it, "there is no promotion after Jerusalem"—though he meant something different by the remark.[38] Motti Golani, in his recent book, describes Cunningham's tenure in Palestine as "a micro-reflection of a macro-reality."[39] The crumbling of the authority of the High Commissioner was the local manifestation of the larger collapse of British power in the post-war world. We might say, adapting Theodor Mommsen's famous remark about the Roman departure from Britain in the early fifth century, that it was not Palestine that gave up Britain, but Britain that gave up Palestine. Both Jews and Arabs professed to want the British to leave. Yet both, in the final moments, appealed desperately to the British for military protection—as the ancient Britons in 410 had implored Rome for protection against the barbarian Picts, Scots, and Saxons.

The last word fell to Cunningham in a farewell address on the Palestine Broadcasting Service, in which he echoed the Emperor Honorius's advice to the Britons: henceforth, they could expect nothing of the empire and must look to their own defenses.[40] Whereupon the station closed forever with a rendition of "God Save the King." As the airwaves fell silent, Cunningham reflected: "Our consciences were clear. But perhaps, at that short range, we missed the full point of what was happening: a page of history was turning over."[41]

Spring Semester 2014

1. *Palestine Royal Commission Report* (Cmd. 5479, London, 1937), p. 43.
2. John Marlowe, *The Seat of Pilate: An Account of the Palestine Mandate* (London, 1959).
3. Diary of Edward Keith-Roach, ch. 4, Middle East Centre, St. Antony's College, Oxford.
4. Salim Tamari and Issam Nassar eds., *The Storyteller of Jerusalem: The Life and Times of Wasif Jawhariyyeh, 1904–1948* (Northampton, Mass., 2014), p. 199.
5. Geoffrey Powell, *Plumer: The Soldiers' General* (Barnsley, 2004), p. 298.
6. Colonel F. H. Kisch (representing the Palestine Zionist Executive), interview by Plumer, 31 Dec. 1926, Central Zionist Archives S25/594.
7. *Palestine Royal Commission Report*, p. 64.
8. G. Stewart Symes, *Tour of Duty* (London, 1946), p. 56.
9. See Plumer to Amery, 28 Jan. 1926; and Amery to Plumer, 16 Feb. 1926, The National Archives [TNA], CO 733/111.
10. Sir John Chancellor to Christopher Chancellor, 29 Aug. 1929, Chancellor Papers, Rhodes House, Oxford, 16/3/2.
11. Sir John Chancellor to Christopher Chancellor, 24 Oct. 1929, ibid., 16/3/37.
12. Sir John Chancellor to Sir Henry Birchenough, draft, Dec. 1929 or Jan. 1930, ibid., 12/7/8.
13. Sir John Chancellor to Christopher Chancellor, 21 Feb. 1930, ibid., 16/3/86.
14. Edwin Samuel, *A Lifetime in Jerusalem* (London, 1970), p. 144.
15. Quoted in Chaim Weizmann, *Trial and Error* (London, 1949), p. 415.
16. Obituary by Wavell in *Journal of the Royal Central Asian Society*, 35 (1948), pp. 6–7.
17. Thomas Hodgkin, *Letters from Palestine, 1932–1936* (London, 1986): Thomas Hodgkin, quoted in introduction by E. C. Hodgkin.
18. Thomas Hodgkin, interview by the author, Oxford, 1970.
19. Hodgkin, *Letters*, p. 101.
20. Samuel, *Lifetime in Jerusalem*, p. 145.
21. Sir Geoffrey Furlonge, *Palestine Is My Country: The Story of Musa Alami* (London, 1969), p. 99.
22. David Ben Gurion, interview by the author, Sde Boker, 16 Jan. 1970.
23. Wauchope to Sir Cosmo Parkinson, 20 Aug. 1937, CO 967/93.
24. Sir Hugh Foot, *A Start in Freedom* (London, 1964), p. 38.
25. Hubert Young, *The Independent Arab* (London, 1933), p. 283 (referring to Curzon).
26. MacMichael to Colonial Office, 2 Oct. 1944, FO 921/153.
27. Martin Gilbert, *Churchill and the Jews: A Lifelong Friendship* (New York, 2007), p. 208.
28. Motti Golani, *Palestine between Politics and Terror, 1945–1947* (Waltham, Mass., 2013), p. 18.
29. Quoted in ibid., p. 172.
30. Sir Alan Cunningham, "Palestine—The Last Days of the Mandate," *International Affairs*, 24 (1948), p. 484.
31. House of Commons Debates, 13 Nov. 1945, 5th ser., vol. 415, col. 1934.
32. Ivan Lloyd Philips, interview by the author, Oxford, 17 Feb. 1970.
33. Wm. Roger Louis, "The End of British Rule in Palestine," in Andrew Porter and Robert Holland, eds., *Theory and Practice in the History of European Expansion Overseas: Essays in Honour of Ronald Robinson* (London, 1988), p. 146.

34. Cunningham, "Palestine," p. 490.
35. Ibid., p. 488.
36. Avi Shlaim, *Collusion across the Jordan: King Abdullah, the Zionist Movement, and the Partition of Palestine* (New York, 1988).
37. Philip Woodruff [Philip Mason], *The Men Who Ruled India*, vol. 1, *The Founders* (London, 1965), p. 15.
38. Storrs, *The Memoirs of Sir Ronald Storrs* (New York, 1937), p. 465.
39. Golani, *Palestine between Politics and Terror*, p. 235.
40. A recording of the speech is in the British Library sound archive: T10348R C4.
41. Quoted in A. J. Sherman, *Mandate Days* (London, 1997), p. 242.

Nancy Lambton

3

Nancy Lambton

JOHN GURNEY

Ann Katharine Swynford Lambton was one of the few outstanding scholars of the Persian language and Persian history that Britain has produced since the subject developed within the wider academic discipline of Oriental languages in the nineteenth century. Early in her career she established a reputation as the preeminent specialist in all matters Persian: language and grammar, history and political thought in the Islamic period, religion, and contemporary political analysis were all considered to lie within her expertise. For many both within and outside the scholarly community, she was the ultimate authority in all these specializations.

Born on 8 February 1912, Ann Lambton, called Nancy by her family and friends, was the second of four children. She was given her third name, Swynford, after the winner of the St. Leger in 1911. Like most Lambtons, she and her siblings were "born in the saddle" and rode "by the light of nature." Nancy attended a day school in Newmarket until she was seventeen. Higher education was hardly necessary for the kind of life that her mother envisaged for her. But Nancy rebelled against the social conventions of her class. She began to read accounts of the great travelers and adventurers of the period, beginning with T. E. Lawrence's *Revolt in the Desert*. A chance encounter around Christmas 1929 changed the course of her life. She found herself seated at dinner next to Sir Denison Ross, the director of the School of Oriental Studies. He encouraged her to take seriously her interest in Oriental travel and suggested that she visit him in London. He introduced her to an entirely different world, one that appealed to her sense of adventure and travel and held out the prospect of greater independence. She set about obtaining the basic qualifications for admission to SOS and studied at a crammer for some months. She was accepted for a one-year certificate course in Persian in October 1930, passed a second-year certificate in Persian in the following year, and then began an Intermediate Arts course, studying Latin, German, and geology at King's College, and Persian at SOS. She progressed to the honors course in Persian, which added Arabic, linguistics, and comparative Iranian philology to the main subjects of Persian language, literature, and history.

An important early influence came from Guy Le Strange, whose experiences of traveling in Persia reached back nearly sixty years. Close to eighty and almost blind, he was delighted to help Nancy through some of her Arabic and Persian texts at the beginning of the honors course, telling her, "You are the most intelligent pupil I have ever had." But the lessons suddenly ended in December 1933 when Le Strange was hit by a bus and died a few days later.

Travel had first aroused Nancy's interest in the Middle East, and she wanted to spend the summer vacation in Persia before her final examinations. The Ouseley Memorial Prize gave her a small measure of financial independence, and she left for Persia in July 1934. This visit of a little over two months indicated those aspects of Persian life that would hold her interest and affection in the future. At Isfahan she lived with missionaries in the Christian hospital compound, but it was in the surrounding mountains that she enjoyed herself most, climbing and walking often by herself. She also was quick to respond to what she then called "the poorer classes"—"hospitable, pleasant, dignified, unassuming people."

After a creditable upper second in her final examinations in 1935, Nancy was encouraged to continue her studies and chose as the subject for her doctoral thesis the social organization of Persia in the Saljuq period. The Agha Khan Travelling Scholarship in 1936 helped her return to Persia. She had a well-defined project in mind—a study of Islamic craft guilds—which made it easier to approach Persians. The governor of Isfahan recommended a learned teacher, Hosein Ali Rashed, with whom she studied Arabic grammar and read some Persian poetry, an experience that for the first time taught her how to appreciate poetry "when explained by someone who really understands it." With the thorough grounding in linguistic studies at SOS, she was also interested in doing some work on dialects. Nancy learned that two young brothers in Isfahan came from an area on the northern borders of the province, and they were prepared to teach her the dialect they spoke between themselves. Nancy stayed some days in Jawshaqan with relatives of the two brothers. It was the beginning of an attachment to the Persian countryside that lasted a lifetime. She immediately liked the genuine friendliness, simplicity, natural courtesy, and dignity of the families there. Later that summer, she spent some weeks living with them *en famille,* joining in the household chores of churning butter, making yogurt, and milking the goats. In the course of those weeks was laid the basis for her extraordinary knowledge and understanding of *Iran profonde,* and these villages in the mountains south of Kashan became a kind of spiritual home to which she was drawn back time and again over the next thirty years.

Nancy then moved to Tehran, but in general it did not make any deep impression on her. In the privacy of her notebooks, she expressed impatience with Tehran life and criticized what she called the Persian mind and its inability to think logically or to synthesize. It was the first sign of a prejudice that grew more marked as the years passed, a certain disdain for the Westernized, metropolitan Persian, in contrast to the affinity she had from the beginning felt for rural life. Back in London, Nancy published two pieces of research that derived directly from these months in Persia. The first was *Three Persian Dialects* (London, 1938), and the second an analysis of a sixteenth-century account of the regulation of the water supply in Isfahan, published in the *Bulletin of the School of Oriental Studies* (1938). Her thesis on Saljuq institutions was completed two years after her return, two months before the outbreak of war.

After nine years of study and examinations, it was not clear what Nancy should do next. There was no prospect of a position in Islamic history at SOS, and several people were already teaching Persian there. She decided to return to Persia and do more research on the topics that interested her. But in early September 1939, her life suddenly changed. After war was declared, the British minister in Tehran enlisted her to work in the press and publicity section of the legation. The move had a momentous impact on her subsequent career. For the next six years, throughout the whole of the war apart from one short leave, Nancy played a central role in the official British presence in Iran. During her previous stay in Tehran, she had not liked what she had seen of diplomats, their concern with status and seniority, the parties, bridge, and formal dinners. She loathed bureaucratic procedures and most of her colleagues. She lived by herself, with a housekeeper, renting a small, damp, uncomfortable house with a leaking roof and no electricity, in an unfashionable part of the town; she dressed as she liked, cycled everywhere, and avoided parties—"the weekly penance"—as much as she could.

She immersed herself in work, which consisted "largely in reading newspapers, supplying material to the press, and making reports on public opinion." She soon had the added responsibility for a news commentary in Persian, an English bulletin, another in German, broadcasts, and propaganda films. She worked long hours, with very few days off.

Her work ethic and commitment to the many tasks entrusted to her as press attaché commended her to Sir Reader Bullard when he came as minister after a few months. With little previous experience of Persia, he quickly saw how invaluable were the services of a young Orientalist who knew the language well and had some knowledge of the country. She saw in him a mentor, with the qualities of rock-like integrity, plain speaking, and moral courage. He disliked "humbug," hypocrisy, "intrigue," and calculating worldliness. A strong bond of mutual respect and trust, even affection, was established between them. After church services at the American Mission Hospital, she would stay to Sunday lunch at the legation, discussing Samuel Johnson, Jane Austen, and Dickens.

Nancy's advice had some bearing on one of the most dramatic episodes of these early years of the war in Tehran, the occupation of Iran by the Allied armies and the abdication of Reza Shah. Alarmed at the somewhat exaggerated number of German agents and the potential threat that they posed to the supply routes to Russia overland from the Persian Gulf, the Allies warned Reza Shah to act against them. When this had little effect, Russian and British troops invaded. It was not an action that Nancy could justify. She felt a sense of shame at the invasion itself and its dubious legality: "The behaviour of the Foreign Office has been jesuitical to a degree. No Persian will ever again believe [us] . . . and I don't blame them. It does not fill one either with confidence or pride." But once it had happened and Reza Shah's behavior became more erratic, Nancy provided the material broadcast by the BBC Persian service, which listed examples of his abuses of power. These were directly responsible for his abdication. It was a masterstroke, devastating in its consequences: "Never, I suppose, have the BBC had such a success, for it was almost entirely due to the Persian broadcasts from London that it happened." Though pleased that Reza Shah was gone, she evenhandedly commented that "it would be unjust to deny that he did a tremendous amount for the country, though unfortunately in later years excesses obscured that fact."

With Persia brought into the forefront of the war effort, the scale of the operation in the Tehran legation was transformed. The city became the center of a vital link in a military and intelligence operation that sustained the Russian defense against the Nazi attack and then reinforced the Soviet army's advance on the eastern front. Nancy's duties multiplied to include all kinds of anti-Nazi, pro-Allied propaganda, broadcasting in Persian, dealing with the Persian press, controlling editors and publishers, recruiting young writers and intellectuals on the left to promote the Allied cause, establishing a pro-British group of supporters among the parliamentary deputies, and influencing the choice of cabinet positions, even that of prime minister. She was at the interface of the British presence and the Persian political elite.

In wartime, the boundaries between this kind of work and intelligence operations were often blurred. Within her department there were undercover members of the Special Operations Executive (SOE), and she knew about some of their activities. She sometimes traveled with them in Persia, visited them in Baghdad and Cairo, and found their company amusing and interesting. She never worked directly for SOE or any other intelligence department, but it was not long before the myth surrounding her began to take shape. She spoke Persian almost flawlessly—well enough, she thought, nearly to pass for a Persian in her broadcasts. In Kurdistan she was once reproached for wearing European clothes instead of her own Kurdish dress. Persian newspapers published her articles and accounts of her attending the Parliament, and less flattering cartoons appeared in the hostile press, as well as the inevitable accusations that she was a spy who knew more about Persian political life than anyone else.

The rough-and-tumble of political involvement in this period exposed Nancy to a different side of Tehran life. In the weeks after the occupation, she described how "the jackals come crowding round," and with them "a certain class of Persian which wants and believes we run the country and wishes to be our slaves." Less vehement in her castigation of these than Bullard, who was contemptuous of almost all Persians to the point that even Churchill commented on it, Nancy drew a distinction between the "falsehood, cowardice, lack of principle and corruption" of those involved in official life, and the "many real virtues" of the best type of Persian, uncontaminated by office or power. She believed that there were some who genuinely wanted reform and progress, difficult though they were to persuade to take an active role. Her hope was for a relatively progressive regime and the emergence of genuine democratic government with real political parties and political programs. These ideas and aspirations were expressed in a series of articles she wrote during the war years for the *Asiatic Review*. She criticized Persians for having no conception of the individual and no capacity for independent thought. In a sweeping condemnation of Persian society, her overall impression was of a nation damaged by the terror of Reza Shah's reign, during which individual freedom had been suppressed and corruption had thoroughly permeated official life. In these years after the abdication, she saw only cynicism, love of intrigue, and political incompetence, rather than a brief interlude of relative freedom and political experimentation.

WHEN THE END OF THE WAR WAS IN SIGHT, Nancy had some apprehension about returning to London. In September 1944, A. J. Arberry, the new professor of Persian at SOAS (by then enlarged to include African studies), encouraged her to apply for a new, AIOC-funded post in Persian. Her appointment started in October 1945. At once Nancy set about creating her own materials for a Persian grammar and a companion vocabulary, which she used for what later became her legendary intensive courses taught to AIOC personnel, government officials, and students. But language work was not her main interest. As early as the summer of 1936, during the first visit to Jawshaqan, she had recorded details about rural life, but it was only toward the end of the war years that she began to reconsider contemporary agrarian problems, gradually realizing that agriculture could play an important part in the regeneration of the country. In the summer of 1944, through an invitation from the Middle East Supply Company (MESC) in Cairo to write a paper on land tenure, her interest was reignited. She planned short visits to areas with different kinds of landholding practices and began to familiarize herself with some of the problems.

From the beginning it was clear where her sympathies lay. Before the war, in small peasant-proprietor villages such as Jawshaqan, she had sensed that there had once existed self-contained, self-governing, relatively stable communities with a corporate sense and some degree of independence. It was these she wanted to encourage. In contrast were the villages owned by landlords. Islamic inheritance laws, insecurity of tenure, and the absence of primogeniture had led to the fragmentation of properties and the destruction of any idea of cooperation in a mutual enterprise. There was no old landed aristocracy or country gentry with a sense of responsibility and an interest in fulfilling their duties generation after generation. Landlords were for the most part absentees living in the towns, with little understanding of the life of the peasant. As a class, she thought them "greedy, short-sighted, ignorant and totally lacking in public spirit." Nancy wanted their estates broken up and redistributed.

An unexpected friendship with Doreen Warriner opened Nancy's eyes to a body of specialist knowledge and theory in the field of land reform. Warriner, several years older and experienced in the agrarian problems of Eastern Europe, was an economist at University College London. During the war, she had worked for the MESC in Cairo. Her visit to Persia in the late summer of 1944 and her travels with Nancy, during which they were arrested by the Russians in Azerbaijan, was the start of a friendship that had a decisive impact on Nancy's subsequent career. Warriner passionately supported the revitalization of a peasant society with a coherent social organization and ethos, whether in Eastern Europe or the Middle East. From this time onward, Nancy's criticisms of the landlord class became more pointed, and her emphasis on the need for agrarian reform more insistent, as part of a thorough, radical transformation of all aspects of society.

The initial idea for *Landlord and Peasant in Persia: A Study of Land Tenure and Land Revenue Administration* (1953), the book that established Nancy's scholarly reputation, came from an invitation in the autumn of 1947 from Chatham House to write on land tenure in Persia, emphasizing both present practice and its historical development. With a year's sabbatical leave from July 1948, she returned to work in Tehran libraries, but she was much happier in traveling, observing firsthand, and interviewing on the spot. From the spring of 1949 until the autumn, she covered great swathes of the country, collecting information from the villages she visited and daily writing up a mass of information. The bulk of her research was completed in the course of a year. Preparing a draft took longer, since she added several historical chapters. It was a remarkable achievement of scrupulous historical research combined with precise firsthand observation and analysis. Regarded by many as a classic in the sixty years since it was first published, it is an indispensable reference work for the history of agrarian life in Iran, as well as an extraordinarily detailed survey of agrarian practice in the first half of the twentieth century. The conclusion contains a passionate clarion call for action. Persia was on the verge of a general collapse, and there was the danger that the wider bonds holding society together would dissolve and leave the country facing the threat of communism. Only a social revolution, a fundamental change in the conception of society, in the relationship of the individual to society, would avert this disaster.

As Nancy had foreseen in the war years, she might not be able to enjoy the quiet return to academic life that she wanted. Her views were sought informally by politicians, the Foreign Office, and the

AIOC. For example, in the Azerbaijan crisis of 1946—a Soviet-supported separatist movement in northwestern Persia—she had given sensible advice to both the Iranian embassy and the Labour Cabinet. Despite a genuine desire to the contrary, she found it difficult to keep aloof from any political involvement. The clearest example of this tendency was her role in the Musaddiq crisis—the most controversial episode of her life. She had come across Musaddiq in the war years, when he was a major political figure with a reputation for personal probity and liberal social views, but she did not know him personally. He had not been within her group of contacts. Indeed, as an anticolonial nationalist, he was strongly opposed to her friends and the old wartime networks. In his reformist social policies and his measures for land reform, Musaddiq's ideas would not have been far removed from Nancy's own, but there could have been no political collaboration. She accepted the predominant British view about Musaddiq. From the 1920s he was usually described as "a demagogue and a windbag." Bullard added that he was epileptic, old beyond his years, and a rich landowner. Before he became prime minister in 1951, Nancy had hastily dismissed his proposals for land reform as insincere, concerned only with preserving his own class interests.

When the movement for the nationalization of the AIOC gathered pace, Nancy became involved, though not out of any great admiration for the company. She had been friendly with its representatives in Tehran, but in principle was prejudiced against big business and had been uncomfortable with the discriminatory social attitudes of the expatriate communities in the oil fields. Like some in the Foreign Office, she was critical of how the AIOC had acted in recent years. Opportunities for a settlement had been missed. But she believed that Musaddiq could not simply appropriate a crucial British interest, perhaps the largest overseas investment in the empire. There had to be a negotiated settlement in which legitimate British oil interests would be protected as far as possible and compensation agreed for what was surrendered. She thought that a compromise could be reached, but Musaddiq had to be removed first.

As soon as the nationalization of the AOIC took place, Herbert Morrison, the Foreign Secretary, sent a warship to Abadan and threatened a land assault. It is likely that Nancy suggested a less reckless response. The embassy, she argued, had been pursuing the wrong strategy by supporting an inherently weak shah and ignoring those who had advanced British objectives in the war years. Iranians' general antipathy against the shah and the corruption of the court had rebounded on the British, who were held to be his protector and guardian. In turn, anti-British sentiment was directed against the oil company, the most visible center of British power and influence. Nancy recommended that her wartime colleague Robin Zaehner, now back in Oxford as the lecturer in Persian after his experiences in Persia and Albania in SOE, should be sent to Tehran at once to reactivate the networks that had proved so effective in supporting British policy in the war years. He was the person, she argued, "to give the Persians confidence and to set the plan in motion." She was optimistic that Musaddiq's position could be shaken "almost immediately" by overt and covert means of propaganda and persuasion, by mobilizing opposition against him, and by supporting those Persians, "the relatively enlightened," whose view of the Persian national interest coincided with British plans. After his fall, a new government could begin serious long-term reform.

Until the files of MI6 are released for this period, it will be impossible to know what informal advice she gave in the months leading up to the coup of August 1953. But it is unlikely that Nancy was directly involved. No evidence has yet emerged that she played any part in the planning of the coup or indeed approved of force, as opposed to propaganda and persuasion, in deposing the Musaddiq government. There are no grounds for describing her as the architect of the 1953 coup, the éminence grise of British intelligence who initiated the whole operation, as has been claimed. In hindsight, however, it is difficult to explain her miscalculation of the strength and nature of nationalist feeling in Iran and of Musaddiq's personality. She did not know the key members of the National Front around Musaddiq, nor appreciate that Persian nationalism was no longer the same phenomenon that she had dismissed as fragile and insincere ten years earlier. In the Azerbaijan crisis of 1946, she had recognized that "what the Persian people desire above all is freedom from interference in their internal affairs, freedom to begin to set their house in order." But when British interests were directly challenged through oil nationalization a few years later, she tried to apply the strategies employed in wartime to a quite different situation.

BY THE TIME OF MUSADDIQ'S FALL and the creation of a new oil consortium, Nancy's standing in the academic world had been confirmed by her appointment to the chair of Persian at SOAS. It had been a rapid elevation. With the publication of *Landlord and Peasant*, followed shortly by *Persian Grammar* (1953) and *Persian Vocabulary* (1954), election to the chair, and the award of a D.Litt. from the University of London, any doubts that she once might have had about her qualifications for an academic career had been comprehensively extinguished. There was, however, no indication in her inaugural lecture of a clear plan for her own research or a wider vision for the field. She had taken on no doctoral students up to this point, and in her own research she appeared hesitant about what direction it might take after *Landlord and Peasant.* Instead of one major topic in mind, she moved between slighter contributions to current affairs journals and a handful of scholarly articles on medieval political thought, administrative history, and the Qajars. There were some signs that she was thinking about a book on the nineteenth century, but for this she needed to return to Iran for several months and resume work on primary sources in Tehran libraries. With another sabbatical year in 1959, some months were spent in Tehran and provincial libraries, looking at material for the Qajar period, but as before, she much preferred to travel, exploring areas she had not visited for some time, walking and climbing, and joining a tribal migration. Wherever she went, she made notes on what she saw of rural and tribal life and agrarian conditions.

The subject of agrarian reform, which embraced both her historical and contemporary interests, provided the impetus for her research over the next decade. As she argued in the final chapter of *Landlord and Peasant,* land reform would have to be part of a wider revolution in society; it could not be considered in isolation. She had no expectation that this might happen. Then quite suddenly the prospect for serious reform was transformed by the appointment of Hasan Arsanjani as the minister of agriculture in a liberal government in 1961. New legislation approved in early 1962 incorporated the two central elements that Nancy had always advocated: breaking the political and social influence of the landowning class and bringing about the emergence of an independent peasantry. It had, she thought, "a touch of genius." At the beginning of the summer vacation of that year, she went to Tehran and interviewed Arsanjani. It helped that the Persian translation of *Landlord and Peasant* had been published, and widely reviewed, the year before. Arsanjani had read it carefully. Their views were very similar, and from the beginning they established a rapport. She thought him "a dynamic man of considerable personal energy, determination, vigour, and toughness." Five days later, he invited her to attend the first distribution of lands to peasants. Nancy became caught up in the excitement and promise of the moment. She wanted to believe that what was taking place would have a profound effect on Persian society. It seemed to fulfill everything that she had hoped for during the last twenty years or more: the transformation of peasant lives, the revival of "an independent, self-supporting, self-respecting peasantry," the elimination of the landlords, the end of their political power, and the rehabilitation of rural life.

Over the next ten years, she spent seven summer vacations in charting the progress of the land reform and cooperative movement. For weeks on end, in a punishing schedule that taxed her physical strength, she crisscrossed much of Iran. In the early years, she was optimistic. She sensed that a new kind of official was emerging, one with a willingness to take responsibility—something quite new in Persian administration. She felt personally involved in this social transformation. She published *The Persian Land Reform, 1962–1966* (1969) when the outcome was still uncertain. In part it was written out of a certain embarrassment, since she had not published a book for over fifteen years. But mainly she wanted to give as much publicity and encouragement to land reform as she could, in the hope that its momentum would be maintained. Doubts had been expressed after Arsanjani's resignation in 1963, and disturbing signs had accumulated in subsequent years that the drive and integrity of the original reform were being diluted. By the later 1960s, the emphasis had shifted toward increased production and greater government control. The new objectives of the early 1970s—rapid mechanization, large commercial farms for cash crops, government corporations, and agribusinesses—were quite different from the original vision of Arsanjani and herself. After the summer vacation of 1972, she never returned to Iran, apart from a brief visit for an academic conference on medieval history in 1977. Any hope for land reform's transforming impact on Iranian society had been extinguished by what she thought was the shah's cynical policy toward rural development.

Nancy returned to her earlier interests in medieval subjects. The period particularly suited her gifts, demanding an unrivaled mastery of difficult Persian prose and an often obsolete technical vocabulary, and a deep understanding of the way in which medieval society, both rural and urban, worked. Her writing reflected the same wide-ranging approach of her earlier articles—Saljuq administration, political thought, agriculture, and Islamic mirrors for princes. On the point of her retirement from SOAS, she published twelve of these articles as *Theory and Practice in Medieval Persian Government* (1980). Almost at the same time, she decided to publish the lectures that she had given for many years on Islamic political ideas. They appeared under the title *State and Government in Medieval Islam: An Introduction to the Study of Islamic Political Theory; The Jurists* (1981).

Nancy retired from the school in 1979, where for well over thirty years she had been responsible for the Persian teaching at all levels, working long hours with beginners, and undertaking heavy administrative responsibilities as head of department for some years. From the 1960s onward, she took on the supervision of the doctoral dissertations of a number of graduates, consolidating her reputation as the most exacting and meticulous scholar in her field. After an unconventional beginning, her academic career had been a stellar success, with a British Academy Fellowship in 1964, followed by honorary doctorates at Durham and Cambridge, and honorary fellowships at SOAS and New Hall, Cambridge. Later she was made an honorary vice president of the British Institute of Persian Studies, to which she had for several decades given conscientious service, and an annual memorial lecture was established in her honor at Durham University.

After moving from London to Northumberland, relieved of the burden of teaching and administration, Nancy was rejuvenated. She settled comfortably into a modest cottage in a hamlet on the northern edge of the Cheviots, with several relatives living nearby. She prepared a series of lectures given in 1981 at Columbia, which were transformed into a substantial monograph, *Continuity and Change in Medieval Persia: Aspects of Administrative, Economic and Social History, 11th–14th Century* (1988), considered by some her most important book. An expanded edition of *Landlord and Peasant* (1991) contained considerable new material about the Mongol period in a long preface. Despite her distance from specialist libraries and her increasingly infrequent visits to London, Nancy remained in touch with recent scholarship. This was particularly important for another task she had set herself in retirement, her work for the *Encyclopedia of Islam* (1960–2009). From the early 1950s, she had dutifully contributed articles to it. She wrote over forty entries in all, tackling long historical periods, important provinces, places, tribes, and technical and administrative terms. Perhaps more remarkable as she worked into her eighth and ninth decades with barely diminished vigor was the noticeable change in her approach as an historian. For the first time she felt able to lighten her style, be less cautious, add a few personal asides and anecdotes, and discuss personalities—at least one or two that, after a lifetime of study, she felt that she had come to understand a little. Quoting Marc Bloch, she saw that "behind the written documents there are men, and it is men that history seeks and grasps." It was far from the administrative and institutional history with which she had begun her career.

Nancy was too reticent and reserved to write or talk much about herself, and left little enough for future historians trying to understand the essence of her personality. She had no small talk; in company there were often embarrassing silences. It was as if she had protected herself beneath a carapace of indifference in an attempt to conceal her own awkwardness. She had difficulty in making any emotional contact, at least outside the few close relationships within her family, and she recoiled from physical touch. In middle age, she assumed the persona of the austere bluestocking, grey hair swept back in a bun or close-cropped, grey herringbone suit with a skirt almost ankle length, thick stockings, and sturdy brogue shoes. Wherever she went, she took her old battered rucksack, packed with a few spare clothes and a Persian text to read. Where she felt at ease, she could relax and enjoy people's company. Once approval was given, total loyalty was expected, and in turn reciprocated, with a surprising warmth and generosity. In her later life there were no limits to the hours she would devote to the aspiring research student struggling with the difficulties of Persian, and well into her nineties she would send back a draft paper meticulously commented on, errors in translation and transliteration corrected. It was a life dedicated to the highest standards of scholarship, which she had learned in her youth and which she felt it was her duty to maintain and pass on. She died on 19 July 2008, and is buried in the churchyard at Kirknewton, close to ancestral Lambton lands and the house where she had lived for nearly three decades.

Fall Semester 2014

A longer version of this lecture appeared in *Biographical Memoirs of Fellows of the British Academy*, vol. 12 (2013).

Siegfried Sassoon

4

Siegfried Sassoon

MAX EGREMONT

The writer Siegfried Sassoon was a compulsive diarist. His notebooks, filled with small rounded handwriting and the occasional drawing or caricature, passed to George, his only child, when Sassoon died in 1967. George lent them to me in the late 1990s when I was writing the elder Sassoon's biography. After George's death in 2006, they were sold to the Cambridge University Library, which has now put them online, digitizing one of the most comprehensive and extraordinary records of any writer's life.

Do these notebooks and their drafts of poems harm his reputation? I think not, although the self-centeredness inevitable in all diaries is even more than usually evident here.

For Sassoon, as he became more nostalgic, Cambridge meant youth, romantic yearning, beauty, and his own beginnings as a poet. He had been an idle student at the university before the First World War, failing to win the poetry prize and leaving without taking a degree. In the 1950s, however, he began to visit Cambridge again, and even thought of moving to the town, when George was a student there. He was proud to be an honorary fellow of Clare, his old college. The surgeon and bibliophile Geoffrey Keynes, one of Sassoon's greatest friends, lived nearby.

Sassoon's story is often turbulent, ranging from a sheltered Victorian country childhood to late despair before ultimate consolation in religious faith. Born in 1886 to an artistic Anglo-Catholic mother and a father from a rich Jewish family, he began writing early on, cosseted yet hit hard by the breakup of his parents' marriage and his father's early death.

Introverted, often awkward, Sassoon kept a diary partly, I think, for companionship, feeling isolated from most people by his wish to be a poet and by his homosexuality. He used the diaries to find his way as a writer, recording impressions and making lists of books that he had read. It was as if Sassoon wished constantly to observe himself, to keep track of his "chameleon" personality. He had a romantic view of his destiny. "It is almost alarming the way I draw people to me," he wrote, "and then withdraw into my solitude." Always there was the quest for poetry, for what he called "the still small voice that speaks to the secret heart alone."

The First World War diaries are bound in dark red, some pages stained with the mud of the trenches or the wax of candles that had lit his writing. Although at first excited by the idea of battle, Sassoon, after experiencing the western front, wrote some of the most powerful poetry of the war in savage satires or graphic depictions of desperation and pain. Perhaps no other writer shows in such sensuous detail what it felt like to be in the trenches. Reading poems such as "Counter-Attack" or "To Any Dead Officer," one can sense the fear, the drizzle, the mud, and the deep comradeship.

For Sassoon, the war brought feelings stronger, and stranger, than he had ever known. "Grief can be beautiful," he wrote in 1916, "when we find something worthy to be mourned," describing how his anger after a friend's death from shellfire became "hate" for the Germans and "the lust to kill." Sassoon was a brave officer, winning the Military Cross. The diaries also have the draft of his 1917 protest against the war's aims, which led to him being sent to Craiglockhart Hospital to be treated for shell shock, where he met his fellow poet Wilfred Owen. Wounded on returning to the front in the summer of 1918, Sassoon wrote of his state of mind in a London hospital, on the edge of a breakdown: how "the arrogant, secret pride of youth says, 'I'll go back and get killed'—just to spite these old men," or civilians at home who had no idea of the war's reality.

Sassoon became identified with the war. He regretted the lack of interest in his later religious and devotional poems, and the path to these is shown in the diaries. After an adventurous 1920 lecture tour in the United States, he found it hard to settle on a satisfactory life in Britain. Devoted to his conventional mother, Siegfried dreaded hurting her by becoming involved in a public scandal because of his open affair with the capricious, aristocratic artist Stephen Tennant.

In 1933, having been rejected by the neurotic Tennant, Sassoon hastily married Hester Gatty, wondering, as if predicting doom, "how could she ever be happy with such an ultra-queer character as I am?" They began an (at first) idyllic life in a Wiltshire country house with their adored son, George. Gradually, however, the atmosphere darkened as the marriage failed. From the end of the 1930s until his conversion to Roman Catholicism in 1957, which seemed to solve everything, Sassoon often felt oppressed by "a bullying barbarian of a world" where his traditionalist poetry had apparently been eclipsed by T. S. Eliot's and Ezra Pound's modernism. These diaries show a man filled with wonder at life who could also be overwhelmed by what it brought to him.

Three volumes of Sassoon's diaries (the ones from 1915 to 1925) were published in the early 1980s, edited with discreet piety by his friend Rupert Hart-Davis. But these stop before Siegfried's obsessive romance with Tennant, and they are a bit dull. It didn't help that the transition of most handwritten diaries into cold print deadens their impact, like a reduction in voltage.

Cambridge's new digitized versions give a much more complete and atmospheric view. To see the writing and the drawings on screen is not as good as handling the notebooks, but is certainly the next best thing. It is funny to think what Sassoon's own reaction might have been. A technophobe dismayed by the modern world and its machines, he used to shout into the telephone, thinking this was the only way to be heard. Yet Siegfried Sassoon wanted to be remembered and would, rightly, have trusted Cambridge to do this well.

How is Siegfried Sassoon seen now? I believe that his work still has great relevance. Our time, after all, is a period of centennial anniversaries of events that he witnessed and wrote about unforgettably: the start of the First World War in 1914, the Battle of the Somme in 1916, his protest against the continuation of the war in 1917, and then the war's end in 1918.

In a sense, the war has become Sassoon's war. From the 1960s (when the British establishment and its record became increasingly challenged), the version of the western front given by Sassoon and Wilfred Owen and other admired war poets—of needless suffering, of innocence betrayed by a misguided high command—has, to the despair of many historians, remained popular. Field Marshal Sir Douglas Haig and others have become identified with Sassoon's "The General," who, in the poem of that title, "did for" his men with "his plan of attack." Soldiers are thought of as wearily going over the top into a sodden, muddy no-man's-land in an atmosphere of despair and misery that are hard to reconcile with the eventual victory.

The war poems have, I think, have survived better than the prose. Sassoon's only partly fictionalized autobiography, the *Memoirs of a*

Fox-Hunting Man (1928), although beautifully written, is perhaps too remote from the twenty-first century to connect strongly with young readers; nonetheless, the descriptions of the trenches in it and its successors—*Memoirs of an Infantry Officer* (1930) and *Sherston's Progress* (1936)—still evoke how the war felt. His importance, however, should not be doubted. Siegfried Sassoon was a vital witness to perhaps the most cataclysmic event of the twentieth century, the trigger for tragedies such as the Holocaust, Stalinist communism, and Hitler. Although ostensibly a conservative writer, he challenges, and attempts to define, the spirit that made this new world.

Fall Semester 2014

A version of this lecture appeared in the *Wall Street Journal,* 22 September 2014.

Clockwise from top left: John Maynard Keynes © National Portrait Gallery, London; Virginal Woolf © National Portrait Gallery, London; Lytton Strachey © National Portrait Gallery, London; Leonard Woolf

5

Bloomsbury's Memoir Club

ROSEMARY HILL

From its first meeting, in March 1920, the Bloomsbury Group's Memoir Club was on the lookout for incidental self-revelation. On that occasion there were seven speakers. It was "highly interesting," Virginia Woolf wrote in her diary, adding: "Lord knows what I didn't read into their reading." Supposedly a secret society, it largely remained so until after the Second World War. The first and most enduring members were Molly and Desmond MacCarthy, Roger Fry, John Maynard Keynes, Vanessa and Clive Bell, Duncan Grant, Virginia and Leonard Woolf, Lytton Strachey, and E. M. Forster. Mary Hutchinson and Sydney Waterlow were also invited but fell by the wayside. Even by Bloomsbury standards, it was an exclusive set. The members were all related by blood or marriage or, which weighed more heavily with some of them, by friendships formed as Cambridge undergraduates. As they aged and became, to varying degrees, public figures, the club offered privacy. It held all the comforts and the terrors of intimacy. Forster was always ambivalent about it. His memoir of his experiences in Egypt and his love for Mohammed el Adl were not read to the club, though his Indian recollections were; they left, Virginia Woolf thought, rather too little to the imagination. She herself, after the second club meeting, at the Bells' house in Gordon Square, was on the receiving end of the club's interest, and regretted it: "Why did I read this egotistic sentimental trash! . . . What possessed me to lay bare my soul!" Yet in various forms and with a shifting membership, the club survived until Clive Bell's death in 1964.

Some of the papers it heard are now lost, and most that survive have been published among their authors' other works. S. P. Rosenbaum, of the University of Toronto, left unfinished at his death in 2012 a project to reconstruct as far as possible the club's history and to republish the existing papers in a single accompanying volume. He got no further than outlining the first part of the historical section, but while far from complete, his notes make a convincing case for reconsidering the memoirs in context, as a group of essays with internal connections and, especially in the early years, as a response to a particular historical moment. Much is irrecoverable. Talk, as Woolf wrote in one of her contributions, is ephemeral: "Even talk of this interest and importance is as elusive as smoke. It flies up the chimney and is gone." Much of the club's atmosphere has inevitably evaporated: silences, tones of voice, the laughter that greeted the beginning of Woolf's first paper and abruptly died away into what she construed as "a kind of uncomfortable boredom." And then there are the things that were not said because they were too obvious and already known. For all of which, in reconstructing as far as possible the order of the papers, and in considering who was listening as well as who was speaking, Rosenbaum's outline, supported by James Haule's editorial framework, puts together an interesting picture. (All quotations in this lecture are from S. P. Rosenbaum, *The Bloomsbury Group Memoir Club,* ed. James Haule, 2014).

One account of the club's origins has it that Molly MacCarthy wanted to find a way of forcing her husband, an incorrigible procrastinator, to produce something. On this front, it was a failure: Desmond never wrote his memoirs. Once when it seemed that he was reading to the club from a manuscript contained in a dispatch case on his knees, it transpired, when he dropped the case, that it was empty. The great leather-bound ledger that Woolf donated for the club records was similarly found years later to be blank. It was clearly not procedure that made the group endure. The scope for subject matter was elastic; papers might be autobiographical or biographical and treat of historic or recent events. The most important rule was complete frankness, which, since it applied to audience members as well as authors, was only erratically observed.

As Haule remarks, "It was no place to go for comfort or support, certainly not applause." The members were competitive and often disinclined to see the merits of one another's approaches. Clive Bell and Keynes were mutually antipathetic, Bell irritated by the "cocksure economist" and Keynes patronizing to the rakish, "gay dog" critic. Keynes also mortified Woolf by telling her that her memoir of George Duckworth, later published as "22 Hyde Park Gate," was the best thing she had ever done. He advised her bluffly to carry on in that vein, "write about real people & make it all up," causing her to reflect that "if George is my climax I'm a mere scribbler." She in turn found Keynes's *Economic Consequences of the Peace* remarkable as "a book that influences the world without being in the least a work of art," concluding with a shrug: "a work of morality, I suppose."

What held them together was the shared experience of decades and the indefinable but indisputable Bloomsbury cast of mind. If the club did not always fulfill the need that Woolf felt to "believe your impressions hold for others," it must have done so more often than any other audience she faced. For most of the members, except the underperforming Desmond MacCarthy, there was a habit of memoir writing somewhere in the background, either in their families or in their membership in the Cambridge secret society, the Apostles. Rosenbaum locates the club's origins in the university group, whose meetings were similarly exclusive and committed to frankness. It was there that the young Lytton Strachey, part of a vast family that was in a constant state of self-memorialization, first demonstrated his precocious biographical talent. Virginia Woolf and Vanessa Bell grew up in the heavy shadow of their father, Leslie Stephen, who was not only the founding editor of the *Dictionary of National Biography,* but also the author of a private memoir that his children called the Mausoleum Book, written for his family after the death of his wife. Keynes's mother had written a similar family book; Fry's father had published an autobiography.

When the club was founded, its members were approaching midlife, the usual time for reminiscence to set in. In 1920 they were all in their late thirties and early forties, with the exception of Fry, who was much the oldest at fifty-four. What Rosenbaum's reconstruction of their early meetings reveals is that the loudest silence, the thing barely mentioned because so all-pervasive, was the First World War. While none of the papers directly addressed the experience of the war, it not only formed the background to the club's formation, but also marked in itself a stage in the life of Bloomsbury. Though for the most part they were only in early middle age, the founding members often felt older, for they were all children of the nineteenth century. They dated, as Forster wrote in a memoir of Woolf, from a time when "the earth was still horizontal and the buildings perpendicular." Now they were "sharply cut off," in Woolf's phrase, "alienated . . . from the past and . . . perhaps too vividly conscious of the present." As writers, they sensed a severing of the arteries of literary tradition; the authors of the prewar years had inhabited another world: "It seemed to them that they were to go on living like that, and writing like that, for ever and ever. Then suddenly, like a chasm in a smooth road, the war came."

Bloomsbury was interestingly and at times uncomfortably placed across the chasm. As an idea, it was perhaps not middle aged, but certainly no longer young. It was talked of, Woolf noted, variously admired, derided, and defined, "in newspapers, in novels, in Germany, in France—even I daresay in Turkey and Timbuktu," and yet it too was a product of the unimaginably distant past before 1914, the last years of the distended nineteenth century. The aura of the Stephens' home at 22 Hyde Park Gate still hung about the club, and Woolf's paper on her childhood and Strachey's on his, the complementary "Lancaster Gate," were among the first to be read. In their accounts of the households in which they had grown up, they returned to the "tangled and matted emotion" of their earliest memories. The bloated houses, heaving with large, complicated families and hemmed in by dark and heavy furniture, were revisited, the impacted feelings teased out. As biographers, they were after the "atmosphere," which, rather than a mere "vulgar succession" of events, was for Strachey "the significance of a personal history." As adults who had succeeded in escaping their parents, they looked back on the social order they had wanted to overturn to find it not merely toppled but utterly destroyed, and they looked back with ambivalence.

The gulf made by the war was in one sense a defense, a historical moat. Safe on the far side, Bloomsbury could reflect on the nineteenth century, knowing it was finally over, and from that distance revolve Strachey's "riddle of the Victorian age" with more forgiveness. In August 1914, in the course of anatomizing Matthew Arnold in the *New Statesman* ("He might . . . have done some excellent and lasting work upon the movement of glaciers . . . But no; he *would* be a critic"), Strachey had reflected that "the Age of Victoria . . . has the odd attractiveness of something which is at once very near and very far off; it is like one of those queer fishes that one sees behind glass at an aquarium, before whose grotesque proportions and sombre menacing agilities one hardly knows whether to laugh or to shudder; when once it has caught one's eye, one cannot tear oneself away." His *Eminent Victorians* was published just before the Armistice in 1918. A knocking down of shibboleths, human and literary, a blowing apart of the "lives of great men" school of biography, it was his own war effort.

By the time the Memoir Club was formed, neither the Age of Victoria nor Strachey's youth were so mesmerizingly close. "Lancaster Gate" is a compound of relief, regret, and a certain tenderness, evoked in the opening by Strachey's account of a recurring dream. In it he is once more in the house at Lancaster Gate. Asleep, he is "positively delighted" to be back, though the feeling seems paradoxical: "In my waking life, I have never for a moment, so far as I am aware, regretted our departure . . . and if . . . we were to return to it, I can imagine nothing which would disgust me more." On waking, he is relieved to find that the happiness he felt a minute before in the dream is an illusion. It is a brilliantly economical image of reminiscence. To be in and out of the past, to revisit, as a guest, what seemed at the time to be only "restriction and oppression," is one of the pleasures of memory and autobiography, made possible by the certainty of escape. That "perhaps too vivid" consciousness of the present in the interwar years gave the club the ideal vantage point for retrospection, as individuals and as a group. In 1928, in Woolf's paper "Old Bloomsbury," she wrote with an elegiac air of the "lustre and illusion" of "those last years before the war," ending with a note of defensiveness about the brave new world that was no longer new: "Old Bloomsbury still survives. If you seek a proof—look around."

"Lancaster Gate" and "22 Hyde Park Gate" both end in bedrooms, Strachey finding the naked Duncan Grant in his and deciding not to do "what the opportunity so perfectly offered," Woolf surprised in hers by her half-brother George Duckworth, two moments on the threshold of adult experience characterized by ambiguity. When it came to considering historic lives, the club members found themselves similarly attracted to fracture, to lives that spanned historic divides and the psychological consequences. Of Isaac Newton, some of whose papers he owned, Keynes wrote:

> He was not the first of the age of reason. He was the last of the magicians, the last of the Babylonians and Sumerians, the last great mind which looked out on the visible and intellectual world with the same eyes as those who began to build our intellectual inheritance rather less than 10,000 years ago. . . .
>
> . . . In vulgar modern terms Newton was profoundly neurotic of a not unfamiliar type, but—I should say from the records—a most extreme example.

Strachey found something of the same attraction in Newton's older contemporary, the biographer John Aubrey. Strachey saw himself as the product of an "embryonic generation" almost as remote now from the Victorians as Aubrey had been from the Middle Ages, yet just as Aubrey was haunted by the lost world of medieval magic, so Strachey and the other club members heard echoes of the nineteenth century.

Rosenbaum does not make enough allowance for these nuances in Bloomsbury's shifting view of its own past. Max Beerbohm, writing about Strachey in 1943, eleven years after his death, warned of the danger that he would come to be seen merely as a "debunker" and that this was "not only vulgar [but] silly." To some extent, the fear has proved justified. Strachey's caricatures have been taken literally, his legacy sometimes coarsened to cliché. Rosenbaum writes, for example, that "the Victorian essence of the Frys' family life may be conveyed by the fact that none of his six sisters married," without pausing to consider how lifelong spinsters and large families can both characterize the "essence" of Victorianism.

Writing in 1928 about Macaulay, Strachey gave a better sense of his own modus operandi when he said that the important qualities of a historian were to have "a capacity for absorbing facts, a capacity for stating them and a point of view." A point of view, he went on, "by no means implies sympathy": "It is curious to observe how many instances there are of great historians who have been at daggers drawn with their subjects."

THE COMPOUND OF SYMPATHY AND ANTIPATHY in the Bloomsbury Club memoirs is what makes them rich. They bristle with points of view; daggers are often drawn. Between them, the club's first members created a conspectus of biography in all its varieties: memoir, confession, and history. That, as a form, biography should have held such appeal for a group among whom only Strachey could be characterized primarily as a biographer was also, surely, a factor of the historic moment. To a generation that felt itself to belong to two centuries and increasingly to be living *entre deux guerres*, it had a particular appeal. In 1940, when the second war had finally come, Woolf wrote that the thing that would "survive . . . and cross the gulf" was English literature, a claim that can be made with particular force for the literature of biography. The lives of individuals continue when social systems, moral orders, and intellectual certainties are overturned, and it is within personal experience that the consequences are played out.

How far a character may endure through different ages is the theme of *Orlando*. Keynes's preface to his published *Essays in Biography* is frank about its purpose: to establish "the solidarity and historical continuity of the High Intelligentsia of England, who have built up the foundations of our thought in the two and a half centuries since Locke, in his *Essay Concerning Human Understanding*, wrote the first modern English book." Newton and Aubrey bestrode the fissures of their age and survived, although in Keynes's account the

Newton who found it easy "to drop the 17th century behind him and to evolve into the 18th-century figure which is the traditional Newton," who lived in London and grew fat, was not the genius. That was the earlier, mystic Newton, who inhabited both worlds, "Copernicus and Faustus in one."

From the continuities of divided lives to the multiple facets of biography itself was a short step, and the form, its history, and its practitioners were another constant interest of the club. Montaigne and Aubrey appealed to them, but in the Bloomsbury sense, as Woolf wrote in "The Leaning Tower," it had been "less than two hundred years since people took an interest in themselves." They were the heirs of Boswell, the proto-romantic chronicler of the details of outer and inner life. Boswell was Strachey's heroic alter ego, whom he admired, as Michael Holroyd wrote, "for all the qualities they did not share" and also as an ur-Bloomsbury *épateur* of literary and social convention. It would be difficult, Strachey thought, to find "a more shattering refutation of the lessons of cheap morality than the life of James Boswell." The age of Boswell gave way to the age of the character sketch. Macaulay's, "like steel engravings—unsatisfactory compromises between a portrait in oils and a realistic snapshot," disappointed Strachey. Then came the age of biography as euphemism; the pious memorials, so often written by daughters, were the "Lifes" that Forster thought should be called "deaths," "monuments of piety" of the sort with which Bloomsbury had grown up and which Strachey so effectively turned into a carnival target for knocking down. After *Eminent Victorians* the form was plastic once again.

Rosenbaum is surprisingly uninterested in *Flush* and Woolf's witty variations on the theme of biographical convention. The story of Elizabeth Barrett's spaniel begins with his enormously long pedigree and ends with acknowledgment of the "very few" authorities on which the book is based. What lies between more or less follows Keynes's advice by taking real people (and a real animal) and making up most of the rest. *Flush* was rated by Forster "a complete success . . . doggie without being silly" and exemplifying the Strachean requirement by having a unique point of view, in this case regarding "high poetic personages" from the "altitude of the carpet or the sofa-foot."

Keynes took his own advice so far as to talk about the "plot" of his memoirs. His paper, described by Leonard Woolf as "a kind of secret appendix" to *The Economic Consequences of the Peace,* was in two parts, the second of which, later published as "Dr Melchior: A Defeated Enemy," was the longest ever read to the club; it recounted his experiences at the Paris Peace Conference in 1919. His characters were as important as his plot, and Virginia Woolf congratulated him on their vividness. Some were acutely drawn, such as Admiral "Rosie" Wemyss, with his "comical, quizzical face and a single eyeglass," who baffled the Germans and left them uncertain whether he was "half-witted and imbecile" or "playing a game with them far cleverer than anything conceivable," an English type that, Keynes predicted, would continue "to the end of history" to baffle central Europe.

The memoir was perhaps more a safety valve than an appendix to the public account he had given in *Economic Consequences*. It shows him, as Leonard Woolf put it, "writing in his shirtsleeves for . . . friends." There were cartoon sketches—of a German officer like a broken umbrella—and some daring theatrical effects. A passage he omitted from the published version ironically dramatizes Woolf's conception of English literature as a force that can override historical events. In the melancholy Gothic villa at Spa, with its heavy decor and dense surrounding woods, where some of the negotiations took place, the ominous Wagnerian overtones, Keynes reports, were driven out by the arrival of the Jane Austen–inspired English: "Miss Bates had vanquished Brünnhilde, and Mr Weston's foot was firmly planted on the neck of Wotan." Dr. Melchior himself, somewhat to Rosenbaum's puzzlement, plays little part in the memoir and is entirely absent from *Economic Consequences,* all of which is quite consonant with his function as a literary device, which surely he is, acting as a hinge in an account of the private experience of public events.

Keynes was a bravura performer, Woolf and Strachey were Postimpressionists specializing in still lifes and interiors, and Forster was the club's mosaicist, tweezering each detail into place. In his introduction to *The Life of the Rev. George Crabbe* by the poet's son, he delicately draws out the virtues of an amateur, unwilling, and now almost forgotten biographer. The younger Crabbe, lacking confidence in his ability to write his father's life, had been "assisted" by John Gibson Lockhart, the son-in-law and biographer of Sir Walter Scott and, according to Forster, "the ubiquitous Scot of his generation," as if every generation were fated to have one. Lockhart introduced mistakes and changed things in the general direction of those "lives of the great [that] are usually unreadable because everything is on an enormous scale." Despite which, Crabbe managed to cling to his own modest tastes. He and his father cared about little things: "He liked to hear how once his father had not known how to put on a shirt, and his father liked to tell him; they had sat gossiping over their study-fires for years, so that the pudding is stuffed, as it were, with plums and nuts and other edible oddments which give it the pleasantest flavour." Thus, Forster tucks an affectionate miniature life of the son into the father's with a sense of justice done. In the end, the younger Crabbe had, he concluded, "a good general grasp of his father's character; he presented it rather too favourably, as we shall see, but he did present his father's character and not some one else's."

Whose character is being presented in a biography, whether character or narrative is to be the motive force, and to what extent all biography is autobiography were questions that the Memoir Club—in the days before "life writing" became an academic discipline—enjoyed both in and out of club meetings, which proceeded by fits and starts. Fairly frequent for the first two years, there was then a hiatus before they resumed in 1928. Rosenbaum's incomplete outline more or less ends at that point, so the club's later history remains to be written in detail. No doubt it will have its interest, but inevitably the energy that first drove it sputtered somewhat. Some things remained constant. Vanessa's son Quentin Bell complained to Desmond MacCarthy in 1948 that "Morgan has started resigning from the Memoir Club again." The following year, the publication of Keynes's *Two Memoirs* began the process of making the club's existence known to the world. As Bloomsbury passed from middle into old age, the younger generations reflected on the older, and the older looked further back on themselves. Vanessa Bell read Keynes's letters to her at a meeting in 1957, until eventually the last days of Bloomsbury faded gently into its afterlife as literary history.

Spring Semester 2014

Dylan Thomas at the White Horse Tavern, New York City, 1952. © Granger, New York City—All rights reserved.

6

Dylan Thomas

KURT HEINZELMAN

The year 2014 marked the hundredth anniversary of Dylan Thomas's birth. It is safe to say that in Britain at least, Thomas enjoyed his greatest public attention since his untimely death at age thirty-nine. But that is the problem. For the last fifty years or so, Dylan Thomas had in effect disappeared. Now seems a good time to ask why. Remember, he was once the most emulated, the most celebrated, and the most notorious poet of his generation. After his death in 1953, his widow, Caitlin, made it known that his archive was for sale, and it was enthusiastically acquired by the Harry Ransom Center, then called the Humanities Research Center. To this day, the HRC's collection is the principal Thomas archive in the world, holding well over 50 percent of all archival material extant. One sign of Thomas's disappearance, therefore, was that the HRC hosted no public exhibition and no academic programming in the centenary year except for a forty-minute Poetry on the Plaza event that I organized. Further evidence of his disappearance is that when Thomas's last remaining notebook in private hands, an archivally important one, went up for auction in December, the HRC did not bid.

I cite these developments in the stock market of poetic letters only because they reflect the precipitous decline in Dylan Thomas's stature among poets and other interested purveyors of poetry, at least in America, and I take the celebrative opportunity of the Thomas centenary to query how celebrity, value, and influence are related.

One poem by Dylan Thomas is undoubtedly popular, has stayed popular for half a century, and is also critically acclaimed as one of the greatest villanelles in English letters. We all know the one. After the Denver Broncos lost the Super Bowl last year, an AP writer led off his story, "Peyton Manning [the losing quarterback] went gently into that good Jersey night."

Maybe the very quotability of "Do not go gentle into that good night" tells us something, though, about Thomas's disappearance. Thomas still appeals perhaps to those who are coming to his poetry for the first time, or coming to it one poem at a time, engaging with his work as readers rather than being already deterred from or attracted to Thomas because of his tabloidian history. It is that history, always swirling about Thomas's life and his poetry's reception history, that is invoked in *American Smoke* (2013) by the Anglo-Welsh writer Iain Sinclair: "This crumpled, swollen-bellied man with stained nicotine teeth was the original postwar performance poet, playing to packed crowds, and losing, in the sweats and fears of hypnotic projection, all sense of self. The preacherly mannerisms of his Methodist ancestors, and the seductive rumble and thunder of voice from the abused instrument of body, mesmerized the uptown poetry mob." How distant all this now seems from current poetic practice and from the more antiseptic attention of contemporary creative-writing mobs who, despite their tattoos and piercings and ripped jeans, listen far less sweatily.

To witness how Thomas now looks to the young, let me cite two contemporary poets from different sides of the Atlantic. The English poet Glyn Maxwell tells this story:

> One morning long ago in Boston town Professor [Derek] Walcott said I played melodies with my right hand but my left hand just lay there. Another time, in his tiny wooden office on a Tuesday morning in November sunshine, he surveyed a forty-line lyric I'd written about me. He'd made us memorise Dylan Thomas's short poem 'Twenty-four years remind the tears of my eyes' and well, I'd had a birthday just that week, my 25th, so I'd done the obvious but gone on way longer. He frowned, ringed a little phrase with his pencil and then quoted with evident scorn: "caving into sleep . . . caving into sleep? *caving*—into—*sleep*?" Knowing what was coming, I said "yes I suppose . . . that's pretty rubbish now I look . . . " He slid the poem back to me. "It's terrific, the rest is shit."[1]

Here is the poem that didn't give Maxwell much joy:

> Twenty-four years remind the tears of my eyes.
> (Bury the dead for fear that they walk to the grave in labour.)
> In the groin of the natural doorway I crouched like a tailor
> Sewing a shroud for a journey

> By the light of the meat-eating sun.
> Dressed to die, the sensual strut begun,
> With my red veins full of money,
> In the final direction of the elementary town
> I advance for as long as forever is.

Maxwell does say he may have learned something—namely, that his own birthday poem had "gone on way longer"—but I doubt that the lesson of brevity was the sole reason Walcott assigned this memorization exercise. Thomas uses rhetorical flourishes that an up-and-coming young poet might shake his head at and think are rubbish, like "caving into sleep." I am thinking of the first line, with its oddly skewed way of saying that time has been wasted and perhaps little is left, or "the meat-eating sun," or that bizarre line about "red veins full of money." And even the wonderful last line may sound to a young poet trying to "make it new" like an old-fashioned rhetorical flourish with too much trombone glissando. I trust that one intent of Walcott's assignment was to say, "Listen, ephebe, you can't imitate this, but you can *learn* from it."

Michael Robbins is a young American poet who contributed a column to a recent issue of *Poetry* magazine devoted to why contemporary poets might hate their modernist predecessors. Robbins is snarkier than Maxwell; let us call his sport "Mocking Thomas." Here he is speaking of Thomas's rhetoric:

> They appear to be the names of heavy metal bands: Plague of Fables; Star-Flanked Seed; Serpent Caul; Murder of Eden; Altar of Plagues; Seed-at-Zero; The Grave and My Calm Body; Dark Asylum; Mares of Thrace, Herod Wail; Christbread; Binding Moon; Red Swine. In fact they are phrases culled from Dylan Thomas's poems—except that I threw two actual metal bands in there. Didn't notice, did you? . . . In Thomas's work, self-seriousness *is* the major trope. Everything is intoned from on high. . . .
> . . . All that's at stake for Thomas is whether his self-pity has been gorgeously enough expressed.[2]

But then comes a gratuitously poignant moment as the writer confesses, "That's what I hate most about Thomas: if you care about poems, you can't entirely hate him." Even as a backdoor compliment, this is weird, considering that the website maintained by the Poetry Foundation, the publisher of *Poetry* magazine, shows that the poem on their site with exponentially more hits than any other English-language poem is by Dylan Thomas. Yes, it is that "good night" one, with its "rage, rage against the dying of the light" and without any of the high-toned phrases this critic mocks.

The question for me is not whether Dylan Thomas has become irrelevant—irrelevant, I mean, in the sense that he has disappeared from networks of current poetic affiliation and contemporary creative practice—but why, and when. It has often been said that the decade following Thomas's death in 1953 was one "in which the rhetorical, the bardic, and the orphic were under heavy interdiction in England as the Movement's aesthetics took the field."[3] There is some truth to this, although the key phrase here may be "in England." Elsewhere, as Seamus Heaney puts it, Thomas's poems remained vital: "They opened a thrilling line between the centre and the edges of the Anglophone world. For all us young provincials, from Belfast to Brisbane, the impact of Thomas's performance meant that we had a gratifying sense of access to something that was acknowledged to be altogether modern, difficult *and* poetry."[4] John Tranter, the fine Australian poet, journal editor, and tireless anthologizer of modern verse, remembers, in an e-mail he sent me, how he, like other poets Down Under, were influenced by Thomas early on but that "he just didn't fit in the 1960s: think Dylan in Carnaby St.: no way." Or in Heaney's words, "Dylan Thomas is by now as much a case history as a chapter in the history of poetry."[5]

To begin to understand why, notice how Robbins's complaint about the bombastic nature of Thomas's diction, its heavy breathing, turns into an ad hominem attack as the essayist equates Thomas's style with narcissism, sliding the poetry's rhetorical technique into disdain for the poet's self-indulgence. Never mind that Robbins sees self-pity where Sinclair sees Thomas "losing . . . all sense of self." Tabloid dissing and Dylanolatry go hand in hand, may even feed off each other, precisely because historically they occurred concurrently—that is, the hagiographic elevation of Thomas as a kind of mystic Welsh bard, touched by *furor poeticus,* the sublime "rage" that his elegiac villanelle for his father called for, *and* the "case history" vilification of him as a perpetual juvenile delinquent, womanizer, boor, and drunk. The result is that a nuanced understanding of Thomas's artistic legacy as a poet is still difficult to attain.

Let us start our search for nuance with Robert Graves's notoriously unnuanced debunking of Thomas as "a demagogic Welsh masturbator who failed to pay his bills."[6] The "Welsh" part of this accusation is undoubtedly a nationalist or classist slur, but I want to focus on the "demagogic" and "masturbator" part because these words must be rooted in Thomas as a speaker, as a performer. Graves elsewhere says of Thomas that as a performer, "he could put on the *hwyl,*" or what Derek Mahon, one of Thomas's most sympathetic readers, calls

"Welsh pulpit declamation."[7] But when Graves says Thomas "put *on*" this rhetoric, it is still a put-*down*, even as Graves adds, "When I listened to him broadcasting, I had to keep a tight hold of myself to avoid being seduced." Some may wish to picture how you hold onto yourself while listening to a masturbator; others may note the subtle gendering here of Thomas as a seductive, emotionally loose poet against whom Graves has to "manfully" resist; but I would like to examine how and why a voice that was once almost erotically appealing became appallingly demagogic.

I suggest two reasons, neither of which, to the best of my knowledge, has been developed before. The first arises from the sometimes understandable complaint that his work suffers, in the poet Charles Tomlinson's words, from a "halo of imprecision," although this complaint may misconstrue what always was a dominant rhetorical feature of Thomas's work.[8]

In classical rhetoric there are five canons, two of which are style (*elocutio*) and delivery (*pronuntiatio*). Both of these are pertinent directly to hortatory discourse, and both are among Thomas's acknowledged strengths. Moreover, hortatory discourse is especially prevalent during war years, and was certainly so in the period sometimes called Churchillian, which Thomas lived through as a young man and a productive poet. Here is a classic example of hortatory verse. Note especially the last word:

> In peace there's nothing so becomes a man
> As modest stillness and humility,
> But when the blast of war blows in our ears,
> Then imitate the action of the tiger.
> Stiffen the sinews, conjure up the blood,
> Disguise fair nature with hard-favoured rage.

Henry V's use of "rage" in Shakespeare's play means not just Iliadic wrath but also the ability to transform a "modest," palliative self into a ferocious one, as in "Do not go gentle." Thomas's poem for his father came six years after the war was over, but it shared with many of the poems composed between the hysterical pre-war years and the no less hyperbolic post-war period a rhetoric heightened by the discourse of exhortation: for and against appeasement, for and against Germany, the Soviet Union, Ireland, Franco, and so on. Even if not explicitly hortatory in intent, such rhetoric often performs itself in a declamatory mode. Is there a huge rhetorical distinction between Neville Chamberlain's "Here [in my hand] is the paper which bears his [Herr Hitler's] name" and these lines from one of Thomas's finest pre-war poems, "Great is the hand that holds dominion over / Man by a scribbled name"? Well, yes—Thomas's sentence is more plangent. Call it Churchillian *avant la lettre*.

There are many poems like this, in which the declamatory mode, born of or nurturing a hortatory style, trumps logical *dispositio*, the arrangement of argument, or even the discovery of content (*inventio*), the other two most important canons of rhetoric. In due course, readers came to understand these inherently declamatory utterances, which they once may have heard as refreshingly hortatory, as "a freak of exaggerated orality."[9] And they are, of course—not "freaks" nor "exaggerated," for those are value judgments, but certainly feats of "orality," for this mode of rhetoric has always worked most effectively as oral delivery.

Thomas's most freakishly hortatory-declamatory poem may be one that doesn't look like it at all. "In My Craft or Sullen Art," written in the late summer of 1945, is a kind of postscript to the war he hated so much for having left him so profoundly conflicted about whether to support or condemn it. That hortatory impulse, which he did exercise explicitly during the war by writing propaganda films for both "praise" and "wages," is here so channeled that the rhetorical impulse becomes self-exhortation, a declaration of his own poetic intentions. What makes the poem thoroughly declamatory is that its ultimate subject is not the poet but those for whom the poet writes. Here are the opening lines:

> In my craft or sullen art
> Exercised in the still night
> When only the moon rages
> And the lovers lie abed
> With all their griefs in their arms,
> I labour by singing light
> Not for ambition or bread
> . . . .
> But [for] the common wages
> Of their most secret heart.

Note again the code word "rages." How does the moon "rage"? By waxing and waning? Lifting and lowering tides? The point is that a moon rages quite differently from the rage required to wage war, whether against a physical enemy like the Axis powers or against the decay of the physical body. Significantly, it is not the verb *to wage* but the noun *wages* that Thomas here rhymes with *rages*, wages in the sense of pay for labor, as by the BBC, but here those wages are accrued only by "lovers, their arms / Round the grief of the ages," and not by the rest of us, still fixated as we are on the grief caused by military armaments.

This poem, I surmise, survives in the Thomas canon because its high declamatory style is, in effect, undone, or dismantled, by the poem itself, which goes on to disclose that these lovers, Thomas's putative listeners, neither need nor want his art because they have, in their embracing arms, sufficient strength and solace. What happened generally, I think, with Thomas's declamatory/hortatory style is that it simply fell out of fashion; the question of how a solitary (which is one meaning of *sullen*) poet crafts poetry in a sullen (using the more common meaning) world of atom bombs no longer seemed a burning issue; and the heatedness of exhortation no longer fit the enveloping Cold War chill: in short, this style had the stink of a world that war-weary adults wanted to forget, and that a new generation of ironic, Aquarius-bound youngsters in the 1960s had no tolerance, no ear, for. Sure, Dylan Thomas's face graced Peter Blake's 1967 *Sgt. Pepper* album cover, but so what? So does a garden gnome: goo goo g'joob.

A second reason for Thomas's disappearance was a paradoxical one: he became popular. Like the Beatles, say, several generations later, his poetry sounded new, sounded like nothing anyone else was producing. He had made it new, the High Modernist compliment, and his newness was as true on the page as it was in his seductive voicings. But newness may cut too deeply. In America, once the thrill of Thomas's newness wore off, his work could be seen as arising out of a native strain of popular performance poetry that went back through Edna St. Vincent Millay to Vachel Lindsay, poetry that was very much out of fashion by the 1960s and, in the view of some, beneath contempt.

Another reason was suggested to me when I heard Kevin Powell at the Nuyorican Café in New York's Lower East Side, one of the birthplaces of contemporary slam poetry, bear witness to how important Thomas was to the slam phenomenon. Slam poetry is certainly a public poetry, but it is not only about performance. It is about competition. Slam poetry events are always judged, and there is a monetary prize at the end of the evening. Maybe Thomas created, by his very success and seductive orality, an aura of competitiveness among his peers, something that slam poets might relish but that so-called print poets don't like or don't like to admit liking, even when they are inevitably being competitive. As Robert Creeley has dryly put it, "Poets are a company and poetry must finally be a tribal art despite the fierceness of contest, which sometimes preoccupies its persons."[10]

We can see some of this conflicted dynamic being worked out, however unconsciously, in a 1963 collection that was meant unequivocally to celebrate Thomas, to praise and not to bury him, but that ends with such contradictory messages that one can see, with fifty years of hindsight, Thomas's influence already dimming. Even the title, *A Garland for Dylan Thomas*, suggests trouble. Historically, a garland is a metaphor for anthologies or chapbooks and harks back to the ancient notion of the garland as a reward for the victor in a competition. The editor of the collection, George J. Firmage, further hypes the rhetoric of garlanding when he writes in his preface about Dylan's death: "Not since the death of Keats had there been such universal mourning for the death of a poet."[11] This is an unfortunate analogy, for a couple reasons. First, there was no "universal mourning" for Keats aside from Shelley's pastoral elegy "Adonais," a poem that never names Keats. And second, in Keats's own poem "Ode on a Grecian Urn," we find garlands figured this way:

> Who are these coming to the sacrifice?
>   To what green altar, O mysterious priest,
> Lead'st thou that heifer lowing at the skies,
>   And all her silken flanks with garlands drest?

This garlanded beast is to be sacrificed.

Firmage intends to save Thomas with his gathering of "84 poems by 78 poets selected from almost 150 written in tribute to Thomas over the past ten years." To save him from what, though? According to Firmage, after the universal mourning of 1953 came the fall into literary criticism, a period when "the so-called literary critics who, for the most part, had never had a word, good or bad, to say about Thomas' creative output of nearly 20 years, suddenly found it fashionable to say something and, unfortunately in many cases, did" (p. xv). Whatever truth there may be in this summary statement, *Garland*'s way of rebutting this history of sacrifice on the altar of literary criticism is odd. Speaking of the contributors to his anthology, Firmage states, "The genuineness of the[ir] poetic statements ... is a living testimonial to the 'craft and sullen art' of the man who inspired them. For a poet, after all is said and done, should be judged only by his peers." That last sentence is highly dubious, but it reveals Firmage's anthology to be, first and foremost, a competitive book, fighting already against the negative reception history that would last until, well, last year.

One way you can tell that an author is protesting too much is when he makes errors not just of fact and logic but also of attention.

Thomas's poem "On My Craft or Sullen Art," which is printed on the page directly after Firmage's preface, says quite explicitly that Thomas thinks he is writing for the approbation of lovers, not for fellow poets. Many of the poems in *Garland,* however, prefer Firmage's premise that Thomas is fundamentally a poet's poet, encouraged perhaps by Thomas's own communitarian love of performing his fellow poets' poems. But these eighty-four poets produce a tribute that is more often than not either bad imitation or backhanded praise, as when John Ciardi, once the very powerful poetry editor of the *Saturday Evening Post* and then director of the prestigious Bread Loaf Writers' Conference, through which many young poets passed, calls Thomas "our angel of defeat" (p. 23). Is such an epithet, honorable though Ciardi intends it to be, likely to inspire up-and-coming, eager-to-succeed generations?

TO BE FAIR, LET ME CONCLUDE by looking at one example of what I would call a largely successful application of Thomas's poetics, but one that also shows the limits of influence. It is an early poem (1965) by the Australian Les Murray, and the poem it echoes is Thomas's "Fern Hill." The poems are about the same length, both too long to quote in their entirety. Most will remember, though, the floating, languid rhythms of "Fern Hill," its sometimes startling imagery combined with wide-eyed optimism:

> Now as I was young and easy under the apple boughs
> About the lilting house and happy as the grass was green,
>   The night above the dingle starry,
>   Time let me hail and climb
>   Golden in the heydays of his eyes.

And we will remember his love for the particulars of this rural scene:

> And as I was green and carefree, famous among the barns
> About the happy yard and singing as the farm was home,
> ....
>   ... I was huntsman and herdsman, the calves
> Sang to my horn, the foxes on the hills barked clear and cold,
>   And the sabbath rang slowly
>   In the pebbles of the holy streams.

And we will remember his attention to birds and horses:

> As I rode to sleep the owls were bearing the farm away,
> All the moon long I heard, blessed among stables, the
>   nightjars

> Flying with the ricks, and the horses
> Flashing into the dark.

And of course there is the famous closing couplet:

> Time held me green and dying
> Though I sang in my chains like the sea.

In Murray's poem a boy and his pony go riding after a hailstorm. The poem is called "Spring Hail":

> This is for spring and hail, that you may remember:
> for a boy long ago, and a pony that could fly.
>
> We had huddled together a long time in the shed
> in the scent of vanished corn and wild bush birds,
> and the hammering faltered, and the torn
> cobwebs ceased their quivering and hung still
> from the nested rafters. We became uneasy
> at the silence that grew about us, and came out.
>
> . . . .
> Sheep trotted and propped, and shook out ice from their
>   wool.
> The hard blue highway that had carried us there
> fumed as we crossed it; and the hail I scooped
> from underfoot still bore the taste of sky
> and hurt my teeth, and crackled as we walked.
>
> . . . .
> I sat on a log then, listening with my skin
> to the secret feast of the sun, to the long wet worms
> at work in the earth, and, deeper down, the stones
> beneath the earth uneasy that their sleep
> should be troubled by dreams of water soaking down,
> and I heard with my ears the creek on its bed of mould
> moving and passing a mothering sound.
>
>> This is for spring and hail, that you may remember:
>> for a boy long ago, and a pony that could fly.
>
> My pony came up then and stood by me,
> waiting to be gone. . . .
> . . . .
> . . . It was time
> to leap to the saddle and go, a thunderbolt whirling
> sheep and saplings behind, and the rearing fence
> that we took at a bound, and the old abandoned shed
> forgotten behind, and the paddock forgotten behind.

> Time to shatter peace and lean into spring
> as into a battering wind, and be rapidly gone.
>
> It was time, high time, the highest and only time
> to stand in the stirrups and shout out, blind with wind . . .
> . . . .
> It was time, as never again it was time
> to pull the bridle up, so the racketing hooves
>
> fell silent as we ascended from the hill
> above the farms, far up to where the hail
> formed and hung weightless in the upper air,
> charting the birdless winds with silver roads
> for us to follow and be utterly gone.

Murray is too good a poet merely to copy Thomas, and it is instructive to see both what he chooses to borrow and how the poets differ. One can hear immediately the same rhythms in both poems—in Thomas, it is a kind of sea-wave music; in Murray, it could be construed as galloping or maybe cantering or trotting, completely appropriate to a poem about "a pony that could fly," as the refrain hyperbolically puts it, and hyperbole is one thing it shares with "Fern Hill." Yet the narrative stances of the two poems are quite different. Thomas's poem is unabashedly personal, its "green" faith totally identifiable with the "young and easy" speaker. Most of Murray's poem is spoken by a boy as well, but the chorus distances the poet from that boy: "This is for spring and hail, that you may remember: / for a boy long ago." "Fern Hill" is often criticized for its relentless optimism, for its excessive pastoralism, and for its naïve nostalgia (naïve because it is about a relatively young man recalling his own youth). Murray's refrain forestalls such criticism by a distancing device that separates the boy who acts and speaks from the poet who records for the sake of remembering.

One also notes in Murray an attempt at vowel linkages like *hill/ hail/hung*, suggesting the Welsh practice of *cynghanedd*, which Thomas uses in "Fern Hill." The invocation of "time" in Murray's poem also echoes Thomas, but it seems rather melodramatic and a bit comic here: "It was time, high time, the highest and only time / to stand in the stirrups and shout out." One can often tell that a poem is borrowing too faithfully when it loses touch with its own composing practice, when it stops listening to itself because it is listening so hard to its predecessor. I think that is the case here with *time*, and also earlier when the speaker says, "I heard with my ears." The mature Murray would never be so deaf to his own redundancy.

Finally, I think the greatest strength of Murray's poem, compared to Thomas's, is also its greatest weakness: the portrayal of landscape. Murray's landscape is a drought-hardened, winter-chilled opposite of Thomas's green world. Murray's highway is hard and blue, and although this is a spring hailstorm, it is still cold enough that the ice stays unmelted in the sheep's wool. Yes, like "Fern Hill," "Spring Hail" is decidedly rural, but with the possible exception of those "bush birds," whatever species they may be, it is a countryside without local specificity. I don't mean that the place is unreal—we know it is New South Wales, but it could be as easily my native Wisconsin or Dylan's own South Wales. By contrast, Fern Hill seems a more specific place. For all the nostalgic, Edenic imagery in the poem, Thomas's birds are exactly identified as owl and nightjar; his foxes bark; his horses whinny; there are ricks in the field and pebbles in the stream. Apple trees appear not because this farm is symbolic but because apples grow in Wales. I am not saying that Murray's poem would be better if it had a kangaroo in it; I am only pointing out that when a poem lacks a local habitation and a name, its portrayal of memory becomes more mythopoeic than personal. The specialness of the memory seems compromised.

Precisely because Murray's "Spring Hail" is a good poem, it may serve as a limit case for the effect of influence. One reason for looking at how a poet's influence waxes and wanes over time is to assess the competing forces of popularity, aesthetic innovation, and enduring value. British readers continue to rate "Fern Hill" as one of the best-loved poems in the language; "Spring Hail," I would argue, mainly shows how limiting the direct imitation of a predecessor poet can be. Which raises a couple of critical questions for reception history. Does a poet's influence upon those who follow him diminish in proportion to how successfully these followers show through their imitations exactly what cannot be imitated? If so, then is that decline in influence the paradoxical vanishing point at which the older poet's work looks to be most valuable?

Well, maybe the rediscovery of Thomas is not over yet.

Spring Semester 2015

1. Glyn Maxwell, *On Poetry* (London, 2012), p. 51.
2. *Poetry*, 201, no. 4 (Jan. 2013), p. 449.
3. Terence Brown, "The Irish Dylan Thomas," *Irish Studies Review*, 17, no. 1 (Feb. 2009), p. 49.
4. Seamus Heaney, *The Redress of Poetry* (London, 1995), p. 124.
5. Ibid.
6. Quoted in John Goodby and Chris Wigginton, eds., *Dylan Thomas: New Casebooks* (Basingstoke, 2001), p. 5.
7. Derek Mahon, *Selected Prose* (Loughcrew, Ireland, 2012), p. 149.
8. Charles Tomlinson, *Metamorphoses: Poetry and Translation* (Manchester, UK, 2003), p. 8.
9. Ivan Phillips, "I Sing the Bard Electric," *TLS*, Sept. 19, 2003, p. 14.
10. Robert Creeley, preface to Denise Levertov, *Selected Poems* (2002), p. xiii.
11. George J. Firmage, ed., *A Garland for Dylan Thomas* (New York, 1963), p. xv.

Philip Larkin, 1968 © National Portrait Gallery, London

7

Philip Larkin

JOSEPH EPSTEIN

The other morning on C-SPAN, I saw at the Library of Congress our current poet laureate, a man of nearly eighty, long white hair parted in the middle, reading incomprehensible verse in a deep southern accent to an audience bored periwinkle blue, and at first wondered whether this might this be a skit from *Saturday Night Live* or a bit from an old Ernie Kovacs show.

Which is another way of saying we live in a distinctly unbardic age, in which poetry itself often seems, not to put too fine a point on it, preposterous. The last half century or so has not seen poetry, nor many serious poets, flourish, at least not outside universities. Poets worthy of the attention of serious readers, and not merely of that captive audience that shows up under duress every September in classrooms, have been a small minority: Elizabeth Bishop, L. E. Sissman, Donald Justice, Richard Wilbur, Howard Nemerov, Anthony Hecht, Philip Larkin, and that is about it.

Of this group, only Larkin passes the ultimate test of having written poetry that is memorable. Only Larkin understood how inhospitable to poetry is the current age. Only he in his poems set out to give his readers neither puzzles nor punishment but pleasure. Poetry, like all art, he held, "is inextricably bound up with giving pleasure, and if a poet loses his pleasure-seeking audience he has lost the only audience worth having." Larkin never gave poetry readings, never taught poetry, never wrote about it at significant length. He turned down opportunities to be the Oxford Professor of Poetry and to be Poet Laureate of England. He was content to write unforgettable poems and never play the official role of poet.

Larkin's poems on first reading may seem dark, depressive even. "Deprivation is for me," he said, "what daffodils were for Wordsworth." The imperfection of life was his subject, the inadequacy of his own endowments for living it, his context. Sometimes the darkness can be overdone. In the poem "Dockery and Son" (1964), he writes, "Life is first boredom, then fear," to which one wants to reply, "So stop complaining, have a beer." The next line reads, "Whether or not we use it, it goes," to which the only proper response is, "Stop your blubbering and wipe your nose."

Yet for the vast most part, far from being depressing, Larkin's poems, written with a wondrous precision and lucidity, and a comic élan that can produce outright laughter, have the effect of lifting one's spirits, as truth telling often does. Not only aesthetically but in just about every other way, Larkin was a man set against his time: modernism in the arts, left-wing politics of the kind that appeals to academic intellectuals, admiration of youth—none of it was to his taste. This unfashionableness, as we shall see, has cost him.

Philip Larkin was haunted by death, as perhaps all of us with normal attentions spans are, but more than most. Fear of marriage, or what it would do to him personally, was another major inhibitor in his life. In his poem "Love" (1962), he wrote: "How can you be satisfied / Putting someone else first / So that you come off worst? / My life is for me. / As well ignore gravity."

"I think writing about unhappiness is probably the source of my popularity, if I have any—after all most people are unhappy, don't you think?" he told an interviewer. Self-depreciation, self-mockery, self-doubt, came naturally to him. Aging, depression, failure, senility, mortality: from these unpromising subjects he made riveting poems. "The ultimate aim of a poet," he wrote, "should be to touch our hearts by showing his own."

Monica Jones, the woman with whom Larkin had a relationship that spanned decades, wrote to him after the publication of *The Less Deceived,* the collection of poems that in 1955 made his reputation, with prophetic correctness: "I'm sure that you are the one of this generation! . . . I feel more sure of it than ever before, it is you who are the one." He too was confident of his own future fame. When he missed a visit from the Queen at the opening of the Hull University Library, of which he was chief librarian, he wrote to his mother: "Ah well, one day I shall meet her as Philip Larkin, not the paltry librarian of a piffling university." He knew his quality. "I don't think I write well—just better than anyone else," he wrote to Anthony Thwaite.

Philip Larkin died in 1985 at sixty-three, the same age as his father, a parallelism he prophesied. His last years were not easy ones. He lost much of his hearing and suffered impotence, both sexually and artistically. The year before his death, he wrote to his friend Kingsley Amis: "So now we face 1982, sixteen stone six, gargantuanly paunched, helplessly addicted to alcohol, tired of livin' and scared of dyin', world-famous unable-to-write poet, well you know the rest." He was not exaggerating his fame. A television profile of him was done on the BBC. Honorary degrees rolled in. He was awarded the Queen's Medal for Poetry. His portrait was commissioned by the National Gallery. He had a carefully cultivated oeuvre that included a dozen or so imperishable poems, one among them, "This Be the Verse" (1971), the funniest poem in the English language. At his death, Philip Larkin's reputation seemed solid and secure.

Not long after, the house came down. Nineteen ninety-three was an annus horribilis. The previous year had seen the publication of *Selected Letters of Philip Larkin, 1940–1985,* edited by Anthony Thwaite, and *Philip Larkin: A Writer's Life,* by Andrew Motion. (Both men had been chosen by the poet as his literary executors.) The letters were filled with jokes about women, put-downs of Labour politicians and student radicals, an interest in pornography, regret over the loss of the British Empire, and more. He complained that getting a woman into bed was "almost as much trouble as standing for parliament." The critic A. Alvarez, who badly misread Larkin's poetry, he called "El Al"; the novelist Salman Rushdie, "Salmagundi." He referred to *Catch-22* as "the American hymn to cowardice," the IRA as "these mad, murdering, Irish swine." The word *wog* often appears in these letters. Their publication laid Larkin open to the kind of critics and biographers who would cherry-pick unacceptable opinions in order to attack him.

In Motion (Poet Laureate, 1999–2009), he found such a biographer. If there was anything ostensibly degrading, however derisory, to be said about Larkin, Motion found it and worked it into his biography. He claimed that Larkin detested his parents; he made him out to be a racist, a right-winger, an exploiter of women. In the Motion biography, Larkin is nailed to the cross of political correctness. How could a man holding such views, the reasoning ran, be a great poet?

Not the least value of James Booth's recent biography of Philip Larkin is the antidote it supplies to Motion's. Booth takes a few swipes at Motion's obtuseness, but his *Philip Larkin* is, far from a polemic, true to its subtitle, exploring Larkin's life, art, and love. The author achieves a proper balance, rare in books about writers, between the life and the art, always intent on showing how the life influenced the art, which in the end ought to be the only reason for interest in the life.

Booth is wise enough to distinguish between indiscretions in letters to friends and actions in the world. He also has the sense of humor—so evidently missing in Motion—required of anyone who writes about Larkin. Booth's biography reveals a three-dimensional Larkin who is more complex and subtler in every way than Motion ever dreamed possible.

Larkin may have written the immortal line about how one's mum and dad eff one up, but he nevertheless liked his parents and was himself a model of the good son. He admired his father's competence—he was a civil servant in Coventry—and appreciated that he introduced him, at any early age, to literature of a sophisticated kind. Larkin cared for his mother through her long widowhood (she died at ninety-one), and wrote to her at least twice a week; Booth notes that there are more than four thousand of his letters to her in the Larkin archive. His parents, meanwhile, according to his ten-years-older sister, "worshipped him."

"I wouldn't want it thought that I didn't like my parents," Larkin told Miriam Gross, who interviewed him for the *London Observer*. "I did like them. But at the same time they were rather awkward people and not very good at being happy." Their marriage turned him into a misogamist, seeing in marriage a kind of shared prison, reducing the potentialities of both parties. If Larkin was in any way disappointing to the five or so women with whom he had serious relationships, it was owing to his inability to assent to marriage. Not that he was entirely happy with his bachelor life. He often wrote, in poems and in letters, of the possibility that he had missed out on the fuller life provided by wife and children. But he couldn't pull the trigger on marriage. Married or single, neither, for Larkin, was a true solution, but he went with single.

That the three women with whom he had longtime affairs wished to marry him is not alone a sign of a nesting instinct in women, but also a testament to Larkin's decency, tenderness, kindness as a lover. Whatever he may have said jokingly in his letters, many of them to Kingsley Amis and to Robert Conquest, in his actual treatment of women he was as far as possible from being a brute. When Monica Jones became ill, he brought her to Hull, established her in his apartment, and cared for her in a devoted, husbandly way. When the seriously Catholic Maeve Brennan, another of the women with whom he had a lengthy relationship, made plain that she held strong views on premarital sex, Larkin seems by and large to have acceded to these views. No one did more than he to revive the reputation of the novelist Barbara Pym. Despite the misogynistic bluster of his letters, he was charming and attentive to women, around whom, his biographer avers, he always felt most at ease.

As for Larkin's politics, they were scarcely central to his art or his personality. He was supposed to be an ardent nationalist in politics, yet Booth quotes a letter he wrote to Monica Jones in which he remarks, "My God, surely nationalism is the surest mark of mediocrity." Larkin was not a right-winger; he was instead anti-Left, which is not at all the same thing. As for his alleged racism, this is a label that should not be stuck upon a man who adored the music of Fats Waller and Duke Ellington and thought Louis Armstrong a genius.

"Books are a load of crap," from his poem "A Study of Reading Habits" (1964), is another of Larkin's best-known lines, and one that went a long way to establishing his reputation as a philistine. The notion is absurd for any poet whose major influences were Auden, Yeats, Hardy, and the French symbolist Jules Laforgue. What he was opposed to, as he made perhaps too plain in the introduction to *All What Jazz* (1970), his collection of writings on jazz, was modernism in the arts, as represented by such figures as Ezra Pound, Pablo Picasso, and Charlie Parker. He disliked such arts "not because they are new, but because they are irresponsible exploitations of technique in contradiction of human life as we know it." He could be amusing about such art. He called Kafka's *The Trial* "that gloomy convincing piece of bulls—." He thought Robert Lowell "balmy," and never passed up a chance to mock Ted Hughes, whom he thought "no good at all."

Larkin's views have been too often conflated with the coarser outlook of Kingsley Amis. The two men, Booth shows, were not as close as Motion and others believed. At Larkin's funeral, Amis remarked, "I sometimes wonder if I really knew him." The answer was that he didn't. Until now, with the publication of Booth's biography, no one did. *Philip Larkin: Life, Art, and Love* is a salutary reminder that biography need be neither iconoclastic nor reveal dark secrets in order to help readers understand the subtle richness of a complex man.

Fall Semester 2014

A version of this lecture appeared in the *Wall Street Journal*, 28 November 2014.

Keith Thomas in Jamaica

8

Army Life

KEITH THOMAS

I sometimes have bad dreams about being back in the army. It is not that the experience of National Service was entirely unpleasant; indeed some of it was highly enjoyable. But even at the best of times there was a sense of living in an open prison. In my case, this oppressive sense of unfreedom lay in the knowledge that it would be many long months before I would see my family again or take up my scholarship at Oxford. It was a miserable moment when I looked out of the window of the train carrying us to the troopship in Southampton, only to see the towers and spires of the university city flash past, so near and yet so remote.

Until the publication of Richard Vinen's superb history *National Service: Conscription in Britain, 1945–1963* (2014), the best accounts of the experience were fictional: David Lodge's *Ginger, You're Barmy* is a particularly successful evocation of the miseries and absurdities of the conscript's life. Yet Vinen, who was born in 1963, when the last national serviceman was demobbed, draws on memoirs, interviews, and official records to evoke and analyze past experience in a way that will command the unqualified assent and appreciation of those who were there at the time. If anyone wants proof that historians really can recover the truth about the past, this book will provide it.

My own experience was exactly what Vinen would have predicted for a shy if upwardly mobile grammar school boy. I was conscripted in 1950, just after the period of service had been increased from eighteen months to two years because of the Korean emergency. My future college insisted that I should do my National Service before coming up. It was a sensible rule, since I would have sunk without trace had I been plunged at the age of seventeen into the sophisticated world of post-war Balliol, but it meant that I was a year younger than most of my fellow conscripts.

I did basic training in the infantry at the Welsh depot in Brecon. I failed the officer selection board, and was transferred from the Welch Regiment to the First Battalion of the Royal Welch Fusiliers, where I became an orderly room clerk. This was a piece of good fortune for me, but not for my former companions in the Welch Regiment, who went to fight in Korea, a destination from which some of them never returned. By contrast, the RWF sailed to peaceful Jamaica, where I spent the next eighteen months, eventually reaching the rank of corporal. (I discover in Vinen that I was saved from Korea because only those aged nineteen or older could be sent there.) Demobbed in 1952, I had to attend Territorial Army summer camps for the next three years, by then as an officer in the Royal Engineers.

My first fortnight of basic training was traumatic. Immediately on arrival, we were lined up to be vaccinated and then given four roughly administered injections. The painful swelling in my arm was as nothing compared with the horrors of the barrack room. I had never been away from home before and, having grown up in the countryside, knew little about the industrial working class. I found myself surrounded by miners, steelworkers, and laborers who had never possessed pajamas, who when they spoke of "books" meant the *Dandy* or the *Beano,* and whose conversation was an unbroken stream of obscenity. The gloom was leavened only by the banal pop songs of the day, sung repeatedly as we sat blancoing belts and polishing boots: "A man without a woman is like a ship without a sail, / A boat without a rudder or a fish without a tail." None of this would bother me now; indeed, after years of studying what historians call popular culture, I would find it interesting that the song "Silver Dollar," composed in 1907, should still have been around in 1950. But I had led a sheltered life, and in my priggish innocence it seemed as if I had been plunged into a Dantesque hell.

There were other humiliations. In the tests designed to identify those of subnormal intelligence, I proved unable to assemble a bicycle pump. Years later I discovered that this failure put me in a distinguished succession. Tom Harrisson, ornithologist, explorer, and a founder of Mass-Observation, is only one of several notables who had a similar experience. Even so, my mechanical ineptitude lent a singular irony to my eventual posting to the Royal Engineers.

Things got better when I was moved to a hut filled mostly with grammar school boys who were regarded as potential officers or NCOs. Basic training, however, continued to be unpleasant. I didn't mind the square-bashing (drilling on a barrack square) or even the bayonet practice: plunging one's weapon into a sack of straw never for a moment felt like the real thing. Sleeping out in the snow on an exercise in the Brecon Beacons was quite exciting. But the threat of being "back-squadded"—having to do the six weeks all over again—hung over me, because to complete the course you had to pass PE, and I couldn't climb a rope however hard I tried. But of course, when the time came, nobody cared whether I could climb a rope.

"Clerks," Vinen writes, "were usually men who were too well educated to stay in the ranks but too plebeian, obviously lacking in martial qualities or rebellious, to become officers." Far from being rebellious, I was in those days obsequiously conformist, and my parents (a successful tenant farmer and a former schoolteacher) would have bridled at the suggestion that they were plebeian. But I was certainly lacking in martial qualities. In the test for potential officers, the squad under my hesitant leadership, when required to transport a huge log across a bridge, managed to drop it into what was supposed, for the purposes of the exercise, to be a raging torrent below. When asked at my interview whether I could imagine myself leading men into battle, I was unable to give a convincing reply. I knew nothing about the army. No members of my family had ever done military service—agriculture was a reserved occupation—and Welsh grammar schools did not have cadet corps. When I was posted to the Territorial Army, I was sent to another officer selection board and passed easily, but by then I was a young gentleman from Balliol.

Vinen, who is very interested in class, stresses that the army had a firmly binary structure into which grammar school boys did not fit easily. There were officers and there were other ranks, with nothing in between; warrant officers were drawn from long-serving members of other ranks. In the regular army, the officers typically came from the upper middle class and landed gentry, and the other ranks from the rough end of the working class. This left little room for the people in the middle, who, as in Hilaire Belloc's poem, looked "out of place and mean, / And horribly embarrassed."

The troopship *Dilwara*, in which the battalion traveled to Jamaica, had been built in 1936. With its strict segregation of officers, who sailed in first-class luxury, and other ranks, who were crowded together in squalid conditions below the water line, it embodied the social assumptions of the pre-war era; and its sadistic staff resembled prison guards. I managed to lose my meal ticket. I found it again, but it was taken for granted that I had stolen it, and for the rest of the voyage I was ignominiously marched to and from the canteen.

Once arrived in Jamaica, however, the orderly room clerks, because of their socially anomalous position, had rather a good time. We were a congenial little band with our own barrack room. I was allowed to keep a sizable library in my locker (though my reading was not as highbrow as my fellow historian Peter Burke's during his stint as a pay clerk in Singapore, which in a typical two days, Vinen tells us, included Galileo, Gide, and Rimbaud). Although subject to weekly parades and periodic kit inspections, we were excused weapons training and most other military duties. We also enjoyed a certain cachet, because it was widely assumed that we were privy to the battalion's secrets. We enjoyed reading the confidential reports on junior officers, and we received extra helpings in the cookhouse because the cooks, who were mostly regular soldiers on long-term postings in the Caribbean, wrongly believed that we were in a position to help them bring their families to Jamaica from Britain or get them special leave to go home.

The battalion's official duty in Jamaica was to assist the civil power, that is, to uphold the status quo during what turned out to be the last years before decolonization. Under the labor leader Alexander Bustamante, pressure for Jamaican independence was mounting, and there were anticolonial demonstrations all over the Caribbean. The RWF had one company permanently stationed in British Honduras, where dissatisfaction with British rule was particularly intense, and from time to time the battalion was required to send other troops to curb protesters in Antigua, Grenada, and British Guiana. But such encounters were nonviolent, and there was no parallel to the atrocities involving national servicemen in Malaya, Kenya, and Cyprus.

As well as learning how to disperse rioters, the soldiers performed ceremonial duties such as mounting a guard of honor for the arrival of the new governor, Hugh Foot. They also helped out in moments of difficulty, such as the emergency triggered in August 1951 by Hurricane Charlie. This was Jamaica's greatest natural disaster of the twentieth century, with seventeen inches of rainfall in a few hours, gusts of 125 mph, more than 150 deaths, and thousands of injuries. It was the only occasion when the orderly room clerks were issued live ammunition. The wind had blown down the walls of the local prison, and seventy inmates, some of them due to be hanged that week, escaped to the hills. We were sent to find them. To our relief, we failed to do so, though we managed to lose one of our number, who spent the night wandering in the hills.

As the 23rd of Foot, the Royal Welch Fusiliers were not without social pretensions or, indeed, literary ones; I took vicarious pride in knowing that it had been the regiment of Robert Graves, Siegfried Sassoon, and David Jones. They had no successors in my time. In Jamaica the officers lived a cheerfully philistine life, playing polo, attending cocktail parties, and spending weekends on the beaches of the north coast. The other ranks took their pleasures where they could find them. For the regular soldiers, this usually meant the brothels of Kingston. On return to camp, they were required to attend the grandly named Prophylactic Ablution Centre. Those who failed to do so and then contracted VD could end up in a military prison. An additional deterrent was the rumored treatment for gonorrhea, said to involve an instrument resembling a folded umbrella, which was inserted into the sufferer's penis, opened up, and then pulled out.

My own life was nothing if not chaste. I didn't smoke or drink beer, or even tea or coffee. Duties in the orderly room were undemanding, and I spent much of my leisure time playing cricket. On one occasion we played against a side that included Alf Valentine, the young spinner who took eight wickets in the first innings of his first Test against England in 1950. Unfortunately, it poured with rain. Undaunted, our hosts poured petrol on the pitch and set it alight. A huge pall of black smoke rose over the ground, and we resumed play on an extreme version of a rapidly drying wicket. Jamaican cricket involved a good deal of audience participation, and my own delivery of slow leg breaks was frequently accompanied by cries of "Mash him up, man! This is no bowler!" The battalion's cricket coach was a former West Indies Test cricketer who a few years later was hanged for murder. By that time, I was at All Souls, where one of my senior colleagues was a member of the Judicial Committee of the Privy Council that rejected his appeal.

"Join the army and see the world," said the recruiting posters of the day; and in Jamaica even clerks had some opportunities to travel. We twice climbed Blue Mountain Peak (7,400 feet high, but covered in mist when we got there). We also spent idle days by the white sands and transparent blue waters of Doctor's Cave in Montego Bay. A more daring trip was to the Cockpit Country, home of the Maroons, descendants of escaped slaves who in the eighteenth century had, after several wars with British troops, been allowed to remain in this remote and inaccessible area in a state of semi-independence. It was said that no white men ever went there. After a long trek on foot, we arrived unheralded one evening at the Maroon town of Accompong, causing consternation. We were ushered into a large barn, where, by the light of oil lamps, we were interrogated about the reasons for our intrusion and involved in a lengthy, arcane, and on both sides seriously underinformed debate about whether the treaty of 1738 allowed us to be there. Understandably, the Maroons decided that it didn't.

Almost as exciting was a visit in March 1952 to Guantánamo Bay, then as now a base for the U.S. Marines, though without its later associations. A friend and I managed to attach ourselves to the battalion's rifle team, which was traveling to Cuba on the cruiser HMS *Sheffield* for a shooting match against the Marines. We were amazed by the luxurious facilities on the American base, and after the postwar austerities of our army food, which mostly came out of tins, we were thrilled to discover unlimited supplies of steak, chops, chicken, and ice cream. We also learned that an American recruit in training was paid as much as a British lieutenant after four years' service. There was a marked contrast between our bored cynicism and the determined attitude of the Marines. To our astonishment, they actually enjoyed being soldiers and even spent their pocket money on sending away for books on weapons training.

Our time in Cuba coincided with the military coup that brought back the dictator Fulgencio Batista. But though we traveled by bus up the island as far as Camagüey and saw a good deal of decaying baroque splendor, the revolution eluded us. We spent a week cruising on the *Sheffield* while its crew practiced firing their ear-splitting six-inch guns. Living conditions were infinitely worse than on the *Dilwara*. Each mess deck, about fifteen yards square, accommodated forty men. There was no fixed place to sleep; ordinary seamen hung their hammocks anywhere or just flopped down on the floor. The watch system meant that no one got a complete night's sleep anyway. It was easy to see why Samuel Johnson thought that a sailor's life was like being in jail with the chance of being drowned.

I wrote home regularly, and my mother kept my letters. Reading them sixty years later, I feel intense embarrassment. The writer's views on politics and race are callow and distasteful. Repelled by Kingston's crowded and filthy conditions, this bigoted youth attributed the poverty that surrounded him to the inherent idleness and fecklessness of black Jamaicans. He was equally scornful about their desire for self-government. A character in Ian McEwan's novel *The Children Act* remarks that all of us had beliefs at the age of seventeen that would embarrass us now. Vinen found that it was not unusual for former national servicemen to be shocked when they reread their diaries and letters. He tells us that Paul Foot (Hugh Foot's son) found it painful to read the diary he kept at the time of Suez; he suggests that most conscripts who expressed political opinions merely adopted those of their parents. That was certainly true of me. I went to Jamaica with the views I had imbibed from my father and mother, and I returned with them unchanged. Vinen quotes Peter Burke's flattering suggestion that Jamaica created my interest in anthropological approaches to history, but it is, alas, not true. I had some interesting encounters with Rastafarians, but I saw them then as comic curiosities, not subjects for serious study, let alone respect. It was not Jamaica, but Balliol and All Souls, that widened my horizons and turned me into the leftish liberal I now am.

I remember no discussion of politics in our barrack room, other than the rumor that if Churchill got back in the 1951 general election he would extend the period of National Service to three years. We were thoroughly unpolitical and barely aware that our role was the doubtful one of trying to hold together the crumbling remains of the British Empire. National Service produced very few radical dissenters, and ex–national servicemen seldom became the student rebels of the 1960s. But neither did they necessarily become timid conformists. Their experience taught them that it was futile to protest against orders, but easy to circumvent them in practice. It was in the army that many innocent young men first learned how to "skive," evade responsibility and look out for a "cushy" billet. Vinen rightly concludes that "far from being an institution that took 'bad lads' and exposed them to the brisk regularity of military life, National Service often took 'good boys' and exposed them to a world of profanity, petty crime and almost pathological enthusiasm to avoid hard work."

To fly us home, the army chartered an ancient Avro York airplane operated by a private company called the Lancashire Aircraft Corporation. The War Office had decided that this was the most economical form of transport. It took several days to reach England, with prolonged stops at Bermuda and Gander, Newfoundland. A few months afterward, the same plane, carrying the latest batch of troops and their families to Jamaica, disappeared shortly after leaving Gander.

What do I retain from this experience of more than sixty years ago? Not much. I have a shameful taste for military bands and films about army life like *Tunes of Glory*, with Alec Guinness and John Mills. An intense dislike of denim, which I associate with fatigues and servility, has deterred me from ever wearing jeans. I love to hear a Jamaican accent, and despite the island's violence and gang warfare, I still think of its extraordinary beauty. Crucially, what I took away from my National Service was a resolution that when at last I got to Oxford, I would do my best never to leave it.

Fall Semester 2014

A version of this chapter appeared in the *London Review of Books*, 5 February 2015.

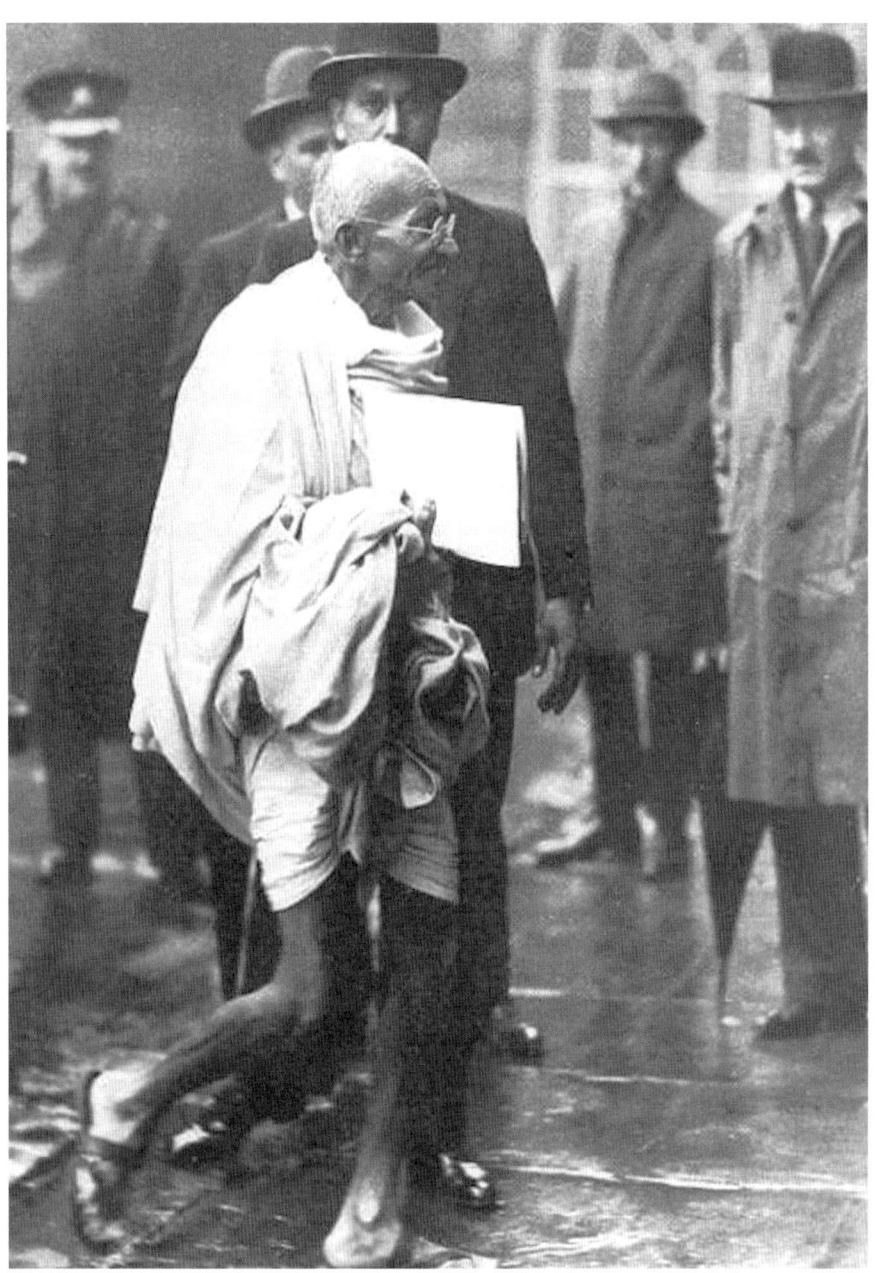

Gandhi in London

9

Gandhi

PERRY ANDERSON

Mohandas Karamchand Gandhi stepped onto the stage of Indian politics upon his arrival in Bombay in 1915, after twenty-one years in South Africa. Though preceded by his reputation as a fearless spokesman for the Indian community there, he had no experience of political life in the subcontinent, and initially confined himself to study tours and setting up an ashram in Ahmedabad. But by the end of the war, his active support of local labor struggles in Bihar and Gujarat, using tactics he had developed in South Africa, had given him a countrywide reputation. Within another two years, he had transformed Indian politics, leading the first mass movement to rock British power since the Mutiny and remaking Congress as a popular political force. After the upheaval of 1919–21, he twice again launched campaigns, in 1930–31 and 1942–43, in size each bigger than the last, challenging the authority of the Raj in successive landmarks of a struggle for national liberation.

In orchestrating these great movements, Gandhi displayed a rare constellation of political abilities, charismatic mobilization of popular feeling foremost among them. In the countryside, adoring crowds treated him as semi-divine. He was a first-class organizer and fund-raiser who rebuilt Congress from top to bottom, endowing it with a permanent executive at the national level, vernacular units at the provincial level, local bases at the district level, and delegates proportionate to population, not to speak of an ample treasury.

Though temperamentally in many ways an autocrat, he did not care about power in itself and was an excellent mediator between different figures and groups both within Congress and among its variegated social supports. Finally, though no great orator, he was an exceptionally quick and fluent communicator, as the hundred volumes of his collected works testify. To these political gifts were added personal qualities of a ready warmth, an impish wit, and an iron will.

But Gandhi's achievements came at a huge cost to the cause that he served. For Gandhi, religion mattered more than politics, which did not coincide with, but subjoined it. But he held no religious office, and his religion was to a peculiar extent homemade, unlike any existing belief system at the time. We owe the first scrupulous account of quite how strange a potpourri this was to Kathryn Tidrick's *Gandhi: A Political and Spiritual Life* (2007), which came out to a deafening silence.

The composition of Gandhi's faith, Tidrick shows, was born of a cross between a Jain-inflected Hindu orthodoxy and late Victorian psychomancy, the world of Madame Blavatsky, theosophy, the planchette, and the Esoteric Christian Union. Garbled ideas from the former—karma, reincarnation, ascetic self-perfection, fusion of the soul with the divine—found occult form in the latter. Little acquainted with the Hindu canon in his early years, Gandhi reshaped it through the medium of Western spiritualisms. His one aim in life was to attain *moksha:* that state of perfection in which the cycle of rebirth comes to an end and the soul accedes to ultimate union with God. The path toward it was "crucifixion of the flesh," without which it was impossible to "see God face to face" and become one with him. If such perfection could be attained, there would be no limit to his command of his countrymen: "When I am a perfect being, I have simply to say the word and the nation will listen."

Crucifixion of the flesh meant far more than the vegetarian prohibitions prescribed by his caste background. Not in food but in sex lay the overriding danger. The violence of Gandhi's revulsion against carnal intercourse of any kind mingled Christian fears of sin with Hindu phobias of pollution. Celibacy was enjoined on all who would truly serve their country: "A man who is unchaste loses stamina, becomes emasculated and cowardly. He whose mind is given over to animal passions is not capable of any great effort." If a married couple gratified such feelings, it was still "an animal indulgence" that, "except for perpetuating the race, is strictly prohibited." Complete continence—*brahmacharya*—was of such transcendent importance that an involuntary ejaculation at the age of sixty-five was matter for an anguished public communiqué. At seventy-seven, he tested himself by sleeping nude with his great-niece. If his conception were to be universally adopted, the logical result would be "not extinction of the human species, but the transference of it to a higher plane."

There were other, no less deadly dangers of more recent origin. Gandhi enumerated some of these in the one consolidated statement of his fundamental beliefs, *Hind Swaraj* (1909). There he explained that machinery "represents a great sin"; that "railways, too, have spread the bubonic plague" and "increased the frequency of famines"; that "hospitals are institutions for propagating sin"; that a peasant needs no "knowledge of letters," which could only make him "discontented with his cottage or his lot." These ruinous innovations were exports of the "satanic civilization" of the West. To restore India to its pristine condition, just one effort was required: "Drive out Western civilisation. All else will follow."

In the years after his arrival on the subcontinent, Gandhi did not insist on such radical atavisms. Sexuality had to be fought, but modernity could be more tactically sidestepped in pursuit of the cause embodied in the title of his work. *Swaraj* was "self-rule." But for Gandhi, self-rule was far from simply political. It was mastery of the passions and of the senses in the ascent of the soul to its appointment with divinity. *Swaraj* was a religious imperative, its political form no more than a means to a higher end. It entailed not a struggle to evict the British from India, but a struggle of Indians with themselves that, if won, would bring the British to reason. The method of that struggle was passive resistance—nonviolence. Gandhi had come upon this conception in Tolstoy, where it was suffused with religious yearning. But his version, satyagraha (a neologism he liked to translate as "truth-force"), was an original development. Gandhi gave nonviolence a distinctively Hindu cast, fusing it with millennial traditions of a radical asceticism and extra-terrestrialism. "Passive resistance" he felt too weak a term for the movement he set out to inspire: truth was not passive—it was a force.

The original politics of the Congress elite had been studiously secular. Gandhi's takeover of the party not only gave it an unprecedented popular basis but also injected into it a massive dose of religion—mythology, symbology, theology. The power of political mobilization in the register of *Hind Swaraj* was manifest. But it posed an obvious problem. Could the Muslim millions be rallied in the same idiom? In South Africa, Gandhi had been a staunch advocate of Hindu-Muslim unity, and no confessional divisions had marred his campaigns of nonviolence there. He maintained that all religions preached the same truths, so there was no basis for division. But in the subcontinent, a long history of conquests and conflicts divided Muslims and Hindus.

For Gandhi, it was impossible to be impartial between the two faiths. Personally, he was perfectly sincere in holding that all religions were equal before the Lord. Politically, one religion was, inevitably, more equal than the other. Hinduism was indigenous to the subcontinent, and peculiar to it. Islam was neither. A dutiful son of his faith, Gandhi declared, "I yield to none in my reverence for the cow," and warned his son against marrying a Muslim on grounds that it was "contrary to dharma" and—a telling simile—"like putting two swords in one sheath." When he announced in 1919 that "India is fitted for the religious supremacy of the world," few could doubt which religion he had in mind.

How then was such a Hindu revivalist to unite Muslims in a common national struggle? On the one hand, he could not do so on a secular basis without denying everything he believed in. On the other, he was realistic enough to know that reiteration of the precept that all religions converged on the same goal, however frequent and well meant, might cut little ice with followers of a prophet who had given famously short shrift to idolatry. The solution he hit on was to rouse Muslims to action against the Raj under the banner of Islam itself.

Under the Raj, Muslims steadily lost ground after the Mutiny. No longer the masters of the region they had once ruled, not fully trusted as soldiers, they stooped with difficulty to bureaucratic employment by the British, had little business experience, and, possessed of an administrative idiom of their own in Persian, did not take readily to education in English. By 1900, it was obvious how far they lagged behind Hindus in government service, industry, and the professions. Alarmed at this downward slide in their community, reformers sought to create a better-educated Muslim elite, and notables, led by the Aga Khan, prevailed on the British to ensure that Muslim votes would not be swamped by Hindu majorities, by allowing them separate electoral rolls and seats.

In the subcontinent, the fall of the Ottoman Empire was perceived by many Muslims as a humiliation that resonated emotionally with their own descent in the world—the last great Islamic power crushed and dismembered by foes, foremost among whom were the British rulers of India. For Gandhi, this was an opportunity to demonstrate Hindu-Muslim unity by rallying Hindu opinion behind agitation to protect the nominal caliph. That more-secular Muslims—Jinnah among them—regarded the issue as not merely irrelevant but thoroughly regressive, a breeding ground for clerical posturing, did not deter him. Nor was he moved by the dismay of friends who pointed out Arab feelings about Ottoman imperialism, not to speak of the fate of the Armenians. What counted was that this was a religious cause in which Hindus could join with Muslims against British injustice. That his fellow Hindus would feel much solidarity over such a strained, remote question was unlikely. But 1919, which saw the formation of an All-India Caliphate (Khilafat) Committee, likewise witnessed Gandhi's first attempt at an all-Indian satyagraha, to protest legislation prolonging wartime powers of arbitrary arrest and imprisonment. Response to Gandhi's call proved patchy and, in the face of harsh repression—including General Dyer's notorious mowing down of an unarmed crowd at Amritsar—faded within a few months.

In linking the issues of the Punjab, under martial law after the massacre, and the caliphate, while making it clear the caliphate had priority, Gandhi launched a mass campaign of Noncooperation with the British in August 1920, promising the nation "*Swaraj* within a Year." Noncooperation would escalate through four ascending levels if the Raj did not yield: first, renunciation of all titles and honors conferred by the British; next, resignation from positions in the civil service; then, resignation from the police and army; finally, refusal to pay taxes. In practice, emphasis fell on a boycott of courts, schools, council elections, and—especially—foreign goods. The campaign electrified the country, drawing in social layers and geographic regions hitherto untouched by nationalist agitation. Mobilizing Hindus and Muslims alike, and engulfing Calcutta and Bombay in tempests of political unrest, the movement posed the greatest threat to British rule since the Mutiny. Desertions from the civil service, police, and army were few. The ultimate weapon in its arsenal was the last: a tax strike. The structure of the Raj depended on the land revenue it extracted from an overwhelmingly agrarian population. Without this, it could not be sustained. On 1 February 1922, Gandhi announced that in the face of British obduracy, he would initiate a refusal to pay taxes in the Bardoli district of Gujarat.

Four days later, police in the small town of Chauri Chaura, in the United Provinces, fired on a crowd protesting food prices, killing three demonstrators; counterattacking, the infuriated crowd put paid to the policemen in the station where they had barricaded themselves. On learning the news of this unthinkable event, Gandhi declared a five-day fast of penance and, to general stupefaction, without consulting anyone, called off the whole national movement. He could do this because such was his aura that Congress had granted him "sole executive authority"—in effect, dictatorial powers—six weeks earlier. No single decision of his would ever be as fateful as this. How did he justify it? He had sinned, he explained, in failing to realize that the Indian masses were not yet spiritually advanced enough to adhere to the nonviolence that he had always said was a condition of obtaining *swaraj* within a year, as he had promised.

It is conventional to take this explanation at face value. Certainly, Gandhi had shown increasing unease at the turbulence his campaign had unleashed. Yet contrary to legend, his attitude toward violence had always been—and would remain—contingent and ambivalent. At the start of his career, as is fairly well known, he twice volunteered for active service (stretcher bearing). When the First World War broke out, he was eager to organize an ambulance corps for the British, and in mid-1918 went out of his way to try and drum up recruits for the inter-imperialist slaughter in Flanders, tramping as far as Bihar in a bid—happily, a dismal failure—to round up more villagers for the trenches. "The ability to use physical force is necessary for a true appreciation of *satyagraha*," he told them. "He alone can practise *ahimsa* [compassion] who knows how to kill"—in fact, the "practice of *ahimsa* may even necessitate killing."

Did he then change his mind in planning the strategy of Noncooperation in 1920? On the eve of the campaign, he expressly allowed for lapses in the struggle: "No general worth the name gives up the battle, because he has suffered reverses, or, which is the same thing, made mistakes." Indeed, so far from flinching at the prospect of hitches, he declared: "I would risk violence a thousand times [rather] than risk the emasculation of a whole race." The remorse at Bardoli was not in any way conclusive. Twenty years later, he would tell compatriots: "We have to take the risk of violence to shake off the great calamity of slavery." In 1942 he informed reporters that in India "rivers of blood" might be "the price of freedom." In 1946, thumping the table, he told the viceroy: "If India wants her bloodbath, she shall have it."

Such is the record. To read it as evidence of mere hypocrisy on Gandhi's part would be a mistake. There can be no doubt that he was, so far as he himself went, sincere enough in his commitment to nonviolence. But as a political leader, his conception of himself as a vessel of divine intention allowed him to escape the trammels of human logic or coherence. Truth was not an objective value, but simply what he subjectively felt at any given time. "It has been my experience," he wrote, "that I am always true from my point of view." His autobiography was subtitled *The Story of My Experiments with Truth*, as if truth were material for alteration in a laboratory, or the plaything of a séance. The result was a license to say whatever he wanted, regardless of what he had said before, whenever he saw fit.

The effects of such a conviction on the political culture of the movement that he led could not but be corrupting. To real intellectual exchange, he was a stranger. He was trained as a British barrister, and argued like one, not as a thinker, changing his brief from day to day. His religious belief in himself was impervious to doubt or objection, guaranteeing that all he said, no matter how apparently contradictory, formed a single bloc of truth, like so many scattered words of God. For while he modified or diluted or inverted positions as time went by, he rarely disavowed directly anything significant he had once said or written. *Hind Swaraj,* its battery of archaisms a stumbling block to those who pointed out that he was using railways and doctors and not actually rejecting schools, he defended to the end. Characteristically, he added: "It is not necessary for me to prove the rightness of what I said then. It is essential only to know what I feel today." Throughout his career in India, he claimed both to rise above consistency—growing "from truth to truth"—and unswervingly to embody it.

Thus, when Gandhi called off the mass movement he had launched, the efficient reason for his sudden retreat lay less in his religious beliefs, whose very fixity allowed for such flexibility, than in his political outlook. The goal of Noncooperation was *swaraj* within a year. What did that mean? A month before his decision at Bardoli, Gandhi spelled out what it did not mean: "Assuming that Great Britain alters her attitude . . . when India is strong, it will be religiously unlawful for us to insist on independence. For it will be vindictive and petulant." What India should seek was a status like that of South Africa, within a commonwealth of equal partners that retained the British connection.

Gandhi did not want to evict the British in India if to do so was to risk social upheaval. Revolution was a greater danger than the Raj. Hinduism bound all who adhered to it into a single interwoven community, in which each was allotted an appointed station. To break its unity by setting one part against another was contrary to divine order. And the movement he called into being in 1919, though extensive, was not comprehensive. The Congress he commanded was a coalition of industrialists, traders, professionals, and better-off peasants; it did not include urban workers or the rural poor, who formed the vast majority of the population. To pit these against their employers or landlords was to divide what God had joined; to mobilize them against their rulers, to risk setting fire to the country. Class conflict was out. In Chauri Chaura, a mob propelled by economic grievances had respected neither the law nor its guardians, in an awful warning of what popular passions might unleash in India.

MUSLIMS, ONCE STIRRED TO ACTION and then unceremoniously abandoned by Gandhi, by and large never trusted him again. Jinnah, a member of Congress long before Gandhi, and the architect of its pact with the Muslim League (of which he was by then simultaneously president) in 1916, had already left the party in a mixture of dismay at the radicalization of its tactics and disgust at the sacralization of its appeals once Gandhi took over. He disliked intensely what he saw as the confessional demagoguery of the caliphate campaign. In 1927, he proposed a pact that would reserve for Muslims one-third of the seats in a central legislature in exchange for a single electorate. Nehru père, charged by Congress with drawing up its constitutional proposals, at first accepted this. Then he produced a report reducing the quota to a quarter and rejecting any reservations in Punjab and Bengal, where Muslims were a majority of the population but a minority of the electorate—elsewhere, they could be "settled by throwing a few crumbs here and there." At an All-Party Conference in Calcutta, Jinnah's attempts at amendments were shouted down.

By 1928, Gandhi, after a spell in the wings, was center stage again, and Congress membership was increasing by leaps and bounds, a recruitment drive lifting it from 80,000 to 450,000 by 1929. Faced with resurgent nationalist mobilization, the incumbent Viceroy, the future Lord Halifax, promised India what Gandhi had by then redefined as the *swaraj* he sought, Dominion Status within the empire. In March 1930, when talks failed to extract fine print from the pledge, Gandhi unleashed his second great campaign of civil disobedience, whose spectacular first act was a march to the sea in defiance of the state's salt tax, recently increased. This time, the response was geographically wider but communally narrower—virtually no Muslims took part—and the repression swifter and greater: 60,000 arrests, including the entire top leadership of Congress. In practice, the tax mostly continued to be collected and little revenue was lost, the main impact coming once again from mass boycott of foreign goods. Unrest was sufficient, however, for the Viceroy to release Gandhi and reach a deal with him to suspend the movement and attend the Round Table Conference on constitutional reform in London, which Congress had hitherto boycotted.

At the conference, Gandhi—unaccustomed to multilateral negotiation—was balked by Muslim and Sikh insistence on separate electorates, and disconcerted by a demand for the same from the Untouchable leader Bhimrao Ambedkar, within what he saw as his own community. Returning empty-handed to India, Gandhi resumed civil disobedience. A tougher British crackdown saw him jailed again, with further mass arrests, and by the spring of 1932 the movement had been defeated, with nothing tangible to show for it. In the summer, London announced that Untouchables would be granted separate electorates. Caste was now, irrevocably, on the table, and for the first time Gandhi's religious beliefs were put to a direct political test.

WHAT WAS GANDHI'S ATTITUDE TOWARD CASTE? He had set it out in 1920–21. Untouchability was a heinous crime. But it was an excrescence that had nothing to do with caste itself, which was not a human invention but an immutable law of nature. There was no element of hierarchy in it. "The caste system is not based on inequality, there is no question of inferiority," for "nature will, without any possibility of mistake, adjust the balance by degrading a Brahmin, if he misbehaves himself, by reincarnating him in a lower division, and translating one who lives the life of a Brahmin in his present incarnation to Brahminhood in his next." There was no need to adjust the balance in this life.

On religious grounds, it was essential to preserve the division of society into four fundamental castes, for it was this that had saved Hinduism from disintegration. To destroy the system would mean that "Hindus must give up the principle of hereditary occupation which is the soul of the caste system." Chaos would result: "The hereditary principle is an eternal principle. To change it is to create disorder." Caste, indeed, was not just the cornerstone of Hindu India. Properly respected, it might be a universal balm: 'It can be offered to the world as a leaven and as the best remedy against heartless competition and social disintegration born of avarice and greed.'

Over time, he toned down such claims. Trying to fend off Ambedkar's attacks, he later explained that the fourfold order of *varna* (classification by occupation) was not to be confused with subdivisions of *jati* (caste), which were a deplorable corruption of it, disavowing the latter as "nothing to do with religion." In due course, he tried to dilute *varna* to make it more palatable to egalitarian opinion, at the cost of emptying it of any content except the irreducible core of its identification with Hinduism itself. This he never abandoned.

The threat to Gandhi posed by the prospect of Untouchables gaining the right to their own electorates thus went much deeper than fear of another British device to divide the national movement, like the separate rolls granted to Muslims. Fundamental questions were at issue. If Untouchables were to be treated as external to the Hindu community, it would confirm that caste was indeed, as its critics had always maintained, a vile system of discrimination, relegating the lowest orders of society to a subhuman existence with which the smallest brush was pollution. Since Hinduism was founded on caste, it would stand condemned with caste. To reclaim the Untouchables for Hinduism was an ideological imperative for upholding the reputation of the religion. But it was also politically vital, since if Untouchables were subtracted from the Hindu bloc in India, its predominance over the Muslim community would be weakened. Most menacing of all, Gandhi confided to a colleague, might not Untouchables, accorded a separate identity, then gang up with "Muslim hooligans and kill caste Hindus"?

To cut off these dangers, Gandhi announced that as "a man of religion" and leader of "numberless men and women who have childlike faith in my wisdom," he would fast to death until the award was rescinded and Untouchables were bundled back into the Hindu electorate. The sensation was enormous. Ambedkar was summoned posthaste to Gandhi's jail in Poona to avert the passing of the Great Soul. His own view of the religion he was being told to embrace was unflinching: "No matter what the Hindus say, Hinduism is a menace to liberty, equality and fraternity"—words few Indian intellectuals would dare utter today. Gandhi, though he had long condemned Untouchability as odious, had never seen it as sufficiently serious to warrant a fast unto death. Granting Untouchables their own rolls was another matter. Against that he would put his life on the line. Under colossal public pressure, and physical threats to him and his community if he stood firm, Ambedkar yielded to Gandhi's blackmail.

A "pact" was reached to give a larger number of reserved seats to Untouchables elected, not by their own kind, but by Hindus at large—depriving the community of political autonomy by ensuring that Congress could pick its Uncle Toms for these places. Of the satyagraha of 1932, Ambedkar wrote: "There was nothing noble in the fast. It was a foul and filthy act. The fast was not for the benefit of the Untouchables. It was against them and was the worst form of coercion against a helpless people," forcing them to "agree to live on the mercy of the Hindus." He regretted his capitulation at Poona to the last.

VICTORY OVER AMBEDKAR COULD NOT alter checkmate by the Raj. For another two years, after civil disobedience had been crippled as collective action, Gandhi persisted with "individual" acts of it, in and out of fasts and prisons, touring and preaching against Untouchability to purify the religion that had invented it. In the spring of 1934, the government lifted its ban on Congress, and a few months later he announced his resignation from the party. The gesture did not mean he was retiring from politics. He was withdrawing to a position from which he could dictate policy when he wished, without having to take responsibility for day-to-day party decisions. He could rely on the incumbent president of the party, the younger Nehru, not to challenge his authority if he chose to exercise it.

By the end of the decade, however, a new cohort was pressing both for Congress to adopt socialism as a goal and for more radical measures to dispatch the Raj. Gandhi had always rejected any talk of socialism, as a breach of the sacred trust in which capitalist property was legitimately held, threatening to have nothing to do with the party if it took it up. The leader of the new left-wing current, Subhas Chandra Bose, stood for a coalition with the Muslim peasant party in his native province of Bengal that was no less anathema to Calcutta businessmen, Hindu chauvinists to a man, than his socialism. The wealthiest of these, the magnate G. D. Birla, not only bankrolled Congress to the tune of millions of rupees, but also was a longtime follower and intimate of Gandhi. When Birla made his feelings known, Gandhi put his foot down and the Congress high command duly scuppered Bose's inter-communal initiative. Not long afterward, Bose was nonetheless elected president of Congress. In the following years he was re-elected, defeating Gandhi's candidate in the first contested election for the presidency in the party's history. This was an unprecedented affront that Gandhi, who was not prepared to let democracy get in the way of his will, swiftly punished, toppling Bose in an inner-party coup and then forcing him out of Congress altogether.

When the Second World War broke out, Gandhi took center stage for the last time. With limited knowledge of, or interest in, the outside world—admiring Hitler as, in his way, a fellow ascetic whose "character is said to be clean" and whose "intellect is unclouded and unerring"—he zigzagged from initial support of the British declaration of war on Germany to requiring individual demonstrations of *satyagraha* against it to suddenly deciding that the British had to be driven forthwith from the subcontinent, come what may. The Quit India movement was imposed by Gandhi on a reluctant Congress leadership. It was his final throw, and this time he not only called for a tax strike but also accepted that violence might break out. Riots erupted across the country, police stations were attacked, rail lines torn out.

For a wave of younger fighters, it was an insurrection for

independence. But Congress had never prepared for one, and the Raj was now on a war footing—the Indian Army swelled to two million troops after 1939. The rebellion, without training or leadership, was put down with fusillades on the ground, strafing from the air, 60,000 arrests, 4,000 casualties. After the event, Gandhi described it as a calamity. His third and last campaign against British rule had ended in a failure as complete as those of the first two. By 1945, he was, politically speaking, a back number. Of the anti-colonial leaders of the twentieth century, few ended their careers with much glory, many among the ruins of their hopes or reputation. An assassin's bullet spared Gandhi a comparable fate, embalming him in the martyr's death that by then he wanted. What has become of his ideals today? A face on a banknote.

Satyagraha was not a success: each time Gandhi tried it, the British saw it off. His great achievement lay elsewhere, in the creation of a nationalist party whose road to power forked off in another direction. For in the end, independence did not come from passive resistance, let alone sexual abstinence.

Spring Semester 2015

A version of this lecture appeared in the *London Review of Books*, 5 July 2012.

Paul Scott

10

Paul Scott

PETER GREEN

I first met Paul Scott at Firpo's bar on Chowringhee in Calcutta in 1944. I was an NCO in what was euphemistically described as "Special Duties," that is, intelligence, but more often meant taking on any odd job for which no one else could be found. Paul was an air supply captain who had been commissioned into the Service Corps, unkindly known to the Rifle Brigade or the Gurkhas as, in the words of his biographer Hilary Spurling, "the Rice Corps, Flying Grocers, or Jam Stealers and generally considered to be about as low as it was possible to get in the Indian Army." We eyed each other's shoulder chips with sympathy over drinks and got on extremely well. I did wonder at the time whether he might not have been trying to pick me up, a suspicion that Spurling's biography and a collection of Scott's letters have done nothing to dispel.

A decade later, with Cambridge behind me, I was trying to break into the London literary world and decided I needed an agent. Summoned for an interview at the firm then known as Pearn, Pollinger and Higham, I found myself facing, across a desk, an elegantly suited gentleman who—I suddenly realized at about the same moment as the penny dropped for him—was none other than my Rice Corps bar companion. We both exploded with laughter, and I became his client on the spot.

So began a literary friendship that lasted, in person or by correspondence, until Paul's tragically early death in 1978. For six years, until he gave up his job to become a full-time novelist in 1960, Paul was my literary agent. We exchanged innumerable critical letters (quite a few of which have found their way into Janis Haswell's collection) about work in progress, together with a kind of running commentary on the rare splendors and all-too-frequent miseries, mostly financial, of the writer's life. (The correspondence is archived at the University of Tulsa, where Paul once taught.) We lunched with each other regularly at Paul's favorite Soho tavern, the Dog and Duck. He was pleasant, competent, sardonic: nice to know, but nothing out of the ordinary. When I moved to the country and came up to town on weekly flying visits, I occasionally stayed with him and his wife, Penny, and their two school-age daughters in Hampstead Garden Suburb.

From 1963 until 1971, my family and I were living in Greece, and after that I took up an academic post in the United States, so during this highly important late period of his career, my friendship with Paul was in essence restricted to letters. It was then, in the early 1960s, that Paul finally discovered his great theme—the twilight and eclipse of the British Raj in India—and retreated further and further, during the decade that it took him to sweat out the four long volumes that emerged as *The Raj Quartet*, into a kind of creative solitude where the fictional world of British India that he conjured up became, more and more as time went on, virtually his sole reality.

The physical and emotional cost was appalling. It was, essentially, as his daughter Carol saw, the prime cause of his alienation from Penny, the breakup of his long marriage. By the end he was (as he told a doctor) eating little, sleeping less, and drinking a quart of vodka a day. When I finally saw him again, after the completion of the *Quartet*—we had invited him to lecture at the University of Texas—I was shocked by the change in his appearance. In 1975, though still only in his midfifties, he was a dying man, and knew it. The completion of that vast and complex project had exacted a horrendous price, of which perhaps the saddest aspect was that Paul never lived to enjoy the fame and success that it brought him.

Paul himself had put it on record, very early: "I mean & intend to become a great artist if I possibly can be." Yet there is nothing about his early suburban life—or, indeed, much of his pre-*Quartet* fiction—that presages the power and the scope of the Indian tetralogy. The son of a commercial artist (the family claimed descent from the engraver Thomas Bewick) who fell on hard times, he was removed from his private school—a far from classy one—at the age of fourteen and set to train as an accountant. He began writing poems and plays that were, as he agreed later in life, better forgotten. The turning point was his army career, which took him to Bengal,

Imphal, and Malaya. But the seed then sown took years to come to fruition, and not before several not-quite-right attempts, such as *Six Days in Marapore* and *The Chinese Love Pavilion,* had been painstakingly hammered out. After the war, having qualified as an accountant, he got a job keeping the books for a new publishing firm, and from there moved on to the literary agency where I met him again. All the time he was writing, and fiction by now was slowly beginning to oust poems and plays.

Paul himself often said that his life, like that of most writers, was a fundamentally dull one. When I started on the first volume of Janis Haswell's collection of his correspondence, which begins in 1940 with him as an army recruit, it was in the hope of proving him modestly wrong. At first I was disappointed. Paul was still plugging away, when he had time from army duties, at what sound like terrible plays and even worse poems, criticized and dissected at tedious length in correspondence with Clive Sansom. His literary standards were relentlessly middle class: "I wish the rain wouldn't look so much like a short story by Maugham. Nobody else has a chance to do anything literary with that man's shadow haunting the scene." The only unexpected discovery was his open discussion of his youthful homosexuality (often managed in the third person: he called his alter ego Ivan Kapinsky) with friends such as Ruth Sansom.

The larger part of Haswell's first volume deals with Paul's postwar life as a literary agent and a working novelist: the years when I knew him best. What strikes me now is how completely professional matters, and the correspondence dealing with them, occupied almost his entire waking life: even the lunches were literary, and almost all his friends were, one way or another, in the book trade. As everyone agreed, he was a brilliant agent who took endless pains over his clients. Many of these letters deal with critical discussions of manuscripts, his own or those of others, which for those outside the charmed circle will make tough reading. (I suspect Haswell inserted so many of them for the benefit of English professors teaching Scott's fiction.) As Paul wrote in 1960, "The bloody trouble is we are only alive when we're half dead trying to get a paragraph right." When he decides to give up the agency and become a full-time writer, there is more about his own problems and less about those of his clients, but the ingrown London world of novelists, reviewers, publishers, and agents remains essentially unaltered.

The turning point came in 1964 when his London publisher, Heinemann, with what can only be regarded, in hindsight, as remarkable acumen, arranged for his return to India on a six-week visit. (Two more such trips were arranged during the years when he was engaged with the *Quartet*.) He was looked after in Bombay by Dorothy Ganapathy, who became a lifelong friend. He stayed for over a week with his wartime *havildar* (sergeant) in a rural village in Andhra Pradesh, where he experienced culture shock in its most extreme form. While in Calcutta, he met Neil Ghosh, product of a British public-school education, who became the model for Hari Kumar in the *Quartet*. Best of all, he found a correct diagnosis of the amoebiasis that he had contracted during the war, with its legacy of "lassitude, depression, insomnia, mood swings, and lack of concentration." For this he sought, and got, curative treatment in Paris. Almost immediately, in the surge of health that followed, his renewed acquaintance with India fresh in his mind, he began to write *The Jewel in the Crown*.

This, the first of the four novels that go to make up the *Quartet*, is set in 1942: the year of the British defeat by the Japanese in Burma and points east, the realization by Hindus and Muslims that the gods of the Raj were by no means omnipotent. We meet several of the main characters, whose lives are changed, for good or ill, by these events, such as Edwina Crane, the elderly missionary, whose sense of progress and colonial idealism is left in tatters after a riot that kills the young Hindu teacher with whom she works, and leaves her holding his dead hand in the rain beside her burnt-out car. We sit in on the striated prejudices of the Europeans-only club, meet socially impeccable Brahmins such as Lady Chatterjee as well as the Eurasian half-castes who talk in what I remember being referred to, unkindly but accurately, as "Bombay Welsh," and who make pathetic claims to have come out from Brighton or Manchester: the simple fact of the existence of foreign rulers and native subjects is seen to penetrate and falsify all human relationships.

The most vivid, violent, and memorable of these relationships is that between the Indian Hari Kumar—resident in England almost all his life, public-school educated, speaking no Hindi or Urdu, and abruptly returned to Mayapore—and Daphne Manners, fresh out from home, the awkward, big-boned niece of a former governor. They fall in love; they stumble through the dreadful minefield of social and racial taboos, and Daphne is raped by a bunch of out-of-town Hindu thugs while making love to Hari in the Bibighar Gardens at night. She cannot admit the affair with Hari without getting him into appalling trouble; but the lies involved are instantly picked up by Ronald Merrick, the district superintendent of police, a major malign figure throughout the *Quartet*, a lower-middle-class English provincial who is a steely upholder of the colonial status quo, which has let him rise to a position of real authority in India. He has also proposed marriage to Daphne, and is all too ready to nail Hari Kumar for a serious offense. The repercussions of the rape in the Bibighar Gardens spread through the entire sequence, affecting everyone, English or Indian, civilian or military, who comes into contact with the case.

What has always astonished me about *The Raj Quartet* is the sense of sophisticated and total control of its gigantic scenario and highly varied characters. The four volumes constitute perfectly interlocking movements of a grand overall design. The politics are handled with an expertise that intrigues and never bores, and are always seen in their effects on individuals. Though Paul saw the inevitability, and the necessity, of an end to the British occupation and exploitation of India, he still could see, and sympathize with, the odd virtues that the Raj bred in its officers. No one—certainly not E. M. Forster—has ever produced a subtler, more nuanced picture of the Raj in action during its last, fraught years, or of the seething, complex, and wildly disparate nationalist forces arrayed against it.

The second volume of Scott's letters takes over as this great novel sequence begins to be written, and inevitably it contains far more than its predecessor to quicken the general reader's interest. Other novelists will not be surprised to learn that many experiences that befall characters in *The Raj Quartet* actually happened to Paul. "*Madame Bovary, c'est moi,*" as Flaubert famously declared. The letters indicate changes of direction: the project starts as one novel, grows to three in the middle of *The Day of the Scorpion,* and becomes a quartet only when *The Towers of Silence* threatens to become too unwieldy—yet the larger whole never loses its overall cohesion.

In 1968, Paul opined that as he grew older, he became "more and more convinced that literature isn't really a fit subject for academic study." Yet a decade later, he astonished himself by emerging as a brilliant and inspired university teacher in the States. Those who claim he was short on humor should read his letters to his daughter Carol, which contain the adventures (with hilarious illustrative sketches) of one Abu Ben Grottso, Camille the Camel, and the sultry Scarlet Sahara. He meets Stevie Smith at a party and drives her home: "What a journey!" he reports. "I've not laughed so much in years." Surprisingly, he turns out to be a close observer of natural life: in a letter to Freya Stark, he talks of the creatures—hedgehogs, foxes, rabbits, magpies, a sparrowhawk—that he watches from his study window. Confronted by an early dissertation on his work, he addresses himself in the mirror: "You mean *that's* what you were saying?" He regales his daughter Sally, only a year before his death, with four detailed, expert pages on how to cook chef-style curry and chicken *pulao*.

There is nothing here to indicate any fundamental, road-to-Damascus change from the efficient agent and struggling, ironic littérateur from the London suburbs whom I knew as my friend and fellow novelist in the late 1950s. We critiqued each other's fiction: his was good, but not in any way really exceptional.

By the time he was well into *The Jewel in the Crown*, I had left for Greece, and so never saw the manuscript. In October 1965, already clearly worried about money, he wrote me, "I think my future largely depends now on what happens to my mammoth novel (about the Indian rebellion of 1942)." He had said much the same thing in 1962 about *The Birds of Paradise*, which I had read: a fictional memoir by an Anglo-Indian raised in India, schooled in England, and scarred as much by heartache as by time spent in a Japanese POW camp. This, I now see, was a trial run for *The Raj Quartet*, though I very much doubt that its author knew it at the time. Maugham still cast a long shadow over these pages. From Haswell's selection, it also emerges that Paul was already drinking very heavily and had at one time at least contemplated suicide.

I HAVE GONE INTO THESE DETAILS in order to highlight the absolute astonishment I felt when I first read *The Jewel in the Crown*, and then, with mounting excitement, each subsequent volume of what was to become *The Raj Quartet*. The style, tone, depth, range, and human understanding had all, at a stroke, undergone a quite extraordinary and enriching metamorphosis. The perception of character, which had previously restricted itself, in essence, to Scott's own literary suburbia, here blossomed into a breadth of understanding that had no trouble with a psychopathic police superintendent, an aristocratic Rajput matriarch, an émigré Russian homosexual acting as chief minister in an Indian Princely State, a highly sophisticated Muslim politician, two elderly spinster missionaries, and a wide assortment of military families brought up, generation after generation, to serve the Raj.

The apparent knowledge of cantonment life, of high-level Anglo-Indian diplomacy, of the inner thoughts and emotional problems of British administrators and Muslim or Hindu nationalists went far beyond what could be learned by research (of which, it turned out, Paul did a great deal, as can be seen in the anonymous reviews he wrote for the *Times Literary Supplement* on all aspects of the Indian political and social scene). What really amazed was the way he never put a foot wrong psychologically over either caste or gender, so an old Indian Civil Service luminary such as Sir Herbert Thompson, on reading *A Division of the Spoils,* instantly assumed that it must have been written by one of his former colleagues under a pseudonym. As Spurling says, when the truth was out and Paul had his first of many lunches with the Thompsons, he felt "the strange sensation of stepping through the looking-glass into a world he had so far projected only in his imagination."

The *Quartet* remains a tour de force virtually without rivals. The question is, how? How did this middle-class suburbanite—who left school at fourteen, had no experience of diplomacy or the civil service, in India or anywhere else, and never set foot inside a British university in his life—suddenly, after a solid but hitherto no more than middling literary career, acquire the vision that brought the world of the fading Raj to unforgettable life, in a quartet of novels that for range and power have been compared to Tolstoy? Suggestions have not been wanting, most notably that his experience on the wrong side of the rigid social divisions operating in pre-war London suburbia gave him a sharpened insight into both native caste distinctions and the even more absolute British color bar that he found in India. Others have pointed to his sexual ambiguity (and probable repression of his homosexual side after a bad experience, perhaps drawn on for Corporal Pinker's dealings with Colonel Merrick in *A Division of the Spoils*). There may be some truth in both these theories, but since they stem from Paul's early life, why did they not have the same transforming effect on his early fiction as they are alleged to have done on *The Raj Quartet*? The difference is as total, and as extraordinary, as the still not fully understood process by which a chrysalis becomes a butterfly.

In Paul's case, it seems to have been a visitation akin to speaking in tongues, a literal possession; and this kind of possession can be dangerous. It perhaps explains what his wife misinterpreted as his "expression of hate" when she interrupted him. What he primarily felt was the agony of loss at being brought back out of an all-embracing cocoon: a total creative world in which he had been granted complete insight, social and psychological, into every character and action. After about a million words of this, he was an alcoholic wreck, and small wonder. It is especially interesting that *Staying On,* the short and charming coda to the magnum opus of *The Raj Quartet,* shows no signs of this kind of possession, willed or involuntary: it was written fast and enjoyably, and reads like it, a deft and sympathetic jeu d'esprit created comfortably from the immense experience and ample detritus of its great predecessors. "What will survive of us is love," said Larkin. *Staying On*, written after Penny had left him, is a wonderful exemplification of that wisdom.

Not long ago, after a lapse of some years, I reread them all, and was struck, first and foremost, at how readable—even the disquisition on Hindu political cartoons!—the entire sequence was. "I am large," wrote Whitman. "I contain multitudes." Paul's magnum opus has the same generous, almost Dickensian capacity. There are the great set pieces—Daphne Manners's report to her aunt on the rape in the Bibighar Gardens (I don't agree that Paul was trying to outsmart Forster here); Sir George Malcolm's interview with Mohammad Ali Khan; the interrogation of Hari Kumar by Nigel Rowan and Ramaswamy Gopal, with Lady Manners as unseen witness; Merrick's report from his hospital bed to Sarah Layton of how Teddy Bingham died; Barbie and Mabel at the Pankot Rifles party; Mohammed Ali Kasim's fraught meeting with his son Sayed, a prisoner after having served in the anti-British Indian National Army.

But for me, the most unforgettable moment in the entire sequence of novels comes at the climax of *A Division of the Spoils*, when Mohammed Ali Kasim's other son, the aristocratic playboy and falconer Ahmed, in a train stopped by a bloodthirsty Hindu mob, says to his English friends, "It seems to be me they want," and quietly walks out to his death. Like Captain Oates vanishing into the snows of the Antarctic, like Sydney Carton going to the guillotine to save another man, Ahmed Kasim the Muslim concludes the great work by carrying out, as calmly as he would flight his hawk, the sort of act of self-sacrificial heroism on which his Raj masters particularly prided themselves. It is almost the last thought we are left with: that dramatic moment crystallizes the deepest sense of Paul Scott's great work. After this long saga of "the British coming to the end of themselves as they were," after the racism, the greed, the arrogant memsahibs, the shattered ideals of service, the bloodshed, and the hatred, the image remaining with us is that of the universality, against whatever odds, of human dignity and courage.

Spring Semester 2014

A version of this lecture appeared in the *New Republic*, 17 May 2013.

Sarvepalli Gopal, Madras, 1987. Photograph by Dagmar Louis.

11

Towards Freedom

SUCHETA MAHAJAN

The years after 1947 saw the publication of many books on the "transfer of power" from Britain to India and Pakistan. The authoritative account from the British point of view came with the twelve-volume *Transfer of Power* series (1970–83). Drawn from official historical records pertaining to constitutional relations between Great Britain and India leading up to the transfer of power, the volumes were published at a time of avid interest in Asia, Africa, and Europe in the twin processes of imperial retreat and colonial independence. The project was entrusted to Nicholas Mansergh, Smuts Professor of the History of the British Empire at the University of Cambridge.

The Indian view of the same period is presented in the *Towards Freedom* series (1985–). The Indian government assigned the project, which was conceived "not as a counter to the Transfer of Power volumes but as an independent endeavor," to the Indian Council of Historical Research (ICHR).[1] It was not intended to be an official history, nor did it become one. The series centers on the role of diverse social groups in the anticolonial movement. It draws upon a wider range of sources than the *Transfer of Power* series does, including autobiographies and memoirs of political activists, the private papers of individual leaders and institutions, newspapers, and visual materials.

There are other significant differences between the two series. The *Transfer of Power* presents the retreat of the colonial power as phased decolonization, whereas *Towards Freedom* views independence as the end of a struggle. In the *Transfer of Power,* Partition is seen as a consequence of a communal divide that the British government tried to bridge; in *Towards Freedom,* Partition comes across as the result of the growing communalization of society, which is attributed to the policies of the imperial power, the actions of the communal forces, and the weaknesses of the nationalist forces.

Sarvepalli Gopal (1923–2002), who set up the Centre for Historical Studies at Jawaharlal Nehru University, was appointed general editor of *Towards Freedom*. His influence nudged the series toward the broad, inclusive perspective that informed his other projects, including a multivolume biography of Jawaharlal Nehru that is both a brilliant biography and an insightful history of twentieth-century India. Under his editorship, *Towards Freedom* brought out the many facets of the movement headed by the Indian National Congress, which was more a political platform than a typical party. As edited by discriminating experts on the subject, the volumes became histories in their own right, not merely collections of documents.

The series has had its share of problems. Financial support by the Ministry of Culture ended in 1991–92. In early 2000, two volumes that had been approved by the general editor and were already with Oxford University Press for publication were called back during the tenure of the National Democratic Alliance (NDA) regime (1999–2004). It was claimed that the books had not gone through a review committee. The withdrawal of the books was part of a wider onslaught on cultural and academic freedom by the same reactionary forces that disrupted the shooting of Deepa Mehta's film *Water* that year.

Allegations of large expenditures and delays were leveled at the *Towards Freedom* project by the Bharatiya Janata Party ideologues Murli Manohar Joshi and Arun Shourie. (The BJP was then and remains today the largest faction in the National Democratic Alliance.) An "expert committee," whose members singularly lacked expertise in modern Indian history, was formed to review the books. K. N. Panikkar, editor of the interdicted 1940 volume, hinted that behind the cancellation was BJP anxiety that the volumes would expose its predecessors, the Rashtriya Swayamsevak Sangh (RSS) and the Hindu Mahasabha, as having collaborated with the British.[2] Gopal condemned the government's intervention in academic matters as unethical. For several years after Gopal's death, no general editor was appointed in his place, leading to long delays in publication. Sabyasachi Bhattacharya, who became the general editor in 2006, described the stop-work episode as amounting to "political interference to the detriment of academic autonomy."[3]

The withdrawal of the *Towards Freedom* volumes was met with protests by the academic community. Meetings were held outside the ICHR on 18 February and 25 March 2000 in Delhi, accompanied by protests in Calcutta, Mumbai, Chennai, Baroda, Trivandrum, and other places. There were letters to the press, campaigns on the Internet, and petition drives at four universities in Delhi. In the Rajya Sabha (upper house of parliament), the entire opposition, led by Manmohan Singh, leader of the Congress, demanded discussion on the issue.

IN 2007, I WAS APPOINTED EDITOR of the volume for 1947, arguably the most significant year of the decade covered by the series. The general editor gave me six months to complete the volume, since I had written a book on the period. Also, "only" seven and a half months were to be covered, from 1 January till 15 August 1947. Keeping to the cutoff date was not easy. Political processes, including Partition, migration, and the accession of the Princely States, moved at their own pace. When documenting the spread of Hindu communalism in 1947, I realized I could not take the story beyond the cutoff date of 15 August to its fast-growing phase after September 1947, leading up to the assassination of Mohandas Gandhi. My research on imperialism, communalism, and nationalism covered only part of the story of 1947. In my book *Independence and Partition: Erosion of Colonial Power in India* (2000), I argued for looking at those major political movements as two sides of the same coin. I was against glorifying either one or the other, as many were wont to do. I learned that there were many stories besides the intertwined ones of independence and Partition. Besides political freedom, there were others—notably, social and economic freedom—the struggle for which remained to be fought.

The volume on 1947 expanded as the years went on till it split in three. The first part covers the conflict between imperialist, nationalist, and communal forces. The second part takes the story from 3 June to 15 August, including in its scope the settlement of boundaries and the rehabilitation of refugees, and then moves to the story of the Princely States. The third part focuses on caste, religious minorities, language and literature, education, the position of women, the future of the Congress organization, the functioning of provincial ministries, the economic consequences of Partition, and the movements of peasants and workers.

Of the sources consulted for the volume on 1947, reports from newspapers such as the *Hindustan Times, Dawn, People's Age,* and *Amrita Bazar Patrika* were often the first choice, since they brought out the diversity of opinion in the public sphere. Newspapers carried delightful letters to the editor, hand-drawn maps of proposed boundary lines, and sharp, witty cartoons. A quaint advertisement for a balm was titled "freedom from pain"; it had obviously been inspired by the wider context of freedom from colonial rule.[4]

Private papers of institutions such as the All India Congress Committee (AICC), All India States Peoples Conference, All India Hindu Mahasabha, and of individuals such as the socialist leader Jayaprakash Narayan, Jawaharlal Nehru, and the Mahasabha leaders S. P. Mookerjee and B. S. Moonje, unraveled the intricacy of political processes in this period. The diversity of voices in the public sphere is seen in letters and memoranda to political representatives and institutions. Documents have also been included from published collections of writings and correspondence by Jawaharlal Nehru, Sardar Patel, Mohammad Ali Jinnah, Mahatma Gandhi, and Rajendra Prasad. There are documents relating to the discussions in the Constituent Assembly and its committees on, for instance, fundamental rights and constitutional safeguards, which provide insights into polity and society. Official documents relating more directly to British rule include the records of the Government of India's Home Department, fortnightly reports from each province containing a wealth of information on the nationalist, communal, and popular movements; Cabinet Papers from the Public Record Office; and papers of Viceroys and senior officials from the India Office, including the voluminous Mountbatten Papers.

Parts one and two of the volume on 1947 contain documents relating to the position of political parties on Partition and independence. Participants grappled with the nature of the future Indian polity. Would the country be a Hindu *rashtra* (nation), given that the creation of Pakistan was based on the two-nation theory? What would be the place of minorities in the new state?

Secular forces refused to accept the two-nation theory, even on the eve of Partition. Congress leaders were clear that they had accepted it as an unavoidable political reality, but they did not endorse the principle behind it. The Congress ruled out the establishment of a Hindu state and stood steadfast in the face of attempts to communalize the party as well as the state. Patel insisted that the "state should exist for all, irrespective of caste and creed."[5] Yet the demand for a Hindu state was made stridently after Pakistan was split off, and was later linked to the Hindu Mahasabha's call to murder Gandhi and Nehru, who were seen as obstacles.

In the writings on Partition, responsibility for the division is placed either on the policy of divide and rule or on the age-old rift between Hindus and Muslims, depending on the ideological orientation of the author. Another view was that independence was a compromise between the imperial and colonial ruling classes, for which a heavy cost was borne by the nation. It was argued that the Congress was largely responsible for Partition, since its leaders did not accommodate the demands of the Muslim League; they preferred to stick to their demand for a strong center rather than compromise with the league. Another view was that Partition took place because of the Congress leaders' lust for quick and easy power, which left the people with a sense of betrayal and Gandhi saying that he no longer wished to live for 125 years, as he had earlier declared.

Gandhi's position was different from, though not opposed to, that of the Congress. This nuance is obvious in his suggestion to the Viceroy that Jinnah be made Prime Minister. The hope was that this would satisfy Jinnah's personal ambition and scotch his insistence on a separate Pakistan. The proposal flattered Jinnah, as Mountbatten observed, but the Congress leaders felt it was too risky. Making Jinnah the Prime Minister would mean handing the constitutional arena over to communal, reactionary forces. Many Congress supporters would see it as a betrayal. Finally, even if Jinnah was appeased, it could not guarantee cessation of the demand for Pakistan, since he was no longer powerful enough to do so in 1946. Consequently, Gandhi withdrew his offer.

When Jinnah and Gandhi issued a joint appeal for peace in the middle of April 1947, Patel drew the Viceroy's attention to the obvious contradiction—how was peace possible without the withdrawal of direct action? (Direct action, the name given to a series of riots and massacres involving Hindus, Muslims, and Sikhs, arose out of large-scale demonstrations in Calcutta in August 1946 for a separate Muslim state.) The implication was that Jinnah's appeal for peace was insincere, an assessment that Gandhi agreed with.

By the middle of 1947, Congress leaders were clear that any attempt to conciliate the Muslim League was not getting anywhere. Nehru saw Jinnah's greed for political power as insatiable. As he put it, "We are up against something which is neither political, nor economic, nor reasonable, nor logical."[6] Patel categorically ruled out further appeasement and stressed that there would be no place for communal representation in independent India.

One view in the Congress was that Partition could be avoided by imposing unity—if needed, by force. But Nehru felt that communal violence could not be countered by politically directed violence and would in fact result in a civil war. He said as much in a speech at the All India Congress Committee session on 15 June 1947. A couple of months earlier, Congress president J. B. Kripalani had told the Viceroy, "Rather than have a battle we shall let them have their Pakistan."[7] Also, in the absence of state power, imposing unity by force would have meant street battles among volunteer armies of communal forces.

Thus, given the inevitability of Partition in mid-1947, the Congress attempted to make it more palatable by describing it as based on the principle of self-determination. Gandhi said that the Congress's decision was based on the views of all communities. Nehru explained that it was the consequence of the desire of some groups to not be a part of India. Kripalani declared at the Congress Working Committee (CWC; the party's executive body) meeting on 1 June 1947 that since the Cripps Plan of 1942, the Congress position had been that no part of India would be coerced into remaining within the union.

For the Congress leaders, the finality of the settlement was very important. Hence, they were dismayed at the ambiguous stand of the Muslim League and the communal position taken by Jinnah in a message broadcast on 3 June.

There was some hope for the possibility of reunification after tempers had cooled and people on both sides realized that their concerns were much the same. Nehru appealed to the people not to accept Partition in their hearts: "We have often to go through the valley of the shadow before we reach the sunlit mountain tops."[8] The AICC resolution on the 3 June Plan stated that the acceptance of Partition was a temporary measure to curtail violence. But such wishes and announcements were fantasies. The steps taken for Partition—population transfers, the division of the army, and the sanction by Parliament of the transfer of power to two dominions— made it irreversible. Interestingly, unlike his colleagues in the Congress, Gandhi preferred for the British to "leave India to anarchy, rather than as a cock pit between two organized armies."[9]

For Congress, Partition would mean having a free hand in the remaining part of India, 80 or 90 percent of the country, as Nehru put it. Both Patel and Jayprakash Narayan, the socialist leader, looked forward to an Indian union with a strong center. There was anxiety among political leaders that after Partition, an impetus toward fragmentation would remain strong. The British government had insisted on the freedom of states and provinces to choose whether to join the union. But since the Viceroy wanted to limit Partition to only two dominions, the 3 June Plan was accordingly altered: the option of independence for the Princely States or the provinces of British India was withdrawn. While a federal polity and decentralization are today seen as desirable assets for unifying a nation, in 1947 a strong center was taken to be essential.

The Congress accepted Partition on the grounds that it reflected the will of the people and that there was no getting around it. At a prayer meeting on 4 June, Gandhi said that the Working Committee had agreed to the division of India not because of the threat of coercion or violence, but because it could not get around the Muslim League. In addition, Congress leaders felt that Partition was preferable to civil war or balkanization. Moreover, Congress's acceptance was an implicit acceptance of its inability to draw the majority of Muslims into the national movement.

The documents on this subject support Gandhi's assessment that both Hindus and Muslims had traveled quite far from the path of nonviolence by that time. He said that he could not oppose the Congress, because it represented the people, who by then had become communal.

Gandhi held prayer meetings every evening during his stay in Delhi in the summer of 1947. After the prayers, he would answer questions from members of the audience. One asked why he did not start a mass movement against communalism and Partition. It is a charge that has been brought against Gandhi by later commentators too. Some historians have argued that an anti-imperialist movement at that time could have forged Hindu-Muslim unity, or that an anti-communal movement could have exposed communal forces. But Gandhi was aware of his limitations at a time when both ordinary people and the cadres had become communalized. As he famously said: "I have never created a situation in my life . . . People say that I had created a situation, but I had done nothing except giving a shape to what was already there. Today I see no sign of such a healthy feeling. And therefore I shall have to wait until the time comes."[10] Contrary to the prevailing mythology on the subject, it was the communalization of the people that contributed to Gandhi's helplessness; it was not the Congress leaders' lust for power that alienated and marginalized him and kept him out of the negotiations for the transfer of power. Congress leaders were keen on an early transfer of power for political rather than personal reasons. They wanted to lead the country out of a cul-de-sac created by the intransigence of the Muslim League.

Records suggest that Gandhi, far from being alienated from the Congress, was consulted on political developments when he was in Noakhali, in East Bengal. Gandhi dismissed any rumors of his disenchantment with Nehru by speaking very highly of him: "He renounces things as easily as a snake its slough."[11] At Kripalani's and Nehru's request, he came to Delhi, met the Viceroy, and participated in the All India Congress Committee meetings between May and June 1947.

He set aside his principled objection to Partition and exhorted Congress members to come together to accept its painful but inevitable reality. As he said at the AICC meeting of 14 June:

> Our constitution permits it and your duty demands it that if you feel that the Working Committee is in the wrong you should remove it, you should revolt and assume all power. You have a perfect right to do so, if you feel that you have the strength. But I do not find that strength in us today. If you had it I would also be with you and if I felt strong enough myself I would, alone, take up the flag of revolt. But today I do not see the conditions for doing so.[12]

Eventually, then, Gandhi and Congress came to accept that their efforts to counter communalism and stop communal violence were not able to stem the tide. Gandhi's struggle to restore communal harmony in Noakhali, Bihar, Calcutta, and Delhi was the stuff that sagas are made of. He went about the country, seeking to bring succor to the victims of violence, all the while trying to save the unity of India. He censured Hindu mobs in Bihar and tried to bring harmony in Noakhali. Though Gandhi and the Congress leaders accepted Partition, they did not accept the two-nation theory or the idea of a Hindu nation. His writings during this period provide a moving account of the times, and those by his disciples and critics help shade in the sketch.

THE *TOWARDS FREEDOM* SERIES has a political significance beyond its academic relevance. Secular and communal interpretations of history continue to contest the nature of the freedom struggle in particular and of Indian history in general. The year 2014 saw a communal regime come to power with a clear majority. This victory emboldened the government, the BJP, the National Democratic Alliance, the Rashtriya Swayamsevak Sangh, and affiliates such as the Akhil Bhartiya Itihas Sankalan Samiti (All India History Compilation Committee) in their attempts to communalize the writing of history. The stated aim of the Samiti is to rewrite the history of India from a "national" perspective. Its "theories" claim, for example, that places like the Vatican, Westminster Abbey, and similarly iconic structures around the world, including the Taj Mahal, were actually temples of Shiva and that Christianity and Islam are derivatives of Hindu philosophical thought.

Increasingly, members of the RSS are being appointed to head premier research and academic bodies, and RSS-minded organizations are seen influencing education and determining the contours of public space. The chief qualification of most of the new members of the Indian Council of Historical Research is their ideological affinity with the RSS. Their work includes writing history to support the political stance of the BJP, such as "proving" the existence of the Ram temple at Ayodhya, at the contested site of the Babri Masjid, which was destroyed by members of Hindu communal organizations in 1992.

The Shiksha Sanskriti Utthan Nyas (Trust for the Uplift of Education and Culture) and the Shiksha Bachao Andolan Samiti (Committee for the Save Education Movement), which push for "Indianizing" the education system, including history textbooks, are headed by Dinanath Batra, whose books have been prescribed in schools in the state of Gujarat, even though they do not meet any standards of scholarship. Batra is the person who started the petition demanding that *The Hindus: An Alternative History* (2009), a much celebrated book by Wendy Doniger, be banned. The publisher, Penguin Books, chose to pulp the book rather than take on Batra. The newly elected BJP government of Haryana has publicly declared that it intends to consult Batra on education policy.

Under the new regime, one can see the revival of communal goals. While celebrating the victory of the BJP government, a minister of the state of Goa claimed that it would now be possible to develop India as a Hindu nation. A colleague of his added that India was already a Hindu nation in its culture. These statements have an uncanny resemblance to ones made in 1947 when, following Partition, many leaders wanted the Congress leadership to declare India to be a Hindu state.

Another strategy of the regime is the selective appropriation of nationalist icons, which is particularly important to a political formation that espoused loyalism and did not stand on the side of the nation during the national movement. Along with Gandhi, to whom lip service is being paid, the Congress leader Vallabhbhai Patel is glorified as the "Iron Man" and set up as a counterpoise to the much-maligned Nehru. Documents in the *Towards Freedom* volume on 1947 bring out how the three leaders, with their different political styles, were united in their sturdy fight against imperialism and communalism. Dividing their legacy and selectively appropriating them is clearly part of a political agenda, unsupported by the historical record. Fortunately, the experience of the secular forces in the face of the communal challenge in such troubled times as the Partition of India is now available to us as an intellectual resource for today's struggle.

Fall Semester 2012

1. Irfan Habib, review of Sucheta Mahajan, ed., *Towards Freedom: Documents on the Movement for Independence in India, 1947,* pt. 1, *Studies in People's History,* 1, no. 1 (2014), pp. 122–25.
2. K. N. Panikkar, interview, *Frontline,* 17, no. 5, 4 Mar. 2000.
3. General editor's preface, in Mahajan, *Towards Freedom: Documents on the Movement for Independence in India, 1947,* pt. 1 (New Delhi, 2013).
4. *Searchlight,* 15 Aug. 1947, in *Towards Freedom, 1947,* pt. 3, ch. 56, doc. 42 .
5. Sucheta Mahajan, ed.,*Towards Freedom, 1947,* pt. 2 (New Delhi, 2015), ch. 34, doc. 3.
6. *Towards Freedom, 1947,* pt. 1, ch. 19 (A), doc. 24.
7. Ibid., pt. 1, ch. 15, doc. 23.
8. Nehru to Cariappa, 29 Apr. 1947, in *Selected Works of Jawaharlal Nehru,* 2nd ser., vol. 2 (New Delhi, 1984), p. 377.
9. *Towards Freedom, 1947,* pt. 2, ch. 26, doc. 82.
10. Quoted in N. K. Bose, "My Experiences as a Gandhian—II," in M. P. Sinha, ed., *Contemporary Relevance of Gandhi* (Bombay, 1970), p. 53.
11. *Towards Freedom, 1947,* pt. 2, ch. 26, doc. 47.
12. Ibid., ch. 26, doc. 51.

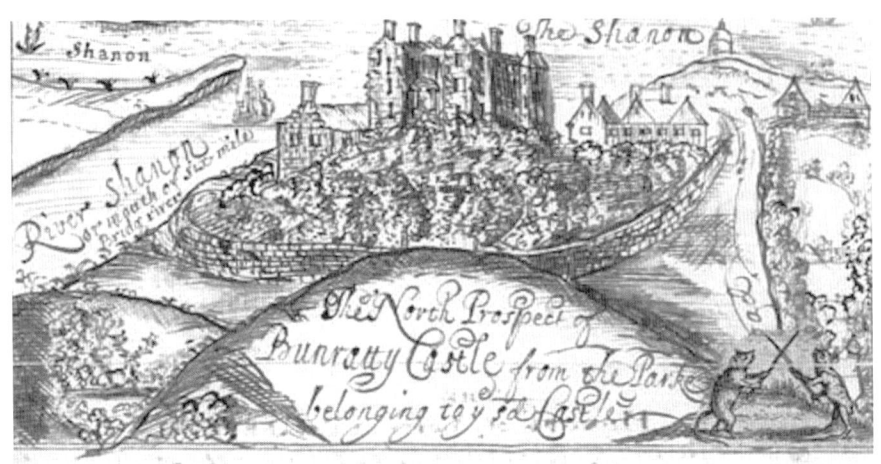

MAKING IRELAND ENGLISH

THE IRISH ARISTOCRACY IN THE SEVENTEENTH CENTURY

JANE OHLMEYER

Making Ireland English: The Irish Aristocracy in the Seventeenth Century, by Jane Ohlmeyer

12

Reflections on Early Modern Ireland

JANE OHLMEYER

In early modern Ireland, the peers were a class of nobility who enjoyed a title—as duke, marquis, earl, viscount, and baron—awarded to them by the English monarch, and had the privilege of sitting as temporal lords in the Dublin parliament. The greater lords, who formed the ruling aristocracy, quickly established themselves as the dominant social group in Irish society. During the early decades of the seventeenth century, the Stuart crown trebled the number of Irish peers. In *Making Ireland English* (2012), my focus was on the "resident peerage," roughly seventy families whose fortunes I tracked over three or four generations. In this lecture, I reflect on the main points and themes of the book in relation to some of the criticism and comments it generated. For example, one reviewer suggested that the nonresident peers should also have been included in my study.[1] While a number of nonresident peers represented significant points of contact with the royal court in London and enlarged the marriage market, their lack of landholdings in Ireland explains why they received such brief treatment (those who held lands and titles in both Ireland and England were, of course, included).

With this inflation of honors, itself an exercise in social engineering, James I created a peerage that comprised, in roughly equal numbers, Catholic and Protestant lords. It was an ethnically diverse body too, made of men from a variety of backgrounds: Gaelic Irish (like the O'Briens of Thomond and the MacCarthys of Muskerry), Old English (like the Fitzgeralds of Kildare, the Butlers of Ormond, and the Bourkes of Clanricarde), New English (like the Boyles of Cork and the Annesleys of Anglesey), and Scottish (like the MacDonnells of Antrim and the Hamiltons of Clandeboy). Even though many came from humble backgrounds and were regarded as upstarts and arrivistes, these were men of money, power, prestige, and privilege. The peers lived nobly, conspicuously, and according to shared notions of honor. They acted as cultural brokers, dressing in the latest London fashions, speaking English (though a significant number were native Irish speakers or bilingual), and living in "great houses." Whatever their backgrounds, these titled families, especially the ancient houses, held a disproportionally large amount of Irish land, at least 18 percent in 1641 and rising to 26 percent by around 1670. The richest aristocrats in Ireland were on a par with the most prosperous English or Scottish lords.

These peers were charged with making Ireland English, rather than "British." My emphasis on anglicization (rather than "Britishization") generated comment. One reviewer wanted me to develop further the arguments around "Anglicization" and "empire."[2] But I never intended *Making Ireland English* to be a general study of imperialism in Ireland, but rather a study of the contribution that the landed peerage, as agents of imperialism, made to that venture. Another reviewer commented on the relationship between my book and Nicholas Canny's magisterial study *Making Ireland British, 1580–1650* (2001), and asked where my book has left "British history."[3] I am a great admirer of Canny's remarkable corpus of scholarship, including *Making Ireland British,* and was honored to be included in his recent Festschrift.[4] Aspects of Stuart rule in Ireland undoubtedly had a "British" dimension, and James I in particular had a vision for his three kingdoms that undoubtedly included Ireland. But "English" agendas, not "British" ones, very quickly predominated. As the century passed, the Irish peers, including those of Gaelic and Scottish provenance, Catholics as well as Protestants, touted their "Englishness," alongside their "Irishness" and "Scottishness," but never their "Britishness" (admittedly, the use of "British" was used as a badge of identity lower down the social order). Where I feel that my book does make a genuine contribution to "British," or three kingdoms–four nations, history is that it opens the way for wider comparative studies with England, Scotland, and Wales and across the British Empire.

As landlords, developers, entrepreneurs, politicians, bureaucrats, and military commanders, the peers served as regional and national powerbrokers, exercising influence in Ireland and beyond. From the Crown's perspective, the peers served as effective instruments in its efforts to "civilize" and anglicize a particularly troublesome colony, which, with its large Catholic population, represented a constant security threat to Protestant Britain. In this sense, the peers acted as a "service" nobility, something that a number of reviewers picked up on. One felt that I should have looked more closely at the role a service elite played in the formation of an imperial state.[5] Another suggested that it was inappropriate to apply the "idea, popular among historians of continental Europe," to Ireland.[6]

Whatever one's views on the utility of the concept of service nobility, the level of mutual dependence between the monarch and the titled nobility in Ireland was striking. This was an age of personal monarchy, and the king relied on these lords in his task of ruling Ireland and supported aristocratic landed interests in order to promote regional stability and domestic security. For their part, the peers saw the Crown as the best source for securing titles, land, and wealth. Time and again, the peers paraded their loyalty to the Stuarts. Of course, at moments of intense political tension or during periods of military crisis, as during the 1640s and after 1688, relations between the sovereign and many of his titled subjects broke down. Yet even within these crises the majority of Irish nobles preferred to operate within an imperial context, and their dogged loyalty to the house of Stuart is one of the most striking themes of these years.

My argument that the aristocracy displayed "collective behavior" attracted comment. I suggested that despite the very real ethnic and religious differences, a significant level of social and cultural integration occurred. Shared notions of honor, educational experiences, and Continental travel, together with marriages, kinship links, and economic interdependence, forged common senses of nobleness. They also shaped the members of the aristocracy into a coherent body, with a communal identity, which served to preserve much of their authority and influence, and emphasized the exclusivity of their rank. One reviewer challenged this notion of "collective behavior," and another suggested that religion complicated it much more than I allowed for.[7] Religion did indeed complicate it—especially at times of crisis, when religious tensions came to the fore—but this should not detract from the numerous other instances of collective behavior, even if this disrupts the traditional sectarian narrative that characterizes some of the writing of seventeenth-century Irish history.

My book was intended to be disruptive in other ways. Despite the Irish aristocracy's importance for understanding state formation, it has been little studied as a collective. There has been some excellent work done on lordship, individual peers, marriage, death, and honor. But the question remains why historians of early modern Ireland have not studied the aristocracy as a collective or assessed their contribution to state formation. First, the unevenness of the archives and the absence of private papers, especially for the lesser Catholic houses, have proved a major and understandable deterrent. Second, the focus of much research on early modern Ireland has, until relatively recently, been on political and military history at the expense of social, economic, and cultural history. Third, the association of the aristocracy in Ireland with English imperialism made it an unpopular subject of study among Irish historians. During the Irish civil war of the twentieth century, the "big house," which stood as an uncomfortable reminder of a colonial past, became a military target; writing the histories of their titled occupants did not sit well with a tradition that was republican and nationalist. This attitude is changing as a new generation of scholars re-evaluates nobles' contributions to the development of early modern Ireland and engage methodologies pioneered by scholars of early modern England and Europe. One reviewer suggested that *Making Ireland English* "marks the end of what seems to have been an unspoken prohibition against work on the subject."[8]

The seminal book on the nobility in the Stuart kingdoms, and one that certainly inspired me, was Lawrence Stone's *The Crisis of the Aristocracy* (1965). Informed by rigorous analysis of extant archives and by methodologies pioneered by the *Annales* school of French social history, Stone argued that the English nobility, during the later sixteenth and early seventeenth centuries, underwent an economic, political, and intellectual crisis that shook the very foundations of Stuart society. Despite the hostile reception Stone's study received in some quarters, it helped transform how historians studied nobilities. While it is now clear that Stone's emphasis on "crisis" proved something of a distraction, the controversy it generated had the positive benefit of stimulating further research into nobilities across early modern Europe. The focus of this new research is more conceptual: the nature of noble status and how was it acquired; noble demography and family structure; the importance of the wider lineage, marriage, and inheritance; attitudes to violence, education, and culture; patterns of office holding, and so on.

Equally important is the current emphasis on consolidation and continuity, which has effectively replaced the theories of aristocratic decline and crisis promoted by a generation of scholars working in the 1960s and 1970s. Recent research points to the endurance and adaptability of many English lineages, even Catholic ones, and has drawn attention to the survival strategies that enterprising aristocrats developed to ensure the long-term sustainability of their lines. Keith Brown's work on early modern Scotland points to the continuity, success, and durability of nobilities in the face of political and economic instability. The commonalities with Ireland, especially with regard to the continuities of good lordship, the centrality of land, noble commitment to service, marriage patterns, trends in conspicuous consumption, economic innovation, concepts of honor, and the emergence of a distinctive aristocratic culture, are striking. The similarities between aristocratic experiences in the composite Stuart monarchies should not surprise, since the Irish peerage was modeled on that of England and the human interactions between the kingdoms were constant. For example, over a third of resident Irish peers married English women, especially as first wives, aiming to increase their social status by intermarrying with members of the English nobility, landed gentry, or prosperous merchant families. These unions also facilitated assimilation and integration.

Less well documented but equally pertinent are wider parallels. Ireland's status as England's first "colony" and the fact that the nobles acted as agents of empire allow for comparisons with the territories governed by other early modern expansionist states and empires. Recent research suggests that the Spanish Habsburgs ruled their dominions in South America and interacted with their political elites there much as the Stuarts did in Ireland. The relationships that the Austrian Habsburgs enjoyed with their nobles in Bohemia and Lower Austria offer some interesting points of comparison with Ireland. Throughout the Austro-Bohemian lands, a redistribution of estates to favored individuals occurred, akin to the Irish land transfers, which resulted in the emergence of a new service nobility that owed its primary allegiance to the Habsburg monarchy.

Identifying differences is as important as examining the similarities. The fact that many peers in Ireland practiced a religion different from that of their king would not have been tolerated elsewhere in contemporary Europe. In Bohemia, only Catholics could hold land or serve the king, which resulted in mass conversions, since this was nobles' only means of surviving and demonstrating their loyalty. In other words, securing the lineage and its continued economic and political prosperity mattered more to most Bohemian nobles than their faith.

The choices facing lords in Stuart Ireland were never that stark, and as a result, ambiguity flourished and religious pluralism was ubiquitous. Despite requiring officeholders to take the oath of supremacy and securing conversions wherever possible, the Crown effectively tolerated the Catholicism of the established lords, elevated active recusants to the peerage, and promoted the interests of these families at court. One reviewer noted that these sorts of accommodations were "similar to those that allowed the Ottoman Empire to endure."[9] Similarly, in the Mughal Empire from the mid-sixteenth century (the reign of Akbar) until the mid-seventeenth century (and the reign of Aurangezeb), de facto religious toleration characterized Mughal rule in India. As in Ireland, the Mughal nobility was a composite body, comprising Muslims and Hindus and a variety of ethnic groups: Muslims from Central Asia who had come to India in the early sixteenth century, native Indian Muslims, the Rajput (Hindu rulers of Punjab), and other indigenous lords. This service nobility was loyal to the regime and always ready to serve the emperor on the battlefield or as trusted officials. In other respects, the Mughal nobility was very different from its Irish counterpart. There was nothing in Ireland comparable to the assignment system, which made the Mughal nobles so financially dependent on the state. The fact that, in theory at least, the nobles held no hereditary titles or lands also allowed the emperor to exercise greater authority over them than the Stuart monarchs could over the Irish peers. But whether in India or Ireland, we have much to learn from looking at the operation of early modern empires and the role that the elite played, even if the scales of such empires might be very different.

LET ME CONCLUDE BY NOTING some of my current projects that have grown out of *Making Ireland English*. I am editing Edward Hyde, Earl of Clarendon's "A short view of the state and condition of the kingdom of Ireland from the yeare 1640 to this tyme," which was published in 1720 under the title *History of the rebellion and civil wars in Ireland*. "A short view" offers a muddled narrative of the course and conduct of the war in 1640s Ireland and the internecine politics that gripped the country at home and among the diaspora on the Continent. Compiled, with the assistance of the Marquis of Ormond and others, between 1652 and 1656, while Hyde was at the Stuart court in exile in Cologne, "A short view" is the first substantial defense of Ormond's conduct as lord lieutenant. Its purpose is to reclaim the memory of the war and portray Ormond as a man of honor and a loyal servant to the Stuarts. The importance of memory, honor, and reputation is something that I touched on in *Making Ireland English*, and I welcome the opportunity to explore it further here.

As I was writing *Making Ireland English*, I became increasingly aware of the importance of women, children, and the family, subjects shamefully neglected by Irish historians with the notable exception of Mary O'Dowd. Experiences associated with widowhood particularly intrigued me and explain my current interest in war widows. Recovering the lives of these widows, especially the ordinary ones, is, in the absence of personal sources, a challenge. One unique archive, that of the 1641 Depositions, provides a series of fascinating insights into the lives of 421 widows who deposed (these widows represented about two-thirds of all female deponents). What can these depositions tell us about wartime widows? Who were these women? Where did they come from, and what was their social status? What contribution did they make to the domestic economy of colonial Ireland? And finally, what were their experiences of civil war?

The other group that piqued my interest as I wrote *Making Ireland English* was the brothers and younger sons of the Irish peers. Many faded into obscurity as members of the army, clergy, gentry, and professional classes. Others had stellar careers. For example, Gerald Aungier was a younger brother of the Earl of Longford and the grandson of Baron Aungier of Longford. Between 1669 and 1677, he served as the governor of Bombay and president of Surat. While scholars of India and of the British Empire have acknowledged the importance of Aungier as the founding father of Bombay, none have paid attention to his Irish provenance, nor to how that heritage might have shaped the formation of the Bombay colony. I hope that my study of Aungier will put Ireland on the radar of imperial and Indian historians and demonstrate the extent to which Ireland was a laboratory for empire during the seventeenth century. I am also hoping that it will attract the attention of Irish historians. To date, the focus has been on situating the Irish colonial experience in the context of the English Atlantic world, or of "westward enterprises." This emphasis is understandable given the scale of migration to North America, the importance of commercial links (especially to the West Indies), and the fact that Ireland served as a model for the plantations of Virginia and elsewhere. I want to suggest that we also need to look east and examine the colonial processes in late seventeenth-century Bombay through an early modern Irish lens.

Spring Semester 2015

1. Toby Barnard, review of *Making Ireland English*, by Jane Ohlmeyer (New Haven, 2012), *Irish Studies Review* (2013), p. 227.

2. John Gibney, review of *Making Ireland English*, *History Ireland*, 20, issue 6 (2012).

3. Edward Cavanagh, "Kingdom or Colony? English or British? Early Modern Ireland and the Colonialism Question," *Journal of Colonialism and Colonial History*, 14 (2013); Gibney, review of *Making Ireland English*.

4. "Making Ireland English: The Seventeenth-Century Irish Peerage," in Brian MacCuarta, ed., *Reshaping Ireland, 1590–1700: Colonization and Its Consequences; Essays presented to Nicholas Canny* (Dublin, 2011), pp. 131–46.

5. Brendan Kane, review of *Making Ireland English*, *Renaissance Quarterly*, 67 (2104), p. 1023.

6. Barnard, review of *Making Ireland English*, p. 227.

7. Ibid, pp. 226–27; Patrick Little, review of *Making Ireland English*, "Reviews in History" (www.history.ac.uk/reviews/review/1330).

8. Kane, review of *Making Ireland English*, p. 1022.

9. Barnard, review of *Making Ireland English*, p. 227.

Gin Lane, by William Hogarth (1751)

13

Pleasures of the Poor

NICHOLAS ROGERS

Any discussion of plebeian pleasure or leisure has to confront two historiographical traditions: the Warwick and the Cambridge. The first, promoted by E. P. Thompson and his students, stressed the tenacity of custom in the face of capitalist innovation. The second, promoted by J. H. Plumb and his students, emphasized the commercialization of leisure in eighteenth-century England and the broad acceptance of capitalist advance. The first tended to display what only can be called an allergy to consumerism, a feeling that any concession to working-class buying power and the allure of goods would weaken the case against capitalism. The second tended to occlude the divisive nature of leisure consumption and suggest that the plebs had an investment in the world of goods, however modest. I suggest that the working poor were consumers of a sort, although their emotional investment in the allure of goods was fundamentally shaped and constrained by their purchasing power and the forms of sociability they hoped to sustain in a changing world where hours of work increased as the century progressed. I also suggest that in the public sphere of debate, plebeian pleasure was always problematic, class inflected, and political. This conclusion emerges clearly in the debate over the gin craze, in which matters of work, play, hierarchy, national welfare, and imperial destiny were intertwined.

Of course, the history of pleasure in the eighteenth century is predominantly an aristocratic or bourgeois enterprise; that is to say, its principal subjects are rich or relatively rich people who had the time and resources to enjoy their pleasures and reflect on them. Samuel Johnson defined "pleasure" as "the gratification of the mind or senses" and then nuanced his definition with a quote from the Anglican clergymen Robert South: "Pleasure in general is the consequent apprehension of a suitable object, suitably applied to a rightly disposed faculty."[1] This pompous, sober, respectable definition might have set the bar too high for the habitués of Bath, whose pleasures were likely closer to a Rowlandson burlesque, but the essential point was that "real" pleasure was a matter of refined taste and culture. By extension, one had to have the leisure to enjoy pleasure, leisure denoting "the freedom from business or hurry," to use another Johnsonian definition, and the "power to spend time according to choice."[2]

The majority of the population did not have access to the kind of pleasure readily available in places like Bath and other fashionable spas. They lacked the money, the leisure, and the breeding. Some working poor were marginal spectators at prizefights, for example, watching one of their own punch his weight for the aristocracy. Jack Broughton, of obscure birth, attracted attention as a waterman, winning on one occasion Doggett's annual rowing race on the Thames. His six-foot, two-hundred-pound frame and defensive skills served him well in the prizefights for which he became notorious, although he greatly irritated his patron, the Duke of Cumberland, when he unexpectedly lost to the Norwich butcher Jack Slack in 1750. Cumberland had waged £10,000 on Broughton's victory and was not amused when his protégé packed it in after fourteen minutes, so beaten about the eyes that he could not see. After that, Broughton's career was more or less over.

The poor were not without their pleasures of course, what Dr. Johnson termed "loose gratifications."[3] To the polite world, these were usually dismissed as vulgar diversions or "antics," to be tolerated as an acceptable antidote to toil. There was broad tolerance for the seasonal blowout or revel, especially during the good harvests of the early eighteenth century. "Waste in wild riot what your land allows," ran one line from Pope, "There ply the early feast and late carouse."[4] The harvest celebrations that followed upon the last sheaf were an acceptable reward for backbreaking work, the carousing at Christmas a necessary charity to take the edge off the winter cold. With the decline of living-in servants and the enclosure of common fields, these time-honored festivals lost some of their vitality in the countryside, although they survived. How well remains a moot point, for when local clergy were asked what popular pastimes were practiced in their parishes, they were often surprisingly ignorant of what was going on. In 1752, the rector of Newbury in Berkshire said he knew little of the regional calendar, claiming he had not researched the "antiquities, whether general or local," language that disclosed his distance from the lives and recreations of the laboring poor. The vicar at Speen was similarly silent, although in Cumnor the vicar noted that the St. Luke's Day processions were popular with agricultural laborers because of their charitable doles, and in East Hendred the week before Whit Sunday was remembered as "a sort of wake and time of revelry."[5] More visible than these village festivals were the annual fairs in the towns, which offered their own brands of merriment and disorder, as did the wakes in the Potteries. Indeed, it was, paradoxically, in the emerging manufacturing areas that the traditional holidays were most tenaciously observed. "Common custom has established so many Holy-days," remarked the Reverend John Clayton of Manchester in 1755, "that few of our manufacturing work-folks are closely and regularly employed above two-third parts of the time," an alarmist statement but one that certainly reflects the strong hold that customary festivals had over the incipient working class.[6]

We shouldn't be surprised at this, or by the nature of the complaint. Much of the work under the putting-out system and in the small workshops of the emergent manufacturing districts was task oriented. Rhythms of work were intense and irregular, with time off for workers to relax, drink, and play. The ruling class instituted a large array of sanctions—vagrancy statutes of varying severity, master and servant laws—to regularize work. There was a constant anxiety that unsupervised workers, especially after payday, would simply knock off. Here is John Houghton in 1681:

> When the framework knitters or makers of silk stockings had a great price for their work they have been observed seldom to work on Mondays and Tuesdays but to spend most of their time at the ale-house or nine-pins. The weavers, 'tis common with them to be drunk on Monday, have their head-ache on Tuesday, and their tools out of order on Wednesday. As for the shoemakers, they'll rather be hanged than not remember St Crispin on Monday . . . and it commonly holds as long as they have a penny of money or a pennyworth of credit.[7]

The point is not the accuracy of the observation so much as the exasperation it induced. Plebeian pleasure meant nonwork. Nonwork was a problem if it was unpredictable, irregular, and habit forming, because the working poor were the backbone of the economy. Without them, no food, no manufacture, no trade, no wealth. In an economy in which profit margins and credit ratings mattered, in which contracts had to be fulfilled on time so that merchants and middlemen could synchronize the flow of goods, some regularity was necessary, even in the age of manufacture before the factory, even in the age of sail. Plebeian pleasure was rarely viewed as a consumer good. It was more likely described as a "luxury," a disturbing sign of disposable income, a social evil, a sin, something that had to be displaced into a "love-feast" if you were a Methodist. Even tea drinking could be a problem. Jonas Hanway, the merchant philanthropist who founded the Marine Society, thought tea drinking responsible for weak nerves, scurvy, and bad teeth. It was pernicious to health, obstructed industry, and impoverished the nation. To John Clayton, it was a "shameful devourer of Time and Money."[8]

Twenty years later, in 1770, Hanway was still ranting on about the incessant sipping of tea by the poor, a remark that suggests, like King Canute, he could not hold back the waters (of taste). Workers drank more tea than before, smoked more tobacco, and perhaps even indulged themselves with finer clothes from the secondhand markets. Average incomes seem to have risen just slightly in the years of good harvests in the first half of the eighteenth century, giving working families a little more disposable income. Some writers recommended a relaxation of low-wage theory, in which a "middling scarcity," to use Bernard de Mandeville's term, was meant to keep them industrious.[9] Among other things, a little disposable income, prudentially deployed, could boost domestic production and the war effort.

How far workers bought into the consumer culture of the eighteenth century remains a moot point. There is a cozy pluralism about many definitions of Britain's "consumer revolution" of the time, an elision of very clear class notations of what was worn, what was spent, and what those expenditures meant. This haziness results in part because the main sources of material culture, wills and inventories, are biased toward the middling and upper classes and offer only fragmentary evidence of those below them. Lorna Weatherill has established that quite a number of low-to-middling people were able to buy more household articles, linen, and clothes over the course of the eighteenth century, but how far such modest purchases were characteristic of the working poor remains another matter. Of course, some workers wore flashy clothes: sailors after discharge, splurging their prize money. Prints portray them strutting around in tawdry finery with watches and whores. Some London criminals adopted a similar sartorial arrogance, robbing the gentry and parodying them; men such as William Russel, alias Captain Flash, a coachman who was hanged at the age of twenty-two for stealing a good watch from a squire in 1750. He was described as "a gay, brisk young fellow and making a better appearance than his Brethren of the Whip."[10] But flush tars and metro sharpers hardly make up a consumer culture, even if they suggest some colorful deviations from the normal course of social emulation, conjuring up the sartorial inversion of the demimonde and underworld.[11]

Historians have recently argued that the better-off plebeians bought more than basic necessities, especially textiles, partly as a means of barter in an economy starved of cash, partly as a source of pride and position for Sundays and feast days, to alert neighbors to their "modest competence." Some of them passed clothes and linen down to their friends and relatives as keepsakes of their memory. Some of this investment in clothes and household articles drew hostile comments from conservatives who might have wished to retain the sumptuary laws, that is, clear markers of social position by costume. It led them once more to decry the luxury of the poor, to fear that incipient consumerism would scramble social position and generate socially inappropriate desires. "No sooner did you dress beyond your situation, and aim at a character which did not belong to you," warned one moralist to unmarried women, "than you forfeited the good opinion of those above you . . . and became the sport of those whom you now considered . . . below you . . . Root out therefore . . . if this be your passion, the desire of dress . . . Be contented with your situation and dress neat and decent as becomes it."[12]

Trouble over clothes was gendered: it generally addressed female desires. Upper- and middling-class fears about male patterns of plebeian consumption and leisure tended to zone in on drink. "The pleasure you receive from mixing with your Companions in social mirth," one minister was told by male workers, "is the only true enjoyment you know in life," a welcome respite from a "dull wife and bawling children."[13] Certainly, the eighteenth century saw the growing centrality of the alehouse as a social hub. With the decline of many open markets and hiring fairs, the alehouse became an employment center as well as a place of male, rarely female, relaxation. Larger than their seventeenth-century counterparts, many alehouses offered bowling alleys, ninepins, and a variety of indoor games as well as newspapers, tobacco, and quite possibly a better range of ale and victuals. Crimping landlords used them to corner sailors enmeshed in debt; employers used them to hire and pay workers. "No kind of business is transacted in England," one visitor remarked in 1672, "without the intervention of pints of beer."[14] As guild regulations ebbed, workers used alehouses to organize their combinations. Alehouses lost their Puritan reputation as sites of irreligion and unorthodoxy. Justices of the peace felt more comfortable about their regulation, although in London at least, the jurisdictional complexities of prosecuting the landlords of disorderly houses remained an ongoing problem. Alehouses might not have been respectable sites of sociability, but there is no doubting their social importance. They were on their way to becoming the pub.

THE ADVENT OF GIN DRINKING disrupted this state of affairs and raised new fears about the deleterious effects of plebeian pleasures. The growth in domestic spirits was a response to the government's efforts to curb the importation of French brandy and to boost grain prices in years of good harvests by using the excess grain for spirits production. Relative to beer, spirits were inexpensive. High excise duties on ale and beer pushed the retail price of a quart to three pence or more by 1720. By contrast geneva, or more popularly, gin, first developed in Holland by mixing spirits with juniper berries and citrus fragrances, was cheap. Retailers unscrupulously proclaimed one could get drunk for a penny and dead drunk for tuppence. Gin production and sales were unregulated. The Distillers Company lost its monopoly over the spirits trade, and while wholesale distilling remained in the control of a select few, compound distilling, the rectifying of gin with juices, spices, and berries, became a flourishing small-scale enterprise. The retailing of gin was likewise unregulated for much of the century, whereas beer and ale could be sold only in licensed premises. The result was that drams of gin could be found everywhere, not only in alehouses, taverns, and coffeehouses, but also in chandler's shops, cellars, back rooms, and stalls. Some women hawked it on the street as people were going to work very early in the morning.

In this unregulated environment, spirit production soared: from half a million gallons in 1688 to 2.5 million in 1720, spiking to over 8 million in 1743. These figures are conservative, because illicit stills evaded detection. Since beer production remained comparatively stable at about 3.5 million gallons nationally, there was clearly a switch in popular taste. "Dram-drinking has been a practice among the poor sort because they could be made merry with distilled spirits cheaper than they could with any other liquor," wrote one observer.[15] An investigation ordered by the Middlesex grand jury in 1736 revealed that there were over 7,000 establishments selling beer, wine, and spirits in the metropolis; that is, excluding the City of London and Southwark, which were not part of the survey. Half of these establishments sold liquor only, and many were unlicensed. A subsequent survey by the chronicler William Maitland revealed that dramshops surpassed alehouses in the poorer districts of metropolitan London: in the City without Walls, along the Strand, in St. Giles and Drury Lane, in Southwark, in the southern precincts of Westminster inhabited by soldiers and servants. The highest proportion of dramshops as a percentage of all official drinking establishments was in the area east of Moorgate encompassing Whitechapel and Bow, and in the industrial districts south of the river. In each case the proportion exceeded 63 percent. Indeed, it was only in the City of London within the walls that the figure dipped below 40 percent.

Rudimentary as these surveys were, there was little doubt that gin had penetrated the lives of the working poor. A newspaper editorialized: "It is scarce possible for Persons in Low Life to go anywhere or to be anywhere without being drawn to the taste, and by Degrees to like and approve of this pernicious Liquor."[16] A few commentators thought the concern alarmist and believed the gin craze to be a metropolitan problem, not touching the lives of the rural poor or provincial servants and artisans. Yet the protests against the 1736 Gin Act, which ritually mourned the death of Madame Geneva at the hands of moral reformers, revealed otherwise. Protests were reported in Bristol, Bath, and Portsmouth, and in the textile districts of the West Country and the North. At Norwich, "several People made themselves very merry on the Death of Madam Gin, and some of both Sexes got soundly drunk at her Funeral, for which the Mob made a formal Procession."[17] In the light of such impressionistic evidence, gin drinking was clearly catching on.

Some historians have suggested this was not a dire predicament. Rather than characterize the gin mania as the first modern drug craze, they claim it denoted economic health, evidence that wide sections of the working poor had some disposable income after decades of good harvests and fairly buoyant industrial demand. Much of the hype about gin, so the argument goes, was the work of moral crusaders, men like James Oglethorpe and Sir James Jekyll, who supported the Society for Promoting Christian Knowledge and other philanthropic ventures, including the new colony in Georgia. While there is some truth to this, it should not detract from the deep class anxieties that the gin craze provoked among the elite.

So why the fierce clamor over gin? First, gin consumption was unregulated, and so it had the potential to dissipate, even destroy, the energies of the working poor. Second, it was difficult to police. Legislators, broadly divided into moral crusaders and fiscal pragmatists, could not find the right formula for controlling the craving for spirits, and they witnessed massive resistance to the normal mode of surveillance, informers. These reward seekers were attacked, threatened, and subjected to various forms of retribution. In the aftermath of the 1736 Gin Act, when some 12,000 accusations were made against irregular retailers, there were some conspicuous instances of hazing. One informer was "set upon an ass" and humiliatingly pelted with mud and offal up and down Bond Street. Another was carried in effigy around Hanover Square "upon a Chair-Pole" with "a Halter about his Neck" and finally burnt "in the Sight of a Vast Concourse of People."[18] Henry Fielding was so taken aback by this violent behavior that he came to believe the mob was a "Fourth Estate" that exercised a virtual veto over the legislation of its betters.[19]

Gin drinking generated fears that the working poor were not simply lethargic and work-shy, but also up to no good. Servants shared drams with criminals at street stalls and corners and likely passed on vital information about what was worth stealing from the house and when their masters and mistresses were away. Gin emboldened people to commit crimes. It erased social deference and encouraged theft. Henry Fielding, then a Westminster magistrate, insisted that the rising number of violent crimes in the mid-eighteenth century were partially attributable to gin drinking. Gin, he declared, removed "all Sense of Fear and Shame"; it disposed "the poorer sort" to commit "every wicked and desperate Enterprize." Jonas Hanway likewise thought it gave the poor "diabolical courage," making them surly, disrespectful, and contemptuous of "every consideration, human and divine." Isaac Maddox, the Bishop of Worcester, suggested that popular resistance to the Gin Acts might well produce a "Populace *enflamed* against the present Distribution of Property, and discovering by outrageous Overt Acts, the strongest *Inclination* to bring it nearer to an Equality."[20]

Gin, then, was seen to spawn crime, anarchy, and the risk of social upheaval. It also, paradoxically, incapacitated the working poor from reproducing themselves and fulfilling their national mission, to work and fight for Britain. "Democritus" in the *London Evening Post* believed gin to be a "slow but sure Poison" producing "liquid Fires which dry up the Juices, and destroy the vital Heat."[21] Like other authors, he was concerned not only about the gin craze, the addiction to spirits, but also about the appalling quality of the product itself. Rotgut gin was produced from the poorest materials and was frequently adulterated. It was so ruinous, claimed George Cheyne, that "neither Laudanum nor Arsenick will kill more certainly."[22] Gin destroyed health, slowed reproduction, and threatened to produce a puny, alcoholic race of degenerates.

Quite apart from the sexual immorality that accompanied gin drinking, for there was a lot of talk about inebriates thrown promiscuously together in back rooms, the habit was increasingly defined as a drug problem, a "plague," a "pestilence." It had serious consequences for an island enmeshed in a competition for empire and markets with the Bourbon powers, especially France, whose population was three times as large. Jonas Hanway believed gin partly responsible for the decline in a population that should have surged with the disappearance of major epidemics in the eighteenth century. "What must become of the Infant who is conceived in Gin?" asked Henry Fielding. "Doth not this polluted Source, instead of producing Servants for the Husbandman, or Artificer; instead of providing Recruits for the Sea or the Field, promise only to fill Alms-Houses and Hospitals, and to infect the Street with Stench and Diseases."[23] It was no accident that the gin crisis led to demands for the first national census in Britain, one that could shed light on the dimensions of the craze and its possible resolution. Even when this proposal failed, there were continued demands to encourage marriage and healthy habits to regenerate the nation. We must have a buoyant population for empire, claimed Hanway in 1767, or "suffer in our interest in those dominions, or find supplies in other quarters of the world."[24]

The debate over gin was visibly encapsulated in William Hogarth's famous print *Gin Lane*. Although the site of the print is recognizably St. Giles in the fields, it was not intended and should not be read as an accurate portrayal of this epicenter of the gin epidemic. It is essentially a collage of images representing the evils of gin as they were developed in the popular press: degradation, economic ruin, child neglect, family breakdown, and delirium. In the foreground, a gin-sodden, syphilitic prostitute drops her baby while taking the stuff, and a cadaverous ballad singer quaffs his last dram. In the background, babies are silenced by gin or abandoned by addicted mothers. Amid the uproar outside the spirit shop, one child is horrifyingly skewered by a gin-crazed man. Hogarth said he produced cheap versions of the print to expose "the dredfull consequences of gin-drinking": "Every circumstance of its horrid effects are brought into view, in terrorem, nothing but Idleness, Poverty, misery and ruin are to be seen, Distress even to madness and death, and not a house in a tolerable condition but Pawnbrokers and the Gin Shop."[25]

The full meaning of the text can be gauged, however, only by pairing it with *Beer Street*, as Hogarth intended. *Beer Street* depicts industry and jollity, productive sociability and patriotism. In the first state of the print, Hogarth included a Frenchman hoisted high by a brawny blacksmith. This illustration of the hearty effects of British ale was designed to counter the fear that gin-inflicted punyism would damage British competitiveness. Hogarth subsequently changed this image to a pair of lovers, whose union would presumably produce a healthy crop of children and further the patriotic project of fostering a healthy nation. Throughout the print, in fact, patriotic motifs abound. Builders and tailors toast the king's birthday. Two fishwives read John Lockman's broadsheet promoting the British herring industry, a project designed to reduce the poor rate, create a nursery of seamen, and bring a disaffected Highland Scotland within the British capitalist fold. The juxtaposition of *Gin Lane* and *Beer Street* brought home the debilitating effects of spirit addiction to society and nation, whereas beer drinking could be accommodated within a calendar that offered predictable breaks from the central task of toil.

For all midcentury commentators, toil was central. The first obligation of workers was to work, not to play. Nonwork was a problem, even if it was begrudgingly recognized as essential to rejuvenating working bodies. There was a constant slippage from leisure to idleness and luxury in public discourses about plebeian pleasures. Plebeian pastimes had to be policed: even among potential high-wage theorists such as Josiah Tucker there was an abiding fear that the pleasures of the poor might be uncontrollable and detrimental to the welfare of the country. In 1749, this well-known economist and clergyman feared British workers of both sexes would refuse to work "while they have anything to spend on their vices." While Tucker would not deny workers access to the world of goods, he wanted to set up industrial tribunals to curb exorbitant wage demands that might destroy Britain's international competitiveness.

The gin debate disclosed that upper- and lower-class luxuries were different things. Upper-class luxury and pleasure produced jobs; its fallout was social specific; elite families suffered from upper-class prodigality, but not the nation as a whole. Lower-class luxury was more damaging. "To be born for no other purpose than to consume the fruits of the earth is the privilege . . . of the very Few," averred Henry Fielding. "The greatest part of mankind must sweat hard to produce them, or society will no longer answer the purposes for which it was ordained."[26] Gin drinking was potentially disastrous for the economy and the country. Swilling down bottles of claret, port, and brandy was okay; tossing back drams of gin was not. To be sure, a few midcentury commentators chafed at the double standard. One in 1751 suggested it was wrong to claim that what was fashionable and excusable among patricians was vicious and punishable among plebeians. But such claims were made, and indeed "luxury," which had earlier been linked to the political corruption of the elite, became increasingly associated with the profligacy of the poor. In an era when Britain vied with France for supremacy in the Atlantic, the sinews of war and commerce had to be strengthened. Consequently no one could allow *all* pleasures to be disciplined by the market. Plebeian leisure preferences had to be regulated. To neglect them was too risky to the national welfare. Even as high-wage theory gained momentum, and the sanctity of the market was championed by the likes of Adam Smith, production still took precedence over consumption. It had to be conditioned by criminal sanctions against servants, harsh rules governing pauperism, and what E. P. Thompson described as the "husbandry of time"—an inner compulsion to use one's time profitably and not waste it—a disposition generated by religious sanctions that fostered work discipline and contained desire.[27]

Fall Semester 2011

1. Samuel Johnson, *A Dictionary of the English language*, 2 vols. (2nd ed.; London, 1755–56), s.v. "Pleasure."
2. Ibid., s.v. "Leisure."
3. Ibid., s.v. "Pleasure".
4. Alexander Pope, *Poetical Works* (London, 1839), p. 369, from *The Odyssey*, book 1, lines 479–80.
5. *Bibliotheca Topographica Britannica*, 8 vols. (London, 1780–90), vol. 4, pp. 8 et seq., queries 14 and 17.
6. John Clayton, *Friendly Advice to the Poor* (Manchester, 1755), p. 13.
7. John Houghton, *Collection of Letters* (London, 1681), p. 177.
8. Jonas Hanway, *A Journal of Eight Days . . . to Which Is Added an Essay on Tea*, 2 vols. (London, 1757), vol. 2, pp. 2, 24–31; Clayton, *Friendly Advice*, p. 20.
9. Bernard Mandeville, *A Letter to Dion* (London, 1732), p. 51.
10. Ordinary's Account, 26 Mar. 1750, William Russel (OA17500326), OldBaileyOnline.org.
11. Maxine Berg, *Luxury and Pleasure in Eighteenth-Century Britain* (Oxford, 2007), p. 6.
12. *Advice to Unmarried Women* (London, 1791), p. 39.
13. *An Earnest and Affectionate Address to the Poor* (London 1770), p. 8; Peter Clark, *The English Alehouse: A Social History, 1200–1830* (New York, 1983).
14. The words of Jorevin de Rochefort, cited in Charles Dickens, *All the Year Round*, (7 June 1890), p. 537.
15. *Gentleman's Magazine*, 7 (1737), p. 214.
16. *London Evening Post*, 20–22 Jan. 1736.
17. *Gazetteer*, 5 Oct. 1736; J. A. Chartres, "Spirits in the North East? Gin and Other Vices in the Long Eighteenth Century," in *Creating and Consuming Culture in North-East England, 1660–1830*, ed. Helen Berry and Jeremy Gregory (Aldershot, 2004), pp. 37–56.
18. *London Daily Post*, 5 Aug. 1738; *London Evening Post*, 15 Jan. 1737; see also Jessica Warner and Frank Ivis, "'Damn you, you informing bitch': Vox Populi and the Unmaking of the Gin Act of 1736," *Journal of Social History*, 33 (1999), pp. 299–330.
19. *Covent Garden Journal*, 20 June 1753.
20. Henry Fielding, *An Enquiry into the Causes of the Late Increase of Robbers*, ed. Malvin R. Zirker (Middletown, Conn., 1988), pp. 89–90; Hanway, *A Journal of Eight Days*, vol. 2, p. 85; Isaac Maddox, *An Epistle to the Right Honourable the Lord Mayor, Aldermen and Common Council of the City of London* (London, 1751), pp. 14–15.
21. *London Evening Post*, 4–7 May 1751.
22. George Cheyne, *An Essay on Health and Long Life* (8th ed.; London, 1734), p. 54.
23. Fielding, *Enquiry*, p. 90.
24. Jonas Hanway, *Letters on the Importance of the Rising Generation of the Laboring Part of Our Fellow-Subjects*, 2 vols. (London, 1767), vol. 2, p. 129.
25. BL, Add MSS 27,991, f. 49b, transcribed in William Hogarth, *The Analysis of Beauty*, ed. Joseph Burke (Oxford, 1955), p. 226.
26. Fielding, *Enquiry*, p. 80.
27. E. P. Thompson, "Time, Work-Discipline, and Industrial Capitalism," in *Customs in Common* (London, 1991), p. 88.

George III—Royal Collection Trust / © Her Majesty Queen Elizabeth II 2015

14

The Men Who Lost America

ANDREW O'SHAUGHNESSY

Britain seemingly should have won the American War of Independence. The defeat was an aberration. The country had emerged as a premier global power from the Seven Years' War. It was in the decade *before* the American Revolution that Lord George Macartney referred to Britain's "vast Empire, on which the sun never sets." It had the advantage of a professional military, the largest navy in the world, and ready access to credit. Nelson would later defeat the French Navy at Trafalgar (1805), and Wellington would defeat Napoleon at Waterloo (1815).

British failure is popularly blamed on the incompetence of political and military leaders who have consequently become objects of satire. This is particularly true of their portrayals in the movies and media, which have a greater impact on public perception than books. It is apparent in popular history like Barbara Tuchman's *The March of Folly: From Troy to Vietnam* (1984), which devotes a third of the book to mocking the British. It even permeates scholarly writing and, especially, college textbooks, which use words like "hidebound" and "incompetent." These stereotypes were equally common in Britain. It is a curious thesis because it diminishes the achievements of George Washington and Nathaniel Greene. It also does the British leaders an injustice, recalling David Halberstam's portrait of the American leaders in the Vietnam War in *The Best and the Brightest*. The issue, however, is not that British leaders' posthumous reputations were tarnished, but rather that this emphasis on the role of personalities has deflected from an appreciation of the essence of this war and why it was lost. Based on my book *The Men Who Lost America: British Leadership, the American Revolution, and the Fate of the Empire* (2013), this lecture considers the ten key political and military decision makers who presided over the British loss of America. Rather like a play, the ten biographical chapters of the book are interlinked along a time line that introduces each person at the moment when he was at the center of the war effort. The portraits show the extent to which success was precluded by circumstances, and they cumulatively offer an alternative explanation of why Britain lost America.

George III (1738–1820). George III was not the tyrant depicted in the Declaration of Independence. He had little responsibility for British policy toward America before 1774. He may, though, still qualify as a villain to Americans. After the Boston Tea Party, he became the leading proponent of punishing the rebel colonies, and the driving force of the British war for America. His attitude hardened from the emerging conviction that the crisis had been caused by too much leniency toward the colonies, and forbearance, he believed, had created the impression of timidity on the part of Britain. Indeed, he became the chief proponent of the war. He effectively prolonged the conflict by refusing either to let Lord North resign or to negotiate with opposition leaders who were committed to ending the war, such as the Earl of Rockingham. He kept the government together by dint of his forceful personality and tenacity. He sounded almost Churchillian. He vowed that he would never surrender, calling for sacrifice, enlisting one of his youngest sons in the navy, and changing his favorite royal retreat from a modest palace to a castle—Windsor Castle. He wanted to continue the war even after Yorktown. He twice nearly abdicated rather than accept the loss of America. He was passionate because he believed—together with many of those who opposed the war—that Britain would cease to be a great power if it lost America.

Lord North (1732–1792). It is still an insult in the House of Commons is to accuse the leader of the government of being "the worst Prime Minister since Lord North." North will always be associated with the coercive policies that led to the American Revolution and the loss of America. It is the great irony of his career.

North inherited a revolutionary situation in America that climaxed in the Boston Massacre. He initially did much to diffuse the situation. It was the Boston Tea Party that caused him to adopt a tougher approach to America in the Coercive Acts (1774). He enjoyed overwhelming support in Britain. But when it became apparent that resistance was widespread in America, North soon began to waver and consistently attempted to negotiate a compromise for much of the rest of the war. Despite the opposition of George III, North insisted on introducing his own Conciliatory Proposal (1775) and eventually offered terms, via the Carlisle Peace Commission of 1778, that conceded every demand in return for accepting token British authority over America.

North was an exceptionally capable and gifted administrator and party manager, and a brilliant parliamentary speaker. A particularly able finance minister, he managed to sustain funding for the war. His disarming charm, wit, and urbane manner won him the admiration of critics. He was a successful mediator and broker within the government, which otherwise might have fallen apart. He was the only politician who was acceptable to George III and who commanded majority support in the House of Commons. He protested to his last days that he had constantly tried to resign throughout the war, but the king had never permitted it.

General Sir William Howe (1729–1814). Sir William Howe was selected over the heads of 105 more senior generals to command in America in 1775. Precisely because the government anticipated unconventional warfare, he was regarded as ideally qualified: an expert in light infantry tactics, he had served with distinction during the French and Indian War in America and Canada. He won all the battles in which he commanded, forcing Washington to retreat from New York and New Jersey. He had the best chance of success of any British commander in America.

Howe has mystified historians by his failure to press his advantage in 1776. This hesitation was initially a consequence of conflicting objectives. He had opposed the coercive policies that caused the American Revolution. Questioning the value of a purely military victory, since Britain could not afford a long-term occupation of America, he preferred to offer the olive branch and to delay military action while making peace overtures. In addition, he needed to preserve his army, which could not long sustain the fatality rates suffered at Bunker Hill. His attitude and strategy changed after the Battle of Trenton, when he aggressively pursued outright military victory and succeeded in conquering Philadelphia. The prize proved elusive, however, owing to the Patriots' victory at Saratoga (1777). Howe was blamed for his failure to reinforce Burgoyne. He would in turn blame the failure of the home government to send him explicit orders—a series of recriminations that helped foster the idea that the war was lost through incompetence.

Admiral Lord Richard Howe (1729–1814). Admiral Lord Howe later emerged as one of the most celebrated naval heroes in Britain before Nelson. His career reminds us that there is a very fine line between success and failure. He understood this well, complaining it was "a little hard, that after a man devoted his whole time and talents . . . to the service of his country," that the outcome, "not his conduct, should determine his character: that to be *unsuccessful* and guilty should be the same thing, and that he should be held up as a public criminal."

The admiral was given command of the navy in North America by a reluctant government at the insistence of his younger brother, General Sir William Howe, who, in the absence of a joint chief of staff and a unified command system, appreciated the advantages of close cooperation between the army and Royal Navy. Like his younger brother, Richard Howe was a pioneer in developing the naval code of practice in amphibious warfare in which the navy gave logistical support to the army in beach landings anywhere along the eastern coast of America. He helped introduce the flat-bottomed ships whose bows would go forward to land the infantry. On 22 August 1776, in less than two and a half hours, he and his brother landed 15,000 men and forty cannon on Long Island near the town of Utrecht.

General John Burgoyne (1722–1792). Burgoyne is the subject of more biographies than any other British commander in America during the Revolutionary War. His theatrical personality, his carefully manicured appearance, his bravado and vanity, perfectly suit the stereotype of an aristocratic dilettante who lost America.

His image was very different at the time of his appointment. He was a rising star known as an original thinker and innovator. He had created the first light-horse units in the British Army. He was credited with the successful defense of Portugal against Spain in the Seven Years' War. He was one of the first officers to write about the treatment of ordinary soldiers and to recommend avoidance of frequent corporal punishment. It was due to his humanity that he was affectionately known by his troops as "Gentleman Johnny."

Burgoyne was also a playwright and keen amateur actor whose deft use of language and dramatic flair enabled him to win support for a plan that promised victory in America through an invasion from Canada. His skill at self-promotion convinced George III and Lord George Germain, who were disappointed with the pace of the war and the caution of Sir William Howe. It offered precisely the bold stroke that they eagerly sought. Burgoyne initially seemed to deliver what he had promised. He managed to begin operations within six weeks of his return to Canada. He captured Crown Point and Fort Ticonderoga, which was regarded as the key to control of Lake Champlain and New York. His ultimate failure at Saratoga helps explain the wider British defeat in America. He had anticipated little opposition after capturing Fort Ticonderoga, yet was outnumbered four to one when he surrendered at Saratoga. It was politically expedient for him to blame Germain. The subtext of the evidence that he presented in his defense before Parliament was that failure was inevitable because Britain lacked the necessary support of the civilian population in America.

Lord George Germain (1716–1785). Lord George Germain, the Secretary of State for America and the main architect of the Revolutionary War in Britain, is the most popular target of blame for the British defeat. He was the perfect scapegoat, a reputed homosexual who carried the fatal stigma of having been pronounced unfit for military service at a court-martial for his actions at the Battle of Minden (1759).

Germain told Edward Gibbon that he sought to vanquish the memory of Minden by pursuing victory in America. A gifted bureaucrat, he was skilled at managing the cumbersome system of eighteenth-century administration that provided shipping, supplies, and soldiers for America. He was one of the ablest speakers in defending the record of the government in the House of Commons. He well understood that he was too far away to attempt to manage the war and that sudden developments might change conditions before he could send orders from Britain. He therefore gave wide discretion to his commanders to act on their own initiative, and deferred to the plans proposed by the generals in the field.

Germain contended against major constraints upon his authority, handicaps generally unappreciated in the assessment of his character. The disunity and vulnerability of the government hampered his efforts. He had no direct control of the navy, even though combined operations with the army were essential to success in America. He could only recommend and advise on military policy, to which he had to defer to the Cabinet. His ability to reinforce and supply the army was limited by the rising cost of the war, the budget available to him, and opposition to higher taxes. He had to work with an administrative apparatus that was not equipped for the unprecedented challenge of supplying an army across the Atlantic. To the chagrin of commanders in America, he was obliged to deflect military resources from America to the Caribbean and to Canada.

In 1776, Germain succeeded in sending more troops to New York and Canada than his commanders had requested. He argued that the best chance of success was a knockout blow against Washington. It is a view widely shared by modern military commentators, who believe it did indeed represent Britain's best chance for victory.

General Sir Henry Clinton (1738–1795). General Sir Henry Clinton started the war as a brilliant second-in-command to Sir William Howe. His withering critiques of his superior remain the most incisive accounts by a contemporary of the strategic shortcomings of the campaigns of 1776 and 1777. He foresaw and tried to prevent the disastrous train of events leading to Saratoga. Indeed, it was a characteristic of this war that the seconds-in-command always knew better than their commanders—until they took the top spot themselves and failed.

As commander-in-chief of the British army in America, Clinton was a gifted strategist who grasped the realities of the war and understood Britain's precarious military situation. He displayed his military talents in the hazardous withdrawal from Philadelphia, in which he outmaneuvered Washington. He won one of the greatest British victories of the war in his successful siege of Charleston (1780). He was much more skeptical than Germain of the potential support of American Loyalists. The most cerebral of all the commanders, he identified the key to the war as gaining the support of the population, writing that the British needed to "win the hears and subdue the minds of America." He saw little value in conquering territory only to abandon it later, thereby disappointing and disillusioning local Loyalists.

Clinton particularly understood the importance of British naval supremacy in supporting the army in America. The son of an admiral and a keen sailor, he foresaw the potential for disaster in the event of a lackluster naval effort. In a scenario like the one that developed at Yorktown, he constantly warned that an army operating outside New York was likely to be stranded should the French gain superiority at sea. Clinton insisted that the outcome of the war would be decided in the environs of New York, a view shared by Washington.

Clinton was constantly frustrated while in command. He was asked to achieve the victory that had eluded his predecessor, against greater odds and with fewer resources—Britain was simultaneously fighting a global war against France, Spain, and the Netherlands. He attempted to resign a number of times. But like Lord North, he continued in limbo. Believing that he had been asked to do the impossible, he resorted to outbursts, indecision, and reclusive behavior.

He was particularly preoccupied in later life with the events leading up to the final British defeat at Yorktown. His command had been undermined by the government in London in its preference for Lord Cornwallis, so it is not surprising that the distorted account of events in his unpublished memoirs absolves him of responsibility. He was incensed that the war was lost by a strategy that he had not devised or approved and that ran counter to his basic instincts. He foresaw its potentially catastrophic consequences. He complied with it nonetheless, against his better judgment, only to find himself bearing the brunt of the blame for the disaster. It must have been particularly galling to be saddled with the defeat, even in part, because one of his few orders to Cornwallis had been to fortify a coastal port in Virginia.

Charles Earl Cornwallis (1738–1805). In the movie *The Patriot*, Lord Cornwallis is portrayed as more worried about his dogs and his clothing than about winning the war. The real Cornwallis was indeed the most aristocratic of the generals in America, but he was also the one who burned all his equipment at Ramseur's Mill in North Carolina in a dogged determination to defeat Greene (1780). Far from being obsessed with his sartorial elegance, he hated pomp and fanfare. He was admired by his troops for sharing their deprivations and sleeping outside without a tent. Very much the professional solider, he agreed to serve in America despite his opposition to the imperial policies that had provoked the war. He was one of only six members of the House of Lords to vote against the Stamp Act (1765).

Cornwallis captivated the imagination of members of the government and the newspaper-reading public in Britain with his military exploits in America. In his march from South Carolina to Virginia, he gave the war a new momentum and the promise of victory. He captured or killed much of the southern Continental Army at the Battle of Camden (1780), where he defeated Horatio Gates, the victor at Saratoga. Cornwallis invaded the home state of George Washington, and his troops narrowly missed capturing Thomas Jefferson at Monticello. His daring won him the admiration of Germain, who was exasperated by the seeming inactivity of Clinton.

Cornwallis took a desperate gamble in persisting with his advance despite a dwindling force and lengthening supply lines. He had no patience with the caution of Sir Henry Clinton, who had instructed him to make a priority of defending British-occupied South Carolina. Cornwallis argued that the rebellion in the South was kept alive by supplies and expectations of support from the North. Believing that the best form of defense was offense, he put to test the assumption that a great numbers of Loyalists in North Carolina and the Chesapeake were just waiting to show their allegiance to Britain.

He believed in the kind of bold strokes favored by George III and Germain. He was under pressure for a quick victory from a home government whose survival was increasingly dependent on the outcome of the war.

Cornwallis enjoyed the most successful post-war career of the men who lost America. He became Governor-General and Commander-in-Chief of India and, later, Governor-General of Ireland. His combat days were not over. He personally led the defeat of Tipu Sultan and the capture of Seringapatam in India. He defeated the French and presided over the repression of the risings in Ireland during the great rebellion of 1798. He was made a marquis and later returned to India, where he died while carrying out a peace mission up the Ganges. A statue in his honor was erected at St. Paul's Cathedral.

Admiral Sir George Rodney (1719–1792). Admiral Sir George Rodney was exceptional in that his reputation was enhanced by his service in the Revolutionary War. During the war, he succeeded in capturing or killing three enemy admirals from three European countries. Yet he was also responsible for failing to intercept the French fleet of Admiral de Grasse in the Caribbean, which wound up trapping Cornwallis in Yorktown

In 1781, Rodney had other concerns besides the French fleet. He was presiding at the sale of goods that he had confiscated after capturing the island of St. Eustatius. This nine-square-mile island was the major source of overseas military supplies for the American Revolution. In 1776, its fort fired the first foreign salute to the flag of the United States. Rodney spent three months on the island, during which time the French fleet escaped detection to join additional ships at Martinique. He justified his behavior by saying that the place was a nest of pirates. He believed that the necessity of securing the island had robbed him of the chance to win a victory against the French fleet that might have tipped the balance of the war dramatically in favor of Britain. Rodney returned to Britain instead of pursuing de Grasse. He blamed ill health for his decision, but his first priority on returning home was not to see a doctor but to defend himself in Parliament against Edmund Burke, who sought an inquiry into the admiral's behavior in the Caribbean.

The presence of the French fleet in Chesapeake Bay removed any chance of Cornwallis and his army escaping from Yorktown. Rodney's departure to Britain deprived the navy of the expertise of the most capable admiral in America. In addition, Rodney's actions contributed to the inferiority of the British fleet on the East Coast, because he took some of his ships with him and sent others to Jamaica. Naval command fell to Admiral Thomas Graves, who was defeated in the most important sea battle of the American Revolution at the Chesapeake Capes.

Rodney was not blamed for his role in the events leading to Yorktown, because he won a decisive victory over the French at the Battle of the Saintes in the Caribbean in April 1782. One of the greatest naval victories against the French before Trafalgar, it enabled Britain to obtain generous peace terms from the French and preserved the remaining colonies in the British Empire.

The Earl of Sandwich (1718–1792). As First Lord of the Admiralty, the Earl of Sandwich was the minister responsible for the Royal Navy during the American Revolution. After Germain, he was the civilian politician most blamed for the defeat, since the war was virtually the only one since the 1690s in which the Royal Navy had been defeated by the French fleet. The charge was unjust; Sandwich had advocated a full-scale mobilization of the navy before the outbreak of fighting in America, but his budget was cut until the eve of French entry into the war in 1778. A highly experienced naval administrator, he had begun his managerial responsibilities before some of the other members of the Cabinet were born.

After 1778, Sandwich regarded America as less important than the war with France and the defense of Britain. He complained that none of his predecessors had faced such an impossible situation: the overstretched navy was fighting against the French, Spanish, Dutch, and Americans, and so he had to deploy fleets in the English Channel, the North Sea, the Mediterranean, the Caribbean, the Indian Ocean, and the Atlantic. He had to provide merchant ships with convoys for protection against privateers. The navy had to defend Britain against invasion attempts through the summers of 1779 to 1781. For almost the only time in the eighteenth century, the Royal Navy was outnumbered by the combined French and Spanish fleets. Sandwich's preference was to concentrate his force in Europe, where his admirals might watch the movements of enemy fleets with a view to pursuing them. The strategy risked the danger that enemy fleets might inflict a major blow in America before the arrival of a relief expedition from Britain.

Sandwich succeeded in achieving his main priority, the defeat of France. He helped prepare the conditions that made possible Rodney's victory at the Saintes. It might be said that France was the real loser of the Revolutionary War. It received only minor territorial gains at the Peace of Paris (1783), and was bankrupted by its participation; that catastrophe led directly to the calling of the Estates General and the French Revolution. The memoirist Nathaniel Wraxall said of Sandwich what was analogously true of so many of the men who lost America: the problems of the navy "originated more in the nature of the war than from the fault of Lord Sandwich: the obloquy and the punishment, however, fell upon him."

THE POPULAR PERCEPTION OF BRITISH leadership as incompetent has disguised the extent to which the outcome of the war was in doubt till the very end, and has eclipsed the real reasons why Britain lost America. There were of course many causes, but General Sir Henry Clinton was right in his recognition that in what was ultimately a war of hearts and minds, the British lacked sufficient popular support in America. Britain had an army of conquest and not an army of occupation, which explains why it was able to conquer every American city but failed to take territory in New Jersey (1776–77), Pennsylvania (1777), and the Carolinas (1780–81). The army's difficulty was best illustrated by the war in the South, where Clinton conquered Charleston and Cornwallis defeated the remnants of the Continental Army at Camden in South Carolina (1780). But the army then faced what we would today call insurgencies led by men who have become folk heroes, such as Francis Marion, the "Swamp Fox," and Thomas Sumter, the "Gamecock."

Britain never expected to have to occupy America, since the war effort was predicated on the assumption that the majority of the population supported the Crown. This error was based on seemingly good information provided by American Loyalists like Joseph Galloway, who on the eve of Yorktown said that 80 percent of Americans supported Britain. Like most revolutions, it was also a civil war: Loyalists constituted up to one-fifth of the population, and about 19,000 Americans fought for the British. There were also neutrals, a "silent majority" that might have been persuaded to support Britain. In reality, even contemporaries were never entirely certain about the politics of their neighbors. The very presence of British troops alienated potential support, given their propensity to commit plunder and other crimes. It did not help that the British enlisted the support of German mercenaries, runaway slaves of Patriot masters, and Native Americans.

This was the only war in the modern period in which Britain fought without a European ally, which was a necessary factor in victories from Blenheim to Waterloo. Indeed, during the course of the Revolution, the British ended up distributing forces throughout the world as war broke out with France (1778), Spain (1779), and the Dutch Republic (1780). Much of the rest of Europe was allied against Britain in the League of Armed Neutrality. As a result, British forces were overstretched, and more troops and naval ships were sent to the Caribbean after 1778 than to North America. A fragmented command system further hampered the logistical difficulties of transporting food and supplies from Britain, an unanticipated necessity: the British thought they would capture enough arable land in America to supply their troops. The geographic size of the continent contributed to the problem of overextension, as did the transatlantic distance from Britain. The national debt was always an obstacle to devoting more resources to the war. It was because of the debt that Britain first taxed America.

It is suggested here that conditions virtually precluded a British victory in America. Historians, however, recoil from suggesting that any event was inevitable. They are too well aware of the role of chance and other contingencies. The British might have succeeded against an enemy lacking the leadership of George Washington, the rifle skills of the Patriots, their proficiency in guerilla tactics, and the formation of an army that the most critical British officers later admitted was the rival of any in Europe. Nevertheless, the British never entirely lost the war in America. As George III wanted after Yorktown, they could have continued to fight, since the main British army was still in New York. They had possession of Canada, Savanah, Charleston, Augusta, Pensacola, Detroit, Niagara, and East Florida. As in the Vietnam War, political opinion dealt the deathblow to the war for America. By March 1782, Lord North could no longer secure a majority in the House of Commons. But he and his fellow ministers enjoyed the last laugh, since before leaving office, they arranged the naval expedition of Sir George Rodney that resulted in his victory at the Saintes. Thus, the British politicians and generals who lost America helped lay the foundations of a future empire that was larger than the one in 1776 and would encompass a fifth of the global population by the time of the death of George III.

Spring Semester 2015

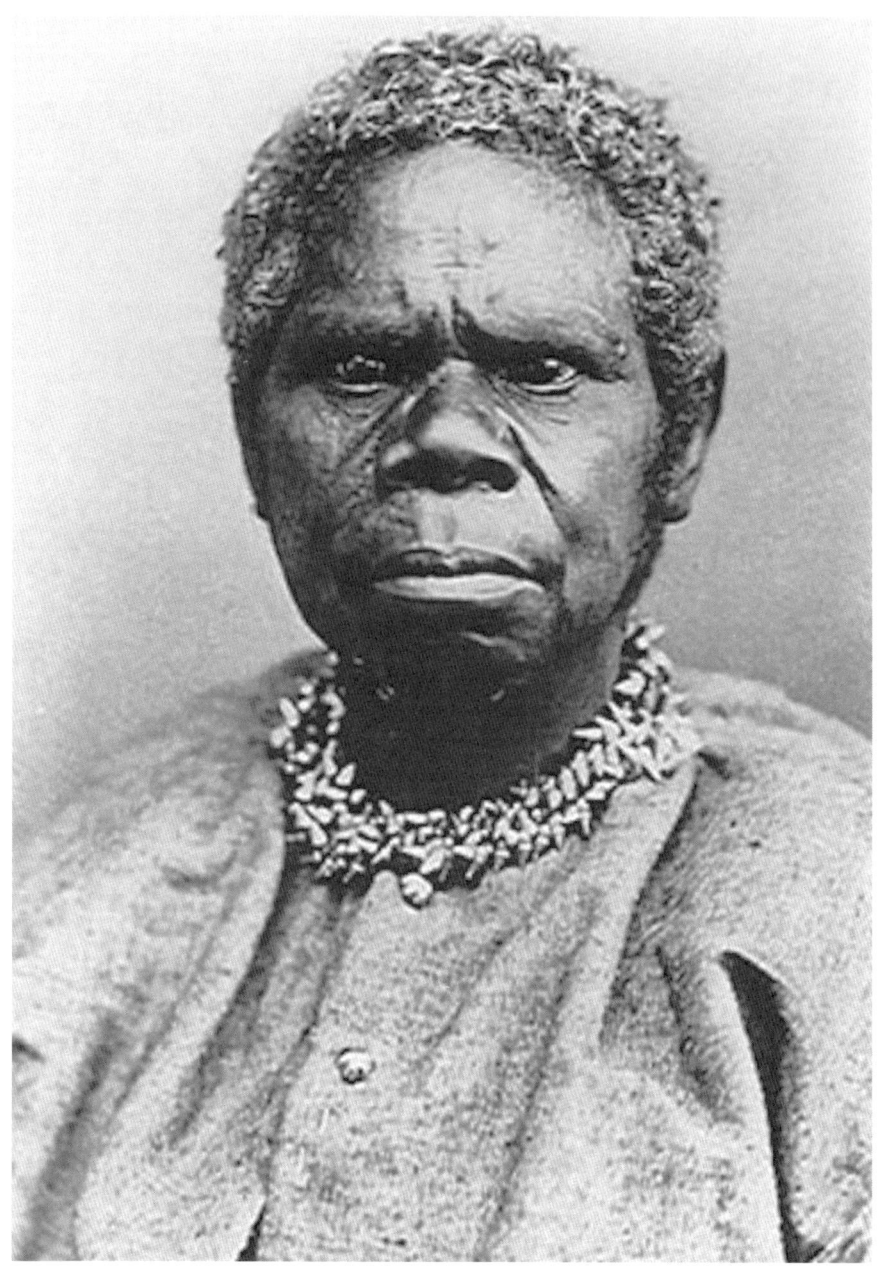

Truganini (c. 1812–1876), generally considered the last Aboriginal Tasmanian

15

Genocide in Tasmania

BERNARD PORTER

The extinction of the native Tasmanians as a result of their first contact with British settlers in the early nineteenth century is well known, and was pretty well known, and widely regretted, at the time. Much about it is obscure, including the numbers involved: most estimates are of 5,000–10,000 aborigines living there at the beginning (in 1803), reduced to nil by 1876—though the last figure omits mixed-race Tasmanians and those deported to the Australian mainland. William Lanne, the titular subject of *The Last Man: A British Genocide in Tasmania* (2014), by Tom Lawson, died in 1869, but two Tasmanian women survived him briefly. (All quotations here are taken from Lawson's book.) There is also controversy over how they met their end, or rather, the relative roles played in that by settler violence, intertribal conflict, exogenous diseases, declining fertility, and simple demoralization—and over the contribution made to the whole tragic affair by the local British colonial authorities. Modern Australian historians seem prepared to accept a large measure of retrospective blame for it on behalf of their nation. A few years ago, their position provoked the almost comically reactionary Liberal prime minister John Howard to inveigh against what he dubbed their "Black Armband" view of his country's history (as opposed to the "proud Gallipoli victim" one), launching the popular debate that became known there as the "History Wars." The main argument was over how many natives were killed by the settlers. Lawson thinks this question doesn't much matter; it was a "genocide" in any case. He is also at pains to demolish the claim often made by even the most critical chroniclers of these events, that Britain—the metropole—was not to blame. In that version of events, the Colonial Office did its best to protect the aborigines. It was the settlers, many of them ex-convicts, who did the damage, against orders and to the great chagrin of those back home. No, claims Lawson; the imperial government was just as implicated. For that reason, he believes that Britain's own record of colonial genocide should be taught in its schools, which makes this book relevant to the (lesser) "history wars" going on now in Britain over how "celebratory" its taught national history should be.

The genocide began, as genocides often did at the time (and perhaps still do), with competition for land between the native population and British immigrants who had been told, first, that Tasmania would be a potential arcadia for them if they put their backs into developing it, and second—and more to the point—that it was empty of "civilized" people, which gave them the right to take it on. Unfortunately for them, it wasn't quite empty of "uncivilized" people, whom they inevitably rubbed up against, with the uncivilized coming off worst. This happened elsewhere too: in North America, of course, and in southern Africa, where native populations were decimated, but never quite wiped out, as is supposed to have happened here. Tasmania is an island, so it was easy to tell when all the natives had been cleared out.

The clashes began just a few months after the arrival of the Europeans, when a group of several hundred aborigines approached their settlement at Risdon Cove, just north of present-day Hobart, probably on a kangaroo hunt, but suspected of hostile intentions by the terrified settlers—wasn't that in the nature of "barbarians," after all?—who fired on them, leaving several dead. The exact circumstances are still unclear, including the number of Tasmanians killed: contemporary estimates ranged from five to fifty; but in any case, the incident bedeviled relations between the two communities for years afterward. Tensions continued, usually as a result of white encroachments on aboriginal hunting grounds, culminating in the full-scale Black War in the late 1820s—Tasmanians against colonial troops and armed settlers, under martial law—which caused most of the damage to the former. There were other massacres too. Some of the European combatants behaved atrociously, and with the clear intention of exterminating the natives. (Lawson provides some gory details—infants' brains being bashed out, and so on.) The usual underlying factors operated here as in all similar cases: need or greed on the Europeans' part, of course, and racist prejudice, exacerbated by fear and paranoia on both sides, together with genuine misunderstandings over what it meant to occupy land. Apparently the Tasmanians had little idea of individual land ownership, which made it difficult for the settlers to assert their claims even if they intended to do it legally. For some of the latter, it was this that proved the aboriginals' inferiority, as though Lockeian concepts of private property were the essential mark of "civilization." At the very least, it justified the Europeans' taking over most of the country and cultivating it in their way (usually with imported sheep), in the interests of agricultural "progress." Tasmanians were inherently *un*progressive, which meant that they were bound to give way to "civilization" eventually. Whether that necessarily meant their physically dying out as a "race," however, as seemed to be their lot, was a moot point.

So far as the British authorities in London were concerned, they hoped not, and—Lawson concedes—probably genuinely. The Black War gave rise to much hand-wringing in Whitehall over the "ignominious stain" on the "honour of their country" that it had brought. Most officials sided with the Tasmanians, accepting that they were the ones who had been provoked. These events happened, remember, at the peak of the antislavery campaign in Britain, when the "humanitarian" lobby was rampant. Instructions from London, usually backed up by local governors, repeatedly enjoined Australian settlers and soldiery to treat the natives kindly. A famous one was Governor George Arthur's proclamation of 1830, circulated among the Tasmanians in comic-strip form, showing, in its last frame, an Englishman being hanged for shooting one of them. (Did that ever happen?) The problem—or just one of them, if Lawson is right—was that Britain didn't have the means to enforce humanitarianism on its subjects abroad, especially when they were so very far away. The problem was moral as well as logistical: would the few available soldiers fire on their kin? This was a systemic flaw in British colonialism in the nineteenth century, and indeed for long afterward: look at Harold Wilson and Rhodesia. Most colonies were run on a shoestring and were expected to finance themselves. Generally, the British depended on native collaborators to help them. Except in India, Britain had nowhere near the troops to impose its will, which explains its repeated military defeats at the hands of the Zulus, for example, and the Maoris—neighbors of the Tasmanians, but much more sophisticated militarily—and even the Indian "mutineers," at first. It was for this reason, and in the absence of a native collaborating class, that Britain so often subcontracted its colonies out to commercial companies and settlers to rule on its behalf; a form of "privatization" *avant la lettre,* with all the disadvantages of privatization, like the surrender of public responsibility and the opening of opportunities for corruption, as well as, no doubt, the benefits. Humanitarians could only fume impotently. That, at any rate, has usually been the British Empire's "alibi."

Imperial authorities did manage some mitigation, but always in the direction of adapting the Tasmanians to their new situation rather than protecting them from it. That was one way of preserving them as a people. So aboriginal children were taken into white folks' homes, for example: often as cheap labor, but at least it kept them alive; in the 1830s and 1840s, a "settlement" was run for the remnants of them on nearby Flinders Island, to Westernize them, basically; and of course the missionaries, always less likely to believe in black people's *inherent* inferiority than most other colonists, played their part. The Flinders Island settlement failed, however, and eventually most remaining Tasmanians were shipped to the Australian mainland, where they presumably merged with other aboriginal tribes. That possible survival is one of the reasons for Lawson's insistence that they never truly "died out."

The point is important to him because it undermines the theory, widely held at the time and still prevalent, he thinks, that their complete extinction somehow proved that the process was "natural," and so was no one's fault, really, but their own. He calls this the "extermination discourse." There is no doubt that this *was* a common view. Lawson seems to think that it was triggered by the Tasmanian situation, but it goes back long before that. In earlier modern times, it was usually applied to the Native Americans. The "natural extinction" rationale was often used to make kind folk feel better about their massacre by European settlers—horrible, but it would have happened anyway—but sometimes to enjoin charity toward them, to "smooth their dying pillows." They may have been wrong—or right: "primitive" peoples are still finding it difficult to preserve their cultures today. But Lawson goes further, claiming that this idea somehow made those who believed it genocidal in *intention*. That is one of his reasons for implicating the British state.

Another rests on his definition of "genocide," which apparently no longer necessarily means literally killing—murdering—a whole "race," which is the popular meaning that seems to have become attached to the word since the Nazis. ("There is no sensible comparison to be made," Lawson concedes, "if one works backwards from the Holocaust.") The 1948 UN convention on genocide went much further, defining it as "acts committed with intent to destroy, in whole or in part, a national, ethical, racial or religious group." That leaves several ambiguities: the "in whole or in part" bit; the "national, ethical or religious" bit; and the word "destroy," which could well be taken to include means short of murder, like the undermining of cultures. We need to be careful here: does Margaret Thatcher's destruction of South Yorkshire's mining community in the 1980s qualify? (Even her bitterest enemies would not accuse her of that.) In the Tasmanian connection, and in a more general colonial one, the word "destroy" might well be stretched to include attempts to re-educate or Westernize or proselytize the natives. If doing so resulted in wiping out a way of life, then it too counts. It is this consideration that leads Lawson to regard British humanitarian efforts to "raise" the Tasmanians in order to enable them to adapt to the "modern world" as not much better than literal genocide. Which obviously—because most of the humanitarians came from there—inculpates the metropole. That is charge number two.

Charge three—the clincher—is that although the British didn't want massacres, they *did* want colonization; and that involved violence inherently. "Colonisation itself amounted, in total, to genocide," according to Lawson. And the British knew it, deep down. That was what all the talk about "naturally dying races" was about. They even "revelled" in it. Behind it was the idea that this doing away with "primitive" peoples was somehow a sign of "imperial British glory and majesty": "What better indication of British might than the destruction of an entire race?" And they were all proud imperialists, weren't they?

This last—the point about the British taking a particular imperial pride in genocide—is provocative, and important if true. But we probably need more evidence. Lawson provides a single quotation (repeated twice) from *The Times* that appears to say something of the kind; but *The Times* was sui generis, hardly the representative of the popular press that Lawson takes it to be. (And these days, with so many old newspapers digitized and searchable, there really is no reason to restrict oneself to it.) The same may apply to Lawson's evidence for the prominent part he believes that Tasmania played in contemporary British culture, as the main source of his extermination discourse: a couple of mainly landscape painters who usually placed tiny natives—significantly, he thinks—in shaded areas; some little-read travel books; one stage play, which was very much on the side of the aborigines (it painted the settlers as the "savages"); skulls hidden away in various collections; and some spears and boomerangs deposited in a little museum in rural Saffron Walden. Lawson may be right, and he puts great trust in his own speculations, but it would be good to have some more empirical evidence too. Likewise with his most provocative argument, and his motive, he says, for writing this book: to show that the Tasmanian genocide of the early nineteenth century is an ever-present element of British "national identity" today—"a part of who 'we' are": "Britain is in effect a post-genocidal state."

"Post" of course can mean many things. It might indicate that Britain has got over all this. But that is not how the prefix is generally used in postcolonial circles today. What Lawson means is that the Tasmanian genocide or its memory still infuses the British present. But his evidence for that claim, too, may be thought rather thin. Essentially, it consists of a little-noticed row about the return of some old Tasmanian skulls, now in British museums, to their descendants, resisted by some curators on the essentially "imperialist" ground that science, being universal, is more important than irrational cultural susceptibilities; and an inconspicuous headstone in the cemetery of Bath Abbey, where, "if you look very closely," you will see the name of Governor George Augustus Robinson, officially "Chief Protector of the Aborigines" in Tasmania, described here as their "Pacificator." If you have to look closely, surely, it can't be all that prominent in modern British life.

There is, however, more. Lawson has one big theory about the significance of the destruction of the Tasmanians to the British of today (and to other colonial nations): it still lies at the bottom of their racial or national amour propre, portraying them as so advanced and progressive that "weaker" nations are inevitably crushed under their wheels. "Such an observation bears repeating," he writes: "the perception of Britain at the apex of human civilisation relied on the memory (and celebration) of genocide." Essential to this view is the myth that the Tasmanians were *entirely* wiped out, which is why Lawson is so anxious to discredit it, along with the interpretation that this annihilation was somehow "natural." It is our memories, albeit vague and deep ones, of the total elimination of peoples like the native Tasmanians that help those of us who were spared to feel that we are history's winners and, therefore, right. That seems plausible, though hard to prove. And difficult, in particular, to ascribe to the Tasmanians' disappearance in particular, when there have been so many others in history, from the Neanderthals on.

The Tasmanian genocide also, however, makes the British feel good in another, somewhat contradictory way. Because it was so far away, allegedly perpetrated by local ruffians rather than true Brits, unplanned, and—let's face it—not as gruesome as the Nazi Holocaust, it does little to undermine the common British assumption that *they* could never have been guilty of such a thing. This attitude is what so exasperates Lawson. His scholarly background is in Holocaust studies. Holocaust studies were instituted, in part, to promote "self-reflection." Instead, because they are presented in Britain, at least popularly—all those Second World War programs on the History TV channel, for example—as exclusively German, the reflection they reinforce is the old self-satisfied one of Britain as a uniquely tolerant and liberal country, in contrast to Germany in the 1930s and 1940s: it couldn't have happened here. So, "counter-productively," in Lawson's opinion, "Holocaust memorialisation is being fed more and more into ideas of British national pride." That is a travesty. (I agree.) The lesson that the Holocaust should really be used to teach—if it is proper for history to be used in this way at all—is how any nation or people can commit atrocities if the conditions are right. It wasn't just the Germans. In different circumstances the British might have been as awful. In certain circumstances—and this Tasmanian one is an example—they were.

That is a valid and important point. It should be taken on board by every history teacher, and (of course) by those who want history to impart patriotism. But it is not exactly Lawson's. Lawson wants to target Britain as a nation, just as wartime Germany is targeted, which is the point of his effort to demonstrate its complicity—governments and people, past and present—in its own genocides. The agent of this collusion was British colonialism, the thing that linked them, which he regards as inherently genocidal, just as Nazism was. But was it? The British committed dreadful atrocities in their colonies, which should be highlighted more; but the purpose of colonialism was not atrocious, and many of their colonies witnessed nothing at all that could be remotely described as genocidal. That was because their indigenes were powerful enough to resist them, as in New Zealand, and because the British needed them to trade with. Even Lawson's loose definition of "genocide" as including the extermination of cultures doesn't always apply. In most of its colonies, Britain wanted to preserve local cultures, partly because it respected them (just a little bit), but mainly because it didn't want to stir the natives up. In the early twentieth century, this policy was called indirect rule. It was colonial nationalists who objected to it the most. They thought—rightly, in the main—that colonialism was straightforwardly meant to keep the locals "in their place."

Elsewhere, even settlers—usually the most atrocious of colonials, and the ones Lawson seems to be referring to ("colonists")—had no reason to exterminate the natives, or even their cultures, if they relied on their labor to work the lands they had stolen from them. Literal genocide happened only in certain colonial situations, usually when there seemed little chance that the locals would fit into the broader colonial or settler scheme. The near extermination of the Native Americans is the best example, followed by the Caribs, the Tasmanians, and the Hottentots of southern Africa under the Dutch. The motive behind it was always individual settlers' land hunger (or greed). It nearly always happened when the metropolitan authority had few means to stop it. Of course, the Colonial Office was ultimately responsible for "pacificating" Tasmania. It can be criticized, fiercely, for not doing better. But that would have involved its being *more* imperialist, in a sense, rather than less. (Or is that too jesuitical?) It was, in a nutshell, private enterprise that did the damage, not the "British state." More generally, it was the rise of global capitalism, with which British imperialism had an ambivalent relationship: facilitating it in some ways, but limiting it in others. That has been a more potent force in modern history generally than colonialism per se—and the main factor behind "cultural genocide," whether in Britain's more resilient colonies or in the South Yorkshire coalfields. It would have got the Tasmanians in the end.

If this book can help put a stop to efforts to overegg the British Empire, made in recent years by leading British politicians, then that is all to the good. It doesn't tell us much more than is already in print about the Tasmanian genocide, as Lawson acknowledges, though its broadly accurate and balanced narrative of that crime will be useful to those unfamiliar with it. As the author insists, however, this is "not a book about Tasmania but about Britain," designed to reveal "the *British* genocidal past" (his italics). On that history, it is certainly thought-provoking. It is an interesting take on the question, tackled from an unusual direction. The Holocaust studies input is valuable. But Lawson's account surely needs to be set in a wider context of colonial history. And whether the British need to feel as guilty as he obviously thinks they should about their "genocidal origins" is surely debatable. Certainly, knowledge of this genocide in Tasmania—and others elsewhere—should prick any feeling of national historical superiority and make the British and others a little more humble when it comes to attacking motes or even Holocausts in the eyes of others. In that regard too, this book performs a valuable service.

Whether it matters to us otherwise, however, depends not only on whether our forebears shared the guilt for these events, but also on the extent to which that guilt can be passed on: the sins of the fathers, and so forth. Then was different from now. It can be argued that we are all far more the products of our contemporary circumstances than of our collective past. Any formulation of national identity ought to be based on that. Myths about the past may play a part in it, which is why it is so important to dismiss the "it couldn't have happened here" one. There is also a case to be made for modern states' making retribution, in the form of compensation, for past national wrongs (though I, as a native of eastern England, am still waiting for the Vikings to pay up). But that doesn't necessarily make those past wrongs—any more than past national virtues—part of *us*, at least without more empirical evidence than Lawson provides here. So far as "alibis" are concerned, we have the best one of all: "Nothing to do with me, guv. I wasn't even born."

Spring Semester 2015

A version of this lecture appeared in the *London Review of Books*, 31 July 2014.

Illustration from *Narrative of an Expedition to Explore the River Zaire, Usually Called the Congo, in South Africa, in 1816* (1818), by James Tuckey

Plate 1. *General Gordon's Last Stand*, George W. Joy (1893)

Plate 2. *The High Commissioner*, Arie Aroch (1966). Photo © The Israel Museum, Jerusalem, by Arraham Hay

Plate 3. *Surrender of Lord Cornwallis*, John Trumbull (1820)

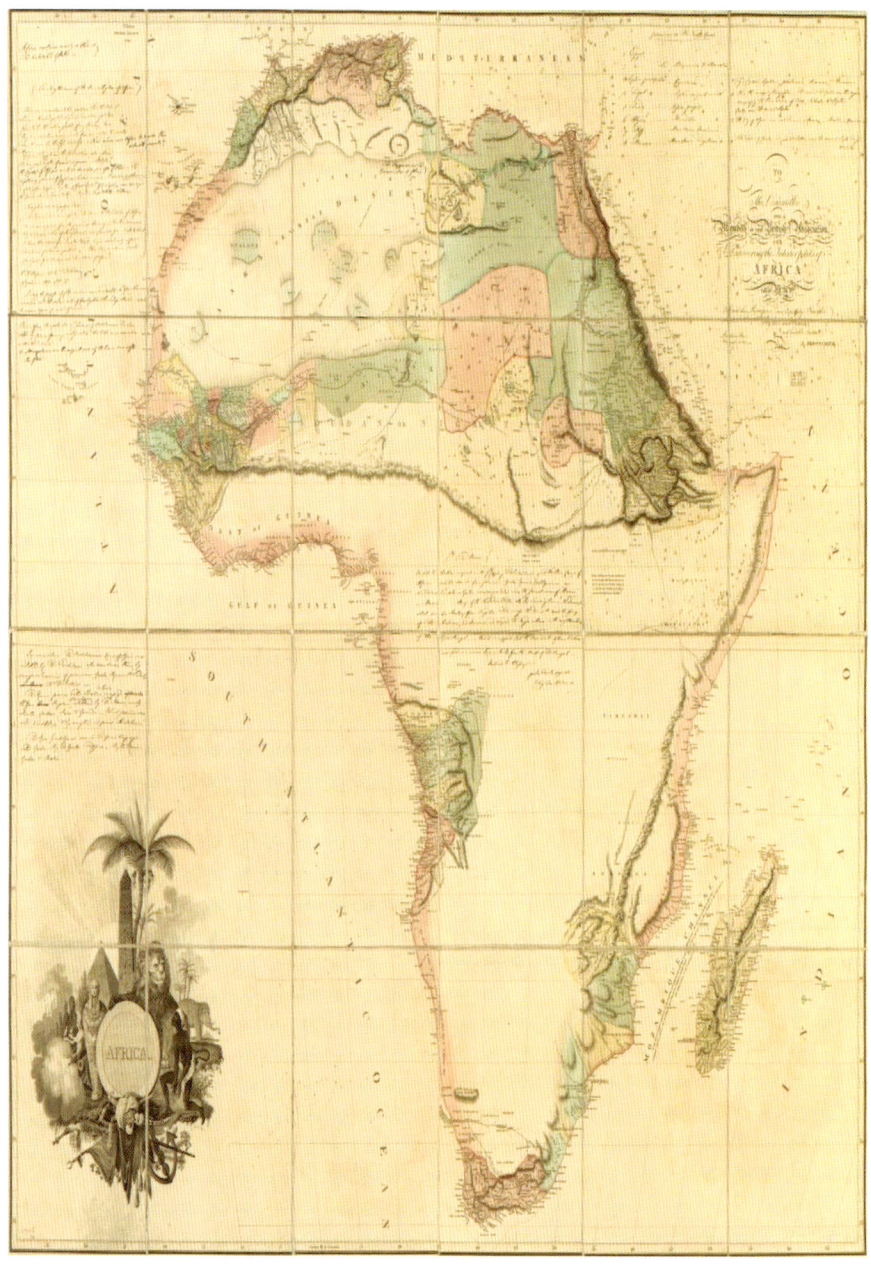

Plate 4. Map of Africa by John Arrowsmith (London, 1802)

16

Lost Expeditions, Lost Histories

DANE KENNEDY

The British exploration of Africa is a story that has been told time and again, often in tiresome detail. There are shelves full of biographies of famous explorers like David Livingstone and Henry Morton Stanley, along with countless other books about British efforts to expose the continent's supposed mysteries. These tales of adventure invariably end in the hero's triumphant return to "civilization" or his brave death in "darkest Africa." Such stories were popular with the Victorian public, and they remain popular today. Yet some of the most ambitious expeditions the British ever launched in Africa received little notice at the time and have attracted almost none since. The main reason for this neglect is that they were ignominious failures. Because they undermine the triumphalist narrative of the West's encounter with Africa, they have been all but erased from historical memory. For this reason alone, they deserve revisiting. They also happen to tell us a great deal about what the British hoped to achieve in Africa, and why their best-laid plans often went awry.

The Napoleonic Wars had barely come to an end when the British government organized and dispatched two large, well-financed expeditions into the African interior. One was a naval expedition whose mission was to sail up the Congo River, break through its barrier of cataracts, and push as far into the interior as possible. The other was an army expedition that planned to march inland from the Guinea coast, establish contact with African states in the interior, and follow the Niger River to its outlet. Europeans still did not know where the Congo River began or the Niger River ended. One of the chief proponents of these expeditions, the Admiralty's Second Secretary, John Barrow, speculated that the two rivers might be one and the same. If so, there was a chance that two expeditions would meet each other on their journeys. That hope, along with all the others that authorities invested in the two expeditions, would be swept away by the implacable realities of Africa.

What we know about the naval expedition comes mainly from the posthumous journals of its commander, James H. Tuckey, and its chief naturalist, Christen Smith, which were published as *Narrative of an Expedition to Explore the River Zaire* (1818). Like many naval expeditions of the era, it was presented as a scientific enterprise, sent out to gather knowledge about the natural world, including its geography, geology, botany, and more. Sir Joseph Banks, president of the Royal Society, one of the founders of the African Association, and the leading proponent of scientific exploration, helped plan the expedition. He recruited Smith, a botanist trained at the University of Copenhagen, and recommended that the famed engineering firm Bolton and Watt build a steamship specially designed to carry its crew up the Congo. The steamship was built, but the weight of the boiler exceeded specifications, making the vessel too unstable for the Atlantic crossing to Africa and its draft too deep for the Congo. So the engine was removed, and the ship refitted for sail. It was accompanied on the journey upriver by a skiff, along with two "double-boats" and several smaller boats. The expedition's scientific agenda, however, remained unchanged. In addition to Smith, the party included a zoologist, a geologist, a marine biologist, and a gardener from Kew. The appendices to the published journals, which include hydrographic observations, an ethnographic vocabulary, and reports on botanical, geological, and zoological specimens, testify to the expedition's scientific ambitions.

At the same time, members of the expedition were motivated by personal agendas. With the Napoleonic Wars at an end, exploration was one of the few avenues by which naval officers like Tuckey could advance their careers. For scientists, too, exploration provided opportunities to establish their reputations, as it did for such later titans of Victorian science as Charles Darwin, Joseph Hooker, and Thomas Huxley. Smith and his team of naturalists leapt at the chance to join the Congo expedition.

Members of the party relished the opportunity to visit a country where the women had a reputation for being, in Tuckey's words, "perfect Otahetians in their manners." That is to say, they were available for sex. Although Tuckey instructed his party to avoid any intimacy with local women, they clearly took no heed. Even before the expedition reached the shores of Africa, Christen Smith reported, "Our young gentlemen of the party dream of the Venuses we should have to admire in the Kingdom of the Congo." To judge from his subsequent journal entries, they were not disappointed. "The women are considered in the light of merchandise," Smith noted, "and a husband generally takes care to make a European pay dear for his bargain." On one occasion, an old woman boarded the ship with her granddaughter, "a little black Venus, the sight of whom kindled an amorous flame in the breasts of several of our gentlemen." On another occasion, a member of the crew "brought on board a weeping girl . . . who was soon followed by another." Even Tuckey was the recipient of a naked girl as a present: she "was very much alarmed," Smith reports, and hid under the captain's bed. What members of the expedition evidently viewed as an opportunity for sex tourism might more accurately be termed a form of sex slavery.

Slavery as it was more conventionally conceived caused the expedition to run into its first serious problem. Africans whose cooperation Tuckey required viewed him with suspicion, fearing that his aim was to shut down the slave trade, on which their livelihoods depended. This was not an unreasonable assumption in light of the British naval patrols that were then sailing in West African waters with precisely this purpose in mind. Tuckey had to give "assurances of not coming to prevent the slave trade, or to make war." Even so, slave merchants at Embomma, the main port at the mouth of the Congo, urged the ruler of the region "not [to] let me ascend the river." One of them "broke out into a violent passion, abusing and calling [the king of England] 'the devil.'" The slave trade had other adverse effects on the expedition. Its chief translator was a freed slave from the region who was able to reunite with his father in Embomma after a decade of enslavement. Although he agreed to accompany the expedition further upriver, he soon deserted, taking four Africa porters with him. For all its claims of scientific neutrality, the expedition found itself inextricably enmeshed in the turmoil caused by the slave trade and its suppression.[1]

The expedition's fatal blow, however, was a result of the region's dreaded disease environment. Tuckey and his men were struggling to bypass the Congo's notorious cataracts by marching overland when, one by one, they began to fall ill. A retreat to the ship was ordered, but then the expedition's porters ran away and people along the river refused to sell them canoes. Tuckey described the return journey as "worse to us than the retreat from Moscow."[2] His journal entries became briefer and less coherent. Soon he was dead. So was Smith, his entire team of naturalists, and over a dozen officers and members of the crew. All had been felled by yellow fever. In the words of John Barrow, who had placed high hopes in the mission, "never were the results of an expedition more melancholy and disastrous."[3]

While Tuckey was a no-nonsense naval officer whose posthumously published journal is a sober and somewhat mundane document, it contains occasional passages of real lyricism that communicate the sense of wonder he must have felt as he ventured into a new and verdant natural world. In an early entry, he describes "the lofty mangroves overhanging the boat, and a variety of palm trees vibrating in the breeze; immense flocks of parrots alone broke the silence of the woods with their chattering, towards sun-set." And the final poignant sentence of his journal is, I think, powerfully evocative: "Flocks of flamingos going to the south denote the approach of the rains."[4]

THE CONGO EXPEDITION WAS A TRAGEDY, but—to borrow Karl Marx's famous dictum—the Niger expedition was a farce. Organized and equipped in the British colony of Sierra Leone, it sailed north to the mouth of the Rio Nunez, from whence it began its march into the interior. The main aims of the expedition were to reach the headwaters of the Niger, follow the course of the river to its conclusion, and establish diplomatic and trading relations with African states along the way. During the Napoleonic Wars, Sir Joseph Banks had urged the British government to lay claim to the Senegambia coast in order to block French advances in the region. Mungo Park's second expedition to West Africa, in 1805, had been intended in part for that purpose: it sought to establish diplomatic and trading ties with the rulers of Sego and Timbuktu and then make its way down the Niger, tempting the Africans they met with the prospects of trade with Britain. Park's fifty-man force rapidly succumbed to disease and violent clashes with Africans, and Park himself apparently drowned in the Niger. The new Niger expedition was meant to redeem Park's sacrifice by fulfilling his mission. It consisted of sixty-nine Royal African Corps troops (forty of them white, twenty-nine black) and thirty-two African civilians, along with an indeterminate number of female camp followers. A caravan of two hundred pack and draft animals carried several field cannon, an arsenal of other weapons, gifts for local rulers, foodstuffs, and other supplies. Scientific considerations took a backseat, though the party did include a German naturalist named Adolphus Kummer.

Major John Peddie, the expedition's original commander, expressed dismay at the quality of his white troops, who exhibited "*vice,* and *dissipation* of every kind." He needed them, however, "to keep the Black men in check."[5] It was not the fear of mutiny that motivated this racial strategy, but rather the fear of desertion. The African recruits had been selected for their knowledge of the languages and customs of the peoples the expedition expected to encounter along the way. The problem was that these men possessed such knowledge because they had been born in those lands and then enslaved, resulting in the cruel odyssey that had led to their current military service. The expedition's officers understandably suspected that "the fidelity of many of them is to be doubted, from the great desire to return to their own country."[6] And, indeed, some of them did just that. One asked for and received an official discharge when he managed to reestablish contact with his mother. Others simply slipped away under cover of darkness, usually taking their firearms with them. The slave trade, then, proved no less problematic to this expedition than it did to the one sent up the Congo.

Disease left its debilitating mark on the expedition as well. Before the explorers left their coastal base camp, Peddie contracted "bilious fever" and died. So did the medical officer. Fevers and dysentery went on to plague the expedition after it set off under a new commander, Captain Thomas Campbell, and a new medical officer, Staff Surgeon Dochard. Surprisingly few men died, however. Dochard prescribed large doses of "the bark" (quinine), which evidently mitigated the effects of malaria. Only five Europeans died on the expedition. (The number of deaths among its African members is not reported.)

While most of the men escaped with their lives, the pack and draft animals did not. Horses, donkeys, bullocks, and camels died off at an alarming rate. They were felled by microbes, parasites, poisonous plants, lions, and even killer bees. This proved to be the expedition's undoing. It had managed to march barely a hundred miles into the interior before losing half its stock. Confronted with this crisis, Campbell ordered the expedition's two field guns and shot buried, and he appealed to local African authorities for porters. The expedition found itself stranded in the Muslim state of Futa Jallon, whose ruler, referred to as the Almamy, proved to be a skilled negotiator. He agreed to provide porters, but then repeatedly withdrew them until the British met his escalating demands for gifts and goods. He also placed crippling restrictions on the route the caravan wanted to take through his territory. It gradually dawned on Campbell that the Almamy had no intention of allowing his party to reach Sego, its intended destination, and for good reason: Sego and Futa Jallon were enemies, and the Almamy feared that the British would supply his opponents with arms. Campbell was informed that the Almamy had received a letter from another Muslim ruler, warning him that "our object in entering the country was the subversion of their religion, for which purpose we had provided ourselves with machines that could kill at any distance."[7] Eventually, Campbell had no choice but to abandon most of the expedition's remaining supplies and retreat to the coast. Once the bedraggled party had returned to its coastal base camp, Campbell promptly died of disease. So did the officer who assumed command in his place, along with Kummer, the naturalist.

End of story? Hardly. In an astonishing act of hubris, the British decided to give it another go. More to the point, they doubled down on the strategy that had proved so disastrous the first time round. Their only adjustment was to set out from the mouth of the Gambia River, roughly a hundred miles north of the previous point of departure. Otherwise, the new iteration of the expedition was almost identical to the previous one. Now under the command of Major William Gray, the expedition relied once again on a large train of pack and draft animals to move its supplies, and once again they succumbed to the environment. Once more the expedition tried to hire porters from the local ruler, in this instance the Almamy of Bondu. This Almamy responded in much the same manner as his counterpart in Futa Jallon: he extorted gifts and other goods from the expedition while working, as Gray noted, "to oppose our further progress." The expeditionary party found itself trapped in Bondu for months as fevers, dysentery, and guinea worms ravaged its men. They soon began to die. In an intriguing aside, Dr. Dochard notes that in some cases he employed "remedies made use of by the natives of Africa, and whenever those were resorted to in time, the disease soon gave way."[8] Unfortunately, he does not specify which disease or what remedies.

In desperation, Gray appealed to the French to help extricate his party from the Almamy's clutches, which they agreed to do. Rather than abandon the mission, however, Gray tried another route to Sego and the Niger, this time through the pagan state of Kaarta, which was at war with Bondu. Once again, his party came under the control of a ruler who had no intention of allowing him to venture beyond his borders. This ruler began to refer to "the whites [as] his tributaries."[9] Once he had squeezed the expedition of its remaining resources, it was permitted to stagger back to the coast. And so the expedition that had first set out six years earlier finally came to an end. Gray noted near the end of his account of the expedition that "whenever I spoke of the Niger, or my anxiety to see it," his African interlocutors "asked me if there were no rivers in the country . . . we inhabit."[10] It was a good question, and he doesn't say how he answered it. But this obsessive preoccupation with the Niger is evident in the tellingly misleading title of his book, *Travels in Western Africa . . . to the River Niger* (1825). In point of fact, neither Gray nor any other member of his party ever set eyes on the Niger.

It was another two decades before the British undertook an expedition into Africa as ambitious as those Tuckey, Peddie, Campbell, and Gray had commanded. What lessons did these costly failures reveal? The most obvious one was that disease posed a serious impediment to British ambitions in Africa. In this regard, the outcome of the Congo expedition in particular reinforced the region's reputation as the "white man's grave." Dochard's apparent success in mitigating the effects of malaria through regular doses of quinine could have given the British cause to suspect that this deadly disease was susceptible to control, but the expedition was so disastrous in so many other respects that no one seems to have taken notice of his discovery. It was not until Dr. William Baikie used quinine to keep his crew alive during an expedition up the Niger River in the 1850s that authorities fully came to appreciate its medical benefits.

The more interesting lessons to be drawn from the failure of the two expeditions were about logistics and local peoples, concerns that the British had seen as separate, but that in fact proved inseparable. While the logistical strategies employed by each expedition were starkly different, they had a common goal: self-sufficiency. For the Tuckey expedition, that goal was pursued by means of a well-stocked ship; for the Peddie-Campbell-Gray expedition, it was the motive behind the large, military-style baggage train of draft and pack animals. The logistical failure of the latter expedition was obvious: when its beasts of burden died, so did its ability to maintain self-sufficiency. Once the expedition turned to Africans for assistance, it became subject to their whims and agendas. The Tuckey expedition seemed far more secure from external forces, at least as long as its members stayed on board their vessel. But all it took for them to see that self-sufficiency slip away was to step on land. The clearest proof of this was when Tuckey and his team had to travel by land in order to bypass the Congo's cataracts.

In both cases, then, the British found it impossible to divorce logistics from local peoples, which meant that they also found it impossible to avoid entanglement in local politics. Local politics, in turn, were imbricated throughout the region in the African slave trade and the British campaign to suppress it. As a result, both the Tuckey and the Peddie-Campbell-Gray expeditions carried political baggage, provoking suspicion among those local peoples and polities whose livelihoods derived at least in part from the slave trade. Both expeditions relied on victims of that trade to assist them as translators, guides, and soldiers, yet their commanders were remarkably naïve about the highly charged political environments it had helped create. Hence, when they found it necessary to appeal to Africans for logistical support, they encountered far more resistance than they seem to have anticipated.

The Peddie-Campbell-Gray expedition faced a further complication that frustrated its ambitions. The region it wanted to pass through was being torn apart by wars between neighboring states. The slave trade was one reason for these wars, but so was the Islamic jihadi movement that was sweeping through West Africa in the early nineteenth century. Islamic states like Futa Jallon and Bondu were at war with pagan states like Kaarta and Sego. It was not in the interest of any of these states to permit a foreign expedition to pass through its precincts into enemy territory. Rather than allow their opponents to gain access to British resources, they squeezed what weapons and wealth they could from the expeditions and took pains to prevent them from making further progress. Campbell and Gray were not unaware of the conflicts tearing the region apart, but they were astonishingly heedless of how their own presence on the scene shaped the political calculations of local rulers. Their claims that they were engaged in the disinterested pursuit of geographic knowledge, and especially knowledge of the Niger, persuaded no one.

In truth, both expeditions were expressions of Britain's imperial ambitions in western Africa. Sir Joseph Banks wanted the British to drive the French from the region, claim control of Senegambia, and establish diplomatic relations and trade agreements with inland African states. John Barrow shared those sentiments and believed the Congo and Niger Rivers would be turned into highways to the interior. Although Gray gave his mission a humanitarian spin, insisting it sought to "improve the condition of our degraded fellow creatures," he believed that the only way that objective could be achieved was by projecting British economic and political influence into the interior of Africa.[11] Tuckey shared this conviction, proclaiming in his journal that "the progress of civilization [in Africa] can only be done by colonization."[12] Yet both expeditions revealed that local conditions created a formidable barrier against British imperial penetration and power. In part, this was due to the African natural environment, notably its disease barrier. But it was also due to the strength, suspicions, and resourcefulness of African states and peoples, who proved capable of obstructing and undermining explorers' objectives at every turn.

The British continued to send expeditions into the interior of West Africa, but they were mainly small parties—usually just two or three Europeans—that relied on indigenous logistical networks and political allies to make their way into the interior, often via the Sahara from North Africa, where the threat of disease was less daunting. When the British finally made another major bid to penetrate the interior of West Africa from its coast, the outcome was no less disastrous than the Tuckey and Peddie-Campbell-Gray expeditions. In 1841, the British government joined with antislavery evangelicals in the exceptionally ambitious and expensive expedition up the Niger River that ended much as Tuckey's Congo expedition had, with many member of the party succumbing to disease. Although the British maintained several colonial enclaves along the Guinea and Windward coast, these possessions did not exert any authority over the interior, and in the 1850s Parliament recommended withdrawing British forces from the region altogether. It was not until the scramble for Africa by competing European powers in the late nineteenth century that the British managed, after a fashion, to fulfill the dream of Banks and Burrow, establishing a colonial presence across significant portions of the region.

What this summary of British involvement in western Africa in the nineteenth century suggests, then, is that Tuckey and Peddie and Campbell and Gray were less anomalous than their subsequent obscurity suggests. Though they did not attain a place in the pantheon of explorer-heroes of West Africa—a group that included the likes of Mungo Park, Hugh Clapperton, John and Richard Lander, and Heinrich Barth—they were no less indicative of British ambitions in the region and of the limitations to those ambitions. They show us that the continent's explorers may have been the harbingers of colonial conquest, but they were hardly successful as its agents.

Spring Semester 2015

1. J. K. Tuckey, *Narrative of an Expedition to Explore the River Zaire* (London, 1818), pp. 110, 109, 266.
2. Ibid., p. 222.
3. Ibid., p. xliii.
4. Ibid., pp. 91, 225.
5. Major John Peddie to Lord Bathurst, 8 Feb. 1816, CO 2/5/26–27, TNA.
6. Captain Thomas Campbell to Lord Bathurst, 7 Jan. 1817, CO 2/5/64.
7. Major William Gray and Staff Surgeon Dochard, *Travels in Western Africa in the Years 1818, 19, 20, and 21 from the River Gambia through Woolli, Bondoo, Galam, Kasson, Kaarta, and Foolidoo to the River Niger* (London, 1825), p. 28.
8. Ibid., p. 140.
9. Ibid., pp. 211, 263.
10. Ibid., p. 349.
11. Ibid., p. ix.
12. Tuckey, *Narrative*, p. 187.

The Reform Club, *Illustrated London News*, November 1890

17

The Reform Club

ROGER BILLIS

To stand in one of the main public rooms of the Reform Club in Pall Mall, London—perhaps the magnificent Saloon, with its busts and recessed portraits of prominent Liberal statesmen of the past, or the capacious Library, where successive Liberal Party leaders and Prime Ministers were appointed—is an experience that reduces some first-time visitors to wonder, awe, and even silence. To convey this experience is perhaps a task best entrusted to a poet of the stature of Siegfried Sassoon, a long-standing member of the club. In a poem composed for Christmas Day 1920, he wrote of the Reform Club:

> In such augustly-thronged environment
> The meanest mind becomes a Parliament.[1]

How appropriate those words seem, since the Westminster Parliament was both the occasion and the inspiration for the founding of the Reform Club. The Great Reform Bill of 1832 bought into force a new attitude to politics and consequently the need for a new kind of private members' club. The anti-Reformers, so to speak, got their retaliation in first. They had been thoroughly outplayed by the Whigs and Radicals in the events leading up the passing of the bill, but quickly responded to the new era and the new challenge. They set up their new club, the Carlton, in 1832 and were soon active from there in canvassing support for their party, known first as the Tories and then, after Peel's Tamworth Manifesto, as the Conservatives. By

1836, they had moved into a sumptuous new building in Pall Mall designed for them by Robert Smirke.

The Reformers were slower off the mark, in part because they comprised a coalition between the landed and predominantly aristocratic Whigs and the more middle-class Radicals, the alliance eventually becoming known as the Liberals. In 1834 they tried to set up something called the Westminster Club, later known as the Westminster Reform Club. It briefly included among its ranks Benjamin Disraeli—then, to his subsequent embarrassment, traversing that much-traveled route from Radical to Conservative—but never attracted a broad enough deputation from the Whig-Radical coalition to become a long-term fixture. The Whigs had their own establishment in the form of Brooks's, that venerable eighteenth-century institution where Charles James Fox had once gambled away £20,000 in a single night, but they were not prepared to share such facilities with the middle-class Radicals, and even if they had, the Radicals, some of whom where Nonconformists, were unwilling to get mixed up with a club that seemed to them a center of wild gambling and somewhat degenerate Regency living.

The Earl of Durham, "Radical Jack" Lambton, who had sat as Lord Privy Seal in Lord Grey's Reform Cabinet, has the strongest claim to the sobriquet "Founder of the Reform Club." In 1835 he wrote to his close ally Joseph Parkes: "Surely the result of this election must convince every Reformer of the necessity of having an Association or Club (call it what you will) in London to counteract the machinations of the Tory Carlton Club."[2] He was joined shortly after by Radicals such as the landed Cornish baronet Sir William Molesworth and Joseph Hume. They formed a group that determined, at a meeting held on Tuesday, 2 February 1836, there should be a Reform Club. Five days later at a meeting held at the residence of the Liberal Chief Whip, Edward Ellice, in Carlton House Terrace, the group resolved: "That a Club be formed to comprise all class of Reformers . . . That the said Club be called 'The Reform Club.'"[3]

Why was such a club seen as necessary by the leading Liberal politicians of the day? First, it was essential to have a common meeting ground for a party that was essentially a coalition. Second, because the facilities for Members of Parliament, the backbenchers at least, were fairly primitive at Westminster, a condition unchanged until the building of Portcullis House in the late twentieth century. Its members needed a place nearby where they could converse, socialize, dine, plan, and plot, and from which they could return to Parliament whenever a vote was called.

Another important raison d'être for a new political club such as the Reform was the registration of voters. The 1832 Reform Act had broadened the franchise, but it was not sufficient simply to be eligible to vote; the act required voters to be registered for a period of six months in the case of freeholders and twelve months for everyone else qualified. The club could act as a general headquarters from which the party leaders could coordinate activities in the constituencies and direct central canvassing during elections.

THE TERM "CLUB GOVERNMENT," used to describe how the nation's affairs were conducted in this period, was coined by Edward Ellice, but it was Norman Gash who, in his *Politics in the Age of Peel* (1953), really defined the expression: "Indeed it would be true to say that the period between the first and second Reform Acts was as much the golden age of the political club as of the private member [of Parliament]."[4]

In the founding of the Reform Club, the Radicals had taken the lead, but if they believed that, as a result, they would gain the upper hand in their alliance with the Whigs, they were to be sadly disappointed. It is instructive to quote Professor Gash again.

> The radicals, particularly those whose forcing tactics had been responsible for making the long-debated project a tangible fact, were naturally gratified at the success of the venture. Yet its very success was a powerful counterweight to the purely radical programme. They had dreamed of capturing the whigs; it is at least arguable that they themselves were ensnared in the net they had woven. . . . Reluctant victims of Parkes' guile as they had seemed to be, it is possible that the whigs in the end could count the foundation of the Reform Club as one of the greatest single factors in prolonging the life of the whig parliamentary party. If Molesworth and Parkes had seriously envisaged the Reform Club as a kind of Trojan horse within the whig camp, the horse was soon docilely eating from the whig manager.[5]

Thus, a club that opened in May 1836 in temporary accommodations came to boast a thousand members with twenty Radicals and fifteen Whigs on the committee, most of the Cabinet being members, and even the more recalcitrant Whig grandees such as Lord Lansdowne joining within a year or two. This was a trend that continued throughout the nineteenth century. Every Liberal Prime Minister from Melbourne (1836–41) to Lloyd George (1916–22) was a member of the Reform, as were a high proportion of their Cabinet ministers, backbench MPs, and other supporters.

A category of temporary member enabled overseas political figures sympathetic to the club's principles to be admitted during their time in England. This opportunity was taken up by two future American presidents: James Buchanan, while American Minister in London in 1850, and Franklin D. Roosevelt, while attending negotiations in London in 1919 after the First World War. A former president, Ulysses S. Grant, was honored with a special dinner at the Reform Club in the late 1870s.

It is important to understand that a nineteenth-century political club was not a modern think tank or a pressure group. It did not engage in fund-raising. The Reform was primarily a social rendezvous for all shades of opinion in the more progressive political party. To perform this function effectively, it needed a first-rate clubhouse, a congenial atmosphere, a well-stocked library, and good food and wine.

Finding a permanent headquarters was one of the key early tasks. To this end, the committee commissioned a competition between five of the leading architects of the day, inviting them to submit plans for a new building with a frontage of 142 feet at 104 Pall Mall. The winning design was submitted by Sir Charles Barry, the architect of the Houses of Parliament. The chairman of the Building Committee was Sir Benjamin Hall, the creator of Parliament's famous clock, Big Ben, to which he gave his name. Barry's original design called for an open courtyard, soon modified into a covered hall studded with individual pieces of diamond-shaped glass. It was an interesting combination: the courtyard was ultimately based on classical precedents such as the Palazzo Farnese in Rome, though adapted to English models, but the roof was entirely innovative, the glass being a sort of Victorian high-tech product.

The main rooms on the ground floor included the Saloon, a spacious hall with a colonnade of twenty Ionic and Corinthian columns and a tessellated pavement with mosaics; the Coffee Room (or restaurant); and off it a private dining room known as the Cabinet Room because, allegedly, Asquith when Prime Minister would summon his Cabinet colleagues there. On the first floor were the Library (originally the Drawing Room), which runs the whole length of the frontage, the Card Room, and the Committee Room, where the general committee could oversee the affairs of the club. Upstairs were two floors of chambers (or bedrooms), and below the Saloon floor were two floors of kitchens, bathrooms, and other facilities.

For all this magnificence, including fittings, the club had originally allowed a budget of £37,500, subsequently increased to £44,000. It was not long, however, before the committee was making expensive alterations to the specifications. Barry spent three years trying to obtain additional remuneration for the altered design before the matter had to be submitted to arbitration, in which he was successful. His clients could afford to admit that their architect had brought off something uniquely satisfying. Here are two judgments, the first by Barry's son and biographer: "Other buildings have risen since on the same or even on a grander scale, both as to size and magnificence of ornament; but still it may be doubted whether its high position has been impaired."[6] Second, the authoritative publication *The Survey of London* records: "To sum up, he created a prototype for the great political Clubhouse, often emulated but never equalled."[7]

Once ensconced in their new home, the members intended not to stint themselves on food or drink. In this cause, they recruited as head chef Alexis Soyer, who later enlarged his fame by writing some celebrated cookery books and organizing some of the club's most famous political banquets.

The kitchens of the Reform Club became one of the sights of London, and Soyer was on hand to provide color, drama, exotic costume, and repartee. As W. M. Thackeray records:

> It was a grand sight to behold him in his dressing-gown composing a menu. He always sat down and played the piano for some time before. If interrupted he remonstrated pathetically. Every great artist he said had need of solitude to perfectionate his works.
>
> Soyer loved fine clothes and when he took the air wore a light-green frock coat, a crimson velvet waistcoat with blue buttons, trousers with a large check pattern, boots with tops of shiny leather, a gold-embroidered cap and a gilt cane . . . He once said, "Cooking is organisation" and at the Reform Club he achieved a nine days' wonder.[8]

Another source provides an example of Soyer's wit: "One day when Lord Melbourne was inspecting the cuisine of the Reform Club and jocosely said to M Soyer, 'How is it you have such a number of pretty female assistants?' 'My Lord,' said Soyer, 'we do not want plain cooks here.'"[9]

With Soyer in charge of cuisine, the club could provide first-class meals in the Coffee Room, grand political banquets to celebrate parliamentary achievements or strengthen alliances, and private dinners for the more epicurean members. No wonder one newspaper wrote: "The impression grows on us that the man of his age is neither Sir Robert Peel nor Lord John Russell, nor even Ibrahim Pasha, but Alexis Soyer."[10]

All the ingredients were assembled for the Reform Club to occupy a position of power, influence, and pleasure in those prosperous and sunny years of the mid-Victorian age. It set up a Political Committee chiefly to promote the political organization of the Liberal Party and to arbitrate between Liberal candidates at parliamentary elections. No one sums up the mood better than Roy Jenkins: "Progressive politics accompanied by solid, even lavish bourgeois comfort was the key note."[11]

Not everyone, however, rejoiced among the visual splendors, general feasting, and air of affluence. The Nonconformist conscience was from time to time challenged, and its worthier members confessed sometimes to a spirit of unease. For example, on entering the Reform Club, the secretary of the Anti–Corn Law League, Mr. Rawson, turned to the radical politician John Bright and exclaimed: "John, John, how can we keep honest if we live in palaces such as this?"[12]

WITH THE CLUB ENTRENCHED as the home of Victorian Liberalism, what could possibly have knocked it off its perch? Part of the general background was the undercurrent of social unrest in England beginning with the agrarian distress of the late 1870s, which brought down Disraeli's second Conservative administration. This led to strikes and growing discontent among the working classes, which in due course prompted the formation of the Labour Party and the passing from the scene of Liberal governments.

The extent to which the Reform Club failed to adapt is exemplified by the formation in 1882 of the National Liberal Club, which, as the name suggests, tried to bring Liberals from the whole country together in a way that the Reform had never accomplished. But how could the National Liberal, with its inferior building and subsidiary location outside clubland, be a challenge? In fact, neither social unrest nor the foundation of a rival club could prepare the Reform for the cataclysmic blow about to fall.

On the 20 March 1886, Joseph Chamberlain, President of the Local Government Board, resigned from the Cabinet in opposition to Prime Minister Gladstone's proposal that Ireland be granted Home Rule. The ensuing general election, four months later, was lost by the Home Rule Liberals. One commentator wrote of Chamberlain: "Twelve months ago he was the bugbear of the Tories and Tory mothers, it was said, used his name as their bogey for frightening naughty children. Today he is their darling and the Times sings Te Deums in his praise."[13]

Chamberlain remains fascinating. It is often said that Churchill was the only man to rat on both parties, but Radical Joe came close to claiming that distinction as well: first on Gladstone and the Liberals over Home Rule, and later on Balfour and the Conservatives over Tariff Reform. His actions on Home Rule split the Liberal Party and the membership of the Reform Club. With his help, the Home Rule Bill lost by thirty votes, forcing Gladstone to seek a new mandate by going to the polls. The election of 100 Liberal Unionist MPs ensured that Lord Salisbury and the Conservatives took office.

There must have been some uneasy moments at the Reform Club between certain members of the Liberal Party's opposing wings, although that was to be expected in any organization formed around a coalition. There were very few resignations at first from the club, and some Liberal Unionist members continued in influential positions. For example, Sir Henry James (the lawyer—later Lord James of Hereford) served in Salisbury's third Conservative administration from 1895 to 1900 while at the same time being a prominent member of the Reform Club's Political Committee and a trustee of the club.

One manifestation of rivalry between the two wings occurred in the so-called Great Portrait Race. The Home Rulers were desperate to have a portrait at the Reform of their hero, W. E. Gladstone, whereas the Liberal Unionists craved a likeness of their leader, Lord Hartington. Each side raised subscriptions, and such was the rivalry that both candidates ran "neck and neck finishing, as one sporting member put it, so that an umbrella would have covered both." Today, a modest reconciliation has been accomplished: both portraits hang on the same wall in the Garden Room.

From 1895, some of the Liberal Unionists agreed to sit in the Conservative administration, and this led to an Indian summer for the political influence of the Reform Club. Once again, Joe Chamberlain was the cause. First, his work as Colonial Secretary made imperialism the major issue of the day. The Liberals realized that they too had to have an imperial policy. Under the Liberal imperialists—predominantly Asquith, Grey, and Haldane—they moved away from the more insular tendencies of Gladstone's day. Second, opposition to Chamberlain's policy of tariff reform and imperial preference was something round which most true Liberals could unite. The thought of combatting higher food prices even attracted some Conservatives, and Winston Churchill crossed the floor to leave the Conservatives and join the Liberals.

These last purely Liberal governments in the period 1905 to 1915 saw a reassertion of the political role of the Reform Club. In particular, it became confirmed as the venue where important ceremonial events and controversial issues involving the Liberal Party were to be settled. The first party leader in that era was the much-underrated

Sir Henry Campbell-Bannerman, who insisted that the party meeting to confirm his installation in that position should be held in the Library of the Reform Club. C-B, as he was often known, expressed his views firmly in a letter to Asquith in 1899: "To go to another Club would be a slap on the cheek of the Reform and we should get all our men blackballed!"[14]

C-B got his way. Two years later, when his leadership of the party was in difficulties, he called a meeting of all Liberal MPs for 9 July 1901 at the Reform Club to face down his critics. One chronicler records: "The meeting at the Reform Club reached a conclusion generally expected. . . . Everyone was in the highest spirits, Sir Henry Campbell-Bannerman was greeted with enthusiasm, and a vote of confidence was unanimously passed."[15]

It was therefore inevitable that in 1908, when Asquith succeeded the dying C-B, the prime ministerial blessing had again to be performed at the Reform Club. One of Asquith's biographers, J. A. Spender, records: "This ceremony was duly performed at the Reform Club on 30th April when Asquith made his first speech as Prime Minister and leader of the party. He spoke briefly and modestly, first paying tribute to his predecessor."[16]

In 1915 the Liberals were forced into a coalition with the Conservatives in order to improve the management of the First World War, and with that event, the last purely Liberal government came to an end. In the poignant circumstances in which Asquith lost power altogether in December of the following year, he felt obliged to return to the Reform to make a valedictory address to leading Liberals and formally to lay down his burden. His successor, Lloyd George, although a Liberal, was not then a member of the Reform, so there was no ceremony for the laying on of hands at the club. An era had passed; the Reform Club was no longer the favorite haunt of the ruling party, and in 1926 it changed its description from being a club for "Liberals" to the rather more nebulous term, in a twentieth-century context, "Reformers."

THE DEMISE OF THE POLITICAL CLUB opened up interesting possibilities. The building was too important and attractive to be neglected. First in were the writers. In fact, throughout the nineteenth century the Reform had been a shining beacon for leading writers, chief among them being W. M. Thackeray and Henry James. Thackeray was an enthusiastic clubman, joining the Garrick and the Athenaeum as well as the Reform. At 104 Pall Mall, he cheerfully enjoyed all that the club had to offer. For example: "It was said that on one occasion, observing beans and bacon on the evening dinner list, he cancelled without hesitation a dinner engagement elsewhere, on the ground that 'he had met an old friend he had not seen from many a long day.'"[17]

Henry James, affectionately dubbed the "American Member," was elected to membership in 1878, an event that he celebrated in true Jamesian style in a letter to his father: "At all events, j'y suis, j'y reste—for ever and a day. It is a precious good thing for me—something of the kind had become indispensable—and makes me feel strangely and profoundly at home here."[18] He did indeed stay at the Reform, taking a room in chambers and for many years residing at the club in what he called his "perch in Pall Mall." James's membership of the Reform was a vital part of his anglicization, which led him, just under a century ago, to become naturalized as a British subject because of his support for Britain's war effort, an event that made it possible for King George V to award him the Order of Merit shortly before his death.

In the years leading up to and after the First World War, an invasion of writers took place. Arnold Bennett was already a member, and his three-volume journals are full of descriptions of club life and encounters there with other famous writers. Here is one extract:

> Wednesday, September 10th [1924]
>
> TS Eliot came to see me at the Reform Club last night, between two of my engagements . . . Pale, quiet, well assured. He works at Lloyds Bank, in a department of his own, "digesting" foreign financial and economic journals. Interesting work he said, but he would prefer to be doing something else. He edits the Criterion, and writes, in the evenings. I said to him, "I want to ask you a question. It isn't an insult. Were the notes to 'Wastelands' [sic] a lark or serious? I thought they were a skit."[19]

By then the floodgates had opened, and writer members included Siegfried Sassoon, Sir Arthur Conan Doyle, H. G. Wells, E. M. Forster, and later on Denton Welch and Simon Raven. It is impossible to generalize about their experiences as club members. Simon Raven reported: "It had a good library, the staff were attentive and it cost a lot less to stay there than a decent hotel." It was also en route to his favorite massage parlor on the other side of Pall Mall.

Along with the writers came the "Press Gang," a group of influential journalists who were editors of daily newspapers and weekly journals and who had their own "round table" in the Coffee Room. In the 1950s an increasingly prevalent and influential group of members came from the senior ranks of the Home Civil Service, the so-called Whitehall mandarins. In his memoirs, Lord Chandos (the former Oliver Lyttleton) lays bare the politician's approach to these encounters: "It is imperative to be on such terms with your senior officials as to know what is being agreed or disputed at lunch in the Reform Club or the Athenaeum by the heads of the Civil Service. An early and unequivocal statement of your own policy often enables your Permanent Secretary to prepare the ground over the sherry in the Club."[20]

Sometimes, however, the politicians could get their own back in minor but short-lived ways. Nigel Lawson recalls how, when Chancellor of the Exchequer, he and his fellow Cabinet minister at the Treasury, John Moore, entered into a sporting contest with two Treasury knights: "Much to their consternation, however, on the first occasion the [snooker] match was held during my time John Moore and I succeeded in beating Middleton and Burns. The two mandarins took care that such a perverse result did not occur again, setting aside time for intensive practice at the Reform Club, that favourite watering-hole of the senior Civil Service, grand in scale and austere in character, with a name that appears to satisfy their modest appetite for change."[21]

Membership was enlivened in the austere times of the 1940s and 1950s by the odd louche character, such as the Cambridge spy Guy Burgess. Legend has it that having been tipped off that investigation and arrest were imminent, he visited the club for one last time before driving down to Surrey, collecting Maclean, and then fleeing into the arms of his Russian controller.

Even though this was the era of economists and mandarins, reform was still in the air. The practice of blackballing, which had excited so much interest in the past, seems to have been phased out in 1932. After that, the candidate books simply record "candidate withdrawn" (usually at the instance of the proposer) instead. Also, the club became more open to use for private functions and the dinners of societies affiliated with the club. Hugh Dalton's diaries are full of entries concerning gatherings at the Reform, with guests such as the distinguished economists Lionel Robbins and John Maynard Keynes. Friedrich Hayek was a member for over fifty years. Leading Labour frontbenchers, including the future prime ministers Harold Wilson and James Callaghan, attended gatherings.

In 1983, the Library was officially made available for private functions. A number of Reform Club societies, including The Austerity (founded 1947), the Economies and Current Affairs Group (founded 1970), and the Thackeray Society (history and literature, founded 1982) began holding regular luncheons and dinners at the club, as well as the Political Committee, whose role has already been discussed.[22]

With the income from these functions, and with funds raised from other sources, such as legacies, members' loan schemes, and accumulated surpluses, the club was able to carry out a series of improvements and renovations to the fabric of the building, including repair of the glass dome and perimeter roofs, the conversion of rooms on the third floor into modern bedrooms and bathrooms, and the complete refurbishment of the magnificent Library.

Probably the most important step occurred in 1981, when the Reform became the first major London club of its kind to admit women on equal terms. Since then, female members have played important roles within the club as committee members, as honorary members, and, in the case of two women, as chairmen and trustees of the club.

IT SEEMS APPROPRIATE TO CONCLUDE with an account of Winston Churchill's short-lived involvement with the Reform Club. His premature departure was, we might say, the mother of all club resignations.

Churchill joined the Reform in the heyday of his period as a Liberal government minister. He had become acquainted with a certain Baron de Forest, who was the adopted son of an Austrian financial wizard and who was elected MP for West Ham North in London. In the same year, de Forest embarked on a disastrous course that was irretrievably to tarnish his standing in polite society: he sued his mother-in-law for slander! Despite the ministrations of no less than four King's Counsel (senior barristers) on his case, including the legendary F. E. Smith, de Forest's only witness failed to corroborate his allegations and the suit collapsed before luncheon on the first day. That farcical outcome led to declarations of open warfare by members of any club against the nomination of de Forest for membership. In 1913, Churchill, as First Lord of the Admiralty, seconded by Lloyd George as Chancellor of the Exchequer, unwisely proposed de Forest for membership of the Reform, with the inevitable consequences.

Churchill's response to de Forest's blackballing was swift and emphatic. On 29 January 1913, he tendered his resignation from the club in a letter to the secretary, being careful to express both his regret at a step that he felt obliged to take and his gratitude for having being elected in the past. For good measure, he acted as proxy for Lloyd George (who later returned as an honorary member on becoming Prime Minister), tendering his resignation too, a procedure not recognized in club rules. But then, as we know, Churchill never did anything by halves. Nearly thirty years later, when Churchill conducted his famous correspondence with President Franklin D Roosevelt to forge the special relationship between America and Britain in the defense of freedom, did either of them at any point recall that one of the things they shared was past membership of the same London Club? I wonder.

Fall Semester 2014

1. Reform Club Archive. The full text appears in Russell Burlingham and Roger Billis, *The Reform Club in History and Literature* (London, 2005), pt. 1.
2. C. W. New, *Lord Durham: A Biography of John George Lambton, First Earl of Durham* (Oxford, 1929), p. 275.
3. Reform Club Archive.
4. Norman Gash, *Politics in the Age of Peel: A Study in the Technique of Parliamentary Representation, 1830–1850* (London, 1953), p. 393
5. Ibid., p. 411.
6. Alfred Barry, *The Life and Works of Sir Charles Barry* (London, 1867), p. 96.
7. F. H. W. Sheppard, gen. ed., *The Survey of London*, vol. 29 (London, 1960), p. 412.
8. Cecil Woodham-Smith, "The Man Who Invented Modern Cooking," *Harper's Magazine*, Dec. 1958, p. 33.
9. F. Volant and J. R. Warren, eds., *Memoirs of Alexis Soyer* (London, 1859), p. 68.
10. *Globe*, 1841.
11. Roy Jenkins, "Edwardian Brooks's," in Philip Ziegler and Desmond Seward, eds., *Brooks's: A Social History* (London, 1991), p. 70.
12. Algernon West, *Recollections, 1832–1886*, vol. 1 (London, 1899), p. 303.
13. *The Popular Guide to the House of Commons and Record of the Election of 1886, Pall Mall Gazette Extra* no. 29 (London, 1886).
14. John Wilson, *C.B.: A Life of Sir Henry Campbell-Bannerman* (London, 1973), p. 292.
15. Henry W. Lucy, *The Balfourian Parliament, 1900–1905* (London, 1906), p. 94.
16. J. A. Spender, *Life of Henry Herbert Asquith, Lord Oxford and Asquith*, vol. 1 (London, 1932), p. 229.
17. Ralph Nevill, *London Clubs: Their History and Treasures* (London, 1911), p. 234.
18. Henry James, *Letters*, vol. 2: *1875–1883*, ed. Leon Edel (Cambridge, Mass., 1978), p. 176.
19. Newman Flower, ed., *The Journals of Arnold Bennett, 1921–1928* (London, 1933), pp. 51–52.
20. Oliver Lyttelton, *The Memoirs of Lord Chandos* (London, 1962), p. 349.
21. Nigel Lawson, *The View from No. 11* (London, 1992), p. 319.
22. The author is indebted to Simon Blundell, the club's librarian, for information contained in this paragraph and elsewhere.

Tsar Nicholas II and King George V, 1913

18

The British Monarchy and the Tsar

JANE RIDLEY

Tsar Nicholas II signed his abdication in the imperial train at Pskov on 15 March 1917. The news did not come as a surprise to Nicky's first cousin George V, who had read Foreign Office dispatches from Sir George Buchanan, the British ambassador in Petrograd, chronicling the autocracy's inexorable slide toward catastrophe. The King's reaction was to draft a telegram of support (19 March 1917): "Events of last week have deeply distressed me. My thoughts are constantly with you and I shall always remain your true and devoted friend, as you know I have been in the in the past."[1] This innocently worded message was held up by the Russian Provisional Government, which hesitated to deliver it, fearing that the King's words would be misinterpreted by extremists and used to damage the Tsar. In consequence, Buckingham Palace ordered the telegram to be canceled, and it never reached Nicholas.

Consider the two cousins. Famously photographed wearing naval uniforms and standing arm in arm at Cowes in 1909 on Nicholas's last visit to Britain, they were so similar that (like their mothers forty years before) they were often mistaken for each other. When Nicholas came to London for George's wedding in 1893, someone asked George whether he had come especially for the Duke of York's wedding. "I am the Duke of York," replied George, "and I suppose I should attend my own wedding."[2] Both were small (George was five foot five or six), trim, and bearded, with the exceptionally small heads characteristic of the Danish family. ("Are you aware that Alix has the smallest head ever seen?" wrote a dismayed Queen Victoria of her daughter-in-law.)[3]

From their shared childhood holidays with their Danish grandparents at Fredensborg, both had been imprinted with a devotion to private, simple family life, and they saw the official world of courts as an unwelcome intrusion. "Dear old Sandringham," sighed George, "the place I love better than any in the world."[4] Both cousins were devoted to and in awe of their larger-than-life fathers, the bearlike Alexander III and the overweight, glamorous Edward VII. Neither received any preparation for becoming sovereign from their fathers. When Nicky acceded in 1894, he wrote: "I am not prepared to be a Tsar. I never wanted to become one. I know nothing of the business of ruling. I have no idea of even how to talk to the ministers."[5]

Both labored conscientiously at their paperwork for many hours each day. They each kept diaries, which startle for the almost schoolboy simplicity of expression. Both married women who were larger than they; but whereas Nicholas allowed himself to be dominated by his histrionic, manipulative wife Alexandra (who was also a first cousin of George's), George kept his wife, the intelligent, shy Mary of Teck, firmly in submission. Both were chain-smokers. Nicholas, age forty-eight, suffered a coronary occlusion on 11 March 1917.

Their last meeting was at the wedding of Kaiser Wilhelm II's daughter in Berlin in May 1913—that final gathering of the doomed dynasties of Europe. They corresponded throughout the war, and in May 1915, George told Margot Asquith that the Tsar was "the best, straightest, most clear and decided man I know."[6] (Edward VII, by contrast, thought Nicholas weak as water.)

None of this was enough to save the Tsar.

On 22 March 1917, a week after Nicholas's abdication, Miliukov, the Foreign Minister in the liberal Provisional Government, approached Buchanan, the British Ambassador. Somerset Maugham, who was sent to Petrograd as an intelligence officer in June 1917, described Buchanan, beautifully dressed in a perfectly cut frock coat, dining in Old World splendor in an embassy that resembled a great country house: "On the other side of the wall was a restless, turbulent population that might at any moment break into bloody revolution, while not 200 hundred miles away men in the trenches were sheltering in their dug-outs from the bitter cold and pitiless bombardment."[7]

Miliukov told Buchanan that he was "most anxious" to get the Emperor out of Russia at once, since "extremists were exciting opinion against His Majesty." Would the King and his government grant asylum in England? Buchanan noted, "The departure of the Emperor would certainly strengthen the Russian Government and help matters to settle down."[8]

Prime Minister Lloyd George met Lord Stamfordham, the King's private secretary, on the same day, and the Foreign Office then wired Buchanan, "readily" offering asylum to the Emperor and Empress in England.[9] When Miliukov received this offer from Buchanan on 23 March, he replied that no final decision had yet been taken. Extremists were agitating against the Tsar leaving Russia. He was now reunited with his family at Tsarkoe Selo, where his children had the measles. He refused to travel until they recovered.

Nicholas shared with his cousin George what Harold Nicolson described as "a bad habit of being ridiculous."[10] In George's case, German measles stopped him attending Queen Victoria's funeral. The measles was the Romanovs' undoing. The moment—that brief chink in the first week or so after Nicholas's abdication—was lost. On 30 March, Stamfordham told Foreign Secretary Balfour that "the King had been thinking much" about whether it was "advisable" for the Tsar and family to live in Britain.[11] Balfour replied that it was not now possible to withdraw the invitation, to which Stamfordham himself had agreed.[12] By then, however, the King's mind was made up. On 6 April, Stamfordham fired off two letters to the foreign secretary. "Every day, the King is becoming more concerned about the Emperor and Empress coming to this country," wrote Stamfordham.[13] The presence of the Tsar "would be strongly resented by the public" and would "compromise" the King and Queen: "We must be allowed to withdraw from the consent previously given to the Russian government's proposal."[14] Stamfordham then descended upon 10 Downing Street for an interview with Lloyd George.

Stamfordham and the King had their way. The politicians demurred. On 13 April, the Foreign Office wired Buchanan that it was preferable for the Tsar to go to France: "There are indications that a considerable anti-monarchical movement is developing here, including personal attacks on the King."[15] Refusal of asylum suited Lloyd George too, since it would make dealing easier with the new Russian government. Buchanan, who had received the same information from the Labour MP Will Thorne, on a delegation to Russia, entirely agreed that if "there is any danger of anti-monarchist movement, it would be far better that the ex-Emperor should not come to England"—this in spite of the fact that the Russian government still wished the Tsar to leave as soon as possible.[16]

When this story was published by Kenneth Rose in his biography of George V in 1983, it caused a furor. The sources were all in the public domain—I have constructed the narrative above entirely from documents in the National Archives' Foreign Office files (the crucial FO 800/205 is digitized—a gripping read). Astonishingly, historians had failed to notice them.

The King's abandonment of his cousin was made more shameful by the cover-up that followed. When George V learned of the murder of the Tsar (18 July 1918), he expressed no remorse. He wrote in his diary (25 July) that he was "devoted to Nicky."[17] On 31 August, the Foreign Office received a telegram giving details of a heap of charred bones that had been found in a mineshaft twenty miles north of Ekaterinburg. Among the ashes were shoe buckles, corset ribs, diamonds, and platinum crosses that had been identified by a former member of the household as belonging to Alicky, her daughters, and the Czarevitch. The telegram spelled out the implication: "It is feared that they were all shot with the Czar and then cremated." A summary was sent to Stamfordham, "omitting gruesome details."[18] The King commented in his diary (31 August): "It is too horrible and shows what fiends those Bolshevists are. For poor Alicky, perhaps it was best so. But those poor innocent children!"[19] George's apparent inability to see any connection between his refusal of asylum and the murder of the Romanovs seems bizarrely amnesiac.

As for Lloyd George, in his *War Memoirs* he was persuaded by Maurice Hankey, the Cabinet secretary, to withdraw a chapter on the evacuation of the Tsar, and in the published version he blamed the Russian government for the refusal of the invitation and made no mention of the King. His biographer John Grigg suggests that his loyalty on the issue goes "some way towards atoning for his often cavalier treatment of the King while he was Prime Minister."[20]

These events raise important questions. Why did the Palace change its mind over asylum? What was the role of Lord Stamfordham? What was the relationship between the Palace and Lloyd George?

STAMFORDHAM REMARKED IN JUNE 1917 that there was no sovereign to whom the truth was more fearlessly told than King George: "There is no Socialistic newspaper, no libellous rag that is not read and marked and shown to the King if they contain any criticisms friendly or unfriendly of His Majesty and the Royal Family."[21] Stamfordham's intelligence gathering has been documented by the historian Frank Prochaska. One of the socialistic papers read by Stamfordham was *Justice* (5 April 1917), which carried an article by Henry Hyndman warning the King against inviting his "disowned" Russian cousins to Britain. This was brandished by Stamfordham in the face of the Prime Minister when he visited Downing Street on 10 April. Stamfordham compiled a file that he titled "Unrest in the Country." It contained letters from a group of advisers, notably John Watts-Ditchfield, the Bishop of Chelmsford. On 5 April 1917, the Bishop wrote to warn the King against backing the Tsar and advised him to meet the Labour MP Will Thorne, who planned to visit Russia and who, as noted above, strongly opposed giving asylum.

Prochaska does not make the connection, but it is surely no coincidence that Stamfordham penned the two decisive letters to Balfour, changing his mind on the asylum question, on the day that he received Watts-Ditchfield's advice. In other words, the King's momentous decision to ditch the Tsar was based on intelligence received from an obscure bishop and a Labour backbench MP. How had this come about?

Watts-Ditchfield came to the attention of the Palace as evangelizing vicar of the East End parish of Bethnal Green. Lloyd George had no time for him. He considered giving political opinions to the King to be "outside his functions," and told Stamfordham that the bishop was "an unconscious tool of the pacifist element" and that his letters to the King were "an unconstitutional appeal to the Sovereign over the head of his ministers."[22] To which Stamfordham huffily replied: "It is only in these ways that Kings can learn what is being said and thought about them in worlds with which they are out of touch."[23] In other words, Stamfordham felt the need to set up his own intelligence networks because he was receiving none from the government.

Cold war had broken out between the Palace and Number 10. Lloyd George admitted that he treated the King "abominably" at this time.[24] "I wonder what my little German friend has got to say to me!" he remarked when summoned to the Palace.[25] Letters went unanswered and appointments forgotten. Lloyd George's secretaries made Stamfordham wait on a hard wooden chair when he came to Number 10. In the Prime Minister's defense, the King must have seemed maddeningly out of touch and fussy. Stamfordham's file in Lloyd George's papers bristles with letters complaining about the Prime Minister's failure to consult the King over matters such as Honors lists or the appointment to the peerage or the Cabinet of such unsuitable figures as Max Aitken (Lord Beaverbrook). The King complained that he no longer received the Prime Minister's letter informing him of Cabinet discussions; instead, he was merely sent the War Cabinet minutes. It sometimes seems as if the King was oblivious that Britain was fighting for its very survival and that the Prime Minister was working twenty-one hour days.

The monarch could have achieved far more by working with his ministers than by opposing them. Buckingham Palace in 1917 was isolated and weak. Within that bubble, however, the royal advisers held sway.

Step forward Lord Stamfordham. A slight, bald man, sixty-eight in 1917, Stamfordham was the son of a Northumbrian vicar. That background perhaps gave him a certain prim austerity and an exaggerated respect for the views of churchmen such as Watts-Ditchfield. He was close to Archbishop Davidson, who was a significant and underestimated royal adviser.

The relationship between Stamfordham and the King is one of the great enigmas of the reign. George's first biographer, John Gore, considered Stamfordham "the great figure in the whole story."[26] Roger Fulford praised Stamfordham for making "an enormous (though insufficiently explored) contribution to the structure of monarchy and to the Government of the country."[27] George himself declared that Stamfordham "taught me how to be King."[28] As Arthur Bigge, he had served Queen Victoria as Private Secretary, teaching himself to write in a bold black script on papers that he dried in an oven for the Queen's failing eyesight. Though not clever, he was known as a man of "simplicity and honesty"; his cautiousness earned him the nickname "Better not."[29]

But there was another side to Stamfordham.

When the news of the Tsar's murder came through, an anxious letter whizzed from Stamfordham's bold black pen to Foreign Secretary Balfour, asking whether the King should attend the Memorial Service of his first cousin and fellow sovereign. Stamfordham worried that this would be seen as antidemocratic and sympathizing with the counterrevolutionaries. Balfour replied that the King should act with natural good feeling, especially because of the tragic circumstances of Nicholas's death.[30] The Court went into four weeks' mourning.

In the new, undeferential world of Lytton Strachey's *Eminent Victorians*, the courtiers' fussiness seemed absurd. When the King visited the front, they treated him as though he was "Queen Victoria *after* the Diamond Jubilee."[31] "It is wonderful that the whole edifice has not crumbled under an avalanche of ridicule," wrote Lord Esher, picturing the "poor little King . . . laid up in bed with a pain in his tummy, having his head held by Derek Keppel." [32]

Stamfordham's fussiness belied a Machiavellian duplicity. Writing to Esher, he pretended to know nothing of the Tsar's fate. "Was there ever a crueller murder," he asked, "and has this country ever displayed such callous indifference to a tragedy of this magnitude? . . . Where is our . . . common decency gone to?"[33] Where indeed.

Esher, a courtier who had spent the war trying to coordinate the military and the politicians, doubtless had a shrewd idea about the asylum business. Maligned by historians for his creepiness and duplicity, he was far more clear-sighted than Stamfordham. But he was not welcome in George's court on account of his ambiguous sexuality and his "cleverness." Owen Morshead likened him to a medicated tomcat: "Manly men did not like Esher . . . honest men, like K. George V and Stamfordham, felt their skin prickle when he entered the palace, as some people react to the unseen presence of a cat in the room."[34] This observation, incidentally, suggests interesting ideas about manliness at the court of George V; but I will resist that rabbit hole. The point I want to make here is that regarding the Tsar, Esher was straight, and Stamfordham the devious one.

Esher refused to play Stamfordham's game. It was moral cowardice, he said, that prevented "our government from obtaining the Czar's release from Miliukov." The King had an important role to play: "But he will have to listen more to the dictates of his own heart, and less to his political advisers. He will have to look more to the simple rules by which his private life is governed, than to the political barometer, that Ministers and advisers are always thrusting into his hand." Flashing the stiletto inside the velvet glove, he told Stamfordham: "The fault is yours, as you asked the question."[35]

Esher was right on the moral issue. The refusal of asylum was a failure of moral courage, a decision dictated by panic and the "political barometer" of the royal advisers, Stamfordham and the Bishop of Chelmsford. But was it the right decision, even if made for the wrong reasons?

THE WAR, AS NICHOLAS II PRESCIENTLY observed in 1914, dealt "a terrible blow to the monarchical principle."[36] In 1910, when the King of Portugal abdicated, Esher had predicted that "monarchies are going to have a bad time": "A war between Germany and Great Britain would end by destroying the monarchies of both."[37] In 1917, George's first cousin Constantine, the pro-German King of Greece, was deposed, and George repudiated him. Queen Alexandra, however, continued to send frantic telegrams to her sister Minnie, the Dowager Empress Marie (mother of Nicholas II), heedless of warnings from the Foreign Office that her communications would endanger the Romanovs by feeding the revolutionaries' fears of a counterrevolution. So concerned was Princess Louise (the younger sister of George V) at "the great danger" of Queen Alexandra's communications with her relations that she wrote privately to Foreign Secretary Balfour, urging him to censor her letters.[38]

At an emotional level, Alexandra anticipated the twenty-first century: this is how we would react today. In 1919, a British battleship was sent to Yalta to rescue her sister from the Crimea. But what George perceived and his mother did not was that the nature of monarchy had changed. The dynastic realm presided over by Queen Victoria and then Edward VII—the supranational extended monarchical family, bonded by marriages of cousins, communicating in the common language of English, held together by (largely German) DNA, by the *Almanach de Gotha*, by letters, by Danish family holidays, by state occasions, and by Faberge eggs—was brutally shattered by the war. To survive, monarchs had to repudiate the dynastic realm and, as Benedict Anderson showed, make terms with official nationalism. Monarchy had to naturalize or perish.

When someone remarked that George must be pro-German because he had a German name, "he started and grew pale."[39] In point of fact, George didn't have a German name; he didn't have a surname at all. No monarchs did. Queen Victoria was vague on the matter. She thought that her surname was Guelph d'Este of the House of Brunswick, from the Hanoverians, and not Saxe Coburg Gotha, as is usually supposed. Her children were registered as Guelph, though Bertie, George's father, was also Gotha. Little wonder that George didn't know his surname. To his dismay, he was advised (probably wrongly) that it was not Wettin, Albert's surname, but Wipper. On Stamfordham's recommendation, the name "Windsor" was adopted, and all German styles and titles renounced, in July 1917. A Bavarian nobleman (Count Albert Montgelas) observed: "The true royal tradition died on that day in 1917 when, for a mere war, King George V changed his name."[40] To be exact: it was the tradition of dynastic royalty that died in 1917. By amputating the German element, George enabled the monarchy to become identified with civic nationalism—that is, Britishness.

The rebranding was opportune. Britishness, like all nationalisms, thrived on conflict with an Other, in this case, the Germans. Britain in 1914 seemed on the verge of fragmenting with the rise of ethnic nationalisms—not only in Ireland, but also in Scotland (a Scottish Home Rule Bill passed its second reading in May 1914) and Wales (with the 1914 church disestablishment bill). Ireland of course rebelled in 1916, but in Scotland the war had the opposite effect: it boosted civic, British nationalism, with above-average volunteer rates and the highest death rate in the nation. Scottish Home

Rule was dropped as ethnic nationalism faded. Central to this British nationalism was worship of the constitution, and especially the monarchy.

As the Scottish independence referendum campaign in 2014 vividly showed, Britishness has become emasculated. Parliament, once the core of Britishness, is now spurned as "Westminster," but the three icons to which even the Scottish National Party nodded were the National Health Service, the pound, and the Queen. Monarchy is still integral to civic nationalism. Earlier this year, when I referred on television to the King of England, I received a torrent of e-mails, some hurt, some abusive, from Scots who complained that talking about the English king was not only incorrect (which is true) but also demeaning to the sacrifices that the Scots made in 1914–18. This Scottish Britishness goes back to George V.

WHEN H. G. WELLS BEMOANED Britain's "alien and uninspiring court," George V famously quipped, "I may be uninspiring but I'll be d––d if I'm alien."[41] The uninspiring part came naturally to him. George's court, as Esher remarked, had none of the glamour and electricity of his father's. The Queen knitted after dinner. "Nothing can be quieter and more domestic," wrote Esher. "We have reverted to the ways of Queen Victoria."[42] At York Cottage, George's family of five, his equerries and ladies-in-waiting and private secretaries, not to mention the servants, squashed into a "glum little villa" on the edge of a pond in the shrubberies at Sandringham.

This, as H. G. Wells, observed was not a dynastic court but a "crowned republic."[43] In 1915, conned by Lloyd George, the King took the lead in banning alcohol at the palace. The menu was dire. Here is a message from the King to his Comptroller of Supply: "Saturday. Minced chicken for lunch. Sunday. Boiled chicken for lunch. A small piece off the breast. Don't send up a whole bird."[44]

It is true that wartime austerity helped mend George's relations with Lloyd George. In April 1917, he lunched at Windsor and "enjoyed it thoroughly," calling it "all so homely."[45] But George V, who had played a central part in the Constitutional Crisis of 1910–11 and then the Home Rule crisis, was marginalized by the war. By contrast with Queen Victoria, who was galvanized by the Crimean War to become Walter Arnstein's Warrior Queen, George was a king in search of a role. Dressing in khaki, as he did throughout the war, didn't quite fix it. "There is such an intense desire to do right," observed one lady-in-waiting. "It is like the piteous spectacle of watching a very good child under an almost unsurmountable handicap."[46] Others were less charitable. The troops dubbed the King and Queen Fertile and Futile. In 1918, Esher visited Buckingham Palace and found it frozen in time. "The same routine. A life made up of nothings—yet a busy scene. Constant telephone messages about trivialities."[47]

How could the monarchy be rescued from irrelevance in the postwar world—especially since the creation of a democratic franchise with the Representation of the People Act of 1918?

WINNING THE WAR WAS CRUCIAL to the survival of Britain's institutions and its monarchy. George V underscored the point when, in June 1919, he went in person to meet Lloyd George at Victoria Station on his return from the Versailles Peace Conference. "There is no precedent for it," said his advisers. "Very well, I will make a precedent," said the King.[48] It was an important gesture. "History," wrote Winston Churchill, "will not overlook the significance of this act."[49]

But peace, as Esher foresaw, brought new challenges. On 4 November 1918, Esher wrote to Stamfordham:

> We stand at the parting of the ways. . . . The Monarchy and its costs will have to be justified in the future in the eyes of a war worn and hungry proletariat, endowed with a huge preponderance of voting power . . . The King and Queen will have to take risks . . . [necessitating the abandonment of many old theories of Constitutional Kingship]. The strength of Republicanism lies in the *personality* of Wilson! And the use he has made of his position. It is a lesson. He has made the "fashion" of a Republic. We can go one better if we try.[50]

How to make monarchy the "fashion," as President Wilson had made republicanism, was the problem George now had to tackle. It was his achievement to rebrand the Crown as integral to the new democracy. By integrating Labour into the two-party system—and especially by forcing Ramsay MacDonald to stay on as Prime Minister of the 1931 National Government—George helped achieve in Britain a national unity that (said Churchill) was the "wonder of the world," containing the explosive force of democracy, which blew away parliamentary government so disastrously in Germany.[51]

George's very uninspiringness was an asset, enabling him to chime with the politics of the centrist coalitions of Baldwin and MacDonald: dull but safe. "He *was* dull, beyond dispute," wrote the royal adviser Sir Alan Lascelles, "but my God his reign (politically and internationally) never had a dull moment."[52] But there was something more. Through his radio broadcasts, and especially the last, in 1935, George achieved what he described as "a personal link between me and my people which I value more than I can say."

Walter Arnstein, that great historian of Victoria's reign, once wrote that "to a surprising degree royal history has been left to non-professionals or non-historians."[53] Yet the institution is central. Events like the murder of the Romanovs have been dismissed by professionals as *Daily Mail*–type stories and urban myths—remember the search for Anastasia. I have tried to suggest that, on the contrary, the refusal of asylum was an integral part—and perhaps the key trigger—of the regrouping of the British monarchy after 1917.

Fall Semester 2014

1. Stamfordham to General Hanbury-Williams, telegram, 19 Mar. 1917, enclosing George V's telegram to Nicholas II, The National Archives [TNA], FO 800/205/CHAR 53.
2. Duke of Windsor, *A King's Story* (London, 1951), p. 129.
3. Quoted in Jane Ridley, *Bertie: A Life of Edward VII* (London, 2012), p. 80.
4. Roger Fulford, *Hanover to Windsor* (London, 9151), p. 158.
5. Anrei Maylunas and Sergie Mironenko, *A Lifelong Passion: Nicholas and Alexandra* (London, 1996), p. 99.
6. *Margot Asquith's Great War Diary, 1914–1916,* ed. Michael and Eleanor Brock (Oxford, 2014), p. 93.
7. "His Excellency," in W. Somerset Maugham, *Collected Stories* (New York, 2004), p. 793.
8. Buchanan, telegrams nos. 364 and 372, 21 and 22 Mar. 1917, FO 371/2998/109, 121.
9. Hardinge to Buchanan, telegram no. 544, 22 Mar. 1917, FO 371/2998/111.
10. Balliol College Archive, Harold Nicolson Diary, 24 Aug. 1949.
11. Stamfordham to Balfour, 30 Mar. 1917, FO 800/205/63.
12. Balfour to Stamfordham, 2 Apr. 1917, FO 800/205/65.
13. The Parliamentary Archives [TPA], Lloyd George Papers, F/3/2/17; Stamfordham to Balfour, 6 Apr. 1917, in Kenneth Rose, *King George V* (London, 1983), p. 212.
14. Stamfordham to Balfour, 6 Apr. 1917, FO 800/205/80.
15. FO telegram to Buchanan, 13 Apr. 1917, FO 800/205/88.
16. Buchanan telegram, 15 Apr. 1917, FO 800/205/90.
17. Rose, *King George V*, p. 216.
18. Forsint, Archangel, to DMI, War Office, telegram, 28 Aug. 1918, FO 800/205/353.
19. Rose, *King George V,* p. 216.
20. John Grigg, *Lloyd George: War Leader* (London, 2002), p. 61.
21. Stamfordham to Revelstoke, 13 June 1917, in Harold Nicolson, *King George V* (London, 1952), p. 309.
22. Lloyd George to Stamfordham, 22 Aug. 1918, Lloyd George Papers, F/29/2/50.
23. Stamfordham to Lloyd George, 25 Aug. 1918, Lloyd George Papers, F/29/2/51.
24. Frances Stevenson, *Lloyd George: A Diary,* ed. A. J. P. Taylor (London, 1971), p. 153.
25. Ibid., entry for 25 Jan. 1925, p. 25.
26. Balliol, Nicolson Diary, 12 Aug. 1949.
27. Fulford, *Hanover to Windsor,* p. 165.
28. Nicolson, *George V,* p. 64.
29. John Gore, *King George V* (London, 1941); W. Kuhn, 'Stamfordham', *ODNB*.
30. Balfour to Stamfordham, 23 July 1918, FO 800/205/305.
31. Churchill Archives, Esher Papers, ESHR 4/9, Philip Sassoon to Esher, 7 Aug. 1918.
32. Esher to Sassoon [1918], in James Lees-Milne, *The Enigmatic Edwardian* (London, 1986), pp. 310–11.
33. Stamfordham to Esher, 25 July 1910, CHAR ESHR 4/10.
34. Owen Morshead to Philip Magnus, 7 Apr. 1964, Charles Sebag-Montefiore Papers.
35. Esher to Stamfordham, 28 July 1918, CHAR ESHR 4/10.

36. Fulford, *Hanover to Windsor*, p. 173.
37. *Journals and Letters of Reginald Viscount Esher,* ed. Oliver Viscount Esher, vol. 3 (London, 1938), p. 25 (6 Oct. 1910).
38. Louise to Balfour, 14 June 1917, British Library, Balfour Papers, Add MSS 49686.
39. Nicolson, *George V,* p. 309.
40. Rose, *King George V,* p. 174.
41. Nicolson, *George V,* p. 308.
42. *Journals and Letters of Reginald Viscount Esher,* vol. 3, p. 48 (16 Apr. 1911).
43. *The Times,* 21 Apr. 1917.
44. Bonhams Sale Catalogue, 19 Mar. 1914, Papers of Jean Marie Claude Barlerin.
45. Stevenson, *Lloyd George,* p. 153.
46. Richard Davenport-Hines, *Ettie* (London, 2008), p. 304.
47. Journal, 16 Feb. 1918, CHAR ESHR 2/21.
48. Stevenson, *Lloyd George,* p. 187.
49. Winston Churchill, *Great Contemporaries* (London, 1937), p. 326.
50. Esher to Stamfordham, 4 Nov. 1918, CHAR ESHR 4/10.
51. Churchill, *Great Contemporaries,* p. 327.
52. Lascelles to Nigel Nicolson, Jan. 1967, in *King's Counsellor: Diaries of Sir Alan Lascelles,* ed. Duff Hart-Davis (London, 2007), p. 433.
53. Walter L. Arnstein, "The Warrior Queen," *Albion,* 30 (1998).

Colonel Edward M. House, c. 1917

19

A Love Triangle: Woodrow Wilson, Colonel House, and the British

JOHN MILTON COOPER, JR.

> *We do so love thee, Colonel House,*
> *Even though you look like a mouse;*
> *Our ardor we can never douse,*
> *We do so love thee, Colonel House*

I cannot resist opening with a parody of that famous verse by the late-seventeenth-century Oxford satirist Tom Brown, whose apocryphal spontaneous translation of a Latin aphorism went thus:

> I do not love thee, Doctor Fell,
> The reason why I cannot tell;
> But this I know, and know full well,
> I do not love thee, Doctor Fell.

This riff on "Doctor Fell" describes full well how early-twentieth-century figures in the British government felt about the American envoy Edward M. House, that native son of Texas who held the honorary title of colonel in the state militia, courtesy of his friend and political patron Governor Jim Hogg. Those Britons knew full well that they *did* love him, and the reason why they could surely tell.

You don't have to look far to find expressions of British affection for this colonel from across the water. Consider these bouquets tossed to the diminutive Texan from memoirs of British leaders during the First World War. Sir Edward Grey, who was Foreign Secretary until the end of 1916, recalled in 1925 that early in the war he and House quickly became "not only friendly but intimate": "I found combined in him a rare degree of wisdom and sympathy." Grey found House's comments, criticisms, and suggestions "valuable" and "fertile" and always "conveyed with a sympathy that made it pleasant to listen to them," adding, "He had a way of saying 'I know it' in a tone and manner that carried conviction of both his sympathy with, and understanding of what was said to him."[1]

In 1933 in his *War Memoirs*, David Lloyd George, who was the strong man of the Cabinet throughout the war and Prime Minister during its last two years, was less fulsome in his praise, but paid House the compliment of likening him to his favorite American: "It is to his credit and that of Mr. Theodore Roosevelt that they both understood that the theoretical aloofness of America no longer had any basis in realities, and that she would be intimately affected by any European upheaval, whether she preferred to ignore it or not."[2] Those encomia almost certainly reflected some diplomatic regard for Anglo-American relations and perhaps a desire not to offend House, who was still living and politically active. Lloyd George later had some less flattering things to say about him.

Consider also laudatory assessments by two other Britons, neither of whom was a government leader and one of whom wrote nearly seven decades after House's death. In his classic eyewitness account of the end of the war, *Peacemaking 1919*, published in 1933, Harold Nicolson declared, "I have the most profound respect for Colonel House—considering him to be the best diplomatic brain that America has yet produced." Seventy-three years later, Godfrey Hodgson, a veteran Fleet Street journalist and fellow of several institutes at Oxford, published a biography that portrayed the colonel essentially as Sancho Panza to Woodrow Wilson's Don Quixote. That characterization of the President reprised one made by John Maynard Keynes in 1919 in *The Economic Consequences of the Peace* as "a blind and deaf Don Quixote" who possessed "all the intellectual apparatus of self-deception." In contrast to Cervantes, Hodgson portrayed the sidekick as the more estimable character. He faulted Wilson for having "failed to confront the awkward realities of the international situation and indeed certain uncomfortable truths about human nature." Echoing Lloyd George, Hodgson depicted House as someone who, by contrast, "took the trouble to study the world enough to confront it as it actually was and to see what could be done not to redeem but to reform it."[3]

Britons loved Colonel House for two reasons. First and obviously, they were reciprocating the affection that he had begun to lavish on them even before the war broke out and that he continued to pile on them continually during that conflict and the peacemaking that followed. To say this Texan was an anglophile understates the case by a mile. There was nowhere else on earth that he would be than in London, where he hobnobbed among the movers and shakers of the empire, which he saw as the greatest force for order and justice in the world. At least from 1913 onward, and perhaps even earlier, he yearned to hitch that empire and his own country together in a partnership that would hold sway in a benevolent global hegemony. Once the world war broke out, House may have briefly shared the wish of most of his countrymen to remain neutral, but that was only because he doubted that Britain and its Allies would need help from across the sea. Once the Germans sank the *Lusitania*, House became an interventionist. Unlike a few of his fellow countrymen, most notably former president Roosevelt and House's erstwhile friend and diplomatic collaborator Walter Hines Page, the U.S. Ambassador in London, the colonel kept those views to himself on the American side of the Atlantic. In Britain, however, he took few pains to mask his sympathy for his hosts, and they could read what he was saying to Wilson, thanks to their having tapped America's and everybody else's diplomatic codes and cables.[4]

Ironically, Britons' other reason for loving House stemmed from his keeping his affection for them quiet at home. Unlike Ambassador Page, whose relentless pro-Allied preaching soon alienated his old friend the President, the colonel could remain close to him. The British saw in House a direct pipeline to the White House and an unrivaled channel for influencing its occupant. On three annual visits to London during Wilson's first term, particularly the ones in 1915 and 1916, the top men in the government made themselves readily available to this unofficial envoy because they believed he had the President's ear and could bend his mind their way. House did everything to encourage British leaders to believe this was so. He once recorded in his diary that the President said, "Mr. House is my second personality. He is my independent self. His thoughts and mine are one."[5] Whether Wilson really said exactly those words is open to question, and it is likely that the colonel was embellishing on his intimacy with President. It is also likely that he repeated such remarks to his hosts in London as he strove to burnish his standing with them.

House's dealings with the British lasted from 1914 to 1919. In addition to making those first three visits, he led two wartime missions overseas, conducted the armistice negotiations, and served as a member of the American delegation to the peace conference. At home, visiting British leaders made House's residence in New York their first stop, conferring with him before they went to Washington to meet with the President, Cabinet members, and other key figures. The British government set up a special channel of communication at the end of 1916 by assigning a young intelligence officer, Sir William Wiseman, to deal exclusively with House. One historian has described Wiseman as "a young House with an Oxbridge accent," and the two men immediately struck up a warm friendship.[6] The Englishman rented an apartment in the building where House lived, and the pair engaged in conspiratorial antics behind the backs of their governments. On their side, the British used the House-Wiseman axis for some of their most important dealings with the Americans, bypassing their successive ambassadors, Sir Cecil Spring-Rice and Lord Reading.

House's diplomatic dealings and his connection with Wiseman gave substance to the love affair between him and the British, but it never ceased to be a triangle. Either literally or figuratively, at the colonel's side always loomed the President. He was what made House important to the British and gave him access and leverage with them. Without Wilson, the Texan would have been just another American anglophile who might have merited some attention and polite indulgence. Wilson supplied the critical ingredient for this love feast. Winston Churchill put his finger on the President's central role when he said in 1927, "Writing with every sense of respect, it seems no exaggeration to pronounce that the action of the United States with its repercussions on the history of the world depended, during the awful period of Armageddon, on the workings of this man's mind and spirit to the exclusion of every other factor; and that he played a part in the fate of nations incomparably more direct and personal than any other man."[7]

The weightiest question about this love triangle is, what did the British get out of it? House without doubt lubricated relations between the two powers, and his link through Wiseman enabled them to bypass cumbersome machinery and procedures. Also, on his own during the summer of 1918, House tried to nudge Wilson a bit closer to what some leading Britons wanted in a post-war League of Nations. The colonel brought back with him from London the report prepared by the jurist Sir Walter Phillimore, and he gave it to the President. When Wilson visited House at the colonel's summer home at Magnolia, on Massachusetts's North Shore, they went over a response to the Phillimore Report written by one of House's advisers. The President drastically revised that response to produce the so-called Magnolia Draft of a covenant (the first time that word was used) for a League of Nations. Wilson's draft showed how much his thinking differed from that of both its British proponents and such leading American advocates of the league idea as former president William Howard Taft and Harvard's president, A. Lawrence Lowell. He also forbade House to share the Magnolia Draft with the British or anyone else. Whether the colonel obeyed that order is not known.

That incident catches the essence of this triangular affair. For all of House's efforts to make the course of his true love run smoothly, in the final analysis the whole business does not seem all that consequential—with two major exceptions. Moreover, the relationship did not last. Wilson's decision to head the delegation to the peace conference meant that he, not House, would do the negotiating on the significant issues. The colonel's sole star turn in Paris came when the President had to take a monthlong break from the conference for a trip back to the United States. As a token of his regard for House, Wilson deputized him to head the delegation in his absence. The colonel busied himself with making accommodating gestures toward the British and French and, thereby, weakening the President's hand when he returned.

Edith Wilson later recalled her husband saying after the colonel's initial briefing, "House has given away everything I had won before we left Paris. He has compromised on every side, and so I have to start all over again and this time it will be much harder, as he has given the impression that my delegates are not in sympathy with me."[8] Mrs. Wilson always disliked and distrusted House, and her memory may have exaggerated her husband's reaction. Still, this recollection has the ring of truth to it. In manner and insinuation more than in substance, House had undercut Wilson during his absence, and afterward things were never the same between the two men. They continued to work together at the conference, but more distantly and formally. After Wilson left the conference on the day of the signing of the Treaty of Versailles, he never met or communicated with House again. The triangle was irreparably broken.

IMPORTANT AS IT MIGHT SEEM, this cooling off between the two Americans was not one of the two exceptions to the relative lack of consequences for the British. At Paris, Wilson reasserted himself and got most of what he wanted in the settlement, despite fights with Lloyd George and the French premier, Georges Clemenceau. The consequential exceptions had come earlier, at the beginning of

1916 and at the end of 1918. They involved the so-called House-Grey Memorandum and the armistice.

The first of those was a document that the colonel presented to Wilson on 5 March 1916, when he returned from his visit to Europe. In it, Grey, the British Foreign Secretary, purportedly stated, "Colonel House told me that President Wilson was ready, upon hearing from France and England that the moment was opportune, to propose that a conference should be summoned to put an end to the war. Should the Allies accept this proposal and should Germany refuse it, the United States would probably enter the war against Germany." The document also gave assurances that this conference "would secure peace on terms not unfavourable to the Allies; and that, if it failed to secure peace, the United States would leave the conference as a belligerent on the side of the Allies." The "not unfavourable" terms included restoration of Belgium, return of Alsace and Lorraine to France, and a warm-water port for Russia.[9]

Even now, nearly a century afterward, it is hard to know what to make of the House-Grey Memorandum. Was it really as important as the colonel made it out to be? If so, what was its aim? Was it a genuine overture toward mediation, or was it a pretext for the United States to enter the war on the Allied side? The one thing that can be said for sure is that House talked out of different sides of his mouth to the British and French, on the one hand, and to Wilson on the other. Not only to his newfound intimate, Wiseman, but also to others in London and Paris, the colonel maintained that the United States was on the verge of going to war against Germany and needed only a propitious occasion to take the plunge. With Wilson, he not only disregarded the President's instructions not to discuss specific peace terms, but also kept Wilson informed of his dealings only in a brief, sketchy way. When he got back, House stressed British interest in ending the war, and in his diary he recorded, "The president placed his arm around my shoulders and said: I cannot adequately express to you my admiration and gratitude for what you have done."[10] Significantly, however, Wilson inserted another "probably" into the memorandum's sentence about the United States leaving the peace conference as a belligerent on the Allied side.

That word "probably" would later stir up a controversy of it own. In his *War Memoirs,* Lloyd George claims that this word "completely changed the character of the proposal" and reflected "the timidity of statesmanship."[11] He meant timidity on the part of Wilson, who cowered before American public opinion, and timidity on the part of Grey, who was afraid to share the memorandum with the other Allies. As with many tales told by Lloyd George, this one does not stand the test of evidence. "Probably" was already in the memorandum, and Wilson's saying it again did not change the document's meaning. Rather, that reiteration showed that he was not seeking a pretext for intervention. Likewise, Grey did share the memorandum with at least one Ally, because he gave a copy to the French ambassador. Most importantly, when Grey brought the memorandum before the Cabinet's War Committee, nearly everybody, particularly Lloyd George, threw cold water on the scheme, and only the Foreign Secretary timidly and equivocally suggested it might be worth considering. The British never did make any reply, formal or otherwise, to the House-Grey Memorandum.

Their lack of response to what the colonel in his diary repeatedly called his "Great Adventure" bitterly disappointed him. He mourned the loss of the golden opportunity he thought he had fashioned, and he believed that its rejection alienated the President from the British. This is another claim that does not stand up to scrutiny. There is no evidence that Wilson shared House's disappointment, and he seldom mentioned the memorandum after he added "probably" to it. Over the next few months, Wilson did grow estranged from the British, but they gave him plenty of other reasons for his cooler attitude toward them. For one thing, the Germans had temporarily reined in their submarines, which defused the war-threatening tensions that had repeatedly flared up since the sinking of the *Lusitania*. This detente had the effect of bringing to the fore mounting tensions over Britain's blockade, particularly the blacklisting of American firms suspected of trading with the Germans and the interception of allegedly suspicious mail bound for Europe. These and other blockade practices prompted Wilson to seek and get from Congress legislation the permitted economic retaliation. Over those tensions hovered the shadow of Ireland, where the brutal suppression of the Easter Rising had besmirched the British image in American eyes the way that the devastation of Belgium had earlier sullied Germany's image. At the end of 1916, the love triangle came close to snapping in two places when Wilson disregarded House's pleas and publicly proposed mediation and a compromise peace, to the chagrin of Lloyd George's newly formed coalition government. Only the Germans' resort to renewed and unrestricted submarine warfare saved the ties between the two men and the two nations.

Ironically, the House-Grey Memorandum heightened the President's admiration for the colonel's skills as a negotiator. Once the United States entered the war, Wilson made House his principal envoy to the Allies, which led to the other big exception to relative lack of importance of his love triangle—the armistice. Defying angry denunciations at home and overriding objections by the British and French, Wilson responded to German overtures toward an armistice. He dispatched House to Europe as his "personal representative . . . to take part in such conferences" as might lead to ending the war. "The president certainly gives me the broadest possible powers," House exulted in his diary. "It virtually puts me in his place in Europe."[12]

After a rough ocean crossing, the colonel found himself in equally turbulent diplomatic waters in Paris. Clemenceau objected to basing an armistice on the Fourteen Points, and Lloyd George balked at any commitment to one of those points, "freedom of the seas." Over a week of hard dealing followed, with Wilson at one point making a cabled threat to start a naval race with the British. The negotiations taxed House's powers of persuasion, but he finally secured agreement to the statement that came to be called the Pre-Armistice Agreement. In it, the Allies accepted the Fourteen Points, which none of them had hitherto recognized, as the basis for making peace, but with the British reserving the right to interpret "freedom of the seas" as they saw fit. Wilson silently assented to the agreement, which was forwarded to the Germans on 5 November and led to the armistice six days later.

This was the colonel's finest hour, and it was pure House. He had brought off a diplomatic coup. His mild, soothing approach had smoothed over difficult patches. Operating on his own three thousand miles from Washington, he had been able to buffer the dealings against the President's more confrontational style, which Lloyd George and Clemenceau would soon taste for themselves at the peace conference. House did more than allay suspicions and lessen resentments. He practiced the kind of creative misrepresentation that some analysts deem indispensable to fractious diplomacy. The abundant records of these negotiations make it clear that, as before, the colonel talked out of more than one side of his mouth. Even the admiring Harold Nicolson criticized House for the different ways in which he used interpretations of the Fourteen Points. In Nicolson's view, these tactics bred a "fundamental misunderstanding," under which the Germans accepted the Fourteen Points as Wilson had stated and elaborated them, while the Allies agreed to the colonel's softening, equivocal assurances.[13] The armistice was Woodrow Wilson's greatest triumph—it shortened the war; it saved countless lives; it avoided vast destruction—and Edward M. House did much to make it happen. But it also showcased the character traits and behavior that led some people to call him "that devious son of a bitch."[14]

THIS BRINGS ME BACK TO the question of what this love triangle really amounted to. The major barrier to assessing House's significance for Anglo-American relations, or virtually anything else about him, is his own account of his importance. The indispensable source for studying the colonel and his thought and actions is his voluminous diary. Everyone who studies this period uses this diary because it richly fleshes out the rest of the documentary record and offers details and insights not found elsewhere. Unfortunately, it is difficult and often impossible to corroborate House's accounts with other sources. The one time it becomes possible to check continually on what he said is in accounts of the peace conference. Then, it seems, everybody was keeping a diary, and two of those diary keepers were much closer to Wilson, his physician, Admiral Cary T. Grayson, and the press secretary to the delegation, Ray Stannard Baker. Their reports and those of some others put House's version of events in context, and they show that the colonel was rarely as important as he thought he was and that he seldom grasped how he and Wilson were drifting apart.

A final way to judge the importance of this Texan and his love triangle is to note what two of its principals had to say about him. In his *Memoirs of the Peace Conference,* published a year after House's death, Lloyd George wrote more fully and a bit differently about the colonel than he had done earlier in his *War Memoirs*. Once more complimentary, the former Prime Minister credited House with playing a most "active, continuous and useful a part" in Wilson's diplomacy: "He was the Claudius of this pacific American Caesar." But judging from the published version of House's diary and letters, Lloyd George found him "under the impression that he not only chiseled and shaped the idol [Wilson] but also pulled the hidden strings that moved it." What was more, "he was ecstatically proud of it." Lloyd George did not agree. He found House an elusive character, amiable and intelligent but intellectually shallow—"nowhere near the same plane as Wilson"—and not the author of his own ideas: "He was essentially a salesman and not a producer. He would have been an excellent Ambassador but a poor Foreign Minister." In his own dealings with House, Lloyd George found him "frank and straightforward," and honorable yet crafty with others: "It is perhaps to his credit that he was not nearly as cunning as he thought he was."[15]

In Wilson's only recorded assessment of House, he said much the same about the colonel. During his courtship of Edith Bolling Galt in 1915, she had taken a dislike to House even before she met him. Some writers have interpreted this instant repugnance as a sign of jealousy of anyone else who was close to her lover, and it probably was. But she also recoiled from the smarmy tone in the letters from House that the President shared with her. "I can't help feeling he is not a very *strong* character," she wrote to Wilson. "I know what a comfort and staff Col. House is to you . . . but he does look like a weak vessel and I think he writes like one very often."[16] Wilson hastened to reassure her about "dear House," although he conceded, "you are no doubt partly right." He told her, "House *has* a strong character," and he praised the colonel's "utter self-forgetfulness and loyalty and devotion" and his ability to win "the confidence of all sorts of men. . . . But you are right in thinking that intellectually he is not a great man. His mind is not of the best class. He is a counselor, not a statesman."[17]

Let me bid farewell to this love triangle here, with those judgments. Colonel House was a man of considerable charm and an incorrigible intriguer. He shunned the limelight and presented himself as a loyal servant of persons greater than himself. Yet he saw himself as the power behind the throne, the puppet master, the silent shaper of great events. As the keeper of his diary and later the fashioner of his image with its publication, he aspired to write not just his own history but also the history of the most important events in the world, casting himself as a central player. In all this, he harbored self-generated delusions of grandeur, which led one detractor to call him "a porcelain chamber pot full of shit."[18] As for Anglo-American relations, this character was fit not for classical or Shakespearean tragedy or for grand opera. Except for the huge stakes and terrible consequences, he belonged in what subsequent generations would call soap opera.

Spring Semester 2015

1. Viscount Grey of Fallodon, *Twenty-Five Years, 1892–1916*, vol. 2 (New York, 1925), pp. 124–25.
2. David Lloyd George, *War Memoirs*, vol. 2 (Boston, 1933), p. 112.
3. Harold Nicolson, *Peacemaking 1919* (London, 1933), p. 15; Godfrey Hodgson, *Woodrow Wilson's Right Hand: The Life of Colonel Edward M. House* (New Haven, 2006), pp. x, xi. Keynes's characterization of Wilson is in *The Economic Consequences of the Peace*, in Elizabeth Johnson, ed., *The Collected Writings of John Maynard Keynes*, vol. 2 (Cambridge, 1971), pp. 25, 32.
4. On House, see Charles E. Neu, *Colonel House: A Biography of Woodrow Wilson's Silent Partner* (New York, 2015); on Page, see John Milton Cooper, Jr., *Walter Hines Page: The Southerner as American* (Chapel Hill, 1977).
5. Edward M. House Diary, Aug. 16, 1913, in Arthur S. Link, ed., *The Papers of Woodrow Wilson*, vol. 28 (Princeton, 1978), p. 178.
6. W. B. Fowler, *British-American Relations, 1917–1918: The Role of Sir William Wiseman* (Princeton, 1969), p. 17.
7. Winston S. Churchill, *The World Crisis*, vol. 3, *1916–1918* (London, 1927), p. 229.
8. Edith Bolling Wilson, *My Memoir* (Indianapolis, 1939), p. 293.
9. House-Grey Memorandum, in Link, *Papers of Wilson*, vol. 36, p. 180, n. 3.
10. Entry, Mar. 6, 1916, House Diary, in Link, ed., *Papers of Wilson*, vol. 36, pp. 262–63.
11. Lloyd George, *War Memoirs*, vol. 2, p. 141.
12. House Diary, Oct. 15, 1918, in Link, *Papers of Wilson*, vol. 51, p. 342; Wilson letter, Oct. 14, 1918, quoted in ibid.
13. Nicolson, *Peacemaking 1919*, p. 16.
14. Jonathan Daniels to John Milton Cooper, Jr., Sept. 6, 1977, Jonathan Daniels Papers, University of North Carolina, Chapel Hill.
15. David Lloyd George, *Memoirs of the Peace Conference*, vol. 1, (New Haven, 1939), pp. 155, 157–58.
16. Edith Bolling Galt to Wilson, Aug. 26, 1915, in Link, *Papers of Wilson*, vol. 34, p. 338.
17. Wilson to Edith Galt, Aug. 28, 1915, ibid., p. 352.
18. Daniels to Cooper, Sept. 22, 1977, Jonathan Daniels Papers.

Royal Welsh Fusiliers, First World War

20

Wales and the First World War

KENNETH O. MORGAN

The French historian Pierre Nora has shown in his *Lieux de Memoire* how ambiguity and contradiction can surround retrospective treatment of a nation's past. So it is with the British centenary commemoration of the First World War. That war, however, was not only a central episode in our military history but also a huge divide in our social, economic, cultural, and imperial history. It brought about a positive new status for women and granted the vote at long last (at least those over the age of thirty). It also witnessed a new centrality for the trade unions in industrial life, the brutal rupture of the Easter Rising in Ireland, and the impact of wartime savagery upon the sensibilities of an extraordinary generation of war poets. In India, war meant a powerful stimulus to the young Gandhi and the swaraj movement for self-government. Within Britain, it meant greater social equality, more occupational mobility, a new impact of the central government on people's lives, and an erosion of pre-war moral values. Several central features of these changes are illustrated by the impact of the Great War on Wales, quite apart from the transformations imposed on Welsh culture and the sense of nationhood. No part of the United Kingdom, indeed, showed more dramatically the revolutionary impact of the events of 1914–18. Liberal Wales and its values were a casualty of total war. In analyzing the British war experience, therefore, Wales should be given its important place.

In the Edwardian years, right down to August 1914, Wales

experienced an unprecedented period of optimism, a golden glow of hope. This came out strongly in August 1911 with the investiture of the future Edward VIII as Prince of Wales. It was a distinctly artificial ceremony, with no historical connection to the events of Edward I's reign. But the excitement and national pride that it aroused were unmistakable. In the monthly periodical *Wales* in August 1911, the Celtic scholar W. J. Gruffydd used the ceremony to sing the praises of the heroes of Liberal Wales, in particular Lloyd George and the litterateur Sir Owen M. Edwards. "The spirit of modern Wales is as fertile in songs of action as in plans of social reform," wrote Gruffydd, with much euphoria.[1]

There was much to justify this mood of celebration. First of all, Wales of the years before 1914 was a land of unprecedented prosperity. The Welsh coalfield continued to boom down to the advent of war. It was the largest coalfield in Britain, with over a quarter of a million miners employed. Its coal exports reached £37 million in value in 1913, the highest total in the world. Cardiff was the greatest coal-exporting port in the world, though in 1913 it was outstripped by its up-and-coming rival Barry, a few miles down the coast. Nothing more vividly displayed the great self-confidence of rural Wales than Llandrindod Wells spa in thinly populated Radnorshire. Its "seasons" had never known such buoyancy. For Llandrindod, the pre-war years were truly its *belle epoque,* Wales's answer to Vichy or Marienbad.

Second, Welsh—more specifically, Welsh-language—literature was never more thriving. A new generation of younger poets had emerged, their presence heralded by the youthful socialist T. Gwynn Jones, whose poem *Ymadawiad Arthur* (The passing of Arthur) created a sensation at the national eisteddfod in 1902. There were brilliant even-younger bards, such as R. Williams Parry and Thomas Parry-Williams, who, in his early twenties, won both chair and crown at the 1912 national eisteddfod. Another cultural milestone came with the publication of a major history of Wales down to the Edwardian conquest in 1283, written by John Edward Lloyd of Bangor. Lloyd applied scholarly rigor to the history of Wales as no one had previously done. At the same time, Lloyd's history, coming from an active Liberal, is suffused with national emotion: the Edwardian conquest is portrayed as a massive cultural and political tragedy. Musical culture also flourished, with the male voice choirs and ladies' choirs of Wales achieving new levels of fame. The manifestly democratic ethos and message of the Welsh choirs was widely praised. Occasional defeats in competitions by English choirs, largely from the north of England, were greeted with disbelief and a sense of national crisis.

Third, Wales was a land of political stability. This was provided by the overwhelming ascendancy of the Liberal Party. In 1906, Wales became a Tory-free zone, with the Liberals capturing every seat in the land, except for the socialist Keir Hardie in the two-member constituency of Merthyr Tydfil (and even he lagged below the Liberal in his vote). The main focus of national pride was naturally David Lloyd George, by 1914 an enormously influential and charismatic Chancellor of the Exchequer, but there were other Welsh Liberals in government: John Herbert Lewis, Samuel Evans, and Ellis Griffith. Under this Liberal hegemony, at a time of much bitterness in English politics, a good deal of the passion of Welsh political life appeared to be diminishing. The Welsh land question no longer aroused the class passion of two decades earlier. The education "revolt" directed against the 1902 Education Act was dying out as church schools were peacefully transferred to the hands of the local authorities. Disestablishment of the church showed signs of becoming a dated issue: Lloyd George was keen that it should be settled on a compromise basis so that Wales could move on to deal with more pressing issues of social reform. For almost fifty years since 1868, the Nonconformist middle class had fought for social equality. By the Edwardian years, especially with the advent of the new "county schools" and the county councils, a democratic revolution in Wales had ensured that that objective had been won.

Fourth, the fact of Welsh national identity was being increasingly recognized at the highest level. There was the federal University of Wales, comprising colleges at Bangor, Aberystwyth, and Cardiff, founded in 1893. There was also the National Library at Aberystwyth. Most striking of all, perhaps, was the neo-baroque National Museum, established on the south side of Cathays Park in Cardiff, one of a range of national monuments created as symbols of the vitality of the newly crowned capital city of Wales, and as testimony to Welsh pride in its history and prehistory. National identity was evident everywhere. For many ordinary people, the national greatness of Wales was most apparent in the field of sport. Boxing produced two world champions, Freddie Welsh of Pontypridd at lightweight and Jimmy Wilde of Tylorstown at flyweight. Rugby triumphs were even more legendary. The national team entered upon a golden age of almost unending victory from 1905, culminating in the historic triumph over the all-conquering All Blacks of New Zealand in December 1905. Welsh patriotism was on full display—but not Welsh nationalism. The Welsh focused on their growing fame in Britain and within the empire. They sought equality within the United Kingdom. Wales was neither separatist nor anglophobe. In short, it was not Ireland.

In one area, this pattern of prosperity and tranquility was emphatically not on display. This was in the history of the labor movement. From 1909 to 1913, South Wales was engulfed in passionate, sometimes violent revolt against capitalist employers, invariably over wages and coal prices. At Tonypandy, fierce battles took place between miners and the local police, the dreaded "Glamorgans." One miner was killed. In 1911, six men were shot down by troops at Llanelli during a railway strike. In 1912, Welsh miners stopped work for a month on behalf of a national minimum wage. There were mighty confrontations between the Miners' Federation and the coal owners, even when they were Liberals such as D. A. Thomas, who owned the pits at Tonypandy. More alarmingly, there were revolts against the miners' own leaders. This was the burden of the Unofficial Reform Committee, led by young Marxist militants such as Noah Ablett and Noah Rees, who produced the famous document *The Miners' Next Step* at Tonypandy in 1912, a call to arms on behalf of workers' control and industrial democracy at the pithead instead of state nationalization.

Even so, this mood of conflict in industrial relations can be exaggerated. Quasi-syndicalist militancy was not so evident elsewhere. The "Lib-Lab" tradition was still powerful. A new generation of miners' agents cleaved firmly to the constitutional, nonviolent path. Even the militants behind the Unofficial Reform Committee owed much to the older culture and values of Nonconformist Liberalism. S. O. Davies had trained to become an Independent minister; Arthur Horner and the young Ness Edwards sought a similar role among the Baptists. Noah Ablett had preached in local pulpits from the age of twelve. For them, the religious revival of 1904–5 had been an inspiration that kindled their socialist faith—and in the end drove them out of the chapels. The Central Labour College and the Plebs League owed much to the populist democracy of the Sunday schools. Keir Hardie in the *Labour Leader* spoke not only of the worldwide unity of the working class but also of the harmony of "the red dragon and the red flag." He understood the socializing force of community. To a degree often underestimated, the Welsh labor movement was still firmly embedded in that tradition when world war broke out.

IN AUGUST 1914, THIS THRIVING, buoyant society was suddenly cast asunder. At the start, Wales displayed much the same jingoism and war frenzy as did the rest of Britain. The official figures, later much contested, showed that Wales had a rate of recruitment, 13.82 percent, higher than that of either England or Scotland. Recruitment was assisted at the end of 1914 by allowing the minimum height required of recruits to fall to five foot three inches, which better catered to the average stature of Welsh men. In all, 280,000 Welshmen served in the armed forces; of these, 40,000 never returned.

The war was alleged to be on behalf of Liberal values. In belligerent speeches at Queen's Hall, London, on 19 September 1914, and later in his constituency in Bangor on 26 February 1915, Lloyd George hailed the courage of "the little five-foot-five nations," "gallant little Serbia and Montenegro," "gallant little Belgium"—and, by extension, gallant little Wales.[2] Much was done to identify the Welsh nation with the objectives of the war. Lloyd George fought hard to create first a Welsh Army Corps, running to over 40,000 men. Then, in late 1915, there emerged from it the Welsh Division, the 38th Division, "one of the most magnificent little armies ever turned out," declared Lloyd George, which first saw action, of a horrific kind, at the Battle of the Somme.[3] Lloyd George could claim to have created a version of his "Welsh Army" despite the stubborn hostility of the mighty Kitchener, Secretary of State for War. Welsh soldiers were heavily involved in titanic battles on the western front in France and Belgium. My own father, serving in the Cardiganshire battery of the Royal Engineers, was among those who fought in Palestine under General Allenby and ended up in Damascus. Welsh patriotic fervor was especially aroused up by the bloody successes of the 38th Welsh at Mametz Wood during the Battle of the Somme and in the capture of Pilckhem Ridge during Third Ypres in 1917. In all, sixteen Welshmen were awarded the Victoria Cross during the First World War, thirteen of them posthumously.

Conscientious objectors were relatively few in Wales, although they had a hard time. The Welsh university colleges built up their Officer Training Corps. Meanwhile, female students in the Welsh university colleges were no less jingoistic, busy in handing out the "white feather" to those they believed were "conchies."[4] Anti-war male students compared the knitting of their needles while making socks for serving soldiers to that of the *tricoteuses* in France in 1789.

The atmosphere could turn very ugly. In Aberystwyth, the eminent scholar Hermann Ethé was driven out of town by a xenophobic mob for no reason other than his German birth. Later the college authorities were to demonstrate even less nobility of spirit, notably in trying to damage the career of the distinguished pacifist poet Thomas Parry-Williams. Eminent Welsh scholars and writers such as Sir Henry Morris-Jones, Henry Jones, and Sir Owen Edwards devoted their academic talents to denouncing the primordial cruelty and racialism of the "Huns" as a race down the centuries. This attitude was especially remarkable for Owen Edwards, who had written poignantly in *Tro yn yr Almaen* (A visit to Germany) of the peaceful culture of the universities of Heidelberg and Göttingen before the war, when the apparently centuries-old tradition of German folk nationalism was not evident to him at all.

The national eisteddfod was especially caught up in the war fever. Lloyd George's speech to the Aberystwyth eisteddfod in August 1916 had a powerful emotional effect when he compared the singing of the Welsh choirs to the nightingales that sang in the darkest hour of the night. An even more moving event came at the eisteddfod held in Birkenhead in August 1917. It was announced that winner of the chair, a young shepherd boy, E. H. Evans of Trawsfynydd in Merioneth, who had written his poem *Y Arwr* (The hero) under the bardic name "Hedd Wynn," had fallen at Pilckhem Ridge a few weeks earlier. In response, the bardic chair at Birkenhead was draped in black. Hedd Wynn, himself almost a pacifist, became forever after a symbol of patriotic sacrifice. A statue was erected at Trawsfynydd after the war, and his simple home was turned into a museum.

Wales and its media during the First World War evoked a Welsh hero of a quite different type—the Christian warrior. One remarkable phenomenon was the Reverend John Williams of Brynsiencyn, an exhibitionist who chose to preach in the pulpit in full military uniform. It was a curious advertisement for the Prince of Peace. For his services as an army chaplain, he was promoted to the honorary rank of colonel. But no one was more passionate in appealing to the most belligerent qualities of the Welsh than Lloyd George. In the first weeks of the war, he seemed becalmed, almost silent in indecision in knowing how to respond to the conflict. After all, he had made his name as antiwar politician, during the South African War after 1899. But the German invasion of Belgium gave his decision a certainty that his earlier membership in the Committee of Imperial Defence had anticipated. A marked change of tone and of role came with his speech to a massed audience of London Welshmen at Queen's Hall in London on 14 September. He poured scorn on "the Hun," "the road hog of Europe." At Bangor in February 1915, he went further still: "Germany would quench every spark of freedom either in its own land or any other in rivers of blood. I make no apology . . . for waging a holy war against that."[5] In the political crisis that beset the Asquith coalition in the winter of 1915–16, he joined with the Unionists to become the leading advocate of military conscription, so passionately opposed by many of his old Liberal comrades.

As Prime Minister from December 1916, he became the uncompromising advocate of the "knock-out blow," the "fight to a finish," and "unconditional surrender." When he moved into 10 Downing Street, his centrality for the Welsh commitment to the war effort was underlined. His household was strongly Welsh in tone and language. His Cabinet Office had as its deputy secretary the Welsh-speaking Thomas Jones; his office secretariat featured Welsh assistants such as John Rowland and, later, Ernest Evans, Evan R. Davies, and Clement Jones. Welshmen who served in key posts included his old adversary Lord Rhondda, who became food controller. The vast majority of his countrymen saw him as a kind of national icon "the man who won the war" or, alternatively, "the greatest Welshman yet born."

This, however, was always a deceptive, incomplete picture. Important areas of dissent were hidden by the public hysteria of wartime, but in the course of 1915, humane Liberal dissent welled up. Thomas Rees, principal of the Bala-Bangor theological college, attacked the mindless anti-Germanism coming from Christian bodies in Wales. The fury aroused by his views led to his being expelled from the Bangor golf club. He continued his crusade undaunted, even though his preaching invitations were reduced. Antiwar men pointed out that Hedd Wynn himself had been strongly pacifist, as the poem "Rhyfel" (War) demonstrated. Indeed his bardic name meant "pure peace." A journal launched in October 1916, *Y Deyrnas*, took up the cause of civil liberties, notably the harsh treatment of conscientious objectors by appeals tribunals, often dominated by landowners. It attacked not just the war but also its social and civil consequences, and worked closely with the pacifist body the Fellowship of Reconciliation. When the armistice came, it turned its attention to the war being waged in Russia against the new regime.

The attacks on civil liberties brought in new allies such as the Liberal MP Llewelyn Williams. An old associate of Lloyd George, he had bitterly denounced German atrocities in 1914, especially the destruction of the great library at Louvain, but was now a passionate opponent of military conscription. In the "khaki election" of 1918, he was an immediate recruit for the Asquithian Liberals. Some Liberals turned to pacifism. The minister George Maitland Lloyd Davies, once imprisoned in Wormwood Scrubs and Winston Green prisons, became a major figure in the Fellowship of Reconciliation. He was later to be elected Christian Pacifist MP for the University of Wales in 1923, a dramatic portent of changing viewpoints among young graduates. Many Liberal dissenters switched to the Labour Party. Welsh intellectuals, especially among the young, were no longer instinctively or necessarily Liberal in their political allegiance.

The moral certainty and social conviction of pre-1914 Wales had been undermined.

The age-old ascendancy of the bishop and the squire over local society was becoming out of date. Both were being disestablished. Very importantly, the cultural and spiritual influence of the Nonconformist chapels was being eroded, especially among the young. The war meant challenges to the old Puritan ethic and the institutions of Sabbatarianism. The mere fact of military conscription from 1916 onward necessarily introduced young serving Welshmen to a distinctly more secular way of life with many, often unsettling, new choices. After the war, the membership of all the chapels showed a steady decline, year on year, particularly in the more anglicized mining valleys and ports of the South. Shortly after signing the Treaty of Versailles in July 1919, Lloyd George finally achieved the disestablishment of the Church in Wales, on the basis of a settlement over the terms of disendowment. To assist with the costs of the commutation of tithe, the Treasury undertook to pay the Welsh Church the sum of £1,000,000. Yet for the chapel congregations, the attainment of their holy grail, pursued for so many decades, seemed almost a nonevent. Ironically, the religious community that most obviously benefited from it was the disestablished church itself, revitalized, more prosperous, and far more the Church of Wales than it had ever been in the past.

Labor dissent during the war was more powerful and aggressive. At first, trade union personalities appeared to subscribe to the conventional "patriotism" of the time. Several miners' leaders, including many miners' agents, were active in recruitment campaigns. *Llais Llafur,* the famous old Independent Labour Party newspaper, changed both its name and its language to become *Labour Voice,* a spokesman for prowar labor. Antiwar men in the ILP faced violent hostility in many of the valleys, as did Keir Hardie himself in Merthyr Tydfil.

Nevertheless, antiwar dissent among workers in the valleys soon built up. After the coming of military conscription in early 1916, so unpopular with many trade unionists, opposition to the war became far more vocal. There was dissent from left-wing bodies such as the Workers' Socialist Federation, and the No Conscription Fellowship became stronger. Several prominent socialists were imprisoned as conscientious objectors. Ness Edwards, as an "absolutist" conscientious objector, was sent by the local tribunal first to Dartmoor and late to Wormwood Scrubs. Only twenty, he was beaten in Brecon barracks and chased naked by soldiers with fixed bayonets. For socialists and radicals protesting against what they saw as an unjust war, doctrines of human rights and the rule of law were contemptuously disregarded in the illiberal, jingoistic atmosphere of the time.

The new mood of protest was not evident in politics at first. In the 1918 general election, the Labour MPs elected, far from being extremists, had supported the war effort. But this concealed a growing surge of industrial and political protest. The 1917 revolutions in Russia were a powerful stimulus to militants, adding to the growing numerical strength and industrial power of the miners' union. Maerdy was popularly named "little Moscow"; the red flag flew at pitheads. When Lloyd George appointed his Commission of Enquiry into Industrial Unrest in 1917, the report on "No. 7 Division," Wales and Monmouthshire, painted an especially alarming picture of deteriorating labor relations and widespread unrest against a background of social deprivation and virtual class war.

By November 1918, the pre-war doctrines of syndicalism and workers' power were again alive and abroad in the valleys. The Central Labour College, based in London, created a new generation of militant young socialists, men such as Aneurin Bevan, Morgan Phillips, James Griffiths, and Ness Edwards, who were to stamp their influence on the Welsh and British world for a generation to come. Unlike its Liberal predecessors, the Labour Party, hitherto sternly male, now gave prominence to women's sections and the Women's Co-operative Guild. Further to the left, the new Communist Party struck roots in South Wales and formed five branches in the Rhondda alone. It was clear that the Welsh working class had changed utterly. The reign of old-generation Lib-Labs was consigned to the labor historians. Welsh miners were to be in the forefront of every strike and lockout. They were turning away from the community values of the valleys and the Welsh nation to the class values of the workers of the world.

THE WALES THAT EMERGED AFTER the Armistice was a far more troubled, tormented nation compared with the confident people of the Edwardian years. There was evidence of endemic decline. First and most obviously, this was true of the economy, especially in the South Wales valleys. The coal mines continued to thrive in 1919 and the early months of 1920 as the growth of the wartime years continued. At the start of 1920, a record 272,000 men were employed in the coal pits of Wales in all grades of work. A terrible rude awakening soon followed. From May 1920 onward, British trade lapsed into a severe decline of both demand and production. By the early 1920s, stagnant trade and high unemployment were prevalent in Welsh coal and the associated steel and tinplate industries, and on the docks of Cardiff, Barry, and Newport. Mass unemployment inevitably followed. There were a few brighter spots. The port of Swansea found new work with the tankers working in the recently constructed BP oil refinery at Llandarcy. But the general picture of South Wales was conveyed by cloth-capped miners having to travel to London, singing to middle-class theatergoers to earn a few pence. In all, 430,000 people, largely able-bodied younger men, had to leave South Wales in the inter-war years, some to work in the new car plants in Dagenham, Coventry, and Oxford, and in the Slough trading estate. Back home, the valleys were officially designated a "Depressed Area."

Less visibly, but no less durably, the vigorous Welsh-language culture of the pre-war period began to decline, too. The linguistic census of 1921 showed an absolute drop in the total of Welsh speakers to 929,000 (37.2 percent), a fall of 50,000 from the census of 1911. It was the perhaps inevitable product of many factors, including the pressures of secularization and anglicization during the social upheavals of total war, and the declining influence of the Nonconformist chapels. This had many consequences for national life. The great male-voice choirs suffered acutely with the migration of robust young singers. Another, less expected consequence of the erosion of this communal world came in sport. Welsh rugby fell sharply away from the high standards of the Edwardian golden age. Many more international matches were lost as fewer sturdy colliers, dockers, and steelworkers were available for the front row, and young men from the few Welsh public schools appeared behind the scrum. In literature, the young pre-war titans who survived the trauma of war still wrote distinguished poetry. But there was nothing in Wales resembling the school of antiwar poets, men such as Wilfred Owen and Siegfried Sassoon, who made so profound an impact in England. Nevertheless, a wider disillusion with pre-war and, even more, wartime values soon became evident among Welsh-language poets and prose authors. There was a significant cultural compensation in the 1930s with a brilliant school of so-called Anglo-Welsh novelists and poets, most notably Dylan Thomas. Some of them achieved international fame. But the consequence of the war was in key respects a loss of cultural as well as economic energy. Wales was becoming not only less prosperous but also less Welsh.

Political and social change was equally profound. The Liberalism of Lloyd George's heyday rapidly evaporated. The temporary ascendancy of the Welsh Prime Minister in the coalition government of 1918–22 soon disappeared as normal party politics returned. He suffered a rapid slump in his post-war reputation, and the Liberals in Wales suffered a huge collapse, catastrophically so in South

Wales, at the expense of the rising Labour Party. In 1923, Labour held almost every seat in South Wales outside Cardiff, as well as Wrexham in the North, along with less durable gains in Anglesey and Caernarfon. The Liberal Party was now manifestly an aging, declining force. Its tally of Welsh seats fell from twenty-one in 1918 to eleven in 1924 and only seven in 1935. The new political titans were Labour men. They were a unique voice of social protest against mass unemployment and despair. This Labour ascendancy was seen equally in local government, where Labour-led local authorities in the 1930s, backed by the co-ops and local civic society, fought a valiant rearguard action against cuts, the means test, and communal decay.

The national ideals of pre-1914 Wales emerged as less vibrant, even if not completely tarnished, after years of patriotic jingoism. So many of their monuments, notably the university colleges, were products of the self-confident, chapel-based, grassroots national pride of the late-Victorian and Edwardian periods. A few responded to this sense of crisis with a wider internationalism. This was seen particularly in the idealistic outlook of David Davies. A passionate supporter of the League of Nations Union in Wales, he personally financed a new chair of international politics at the University College of Aberystwyth. That internationalism was countered by the new and more intense nationalism of Plaid Genedlaethol Cymru, the Welsh nationalist party founded at Pwllheli in 1925 by two distinguished Welsh-language writers, Saunders Lewis and Ambrose Bebb. They poured scorn on pre-1914 "nationalism," which they regarded as hypocritical, pompous, and of no moral worth. They showed how the Treaty of Versailles had paid tribute to the force of nationality while ignoring and betraying smaller peoples such as the Welsh and the Irish. Plaid's counsels were divided during the Second World War. Bebb strongly supported the war and resigned from the party. Lewis saw it "as an English war for English aims" and refused to back it in any way, which seriously undermined his authority and saw him accused of fascism and anti-Semitism. It took a post-1960 generation of nationalists to create a more lasting niche for Plaid Cymru in Welsh life.

THE 1914 WAR LEFT A BITTER LEGACY for Wales. After it was all over, the Welsh, like many other people, were uncertain how to commemorate it. Memorials to the fallen could provoke argument about the competing claims of Wales, Britain, and the empire, for which the Welshmen who had sacrificed their lives were supposed to have died. There was some emphasis on Welshness, but even which language would be used on war memorials could be a source of contention. The size, form, and (especially) cost of memorials could give rise to constant argument. A striking feature of Welsh war memorials is their anonymity, their identification with the worldwide glories of an empire on which an English sun never set, rather than with the democratic "little five-foot-five nations" for whose interests Lloyd George in 1914 had declared that the supreme sacrifice was being asked.

The experience of the First World War in Wales was not wholly negative. New attention was paid to health and housing. There were advances in education, especially higher education, after the Haldane report on the University of Wales, which resulted in a new university college being established in Singleton Park in Swansea in 1922. The status of women improved in some limited areas of professional life, such as education, and it was significantly promoted in the 1920s by idealistic pioneers such as Margaret, Lady Rhondda. But the comparison with the pre-war years remains striking. There was a manifest loss of self-confidence compared with the ebullience of the Edwardian golden age. Devolution has now given Wales a new sense of its creative destiny. But the national vitality of its Edwardian heyday has never quite been replaced. Perhaps Welsh people commemorating the First World War in 2014 reflected too on the faded glory of a world we have lost.

Fall Semester 2014

1. W. J. Gruffydd, *Wales* (June 1911), p. 81.
2. Speeches printed in David Lloyd George, *From Terror to Triumph* (London, 1915).
3. Colin Hughes, *Mametz: Lloyd George's "Welsh Army" at the Battle of the Somme* (Gerrard's Cross, 1982); Wyn Griffith, *Up to Mametz* (London, 1931). Griffith, later a distinguished public servant, served at Mametz as a captain in the Royal Welsh Fusiliers.
4. J. Gwynn Williams, *The University of Wales, 1893–1939* (Cardiff, 1997), pp. 107–8.
5. See, in this vein of religiosity, Lloyd George's speech "The Righteousness of Our Cause," delivered at the City Temple Congregational Church, 10 Nov. 1914.

Krishna Menon, 1950 © National Portrait Gallery, London

21

The United Nations and Colonial Independence

THOMAS MEANEY

It has become fashionable of late to say that the prevalence of the nation-state in the twentieth and twenty-first centuries was not inevitable. A whole generation of historians has sought to recover the full array of alternatives to the nation-state as the dominant political form of the post-war order. For the most part, this recovery effort has meant recapturing the imagining, thinking, and organizing that went into alternative political configurations, whether they were federations, new types of dominions and associations and unions, or various pan-isms. The recoverists see two tragedies in the fate of the nation-state as the ultimate political container for postcolonial peoples.

The first tragedy was, of course, the tremendous amount of violence required to fit many postcolonial peoples into nation-states in the first place. Postcolonial states appeared to repeat the history of their predecessors in their repression, marginalization, and exclusion of social forms deemed irreconcilable with their nation-building projects, which in the case of Africa tended either to subscribe to the decentralized despotism of late colonial rule or to react against it in an even more violent drive toward state centralization. Much of that violence is still with us.

The second tragedy concerned the future possibilities that the rise of nation-states precluded. If, during the first flush of decolonization, large sections of Africa or the Middle East had been able to coalesce into federations or expanded political unions, perhaps this transformation would have made parts of the global South into more formidable members of international institutions. At the very least, they would have been more effective bargainers in negotiations over world trade.

Certainly, this recovery project is admirable and necessary, but it fails to answer a simple question. If there were so many attractive alternatives to the nation-state available in the post-war world, why did virtually all postcolonial peoples end up in one? If so many people, from Tanganyikan shopkeepers to administrators at the Élysée, wanted something else, then how did the nation-state become the obligatory post-war political form? There were several connected and discrete factors, I think, that made it so. First, of course, and especially in the case of France, there was the difficulty of making former colonial subjects into economic equals of their fellow citizens in the metropole. The proposition that the new redistributive politics of the emerging European welfare state would expand to include former colonial subjects was just not going to work for politicians and parties in the metropole. Then there was the fact that the first generation of leaders in Africa and Asia quickly became too jealous of their hard-won sovereignty to make any push for more local federations a real priority. Another factor was "competitive decolonization": the way one empire's scaling back from formal political control could encourage another empire to do so. Additionally there was the new security climate of the post-1945 world. Outside a few contested regions, most states no longer had to be concerned about imperial territorial aggrandizement. Smaller states had a better chance of survival if they received international recognition. Here one could also mention the ruptures of the Second World War, the nationalist aspirations of returning veterans and political elites to the colonies, and other essential ingredients for modern nationalism, such as new technologies of mass communication. The list goes on.

All these factors were important, but the focus here is on one small part of the story: the United States and its design of the International Trusteeship Council. As early as 1941, U.S. planners for the post-war world were bent on making the nation-state the only legible form of participation in the world system because of the failures they attributed, at quite a late date, to the interwar system. There was also the widespread sense that only in a world of independent nation-states—each filled with political content approaching liberal-democratic government—would the old open-door dream become a reality. It is not obvious why U.S. planners thought this was the only way to get there. Nor is it obvious why there was a sudden uptick of interest and convergence in their thinking about the directionality of global history. But by the early 1940s, a fairly radical consensus, molded into shape by Sumner Welles, saw imperialism as at least partly responsible for the Second World War. During the war and the occupations that followed, that consensus came to consider the nation-state the political form best suited not only to the U.S. export market but also to the specific type of knowledge and expertise it was able to bring to occupied zones and countries. To enter into a world system of states in 1945 turned out to be a very different thing from acquiring independence in the interwar years. It meant entering into a new kind of international state structure, the designs of which began had begun percolating in U.S. policy circles around the time of Hitler's shocking conquest of France, which jump-started planners' thinking about the world order. The threat of a new configuration of power in Europe, with Germany applying its own version of the Monroe Doctrine to the continent, was not as troubling to U.S. planners as the possibility of a new European economic order hostile to the principle of the open door.

The future of the colonial world would become the most debated parts of the United Nations Charter. The standard story of UN trusteeships goes something like this: they were the revised, postwar version of the League of Nations mandates system—which had been set up to administer territory won from Germany and other powers during the First World War. These territories—mostly in Africa—accounted for only about 10 percent of all people living under colonial rule. U.S. post-war planners at times fancied imposing international administration on all European colonies after the war, but trusteeship, the standard story goes, was a kind of compromise. It was a way to appease domestic U.S. anticolonial sentiment and to answer the desire for self-government on the part of the colonized, but also a way for the empires to maintain a familiar form of control over their territories.

The final wording of the UN Charter makes no mention of any definite end point of independence or even self-government. But there were significant differences between trusteeships and the old mandates system: the Trusteeship Council, unlike the Mandates Commission, was made up of political representatives from member countries, not staffed by professional experts, as in the league. The council was charged with examining petitions from the trusteeships and presenting reports to the General Assembly, to which it answered. The power granted to the General Assembly of overseeing the work of the Trusteeship Council quickly brought it into direct conflict with the administering imperial powers and thus made the Trusteeship Council one of the more vivid theaters of anticolonial and imperial interchange in the immediate post-war years.

On the one hand, there is an old argument that UN trusteeships were a complete sideshow and made almost no difference in the course of decolonization. After all, several colonies achieved independence before trusteeships were instituted. The opposing, more recent argument is that the trusteeship system shaped the course of decolonization. It did so by serving local anticolonial ends, almost in spite of itself. For example, in the case of the French Cameroons and the anticolonial political party of the Union des Populations du Cameroun, the very process of petitioning may have made separate anticolonial groups aware of one another. The national stature of a figure such as Sylvanus Olympio—the first president of Togo, who made an initial, dramatic appearance at the UN in 1947—was partly produced in this way. (Olympio would later joke that he had seen very little of the United States other than Lake Success, New York, where he lived under a kind of UN-imposed house arrest.) The subjects in trusteeships exploited the tensions between the Trusteeship Council and General Assembly. The council felt pressured to include the perspectives of indigenous representatives in its reports, which irritated the administering powers.

But there is an overlooked element in this sort of opposition. The UN trusteeship system was dreamed up in large part by ambitious U.S. planners at the zenith of anticolonial sentiment during the Second World War. Sumner Welles, Cordell Hull, FDR himself—all had different ideas about the colonial world, but all agreed that formal colonialism had to end. And all of them swathed these visions in copious idealism. Even Hull, the most ardent open-door ideologist of them all, dreamed of a national bill of rights for all countries and an international organization that they could appeal to. The UN was meant to be a clearinghouse for territorial disputes, and so U.S. globalism would have to be willing to cede some of its power to this international system. Part of the deal was that this system would facilitate a world market beneficial to the U.S. economy. In a State Department memo from this time, the American economist Jacob Viner suggested that any U.S. spearheading of decolonization would have to be carefully tempered, since in the eyes of European leaders, the United States still had colonial possessions of its own. Viner recommended a dual strategy of showcasing the independence of the Philippines as a model and gently helping European empires wind themselves down. In the trust territories, the urgent point was that American products, as part of lend-lease, were already flowing there, and there was a worry about domestic effects in the United States were such trade to wane. In 1943, the U.S. consul in Brazzaville saw the prospect of post-war U.S. textile trade with Free French Africa continuing as long as the United States improved the quality of the fabric sent and replaced the woven imagery of warplanes and cowboys with simple tags that said "Made in the U.S.A."

The trusteeship plan was thus always part of a larger goal to bring about a world of independent nation-states without any cover of colonial rule. This plan succeeded, but not in the way the planners thought it would. The negotiations over trusteeship were primarily between the Americans and the British—and much of it constituted a rollback of more grandiose American visions, such as international trusteeship for all colonial territories, not just former League of Nations mandates. In part, this concession was necessary because the U.S. Navy, as British diplomats were all too happy to point out, wanted to hold on to some newly acquired Japanese islands in the Pacific, mainly for security reasons. There was also much confusion over what the words "self-government" and "independence" meant in the post-war world. But my point is simply this: since the General Assembly was given oversight over the Trusteeship Council, which in turn was charged with monitoring colonial performance in trust territories, the architecture of the trusteeship system had little place to go besides independence.

HERE IS A MORE CONCRETE EXAMPLE. One of the most representative tussles in the UN about colonial independence in the 1950s related to the Togoland question. Togoland, a German protectorate before the First World War, was subsequently divided into French and British Togoland mandates. These became trusteeships, and British Togoland bordered the British colony of the Gold Coast. The problem began, as problems often did with UN trusteeships, with petitioning. The Ewe people of the greater region, who were better organized than most other tribal peoples nearby, began petitioning the council for unification of their territory—which would mean the joining of French and British Togoland. The territory had once been unified anyway, after all. In the Trusteeship Council, fierce Soviet representatives and, more importantly, Indian representatives saw an opportunity to pounce. Here was a chance to shame colonial administrators on all sorts of fronts: on the one hand, the Ewe people were clearly not being represented to their satisfaction, but on the other hand, a unified Togoland would save British Togoland from any threat of being absorbed into the Gold Coast.

In the early 1950s there was a persistent concern, voiced by the Indians especially, that the colonial powers would use the excuse of "administrative unions" to absorb trusteeship territories, further adding to their empires. For this reason, the Indians even wanted to expand trusteeships, in the way Sumner Welles had wanted to do back in 1942. The British countered by arguing that their "trust" or "mission" was to see that their trust territories developed economically and socially as well as the rest of their empire did so that such unions could be beneficial. The Americans' stance was more hesitant: they suggested that the best course was a plebiscite of the peoples in both Togolands to see which option they preferred. When Benjamin Gerig, the U.S. representative on the Togo question, made this case, he was told by the British that he had "as much African experience as the cuckoo who winters in Algiers and returns to lay its eggs in the nests of birds at North Latitudes."[1]

So the Togoland problem in 1953 appeared intractable. And three highly representative temperaments toward trusteeship had come into focus in the form of three people. The British Trusteeship Council member, Sir Alan Burns, was a throwback figure. He had been private secretary to Frederick Lugard (the British representative on the Mandates Commission), and later Governor of the Gold Coast, where he was the first to bring Africans on to the governor's council. But he was a defender to the hilt of imperial administration—and its benefits. His book *In Defence of Colonies* (1957) was a direct defense of empire geared toward American readers, whom he took to be in need of some elementary instruction about British benevolence. "A generation or two ago colonial peoples could remember the tyranny and chaos which preceded the establishment of British rule in Africa and Asia," he wrote in characteristically paternal tones. "They were to be grateful for what had been done and were glad enough to be members of the British Empire."[2] The guiding Indian presence on trusteeship matters was Krishna Menon, one of the most brilliant and ruthlessly anticolonial Indian leaders, who early on saw a way to use the UN for Indian purposes, beginning with attacks on South Africa. ("Krishna Menon taught people to use the United Nations," said Michael Foot.)[3] He also knew how to bend the British Empire—and had co-founded one of its admirable products: Penguin Books. The American representative, Benjamin Gerig, was a more obscure, but ultimately quite significant figure. Gerig was an expert on the British imperial economy and one of the few Americans who had a profound sense of how the empire was administered. He had written *The Open Door and the Mandates System* (1930), and he was in tune with many of the original U.S. aims for the Trusteeship Council. He was also a close mentor and friend of Ralph Bunche, who would administer the council for the United Nations.

What is fascinating is how these three temperaments interacted during the Togoland problem. In 1954, the British began preparing the Gold Coast in earnest for independence. While the Soviets went on insisting on Togoland's unification, Krishna Menon saw a new opening. He reversed the Indian course and instead lobbied for Togoland's absorption into the Gold Coast, since the British seemed to be operating in good faith there. Gerig was more or less required to go along with this—since now the anticolonial Menon and the British were in rare agreement. Menon's private justification for the push was that for the sake of economic independence, new states, like his own, should be as large as possible. Since the Gold Coast was going independent along with British Togoland—and finally achieved independence in 1958—the French were put under pressure to deal with French Togoland, which gained independence in 1960.

In 1960, with all of this momentum and with enough fellow anticolonial nations in the General Assembly—nineteen were admitted in that year alone—the Indians, led by Menon, passed the landmark "Declaration on the Granting of Independence to Colonial Countries and Peoples." With its language of "immediate steps . . . to transfer all powers" and its stress on political independence rather than economic readiness for independence, the declaration signaled the fading away of any form of colonial- or U.S.-managed independence. It was the beginning of the end of the UN being thought of as a useful instrument by American politicians and policy makers. To many observers at the time, history seemed suddenly to speed up, and Sir Alan Burns, and even Gerig and Ralph Bunche, suddenly seemed like fossils from an earlier time.

But this story of the gradual Third Worldist appropriation of the General Assembly—which is still a common view about the UN—is in at least one sense misplaced. It is true that the Trusteeship Council in the 1960s, as it became an increasingly vestigial organization, developed into an anticolonial, and then an anti-American, cudgel. And it is true that it started to use the language of anti-racism after the language of anticolonialism no longer seemed to promise as much. But to find a more effective Third Worldist use of the UN, it is probably better to look elsewhere—to the United Nations Conference on Trade and Development, for instance, which tried to revise the terms of the world commodities trade in the 1960s and 1970s.

The real significance of the Trusteeship Council was that it ultimately served some quite old, quite revisionist American ends. That goal was a world of independent nation-states. The U.S. planners for the post-war world, including even Sumner Welles, were too cautious and respectful to ask for the outright independence of European colonies after the war. Instead, they turned to trusteeship as a kind of midwife for independence, one that would allow for some critical exceptions. In the U.S. case, this exception was Micronesia. But the beauty of the system turned out to be that it had been set up in such a way that India and a handful of others could be seen as responsible for the lion's share of anticolonial pressure, while the United States could sit largely on the sidelines as an old wish came into being. Not many U.S. officials thought that it would happen that way, but this structural cunning must be part of the story of how it happened. As the handsome latecomer to the dance, the United States wanted everyone to be single: that wish was largely granted.

Spring Semester 2015

1. Gordon W. Morrell, "The Big Three, the UN Trusteeship Council, and the Early Cold War," in *Imperialism on Trial* (Lanham, Md., 2006), p. 129.
2. Alan Burns, *In Defence of Colonies* (London, 1975), p. 21.
3. Janaki Ram, *V. K. Krishna Menon: A Personal Memoir* (Oxford, 1997), p. 143.

South West Africa

22

South by Southwest: South Africa, South West Africa, and the Commonwealth

MOLLY MCCULLERS

The *Durban* touched down at Jan Smuts International Airport in Johannesburg on 20 March 1961, a golden late-summer afternoon. When Minister Hendrik Verwoerd of South Africa disembarked to a crowd of nearly fifty thousand supporters, he assured them that it was "one of the greatest days of our lives . . . after what has not been a defeat but a victory for South Africa." He referred to South Africa's recent departure from the British Commonwealth. On 15 March 1961, South Africa left or was ejected from the British Commonwealth of Nations. Verwoerd construed the event as a South African triumph. He emphasized that South Africa had "freed itself from the pressure of the Afro-Asian nations who have been busy invading the Commonwealth."[1] The event, he said, "bound [South Africa] closely together in the dangerous period of struggle between white and non-white which lay ahead."

South Africa was expelled from the Commonwealth primarily because of its objectionable and increasingly anachronistic racial policies. But to understand more fully the larger history of South Africa's fraught foreign relations, it is necessary to look outside the country's borders. What has gone virtually unremarked upon by scholars who have examined South Africa's break with the Commonwealth is that Verwoerd succeeded in walking away while maintaining control over South Africa's only colony, South West Africa (often referred to simply as "Southwest"). Examining the South West Africa question—whether the Union of South Africa's controversial League of Nations' Permanent Mandate would be placed under UN trusteeship or annexed by apartheid South Africa—reveals the imperial dimensions of South Africa's racial policies and the Commonwealth's objections to them. As an African settler colony on the periphery of two interconnected empires, Southwest reveals that apartheid was as much a racial as an imperial project, and this imperial dimension of apartheid racism was a significant factor in South Africa's difficult Commonwealth relations. The South West Africa question reveals that South Africa's racial policies were rooted in the pre–Second World War order of empire. The period 1945 to 1961 was one of tremendous change, in which South Africa's racial policies became embroiled with struggles to manage the unfolding process of global decolonization and uncertainties about the changing racial composition of global power and corollary transformations of empire. The South West Africa question magnified the imperial nature of South Africa's racial policies and the racial overtones of its imperial ambitions, greatly contributing to South Africa's growing international isolation.

South Africa acquired South West Africa in 1915 after invading the German colony during the First World War. The Union lobbied to annex the territory at the 1919 Paris Peace Conference during the creation of the League of Nations. Though the league refused this request, South Africa's new Prime Minister, General Jan Smuts, was instrumental in devising the mandates system, which granted South West Africa to the Union as a class C permanent mandate. Although Smuts considered this to be annexation in all but name, time revealed that it was not, in fact, the same thing. Again Prime Minister at the end of another world war, Smuts announced South Africa's renewed plans to annex Southwest at the 1945 San Francisco conference creating the United Nations. Even as he penned the preamble to the UN Charter, which guaranteed self-determination and territorial integrity, Smuts contended that Southwest was an integral part of South Africa and should therefore be formally absorbed by it. He argued that the territory could never exist as a separate state and that "the ultimate objective of the mandatory principle [of eventual independence] is therefore impossible of achievement."[2]

South Africa had been attempting to establish an empire in southern Africa since the Act of Union in 1910 and had been eyeing South West Africa; the British High Commission territories of

Bechuanaland, Basotholand, and Swaziland; and the Rhodesias and Nyasaland. Yet historians rarely consider South Africa an empire, largely because its endeavors at formal imperial expansion failed spectacularly. Admittedly, South Africa was not much of an empire—it had one sparsely populated desert colony over which it could never claim full sovereignty. Still, the South West Africa question illuminated the nature of white supremacy in South Africa and Afrikaner-led governments' ambivalent attitudes toward empire. Although race and empire have been entangled issues in South Africa since the seventeenth century, British conquest and the Second Boer War raised unsettling questions about Afrikaners' racial purity. Afrikaner governments from 1910 to 1961 shared a desire to erase doubts about their whiteness and counteract notions of cultural inferiority by establishing their own African empire; in this way, they could join the ranks of Western powers and mitigate British suzerainty. While concerns about British control dominated South African political struggles in the immediate post-war period, decolonization and African nationalism had become much more pressing threats by the late 1950s. The South West Africa question illustrated how South Africa could rework its imperial techniques to confront this changing situation.

Smuts's annexation plans were immediately controversial. Many UN member states believed South Africa should place South West Africa under UN trusteeship as a requirement of signing the charter. As the environment in the UN turned increasingly hostile, South Africa could not count on Commonwealth support. Although the Attlee government was lukewarm at best, both Britain and Australia supported South Africa's right not to place Southwest under trusteeship; they nevertheless emphasized its moral duty to do so. New Zealand publically shamed South Africa by placing its own mandates under trusteeship in January 1946, stating that mandated territories belonged to the world and not to mandatory powers. But it was India, the Commonwealth's newest member in the making, that became South Africa's main opposition. South Africa's racially discriminatory policies against Indians did not sit well with Indian nationalist leaders. The Indian problem, which Smuts described as "this incubus, which has been with me most of my working life," only worsened when Prime Minister Nehru's sister, Mrs. Pandit, arrived at the UN in 1946 to lead the Indian delegation.[3] The South West Africa question soon became her main avenue of attack against South Africa.

To try to push his annexation plan through the UN Trusteeship Council in 1946, Smuts began marshaling support within the territory. After conferring with opposition leaders in Southwest, Smuts received a unanimous resolution in favor of incorporation from the territory's all-white Legislative Assembly. Britain would, however, countenance support for annexation only if Smuts obtained backing from the territory's African majority. Smuts and the Administrator for South West Africa devised a plan to obtain African agreement in the territory's northern tribal areas of Ovamboland and Okavangoland, which were home to nearly 60 percent of the African population. They would consult the chiefs of each tribal area separately, and once cooperation was obtained, they would explain the situation to the rank and file in order to "obtain the full voice of all." Smuts could gain a clear African majority by asking a handful of chiefs on the government payroll to sign a form letter, which most of them could not read. The African majority would simply be presented with a fait accompli. Smuts thus reported 208,850 Africans in favor of incorporation, to 33,530 opposed.

Though his critics were not impressed with the results of this African "referendum," Smuts might have gotten away with it had it not been for one snag. South West Africa's Herero leaders not only refused to sign the form letter, but also stated their objections to it in petitions sent to the UN and representatives of Britain. Though the territory's roughly 25,000 Herero made up only 10 percent of Southwest's African population, their leader, Hosea Kutako, was the area's most important African political figure. Herero opposition to incorporation stemmed from their colonial history of land alienation and genocide under German rule, which had been followed up by further land alienation and fragmentation under South African rule from 1920 onward. As Chief Kutako's secretary succinctly put the matter, "We reckon that if the Territory is incorporated into the Union, our land will never be returned to us . . . We want our land back and then we want to stay under the protection of the Trusteeship Council."[4]

Although Kutako had previously looked to the League of Nations and the United Negro Improvement Association as possible sources of salvation from South African rule, he recognized that the new United Nations had much greater potential for ending the colonial regime. Kutako's secretary thus sent a petition to the UN: "The whole Herero nation of South West Africa do not wish this territory to be incorporated with the Union of South Africa. We desire to be placed under the Trusteeship of Great Britain."[5] The Herero chief was well informed about the UN and the global situation. Kutako was not only literate but also in frequent contact with the sizable Herero diaspora in the British-controlled Bechuanaland Protectorate, as well as with the protectorate's influential Tswana leader, Tshekedi Khama.

Concerned that annexing South West Africa was simply a stepping-stone along South Africa's way to acquiring the long-coveted Bechuanaland, Khama was the first to try to petition the UN on behalf of Southwest and attempted to travel to Britain and the UN to state his case. The British government refused to submit his petition or to grant him a travel permit, fearing that Khama would strain Britain's Commonwealth and international relations and also internationalize its continued control of the High Commission territories. Khama then asked the Indian High Commission in Pretoria to ensure that the Indian delegation would bring up Herero and Tswana grievances about incorporation at the UN. Khama also put Kutako in touch with the Reverend Michael Scott, a British Anglican priest who advocated for Herero interests at the UN.

Khama's activities, Kutako's petitions, and Scott's advocacy laid bare emergent tensions within the Commonwealth and forced its members to begin to take sides with regard to Southwest. By the end of Smuts's premiership in 1948, the South West Africa question had become about far more than incorporation. First, it revealed Britain's wishy-washiness and the messy state of affairs in the Commonwealth. India and South Africa were openly warring at the UN, a protectorate chief was making international waves, and rural Africans were challenging white overrule. On the one hand, Britain did not want to support measures that would give the UN powers to infringe on state sovereignty, and therefore did not actively work against South Africa. On the other hand, failure to oppose South Africa actively risked alienating the new members of the growing Commonwealth, namely, Pakistan, Ceylon, Ghana, and Malaya. Second, the South West Africa question exposed mounting tensions over the UN's precise functions and powers. By limiting UN representation to nation-states and insisting on the sanctity of domestic sovereignty, Smuts wished to limit UN powers and legitimate South Africa's imperialist aims in Southwest. But Kutako, Khama, Scott, Mrs. Pandit, and others succeeded in allowing the voices of colonized peoples to be heard and made South Africa's domestic affairs, especially its racial policies, the subject of international debate.

South Africa's racial policies became an even more hotly debated subject after Smuts lost the 1948 elections to the Afrikaner Nationalist D. F. Malan and his National Party, which campaigned on apartheid. As many historians have demonstrated, this election was rooted in the political drive for Afrikaner power over English dominance; transforming South Africa from a British Dominion into a republic was the central platform of the National Party. In addition, historians have shown that apartheid was in no way a clearly defined policy or plan at that point. Although 1948 is often considered a major turning point in South African history, there was also tremendous continuity. Malan was as keen on keeping Southwest as Smuts had been, and he resolutely maintained Smut's line that South Africa did not recognize the authority of the UN, and extended this to the British King and the Commonwealth.

Malan's parliament passed the South West Africa bill in February 1949, which gave white residents of the territory six seats in the Union parliament and deleted all references to the mandate in Southwest's constitution. Malan contended that Southwest under UN trusteeship would be "nothing but a festering sore on the body of South Africa."[6] After the bill passed, Malan decided to stop sending the UN Trusteeship Council annual reports on Southwest, arguing that they encouraged the UN to interfere in South Africa's domestic affairs and became "grist for the mill for people like Reverend Michael Scott." Scott, for his part, viewed the South West Africa bill as a violation of Britain's sacred trust and petitioned the King to intervene in the matter. As an indication of the extent to which Britain viewed Southwest as South Africa's affair rather than its own, the King's private secretary sent a copy of Scott's letter to the Governor-General of South Africa, instructing him to take whatever actions he saw fit. Unsurprisingly, Scott's letter went unacknowledged.

Although Malan was prepared to go further than Smuts, he nevertheless continued to press South Africa's case at the UN and attempted to maintain South Africa's position as a member in good standing within the Commonwealth. Malan more or less continued Smuts's policies rather than annexing Southwest (neither the UN nor Britain was in a position to really challenge such a move), which suggests a desire to achieve Afrikaner legitimacy in West. Malan was not prepared to risk ostracism from the West by flouting its rules of international diplomacy, a particularly dangerous move in the early years of the Cold War. Indeed, the National Party's hold on power was so tenuous early on that he could not risk further alienating English-speaking whites, for whom acceptance in British eyes was exceedingly important. His efforts to strengthen South Africa's ties to Britain and the Commonwealth resulted in a significant backlash from republican hardliners in his party, namely, future Prime Ministers J. G. Strijdom and Hendrik Verwoerd. But the passage of key pieces of apartheid-era legislation between 1950 and 1955 intensified international opposition to South Africa and its ongoing efforts to annex Southwest.

Malan attended the 1949 Commonwealth Prime Ministers' Conference in London and was an immediate success. The conference focused on the question whether India could remain in the Commonwealth after becoming a republic. In an effort to lay the groundwork for South Africa's own republican plans and to ameliorate Indian hostility toward South Africa at the UN over the South West Africa question, Malan ardently supported the Indian case. Despite these overtures, India was hardly conciliatory. In 1949, after the passage of the South West Africa bill, the UN asked the International Court of Justice for an advisory opinion whether South Africa was obligated to place Southwest under trusteeship according to the UN Charter. South Africa ignored this opinion. By 1952, the Reverend Scott was lamenting that South African truculence over the South West Africa question, and Britain's failure to oppose South Africa, were damaging Britain's prestige in the Commonwealth, especially among the African and Asian nations. In view of South African recalcitrance on the international court's recommendation, the UN constituted its own standing committee on Southwest in 1953, intending to administer the territory with or without South African cooperation.

SOUTH AFRICA BECAME ONLY MORE uncooperative under the premiership of J. G. Strijdom, which began in 1954. Strijdom distrusted Malan's promotion of ties with Britain, the Commonwealth, and the UN, and his tenure saw the beginnings of South Africa's international isolation. Foreign criticism of South Africa ratcheted up under his regime as apartheid began to enter its "grand" phase and South Africa became known for its increasingly repressive racial legislation. Under Strijdom, South Africa's Native Affairs Department became a state within a state under the guidance of Hendrik Verwoerd, the Minister of Native Affairs and "architect" of apartheid. Amassing hitherto unprecedented powers, Verwoerd's department annexed Southwest's autonomous Division of Native Affairs in 1955 and brought Verwoerd into direct conflict with Chief Kutako.

Their first battle emerged over Verwoerd's plan to reduce the size of Kutako's home reserve, Aminuis, by excising a strip along its western border for white settlers and, as compensation, adding a marginal strip of land known as the Corridor to its eastern border. The catch was that the Corridor may have already been legally part of Aminuis. If the Corridor was part of the reserve, Verwoerd would be illegally shrinking the reserve without the necessary parliamentary authorization. Kutako refused to allow any part of the reserve to be cut off. He petitioned the UN about it in 1956, framing the issue within a larger historical pattern of colonial land alienation. The petition worried the usually unflappable Verwoerd, who admitted to the Administrator of South West Africa that he was "worried that we want to do the wrong thing . . . just to prevent foreign noise." The Corridor soon became embroiled in mounting tensions at the UN, particularly over the International Court of Justice's ruling that the UN could hear oral petitioners on behalf of Southwest, including the Reverend Scott and a handful of African representatives. In response, South Africa left the UN in 1956, maintaining only a skeleton crew there for the next three years.

In the following year, with the Corridor affair still at an impasse, Kutako produced evidence unearthed by the UN Special Committee on South West Africa that administrators of the territory had promised to add the Corridor to the reserve in 1928 and again in 1933. This information discomfited Verwoerd. He frantically wrote to the Secretary of Native Affairs that the Hereros would "claim that the strip of land was theirs the whole time and that they therefore cannot exchange it because it is their land and not crown land." Verwoerd hastened to do damage control, lest "advisers, possibly lawyers, see that [the petition] goes before the UN and possibly elsewhere . . . it will be published that we tried to pull a trick." He noted that Kutako's claims would become "the cornerstone and a danger point of the coming assault by the UN," adding "These allegations are a very good attack point . . . and will be noted against the Union administration in SWA."[7]

The Corridor affair illuminates the crux of the tension between South Africa and Southwest: the demand for sovereignty. The Corridor was not Kutako's main interest; it was another way to express Herero land claims, which were the idiom for demanding Africans' sovereignty over their land and lives. Land claims were therefore their central platform at the UN. Likewise, South Africa's ambivalent foreign relations reflected Afrikaners' demands for sovereignty, which transcended distinctions between Smuts's segregation regime and the National Party's apartheid rule. By threatening to intervene in South West Africa, the UN endangered the fragile imperial claim that granted South Africa entrance into the coterie of Western nations. It threatened the autonomy that Afrikaner Prime Ministers of all political stripes had worked so hard to achieve. Having struggled unsuccessfully to gain an empire, South Africa, least of all its Afrikaner Prime Ministers, was not prepared to become a scapegoat for the Western imperial project. But it was South Africa's very weakness as an empire that made it an ideal target for the tide of nonwhite anti-imperialism at the UN and in the Commonwealth.

Verwoerd ascended to the premiership in 1958 after Strijdom's somewhat premature death. South Africa returned to full participation at the UN that year because of the Trusteeship Committee's "new approach" to Southwest. That year, the UN's Good Offices Committee on South West Africa recommended partitioning the territory, with the northern, African areas to be placed under trusteeship in preparation for independence. Verwoerd endorsed the basic outlines of this plan because, by 1958, African nationalism, global decolonization, and international anti-apartheid sentiments were eclipsing the importance of South Africa's constitutional relationship with Britain in domestic politics and foreign relations. Verwoerd could use the Western discourse of "national self-determination" to achieve territorial apartheid under UN auspices and in the name of independence and decolonization. Unfortunately for Verwoerd, the plan collapsed when the Trusteeship Council voted to hear evidence from Scott and Getzen before the motion for partition could be brought. Although Britain, Australia, and Canada voted against hearing testimony, Eric Louw, South Africa's Minister of External Affairs, blamed India, raging, "The United Nations is being used for the prosecution of vendettas, as a convenient battle ground for the waging of an ideological and propaganda war." While South Africa's odds of getting the motion through were never very good, they plummeted when it was revealed that South Africa had planned to relocate the residents of four or five other reserves to the northern areas before partition. So much for new approaches.

Verwoerd's regime was beset by a series of events beginning in December 1959 and climaxing in South Africa's break with the Commonwealth in May 1961. This tumultuous period began with the Old Location Massacre in Windhoek on 10 December 1959. Africans in Southwest had been engaged in three days of a municipal services boycott and peaceful protests against plans to demolish Windhoek's freehold township and relocate residents to the apartheid township of Katutura. The protests turned violent when police intervened in residents' efforts to enforce the boycott of the local beer hall. A crowd gathered at the location superintendent's office and began stoning the building. When police arrived, they shot into the crowd without warning, killing twelve and wounding forty-four. It was international Human Rights Day.

The massacre became enmeshed with the South West Africa question and stood as an emblem of the brutality of apartheid. These concerns became all the more pressing when Verwoerd announced a few weeks later, in January 1960, that South Africa would hold a referendum on becoming a republic later that year. Given the success of India and Pakistan in becoming republics and remaining within the Commonwealth, achieving republican status was largely symbolic for Afrikaner nationalists. But it was an important symbol of the restoration of Afrikaner freedom and sovereignty in southern Africa—the final end of British overrule. What would it mean for Africans in South Africa and Southwest? Would a republic remove any vestiges of the restraint imposed by nominal British rule? Verwoerd's announcement deliberately coincided with the coming visit by British Prime Minister Harold Macmillan, during which he would deliver his famous "Wind of Change" speech.

South Africa was booming, and the apartheid state was still climbing toward the apex of its power. Consolidating control over South West Africa amid international furor was a critical dimension of South Africa's victory over its former imperial master. Still, Verwoerd was not immune to changing global politics. He began to reframe apartheid as contributing to the development of African nationalism and state building through "separate development" and "homeland" independence. In addition, South Africa would begin to rely on neocolonial tactics rather than formal imperialism to extend its power throughout southern Africa. Verwoerd was not changing policies or goals, merely their packaging. Within a year, he had begun to gloss South Africa's wholesale annexation of Southwest and the implementation of grand apartheid in the territory as "development" and "decolonization."

In response to a massacre in Sharpeville (in the Transvaal) on 21 March 1960, in which white police officers killed sixty-nine Africans, the UN Security Council passed a resolution condemning South Africa. Since several Afro-Asian members of the Commonwealth had helped bring the complaint, Britain worried about the effects of the sanction on Commonwealth relations and its own international policies. If Britain vetoed the resolution in order to protect the principle of domestic sovereignty, Ghana, Nigeria, India, and Malaya might leave the Commonwealth. But if Britain did not veto the resolution, South Africa might do so. What was more, Macmillan feared the resolution would create a "tremendous effort to stoke up similar riots in Rhodesia and Nyasaland or Kenya, in order to put the UK on the dock."[8] In the end, Britain abstained from the vote.

Such was the growing sentiment at the 1960 Commonwealth Prime Ministers' Conference. Eric Louw, who attended the meeting in place of Verwoerd (he was recovering from a near-fatal assassination attempt), posed the question whether South Africa would be able to remain in the Commonwealth if the republican referendum passed in October. Although Nehru expressed concern over the future of Southwest, the meeting declined to answer Louw's question unequivocally. Although members of the Commonwealth were free to choose their own form of government, the meeting refused to make any promises regarding the Union's post-referendum Commonwealth status; otherwise, it could be accused of "interfering in South Africa's domestic affairs." Louw interpreted this tongue-in-cheek statement as an assurance of continued membership, though the other delegates did not necessarily consider it to be so. The referendum passed with a 52 percent majority in October 1960. South Africa would become a republic on 31 May 1961, the fifty-ninth anniversary of the Afrikaners' surrender to the British in the Second Boer War.

The following year, in 1961, South Africa had to formally reapply for membership in the Commonwealth as a republic. As Verwoerd prepared for the meeting that March, he was confident of South Africa's success, but warned the populace that he was "not prepared to buy membership or friendship." Macmillan, however, perceived a growing sense that the procedural question whether South Africa could remain in the Commonwealth as a republic would be used as an opportunity to expel it from the organization. That maneuver could set a dangerous precedent and, Macmillan worried, could lead to the organization's disintegration, thus removing any influence or restraint the Commonwealth could exercise on South Africa. A slighted South Africa could easily threaten the High Commission territories and support white-settler extremists in the Rhodesias and Nyasaland. But in attempting to create a new, multiracial, post-imperial Commonwealth, Macmillan could not afford for the old white Commonwealth nations to side with South Africa against the new, nonwhite members.

The South West Africa question was not a topic at the 1961 conference, even though it was one of several factors affecting South Africa's fraught Commonwealth relations. But its historical legacy became clear in the way the conference played out. South Africa's racial policies were open for discussion, and though everyone criticized apartheid and South Africa had no outright defenders, the approaches taken by the member states suggested a correlation between racial politics and imperial politics. The three states least hostile to South Africa—Britain, Australia, and New Zealand—were the three that currently or previously had mandated territories and dependencies. Since Verwoerd refused to concede an inch on South Africa's racial policies, the recently decolonized Afro-Asian states and Canada took the lead in the offensive against South Africa. As the meeting deadlocked and it became clear that South Africa's constitutional status would provide a platform for criticizing, and being seen to criticize, apartheid, Verwoerd withdrew South Africa's application for Commonwealth membership. In his final statement to the other delegates, he declared "No member with any self-respect—no organization of any kind—could be expected, in the light of the terms stated here and the degree of interference in South Africa's domestic affairs, to continue its membership of a body which has degenerated into such a pressure group."[9]

Verwoerd's plane landed in Johannesburg five days later. He had in many ways won—he had walked out with his small and fragile empire intact, whereas Britain seemed to be bullied by what had been its colonies. It was South Africa's ultimate triumph—for Afrikaners over Britons, for whites over nonwhites, and for English-speaking South Africans, who increasingly supported Verwoerd in ensuring South Africa stayed a white man's country and a white man's empire. Although it is now clear that this was a pyrrhic victory at best, it was no so clear-cut in 1961. The South West Africa question remained an ongoing concern for the next three decades, during which apartheid became even more entrenched. Verwoerd began, informally but effectively, to annex Southwest almost immediately, and would use the territory as a neo-imperial springboard into every African country and conflict from the Congo southward. Although it took a long time for South West Africa to gain its independence (in 1990, as Namibia) and for apartheid to end, they were co-terminal events. South African racism and imperialism rose and fell together.

Spring Semester 2015

1. Hendrik Verwoerd, "Speech on Arrival from London, Jan Smuts Airport, Johannesburg, March 20, 1961," in *Verwoerd Speaks: Speeches, 1948–1966*, ed. A. N. Pelzer (Johannesburg, 1966), 513.

2. South African UN Delegation, "South West Africa Mandate," 7 May 1945, South African National Archives (henceforth SAB) External Affairs (henceforth BTS) 1/18/59, vol. 1.

3. Jan Smuts, "Letter to M. C. Gillett," 26 Feb. 1946, in *Selections from the Smuts Papers*, vol. 7, *August 1945–October 1950*, ed. Jean Van Der Poel (Cambridge, 1973), pp. 42–43.

4. "Minutes of Meeting with Herero Headmen," 6 Mar. 1946, SAB BTS 1/18/59, vol. 3.

5. "Copy of Overseas Telegram, Handed in on 19th March, 1946," from Festus Kandjou to UN Secretary General, SAB BTS 1/18/59, vol. 3.

6. Michael Scott, "Note on Recent Statements of South African Government Spokesman on South West Africa and United Nations," in "South West Africa and the U.N.O.: A Question of Good Faith," ca. 1949, SAB BTS 14/15/2.

7. Verwoerd to Secretary of Bantu Affairs, "RE: Letter from Hosea Kutako," 6 Nov. 1957, National Archives of Namibia, Bantu Administration, 4 HN 1/1/7/4.

8. Harold Macmillan, diary entry for 23 Mar. 1960, in *The Macmillan Diaries: Prime Minister and After, 1957–66*, vol. 2 (London, 2011), p. 281.

9. Verwoerd, "Speeches in the House of Assembly with Reference to South Africa's Withdrawal from the Commonwealth on March 23, 1961," in *Verwoerd Speaks*, p. 529.

Christ Church Meadow

23

Lost Causeways:
Oxford, Experts, and the Motor Age

WILLIAM WHYTE

Universities are only very rarely in the avant-garde of architecture. Seeking solid, even stolid respectability—or just the cheapest buildings money can buy—they tend to eschew the experimental. The times when universities become the leaders rather the followers of architectural fashion are consequently rather rare but also telling. One of those moments occurred in Britain in the two decades after 1957. It transformed universities generally, and Oxford in particular. "It comes as a surprise to most people," observed Alan Bullock in 1977, "to be told that if they want to see a representative collection of the best British architecture of the last twenty years they cannot do better than visit Oxford."[1] The big question, of course, is why. Why should Oxford have so wholeheartedly, though unexpectedly, embraced the modern movement in architecture? To answer this question, I want to look at something that was not, strictly speaking, architectural: a project that was never undertaken, much less completed; and yet a project that can, I believe, tell us a lot about Oxford, architecture, and modern Britain.

At first sight, it must be said that the plan to build Oxford's inner ring road seems a trivial enough topic. Yet the battle over this divisive highway lasted for more than thirty years. So many plans were produced and ultimately rejected that quite early on in the debate the *Sunday Times* was moved to describe Oxford as the "home of lost causeways."[2] So complex were the politics involved that in 1977 a doctoral thesis was written on the subject. And the fight was not just long running but also unusually intense. In Oxford, wrote Hugh Trevor-Roper in August 1955, "all intellectual speculation has given way to the great question of the Road through the Christ Church Meadow, which has totally convulsed City and University alike, rendering all old politics useless and all pretence of scholarship irrelevant."[3] This road was debated in the press and on radio, in Parliament and even in the Cabinet. Strikingly, Prime Minister Anthony Eden intervened personally in the dispute: breaking off from the Suez Crisis to arrange for meetings between interested parties, and then, even as the Israelis mobilized, writing a two-page missive to the head—or Dean—of Christ Church. Little wonder, then, that he received letters like those dispatched by Lord Conesford, a former Cabinet colleague: "If the road is constructed," Conesford declared, "then whatever you accomplish as Prime Minister—and your achievements will, I hope, be great—your Government will be remembered among the vandals of history."[4]

Oxford has always attracted attention. Building in Oxford is an especially sensitive issue. Moreover, as the sociologist James Simmie noted, the debate about Oxford's roads was a good illustration of how an elite university could mobilize its connections. As Trevor-Roper informed Bernard Berenson, "Ministers are being lobbied in country houses, and the fact that half the House of Lords were at Christ Church is not being left unexplored."[5] Indeed, it was "as a Christ Church man myself" that the Prime Minister wrote to the Dean.[6]

But the road proposal spoke to still wider concerns. Not least of the reasons for all this attention was the fact this was a debate about traffic; as Simon Gunn has shown, traffic was a matter of immediate interest to a very wide constituency of people. The number of cars on British roads rose from three million in 1939 to more than ten million in 1960. It was generally accepted by contemporaries that they were living through the "Motor Age" and that it would radically transform life and the towns in which people lived. Yet this onslaught of vehicles raised huge questions for places that wished to solve the traffic problem without damaging the built environment. In that sense, traffic brought together three concerns: modernity, in the form of the Motor Age; history and, especially, preservation; and the reconciliation of both with a sense of Britishness. As the Buchanan Committee, set up by the Ministry of Transport in 1960, put it in the report *Traffic in Towns:* "Our British cities are not only packed with buildings; they are also packed with history, and to drive motorways through them on the American scale would inevitably destroy much that ought to be preserved."[7]

This general problem found a particular purchase in Oxford. It was not just that the city was a magnet for cars—though it was, forming a crossroads for traffic traveling from Birmingham to London and from the East Midlands to the South and Southeast. It was this that led *The Times* to dub Oxford "the Clapham junction of the road."[8] Oxford was also a motor town itself. Morris Motors, which made a quarter of all cars in the country, had transformed the city, producing an unanticipated new urban form. Oxford was divided between Cowley, where the car plant and most of its workers were based, and the ancient city center, increasingly seen as "the Latin Quarter of Cowley."[9] The majority of the people were in Cowley, but the services, shops, and facilities they wanted remained in the older part of town. The ensuing traffic was notorious. A census in 1954 showed that each day more than forty thousand vehicles crossed Magdalen Bridge—the only bridge—into the city center. That they then traveled down the High Street—"a street," as the *Birmingham Post* put it, "that is one of the most famous and beautiful in Europe"—only made matters worse.[10]

Commentators were as one in seeing this as a tragedy for Oxford and a test case for Britain's response to the Motor Age. For the planner Colin Buchanan, traffic was "threatening to break down the entire organization of Oxford as a centre of civilized life."[11] For the editor of the *Oxford Mail,* Oxford had become a "subtopian tragedy," which "points to a lesson for every busy town in the country." "Oxford," he concluded, "has become the classic example of a city in the culminating paroxysm of motorized thrombosis."[12] *Country Life* put it more succinctly, observing that "the Oxford traffic crisis is a matter of national concern."[13]

Thus, when the Oxford City Council decided in 1945 to employ the distinguished planner Thomas Sharp to consider the town's future, it was inevitable that he should focus on traffic as well as wider questions of development. Indeed, by hiring Sharp, whose career would be defined by "the problem of managing the massive growth of motor traffic in existing settlements," Oxford had practically guaranteed that new roads would be a central part of his proposals.[14] *Oxford Replanned,* published in 1948, in fact went much further than just suggesting new transport facilities. It laid out an ambitious program of comprehensive urban redevelopment. But Sharp also addressed the issue of central Oxford's problems with cars and lorries more directly, proposing a new road immediately to the south of the city, running through the meadow that abutted and belonged to Oxford's grandest college, Christ Church. This new road, which Sharp christened "Merton Mall" in honor of the oldest of the Oxford colleges, was designed to take traffic away from the congested and blighted High Street—a street he described as "the greatest and most typical work of art England possesses."[15]

Such a plan was typical of Sharp, who almost always argued for these sorts of "substitute roads" designed to relieve major thoroughfares by drawing off all traffic that did not absolutely need to be on them. It also distinguished his plans from two earlier proposals: one made as early as 1941 by the local architect Lawrence Dale; the other produced a few years later by the city council itself. Dale had proposed "Christ Church Mall": a relief road, or bypass, of the sort that Sharp thought wholly inefficacious, running to the south of Christ Church Meadow and thus avoiding the destruction of a beauty spot. The council's plan was even less invasive of this sensitive semi-rural location, proposing a new road well out of sight of the meadow. Sharp believed that both ideas were insufficiently radical. His Merton Mall would run only a few yards from the colleges, separating Christ Church from its meadow. This was a loss, he admitted—a loss of "one of the pleasantest features of Oxford." But, he concluded, "In face of the difficulties like these in Oxford, some sacrifice must be made somewhere. It is a question of whether High Street shall continue in madder and more murderous congestion or whether the deep peace of one particular spot out of many such spots shall remain."[16]

This solution seemed so obvious to Sharp that he confessed himself unable to understand why it had not been proposed before. "Perhaps," he conjectured, "fear of powerful anger has intimidated anyone who has thought of it."[17] He was right. Each of the three proposals made in the 1940s had their supporters—supporters who would advocate them steadfastly for the next three decades. Each also had their opponents—and none more so, in fact, than Sharp's plan to build Merton Mall. So contentious was the subject that the city council refused to make a decision. Compelled by the 1947 Town and Country Planning Act to produce a local development plan, its draft ignored the problem of traffic entirely.

It was at this point that the national government, in the shape of Duncan Sandys, Secretary of State for Housing and Local Government, intervened. Eton- and Oxford-educated, with a good war behind him, and, as Churchill's son-in-law, superbly well connected, Sandys was a dynamic minister determined to make his mark. In the words of one admiring colleague, he was "a steam-roller—he would grind away in first gear and nothing could stand in his path."[18] In

March 1955, Sandys went to Oxford to discuss the city's draft plans. He arrived on the night before the annual Oxford and Cambridge boat race, dining with the Vice-Chancellor that evening and meeting the city council the next day. A television was specially installed in the mayor's parlor to enable those involved to break off their discussions for the duration of the race. That Cambridge won was perhaps an ominous omen, for Sandys came away disappointed with the meeting, writing to the mayor that he was unwilling to approve the Oxford development plan unless something was done about the High Street. "This is of course," he wrote, "not primarily a traffic problem. It is the question of preserving a priceless heritage of culture and beauty."[19]

That everyone could agree with this assertion in principle was noteworthy. Oxford, in that way, was another illustration of the intertwining of modernism and conservationism that Miles Glendinning, among others, has recently observed. But still more important was the fact that no one could agree on the best way to achieve the minister's goal. There were at least three—and on one count, up to fifteen—rival plans to consider, and the key players in reaching a solution were profoundly split. Both the city council and the university (which had twelve seats on the council) were divided within and between themselves. The city planning officer and the city engineer were at loggerheads. The council committee responsible for planning admitted it was unable to agree on a solution. In the council, one vote on a road through Christ Church Meadow produced a vote of 29 in favor and 29 against.[20] As new proposals were put forward, views changed swiftly; the opposition Labour group fought Sharp's plans in 1948 and then enthusiastically endorsed them in 1955. Decisions were made, and then overturned, with an alarming rapidity.

Within the university, too, opinions were desperately riven. The undergraduate newspaper, *Cherwell*, observed in October 1955 that ten colleges were in favor of a road across the meadow, while fifteen were utterly opposed. But even this was an oversimplification. "Colleges," observed the *Evening Standard*, "are cleft into factions each of which sees cloven hooves beneath the other's gown."[21] Despite the best efforts of the Vice-Chancellor, the university's governing Hebdomadal Council had to agree to disagree. Meanwhile, Congregation—the assembly of the academics at Oxford—voted first against a road on Christ Church Meadow, and then, a week later, that, in extremis, this might be the least appalling option. In the process, as the historian Robert Blake noted, old friends "nearly came to blows," and distinguished academics were reduced to trading insults in the street.[22]

Not least of the problems in agreeing on a solution to Oxford's traffic was the way in which it attracted alternative schemes. The economist Roy Harrod projected a tunnel under the meadow; he wrote to *The Times,* broadcast on the BBC, and lobbied Sandys, who was, as he repeatedly mentioned, "an old friend of mine."[23] Sandys himself tried to float a different approach, visiting Oxford for a private meeting and persuading the leaders of the council to spare Christ Church Meadow by running two new roads to the north and south of the city, which would mean demolishing dozens of houses to the south and one much-loved pub, the Lamb and Flag, on St. Giles. St. Giles, however, was next to Oxford's richest college, St. John's, and also lay close to the wealthier, northernmost part of town. It was this new idea that caused the Conservatives in North Oxford—led by a former Bursar of St John's—to reject road building in Oxford even as the leaders of the city's Conservatives voted Sandys's plan through. It was this proposal, too, that changed the votes of the university, many of whom clearly came to prefer a meadow road to one that spoiled St. Giles.

Above all, the discussion was shaped—and people's votes were altered—by the Vice-Chancellor of Oxford University. The Warden of New College, Alic Smith, was a man conspicuously committed to the improvement of Oxford's architectural amenities. As part of this campaign, he agitated for a solution that would exclude cars, buses, and lorries from the High Street completely. Smith, as Hugh Trevor-Roper maliciously observed, was, "like all who arrive at executive eminence in our universities[,] . . . a past-master of *intrigue.*"[24] His enemies believed that he "cheated and swindled" to get his way.[25] Even his admirers thought him "shameless" in a fight.[26] It was Smith, as Vice-Chancellor, who had dined with Sandys on the minister's fateful visit to the city and who had attempted to square the university behind a road in the meadow through his chairmanship of Hebdomadal Council. And it was, indeed, his plan to close the High Street to traffic that the minister suggested in November 1955. But this proposal made matters only worse, for the shopkeepers of Oxford, who had initially favored a relief road, were horrified at the threat to passing trade that it seemed to present. So too the local Labour Party, which had been persuaded to support a road in the meadow, now came to fear that the closure of Magdalen Bridge would mean cutting Oxford in two, leaving their constituents in industrial Cowley unable to obtain access to services in the heart of the city.

The debate rumbled on for months, provoking much further fury and a ten-day public enquiry. On 24 July 1956, the issue reached the Cabinet. Of its eighteen members, more than half had attended

Oxford, and no less than a third had been to Christ Church. Although legend was later to claim that the agenda read "1. Oxford roads; 2. Seizure of the Suez Canal," the government's sense of priority is revealed by the fact that it was the fifth item discussed, after the Baghdad Pact, but before local government reorganization and economic statistics.[27] Sandys was forthright in presenting his case. "Traffic," he declared, "is ruining Oxford." The only solution, he maintained, was some form of relief road, either to the north or the south of the city, and since the University thought the former worse than the latter, he recommended a version of Sharp's Merton Mall. Anthony Eden was, it seems, doubtful about the proposal, arguing instead that Cowley should be developed with shops and cinemas. "Can't we seal off old city [?]" he went on to inquire. The result of these deliberations was a compromise, one that was, as the Cabinet secretary's notes indicate, "Approved—with regret." Merton Mall would be built; Magdalen Bridge would shut. Despite the "shocking outcry" that Sandys predicted, the High Street would be closed to traffic, and the road run through Christ Church Meadow.[28]

In a masterstroke of misjudgment, the government had agreed on a solution designed to cause the most outrage among the widest range of people. The author of the scheme, Thomas Sharp, was, predictably, pleased. "Thank God for someone with sense and courage," he declared on hearing the minister's decision.[29] The *Architect and Building News*, the *Architect's Journal, Autocar*, and other specialist publications also welcomed Sandys's "sound judgement" on the matter.[30] The Vice-Chancellor and other vocal advocates of the scheme were also presumably content. But the closure of the High Street was simply unconscionable to most city councillors, and the road through the meadow remained unacceptable to a majority of university opinion. Worse still, the minister himself was now widely suspected of duplicity. Even the timing of his decision seemed dubious. "It is no accident," wrote Robert Blake, "that this announcement has appeared right in the middle of the Suez crisis. I cannot believe that Mr Sandys would have got away with it if the Cabinet had been less preoccupied with far greater matters."[31]

The concatenation of the these events—one of global significance, the other of apparently more Lilliputian dimensions—proved irresistible for satirists, like the writer in *The Times* who described an appeal made to UN Security Council "to take urgent action to remove the threat to peace, culture, and human rights contained in the unprovoked seizure of Christ Church Meadow by the British Minister of Housing and Local Government."[32] In truth, however, powerful figures were attempting to mobilize higher powers.

Christ Church instructed lawyers and began to serve a writ against Sandys. Churchill's scientific adviser, Lord Cherwell, who had lived in Christ Church since 1922 and whose windows overlooked the proposed new road, agitated for a Royal Commission. William Beveridge provoked a five-hour debate in the House of Lords, one that attracted speakers including Clement Attlee, Lord Halifax, and the Archbishop of Canterbury, and that went on so long that it risked making the peers late for their dinner; something, as the *Oxford Mail* put it, "that happens on only the most exceptional occasions."[33] So it was that the government backed down. The result was a further enquiry, further recommendations, and yet further outrage, which occasioned more of the same. Multiple proposals would be made, accepted, and then rejected until, in 1978, Labour's environment secretary, Peter Shore, finally killed the plan for a road through Christ Church Meadow for good.

TWENTY-ONE YEARS EARLIER, IN FEBRUARY 1957, Robert Blake had observed, "The Oxford roads question has by now made most observers slightly giddy," and if that was true then, I fear that it might also be true now.[34] In any event, it would not serve much useful purpose to trace this battle any further on in time, much less to pursue it all the way to 1978. Instead, I want to return to the years between 1955 and 1957, a pivotal moment in Oxford's history, in the history of universities, and in British architectural history more generally.

The tactics used by those involved in this debate are highly revealing. They exemplify the ways in which politicians like Sandys sought to avoid public involvement, whereas campaigners and planners hoped to stimulate it. After all, it was the minister who attempted to manage this problem through private meetings and who wrote, at the very beginning of the process, of his efforts "to avoid the necessity for bringing in outside enquiries."[35] This debate also illuminates the multiple modes of engagement open to people who wished to shape the urban fabric around them. Public meetings, letters in newspapers, the consultations carried out by the council, the surveys carried out by the Oxford Preservation Trust, the more private access granted to members of the social and cultural elite—this was a moment in which a variety of actors could, and did, contribute to planning policy. Here, at any rate, is a considerably greater degree of public participation than other historians have found.

The terms of the debate are also noteworthy. All those involved accepted a common frame of reference. All, naturally enough, believed themselves to be acting in the best interests of Oxford. All, inevitably, argued that they were seeking to preserve the beauties of an ancient and historic city. More interestingly, though, all the participants claimed that their position was the one that best reflected the nature of modern life. Their opponents, by contrast, they depicted as reactionaries, unable to comprehend the challenge of modernity. Those who wished to close the Magdalen Bridge were attacked by Labour councillors for "trying to create 'a Vatican City in Oxford' . . . a 'National Trust sanctuary for Dons.'"[36] Advocates of a road through the meadow were condemned for wanting to achieve the "re-Gothicising of Oxford."[37] Writing privately, Hugh Trevor-Roper joked that the Vice-Chancellor hoped to ensure that "the High Street, newly cobbled and grassed, should accommodate only maypoles and morris-dancers and bare-footed monks singing Vespers through the nose."[38] Writing publicly, the Warden of Merton College slammed Smith for wanting to "ride his hobby-horse round the re-medievalised Oxford of his dreams."[39] Yet, as the Vice-Chancellor's allies asserted, the plan he proposed was in fact ultramodern, recommended by latest authorities on the subject. In closing the High Street and diverting the traffic elsewhere, wrote Walter Oakeshott, the Rector of Lincoln College, Oxford would be ahead of the game, providing "something that every city will be driven, before long, to try somehow to secure."[40] "Oxford is not a museum. I think of it as a town and not a tomb," observed the lord mayor in January 1956.[41] Everyone could agree with that, even if they could not agree what that meant in practice.

The ubiquity of this rhetoric was criticized at the time. Indeed, Duncan Sandys's vacillations were explained precisely in these terms. "The one thing that all politicians are frightened of is that they may be thought backward, reactionary, Victorian, not on the spot," wrote the Cambridge historian Charles Wilson.[42] The same was true for the academics, local leaders, and planners who participated in the debate about Oxford's road. All had to embrace the language of modernity. All were competing to be seen as the most modern. Moreover, all were keen to articulate a particularly British notion of modernity. The *Oxford Mail* observed in 1955 that Roy Harrod "fortified the argument against the Christ Church Meadow proposal by terming it an 'express way,' an Americanism with the kind of overtones calculated to counterblast those who prefer to call the meadow road a 'Mall.'"[43] Trevor-Roper similarly opted to call it an "*Autostrada.*"[44] In that sense, the whole controversy was a wonderful illustration of how Britons in the 1950s saw themselves and their country as explicitly, confidently, and distinctively modern.

But there was even more at stake than modernity. The battle over Oxford's roads was a struggle for authority. It raised questions of who was best able to interpret the modern age: locals or "the Gentleman at Whitehall"; politicians or planners; an educated elite or activists, businessmen, and the members of special interest groups.[45] Above all, then, it was about the nature of expertise and the question of which people were most expert. At a basic level, it mattered which experts were involved and what authority they possessed. When St. John's College found itself threatened by plans for a new road, it employed the country's leading town planner, Sir Patrick Abercrombie, as an adviser and expert witness. His arguments against a northern route onto St. Giles were devastating. Christ Church, by contrast, sought help from the elderly, undistinguished, and outmoded architect Arthur Kenyon. No planner, he was evidently overwhelmed by the responsibilities thrust upon him, recommending that the college turn to "authoritative names" like Abercrombie instead and admitting that he thought Sharp's plan a good one—the road through the meadow and all.[46] He was no match for the other experts, and Sandys found him "stupid and irritating." The minister concluded that "he was so irrelevant and raised so many false issues, that he made it difficult . . . to understand what the Christ Church view really was."[47] No wonder Sandys concluded that Merton Mall was the only solution.

The problem for Christ Church, and for all those involved in this debate, was that it was not at all clear who the real experts were. The 1947 Planning Act, which had prompted this whole farrago, depended, in Stephen Ward's words, "to a substantial extent on unelected professional experts."[48] But there were only 1,700 members of the Town Planning Institute, a fifth of whom were as yet unqualified, and 1,400 planning authorities. In fact, the question of who was most competent to advise on town planning was still being fought out between architects, engineers, surveyors, and this newly conceived town-planning profession. In these circumstances, there was little wonder that no authoritative, clinching conclusion could be reached. Any opinion was only ever provisional. The search for the right expert was always ongoing.

All of which helps explain how it was that Oxford—and Britain's other universities—came to adopt modern architecture so comprehensively in the late 1950s. There was a near-universal desire to embrace modernity, and a fear of being left behind. Almost all the people and institutions discussed above would be involved in modernist architectural projects in the decade that followed; the Warden of Merton (who opposed the road) commissioned self-consciously modern lodgings, and the Rector of Lincoln (who wrote in favor of the road) championed the modernist designs for a new Law Library.

Even conservative Christ Church succumbed, erecting a series of buildings by the Brutalist partnership of Powell and Moya. And how was it that all these academics with different and often very divergent views came to share a similar understanding of what modernity looked like? Just as in planning, so in architecture: they got it from experts. In fact, a strikingly small group of people determined what modern Oxford amounted to. Their numbers included the historian John Summerson, who played a decisive role in Oxford's first collegiate example of modernism at St. John's, and the architect Leslie Martin, who became kingmaker extraordinaire, doling out jobs at a dozen institutions to his protégés.[49]

In that way, we can see that Oxford was shaped and reshaped by a cult of the expert: embodiments of the "expert paternalism" that David Matless has seen as characteristic of contemporary planners.[50] Experts were expected to give shape to a general desire to be modem and to seem modern. They were also employed to sell these ideas to the public. These experts, however, were vulnerable to the assaults of rival experts, be they other professionals or locals deploying their local knowledge. This explains why Oxford went modernist and why it did not build a road through Christ Church Meadow. It also helps account for what happened next. For Oxford found that its experts were not so expert after all. The turn away from modernism in the 1970s was as much a loss of faith in the previous generation's experts as it was an abandonment of a particular aesthetic. That, though, is another story.

Spring Semester 2014

1. Alan Bullock, foreword to David Reed and Philip Opher, *New Architecture in Oxford* (Oxford, 1977).
2. *Sunday Times*, 6 Nov. 1955.
3. Richard Davenport-Hines, ed., *Letters from Oxford: Hugh Trevor-Roper to Bernard Berenson* (London, 2006), p. 178.
4. Oxford, Christ Church Archive [CCA], xxviic.1/191.
5. *Letters from Oxford*, p. 180.
6. CCA, xxviic.1/194.
7. Colin Buchanan, *Traffic in Towns: A Study of the Long-Term Problems of Traffic in Urban Areas* (London, 1963), pp. 6, 22.
8. *The Times*, 13 Oct.1956.
9. J. P. R. Maud, *The Times*, 8 Dec. 1938.
10. *Birmingham Post*, 2 Aug. 1955.
11. C. D. Buchanan, *Mixed Blessing: The Motor in Britain* (London, 1958), p. 185.
12. Harford Thomas, *News Chronicle*, 27 July 1955.
13. *Country Life*, 21 July 1955.
14. John Pendlebury, "The Urbanism of Thomas Sharp," *Planning Perspectives*, 24 (2009), p. 13.
15. Thomas Sharp, *Oxford Replanned* (Oxford, 1948), p. 81.
16. Ibid., p. 118.
17. Ibid., p. 114.
18. Lord Orr-Ewing, quoted in N. Piers Ludlow, "Baron Duncan-Sandys," *Oxford Dictionary of National Biography*.
19. CCA, xxviic.1/54.
20. *Oxford Mail*, 7 Nov. 1955.
21. *Evening Standard*, 14 Oct. 1955.
22. CCA, Soc. Dacre 1/2/3.
23. CCA, xxviic.1/235.
24. *Letters from Oxford*, p. 179.
25. Bodleian Library, Berlin papers MS 257/26, Herbert Hart to Berlin.
26. John Sparrow, quoted in *Alic Halford Smith, 1883–1958* (Oxford, 1960), p. 5.
27. Mark Barrington-Ward, "The Story So Far," in Edward Townsend-Coles, ed., *Transport and the Future of Oxford* (Oxford, 2000), p. 10.
28. TNA, CAB 195/15, 24 July 1956.
29. *Oxford Mail*, 22 Sept. 1956.
30. *Architect's Journal*, 27 Sept. 1956.
31. Robert Blake, "Ploughing the Sandys," *Spectator*, 28 Sept. 1956.
32. *Sunday Times*, 5 Oct. 1956.
33. *Oxford Mail*, 13 Feb. 1957.
34. Robert Blake, "Oxford Roads," *Spectator*, 8 Feb. 1957.
35. CCA, xxviic.1/55.
36. *Oxford Times*, 2 Dec. 1955.
37. Robert Blake, *Spectator*, 21 Oct. 1955.
38. *Letters from Oxford*, p. 179.
39. Geoffrey Mure, *Oxford Mail*, 10 Oct. 1955.
40. *Spectator*, 28 Oct. 1956.
41. *Oxford Times*, 27 Jan. 1957.
42. Charles Wilson, *Spectator*, 12 Oct. 1956.
43. *Oxford Mail*, 16 July 1955.
44. *Letters from Oxford*, p. 222.

45. Blake, "Oxford Roads."
46. CCA, xxviic.1/180.
47. CCA, xxviic.1/235.
48. Stephen Ward, *Planning and Urban Change* (London, 2004), p. 102.
49. William Whyte, *Redbrick: A Social and Architectural History of Britain's Civic Universities* (Oxford, 2015), ch. 10.
50. David Matless, "Appropriate Geography: Patrick Abercrombie and the Energy of the World," *Journal of Design History*, 6 (1993), p. 172.

Harold Macmillan, 1959 © National Portrait Gallery, London

24

Harold Macmillan

FERDINAND MOUNT

The first thing about Harold Macmillan was his bravery, and it was the last thing too. In the Great War, he was wounded five times, at the Battle of Loos and at the Somme. At Delville Wood he was hit in the thigh and pelvis and rolled down into a large shell hole, where he lay for the next ten hours, alternately dosing himself with morphine and reading Aeschylus. He wrote home on 13 September 1916 that "the stench from the dead bodies which lie in heaps around is awful." Only a fortnight earlier he had told his mother: "Do not worry about me. I am very happy; it is a great experience, psychologically so interesting as to fill one's thoughts." In North Africa during the Second World War, his plane crashed on takeoff at Algiers and burst into flames. Macmillan scrambled through the emergency exit and then went back into the burning plane to rescue a French flag lieutenant—a fact he doesn't mention in his account of the incident in his memoirs or even in his diary. John McCloy, FDR's assistant secretary of war, described it as "the most gallant thing I've ever seen."

Macmillan wasn't one of those not infrequent war heroes who in peacetime are mild and eager to please. He remained dauntless and daunting in politics. He despised Rab Butler for not having fought (he had a withered hand after a riding accident as a child), he sneered at Hugh Gaitskell for not having any medals to wear on Remembrance Day, and he loathed Herbert Morrison, his first boss in the wartime coalition, for having been a conscientious objector in the First World War, calling him "a dirty little cockney guttersnipe." Macmillan's diary is spattered with abuse of other public figures, often tinged with anti-Semitism. He never hesitated to tell his colleagues or his superiors when he thought they were wrong. He was the only minister who dared to tell Churchill it was time to go, although it was Churchill who had brought him back from the political wilderness in 1940.

He was implacable and proud of it. When his son, Maurice, wondered why his own career had fallen so far short of his father's, Macmillan said: "Because you weren't ruthless enough." When Eden offered him the Exchequer, Macmillan did a Gordon Brown: insisting that "as chancellor, I must be undisputed head of the home front, under you" and that there could be no question of his predecessor, Butler, being accorded the title of deputy prime minister. Barely a year later, after the Suez debacle, he was promising the American ambassador that in return for "a fig leaf to cover our nakedness," he would arrange not only the withdrawal of British troops from Egypt but also the replacement of Eden. When he sacked a third of his Cabinet in 1962 after a run of terrible by-election results, the purge was entirely typical of his undeviating self-interest, although in that Night of the Long Knives it turned out he had been so sharp he cut himself, fatally.

Not surprisingly, throughout his life he was disliked by many and hated by quite a few. At Eton, he received thirteen blackballs in the election for the debating society. The following term, he received eleven. "He is his own worst enemy: he is too self-centred, too obviously cleverer than the rest of us," his fellow new MP from the Northeast in 1924, Cuthbert Headlam, noted after a dinner with Macmillan. "He never will let the other man have his say, and he invariably knows everything better than the other man." This inability to listen gained him a reputation in clubland as a bore and banger-on, despite his undoubted wit and languid charm. In politics, the results of his not listening were frequently calamitous.

Not that he much minded being unpopular. For most of his life he essentially lived alone. His two brothers were years older, and his father was away building the great publishing house. His mother, the bossy and possessive Nellie Belles from Indiana, took him away from Eton when he was only fifteen, fearing he was being exposed to "unnatural practices." J. B. S. Haldane, who was there at the same time, claimed that Macmillan had been expelled for homosexuality; but Nellie seems to have thought it was the school that was out of order, not her son. Being a strict Nonconformist, she was no better pleased when he formed a close affection for one of his tutors,

Ronald Knox, who came within an inch of converting Macmillan to Catholicism. The war saved him from taking this step, which would almost certainly have prevented him from becoming Prime Minister. In his last letter to Knox before leaving for France, he wrote: "I'm going to be rather odd. I'm not going to 'pope' until after the war (if I'm alive)."

Volunteering for the war meant that at Oxford, as at Eton, he stayed only half the course, being "sent down by the Kaiser," as he liked to put it. It seems peculiar in retrospect that he should have retained such obsessive loyalties to two institutions he spent so little time in. Nothing gave him more pleasure than being elected Chancellor of Oxford, and he was disappointed not to become Provost of Eton in 1965 after he ceased to be Prime Minister. He continually referred to the Fourth of June, often to people who had no idea that this was the school's great festival, or to those who pretended not to, like the Harrovian Field Marshal Alexander.

There was something strangely fake about his snobbish carry-on, almost as though he was trying to convince himself that he belonged. Some of his smoking-room metaphors were merely mystifying: for example, when pondering whether Cyprus should be granted full Commonwealth status after independence, he wondered whether the island should "be the RAC [Royal Automobile Club] or Boodles"? When Roger Hollis, the head of MI5, exulted to Macmillan that they had arrested the spy John Vassall, the Prime Minister complained that this was the wrong approach: "When my gamekeeper shoots a fox, he doesn't go and hang it up outside the Master of Foxhounds' drawing room; he buries it out of sight." To which Hollis might legitimately have replied that some gamekeepers had the sense to hang the vermin they had shot on the nearest fence to warn off other predators.

This clubman's chatter dates from his marriage to the Duke of Devonshire's daughter Dorothy in 1920: a giant leg up socially but ultimately a disaster. Both gawky virgins, they were happy for nearly a decade until Dorothy fell in love with Macmillan's fellow MP Bob Boothby and demanded a divorce, claiming that her youngest daughter, Sarah, was Boothby's child. From being regarded as a jolly sort, keen on golf and a dab hand at opening fêtes, Dorothy suddenly revealed unsuspected Wagnerian depths of passion, saying to Boothby: "Why did you ever wake me? I never want to see any of my family again." She had four young children at the time. Years later, Boothby described her as "on the whole, the most selfish and possessive woman I have ever known."

She did not get what she wanted. Macmillan's solicitor, Philip

Frere, pointed out that divorce would be fatal for his political career and recommended a "west wing–east wing" solution, traditional among the estranged upper classes who had houses large enough for the purpose. Until she died in 1966—suddenly, of a heart attack as she was putting on her boots—if they were both at Birch Grove, Macmillan's house in Sussex, they would meet for dinner and then go their separate ways.

Macmillan remained haunted by the affair. In 1975, he went to see Boothby at his flat and asked, for the sake of his peace of mind, to know the truth one way or another about Sarah. In the unbearably painful conversation that followed, Boothby assured him that Sarah was not his daughter because he was always scrupulously careful in his affairs. What Macmillan did not know was that Boothby had just been presented with a tape recorder by the Royal Philharmonic Orchestra, of which he had been chairman for many years. Before Macmillan's arrival, he had been taping a Tchaikovsky symphony from the radio. He had turned off the radio but unwittingly left the tape recorder running on the floor behind a sofa. And so all the agony that Macmillan had poured out to him was on tape, and Boothby played it back to his new wife, Wanda, when she came in, with tears running down his face.

This is how D. R. Thorpe tells the story, eloquently and elegantly, as he does everything in *Supermac: The Life of Harold Macmillan* (2010), an exemplary biography that complements, even if it does not entirely supplant, Alistair Horne's two-volume official life. Horne is better on the military, Thorpe on the political and personal. At every juncture, Thorpe presents the evidence in a scrupulous and equable style. He is charitable, just as he was in his earlier biographies of Selwyn Lloyd and Eden, both of whom had reasons to be resentful of Macmillan's behavior. By not taking sides, Thorpe leaves readers room to come to their own judgment.

I don't think that Boothby, that insatiable seducer of both sexes, left the tape recorder on by accident. I don't mean that he had it in for Macmillan exactly, although it is always hard to forgive those you have wronged, especially when you have been wronging them for years. It is more that Boothby, himself the ripest of old hams, would have been unable to resist the dramatic potential of the scene: the aged former Prime Minister with tears running down his face, and then a few hours later Boothby, the man of feeling, recalling the recalling with tears running down *his* face.

Thorpe tells us that Macmillan never looked at another woman. He dismisses the claim of Sean O'Casey's widow (O'Casey was a Macmillan author) to have had an affair with Harold at the time

Dorothy first fell for Boothby. Quite out of character, Thorpe argues: Macmillan was straitlaced and not much interested in sex anyway. He was lost for words when JFK turned to him during a break in their discussions on nuclear arms at Key West and inquired: "I wonder how it is with you, Harold? If I don't have a woman for three days, I get a terrible headache." What is certain is that Macmillan was deeply lonely. He took refuge in West End clubs to an almost pathological extent: Pratt's, the Athenaeum, Buck's, Guards, the Beefsteak, the Turf, the Carlton—he was in and out of them every day. A member of Pratt's calling in there one evening in the 1960s inquired whether there was anyone in that night. "Nobody at all, sir, only the Prime Minister."

His health, always fragile, gave way during his wife's affair. In the summer of 1931 he had a serious breakdown. There were rumors that he had attempted suicide. He was secretly admitted to the Kuranstalt Neuwittelsbach sanatorium outside Munich. He recovered, but had another bad collapse in October 1943 during an unexpected visit to London from his post in North Africa. He remained an intensely nervous figure, inclined to vomit before big speeches, which was why he always lunched alone before Prime Minister's Questions. The unflappable façade was an amazing effort of the will.

He had become MP for Stockton-on-Tees in 1924 and held the seat almost continuously until 1945; in old age, he took his title from it. Stockton was (and in its center still is) a handsome old market town, transformed when it became the birthplace of the railways and the hub of the iron and steel industry. By the time Macmillan appeared there, unemployment was more than 20 percent and rising (what trade there was had shifted to neighboring Middlesbrough). His principal loathing was not for the Labour Party, which he periodically thought of joining, but for the hard-faced men on his own benches, the industrialists who had done well out of the war—the Forty Thieves, as they were known to Macmillan and his friends. They were mocked in return as "the YMCA." All his life, Macmillan retained a distrust of the City and "the banksters." He claimed in 1936 that "Toryism has always been a form of paternal socialism."

FOR AN UNDENIABLY CLEVER MAN, Macmillan left remarkably little evidence of strategic thought in his voluminous diaries. The latest volume, covering his years as Prime Minister, does little to improve one's earlier impression of an agile but not very original mind struggling to survive from day to day. The enormous length of the diaries remains a problem. In his introduction, the editor, Peter Catterall, states that "omissions have, of course, had to occur to reduce the original text to less than half its length" and that it was "necessary to omit Macmillan's reading, social activities and family life." This strikes me as precisely the wrong way to go about editing this particular diary, perhaps any diary. The value of having the diaries in their entirety must be to give a rounded portrait of this strange, lonely, rather wonderful but also decidedly unpleasant man. Pepys without Mrs. Pepys, the delicious Deb Willet, or the visits to the play would be a far poorer thing.

The diary also contains gaps. Macmillan admits several times that during a real crisis such as Suez or Profumo his diary keeping breaks down. Nor does he seem fully alert to his own memorable moments. All he says of his speech at Bedford in July 1957 is that it "was well reported in the Sunday press, and I think helped to steady things," omitting to record that it was in this speech that he uttered the immortal phrase about most of us never having had it so good. His "Wind of Change" speech he does not mention at all in a skimpy retrospect of his African tour in February 1960. Quite a few entries read like a summary of events drawn up by someone else. Not often do you get the feeling of being there yourself or of learning something new about how it went. Only the odd languid wisecrack convinces you that this is the real Mac. I liked his musing during the Cuban Missile Crisis on "the frightful desire to *do* something, with the knowledge that *not* to do anything . . . was prob. the right answer."

What strikes the reader, above all, is Macmillan's obsessive preoccupation with foreign affairs to the near exclusion of the domestic and economic; a good 80 percent of the diary entries, perhaps more, are concerned with overseas affairs. Pages are filled with the fruitless efforts to save the Central African Federation. Weeks are consumed with overseas visits to prepare the way for a summit until, as Macmillan wearily concludes, "everyone else has visited everyone." The summit then collapses and "all our plans are in ruins." By contrast, it is not until March 1963—after he has been Prime Minister for six years—that he publicly launches a campaign for "the modernisation of Britain."

When we see Macmillan at his best is undoubtedly during the war years, which were covered in a volume published separately in 1984 (*War Diaries: Politics and War in the Mediterranean, January 1943– May 1945*). Those diaries, published pretty much entire, contain fine descriptions of North Africa as well as sharp pen portraits and nippy asides. And besides, they describe an extremely delicate and fascinating mission, told as deftly as it was executed. As ministerial representative at Allied Forces Headquarters, Macmillan had to devise his own peculiar role. Generals, including Eisenhower, who at first wondered exactly what he was doing there, came to respect his panache, energy, and ingenuity. His management of the political chaos in Italy and then of the warring factions in Greece was nothing short of masterly. Richard Crossman, then assistant chief of psychological warfare at AFHQ, concluded in a shrewd single sentence: "I suspect it was in Algiers, where he could do all the thinking and take all the decisions while Ike took all the credit, that Harold Macmillan first realised his own capacity for supreme leadership and developed that streak of intellectual recklessness which was to be the cause both of his success and of his failure when he finally reached No. 10."

IT IS THUS A PITY AND AN IRONY that of Macmillan's service in that war, the only bit that is much remembered is the tragic finale: the handing over of Cossacks and White Russians and Croats at Klagenfurt, Austria, in May 1945. The appalling consequences of this decision—thousands of men, women, and children were slaughtered by Stalin and Tito—remain a black and unforgettable chapter. The accusations against Macmillan personally became progressively more pointed in Nikolai Tolstoy's three polemics: *Victims of Yalta* (1977), *Stalin's Secret War* (1981), and *The Minister and the Massacres* (1986), which fingered Macmillan as part of "the Klagenfurt conspiracy" and an accessory to mass murder. After Macmillan's death in 1986, an independent investigation led and largely paid for by Anthony Cowgill concluded unequivocally that, in the words of one of his team, "Macmillan's part in the story was (a) marginal at best, and (b) that he actually knew very little about the Cossacks in Austria, apart from what he was told at the briefing at Klagenfurt airfield." In *The Repatriations from Austria in 1945,* Cowgill concluded that Macmillan had nothing at all to do with the decision to send back the dissident Yugoslavs against their will. The general decision to repatriate to the Soviet authorities arose from Cabinet decisions dating back to June 1944; it then became part of a quid pro quo agreed to with Stalin at Yalta in February 1945. The operational decisions on handover were taken, he argued, at a military conference in Udine on 26–27 May, by which time Macmillan was back in England. Those who criticize the orders fail to take account of the chaotic and menacing circumstances of the moment. Tito's forces were threatening to overrun Carinthia and Venezia Giulia. The whole war could have reignited in the region.

This is the new consensus on the subject, and Thorpe subscribes to it. Yet, fair-minded as ever, he offers several pieces of evidence to support those who still believe that Macmillan was, at best, guilty of "over-compliance." In his diary for 13 May, Macmillan wrote: "Among the surrendered Germans are about 40,000 Cossacks and 'White' Russians, with their wives and children. To hand them over to the Russians is condemning them to slavery, torture and probably death. To refuse, is deeply to offend the Russians, and incidentally break the Yalta agreement. We have decided to hand them over." The next day, 14 May, General Charles Keightley telegraphed Alexander, the commander in chief: "On advice Macmillan I have today suggested to Soviet General on Tolbukhin's HQ that Cossacks should be returned to SOVIETS at once." As for there being no final authorization for handing over either the Cossacks and White Russians to Stalin or the Croats to Tito until the conference at Udine on the 26th, Lieutenant Colonel Robin Rose Price wrote in his diary on 19 May: "Order of most sinister duplicity received i.e. to send Croats to their foes, i.e. Tits to Yugoslavia under the impression they were to go to Italy." Thorpe does not quote the even more sinister sentence that follows in Rose Price's diary: "Tit guards on trains hidden in guards van." It is not unreasonable then to suppose that the essential decisions were taken not at Udine, which looks more like a rubber-stamping, but during the two hours Macmillan spent on the airstrip at Klagenfurt. Whether other orders could have been given in the circumstances of the time remains debatable, but "marginal" isn't quite the right word to describe Macmillan's role.

What he cannot be acquitted of is callousness. Which is shown by a curious coda to the miserable story. Macmillan's diaries break off (not to resume until 1950) when he flies home on 26 May 1945 to become air minister in Churchill's caretaker government. Thorpe, like previous biographers, assumes that this was his final farewell to the mountains and lakes of Austria. But William Dugdale, in his memoir, *Settling the Bill* (2011), describes being deputed to organize a Fourth of June dinner in an orchard by the banks of the Wörthersee. Sixty or seventy Old Etonian guards officers were invited to sing "Floreat Etona" and toast the Old Coll in slivovitz, along with the army commander, General McCreery, Field Marshal Alexander, and Harold Macmillan. Nothing, it seems, would have deterred him from flying halfway across the ravaged continent to celebrate the two institutions he loved best, Eton and the Grenadiers. At the end of dinner, Macmillan was accosted by Rose Price, aflame with drink and an almost Homeric rage, and lambasted for ordering his battalion to send the Cossacks to their death. Dugdale records beautifully how Macmillan, a cigarette drooping from his lips, turned his strangely flappy hands (weakened by war wounds) outward in that gesture we came to know so well and replied: "How else are we to demonstrate our loyalty to Stalin and the Russians?" Thus, long before the controversy reawakened in the 1980s, Macmillan was made forcibly aware of the repugnance the orders aroused among the soldiers who had to carry them out. What is so striking is that he had no hesitation in returning to the scene of the crime only nine days later.

Again and again, one notices the callous insouciance, which, as Crossman spotted, was both his strength and his weakness, leading him to overcome, seemingly without effort, "little local difficulties" that might have unhorsed more careful operators, but also drawing him into wildly optimistic miscalculations that generated terrible outcomes. The part he played at Suez certainly seems to fit that description. As Chancellor of the Exchequer, he was desperately keen to establish that the Americans would back Britain in the use of force. He hammered home as forcefully as he could to Bob Murphy, his wartime comrade who had come to London on Eisenhower's behalf, that the government had decided to drive Nasser out of Egypt and that Parliament and the people were behind them. He told John Foster Dulles, the Secretary of State, the same thing. "We are committed to a peaceful settlement of this dispute, nothing else," Eisenhower said at a press conference on 5 September. But Macmillan refused to believe this or to grasp the fairly obvious fact that all Ike cared about was being reelected in November. In Washington at the end of September, Macmillan saw Eisenhower, Dulles, and George Humphrey, the U.S. Treasury Secretary. Yet he still could not grasp that, in Humphrey's words after the invasion, "You'll not get a dime out of the US government until you've gotten out of Suez." Roger Makins, Macmillan's private secretary, who took notes at the meeting with Eisenhower, was amazed by the rambling, unfocused nature of the conversation and thought Macmillan was wholly unwarranted in his subsequent optimism about American support. Ike was rambling on purpose in his typically devious way. Macmillan just failed to listen.

Thorpe acquits Macmillan of the charges usually laid against him regarding Suez: that he was "first in, first out," that he pushed Eden into a disastrous venture that he knew would fail, that he exaggerated the ensuing economic crisis, and that he poured his energies into outmaneuvering Butler for the succession. Fair enough, but Thorpe also makes light, much too light, of the secret collusion with the Israelis. Contrary to the long-prevailing misconception, he tells us, the Cabinet was informed of Lloyd's meeting at Sèvres with the French and the Israelis—which serves only to implicate the lot of them. Then he wheels on the historians Robert Blake and Andrew Roberts to argue that secret diplomacy and suppressio veri are necessary to the successful prosecution of war: in Blake's words, "no one of sense will regard such falsehoods in a particularly serious light." This sort of unabashed realpolitik is undermined, even exploded, by the final Suez dispatch from the supreme military commander, General Keightley, last seen in Klagenfurt: "The one overriding lesson of the Suez operation is that world opinion is now an absolute principle of war." Where military action is undertaken for moral reasons, to right a wrong or to turf out a tyrant, any hint of deceit is fatal (see: Iraq passim). The gravamen of the charge against Macmillan is different: namely, that he was the only British minister to talk to all the top Americans and that he completely and disastrously misread their intentions.

Macmillan's political vision may have been impaired, but his eye for the main chance remained undimmed. He was, quite simply, a magnificent intriguer, opaque when he had to be, brutally swift to jump through any window of opportunity, smashing the glass where necessary. Enoch Powell described the way Macmillan destroyed Butler's chances of succeeding Eden when they both appeared before the 1922 Committee (a committee of Conservative MPs) in January 1957 after Eden had flown off to Jamaica as "one of the most horrible things that I remember in politics" (and he ought to know). Macmillan saw off Butler again, just as effortlessly, in the race to succeed himself in 1963. In his usual charitable way, Thorpe acquits Macmillan of organizing Alec Douglas-Home's startling triumph. As in 1957, he argues, the parliamentary party would not have Rab Butler at any price, and Home was the candidate that fewest people objected to and so the one best qualified to keep the party united. Yet Thorpe once again provides us with the materials to come to a rather different conclusion.

Compared to his dithering over the preceding months about whether he should resign, Macmillan moved with great rapidity once his prostate trouble was diagnosed. Contrary to previous misconceptions, he was told by his consultant urologist Alec Badenoch before he resigned that he didn't have cancer. The reality was that he was desperately tired and was glad of the medical excuse to pack it in. He told Badenoch that the illness "came as manna from heaven—an act of God."

But he was by no means done for. Consider the calendar. The Lord Chancellor, Lord Dilhorne, had asked all the Cabinet ministers at the beginning of September whether they wanted Macmillan to carry on and, if he decided not to, who should succeed him; all but three wanted him to carry on, and nobody mentioned Home as a successor. October 4: Macmillan discusses possible successors with his son, Maurice; again no mention of Home. On the night of 7–8 October he is taken ill. On the afternoon of the 8th he is diagnosed and in the evening taken to hospital. The next morning, the 9th, he talks to Home about the announcement of his resignation and raises, for the first time, the possibility that Home might make himself available. At the same time, Selwyn Lloyd sets about spreading Home's claims. By the 11th, Lloyd has converted Dilhorne and Martin Redmayne, the chief whip, and is walking along the prom at Blackpool with them, plotting what to do next. These two men would be responsible for canvassing opinion: Dilhorne doing the Cabinet (for the second time), and Redmayne the Tory MPs. By Tuesday the 15th, it is agreed that these soundings should include three questions: who is your first choice, who is your second, and who would you oppose? Then, after Lord Hailsham makes a fool of himself at Blackpool, a fourth is added: what do you think of Lord Home as leader? That same day, before the soundings are actually taken, Supermac composes what becomes known as the "Tuesday memorandum" for the Queen. It is a dithyramb for Sir Alec, comparing him to the heroic Grenadiers of 1914 and lauding his qualities of judgment and selflessness. He also makes a note in his diary after another meeting with Maurice and the party chairman, Lord Poole: "The basic situation was the same—the party in the country wants Hogg; the Parliamentary Party wants Maudling or Butler; the Cabinet wants Butler." But what they all got, only three days later, was Home.

Almost at the end of his book, Thorpe tells us, though without giving a source, that "Macmillan and Home both came in time to think that it might have been better if Rab Butler had become prime minister in 1963." I would go a lot further. It might have been better if Butler had succeeded Eden in 1957, or even Churchill in 1955. The country would undoubtedly have been better governed. There would have been no Suez, no inflationary stampede, no botched attempt to join the EEC, but rather a careful development of a European Free Trade Area. Social reform and economic modernization would have been pursued more seriously and systematically. It would have been a soberer time, without the showmanship with which Macmillan delighted some and repelled others. We would not have been told we had never had it so good; but we might have been better off.

Alas, the qualities required for being Prime Minister are not the same as those required for becoming one. Butler had all the charisma of an old flannel. Supermac in his heyday was a class act. In his later years, the satirists got at him, and to the young he was a somewhat moth-eaten comic figure. Thorpe tells us at the end that "Macmillan *was* a great prime minister for much of his time in Downing Street." There is a certain desperation about those italics. What was his legacy, after all? Premium Bonds and the Beeching Report. Macmillan said of Eden, quite rightly, that he had been trained to win the Derby of 1938 but had not been let out of the stalls until 1955. If you change the dates slightly, you could say much the same of Macmillan. His best years were already behind him when he reached the top at the age of sixty-two. And somewhere at the back of his mind, I think he knew it.

Spring Semester 2015

A version of this lecture appeared in the *London Review of Books*, 8 September 2011.

British armed forces in Borneo, 1964. Photograph in the collection of the Imperial War Museums

25

The Last Colonial War

DAVID RAMSBOTHAM

Britain's last colonial war, the 1962–66 undeclared war between Indonesia and Malaysia, could be said to have its origins in a rivalry between the British and the Dutch. Britain first became involved in the Far East in the seventeenth century, and Holland had been there since the early sixteenth. The most obvious manifestation of the rivalry was commercial competition between the British East India Company, which, besides running India until the mutiny in 1857, established trading posts on the Malay Peninsula, and the Dutch East India Company, which held a number of coastal strongholds on Java, Sumatra, Timor, New Guinea—or Irian—and other islands of the vast Indonesian archipelago. After the Dutch East India Company was declared bankrupt in 1800, its strongholds were administered as a colony called the Dutch East Indies. The boundaries between them and British Malaya—which, including Singapore, was administered from London as a crown colony called the Straits Settlements, from 1826—were formalized by treaty in 1824.

On Kalimantan (Borneo) the Dutch concentrated on the south and east, and the British on the north and west, the boundaries again formalized by treaty (but not until 1891). The governance of the three British North Borneo territories was very different from that of the Straits Settlements. Sarawak was run by the "white rajah" Brooke family—an English adventurer, James Brooke, having been given the title by the Sultan of Brunei in 1841 as a reward for putting down a rebellion. Sabah, previously under its own sultan, was from 1881 run by the British North Borneo Company. Brunei, under its sultan, became a British protectorate in 1888.

And then came the Second World War. Malaya was invaded by the Japanese on 8 December 1941, fifty minutes before Pearl Harbor was attacked, and the peninsula had been captured by 31 January 1942, after what can only be described as a wholly ineffective defense by outnumbered and outfought British forces. Singapore was overrun in a mere eight days in February 1942, its defense not helped by the fact that all the main guns protecting the naval base faced out to sea, whereas the Japanese attacked from mainland Malaya. Sarawak was attacked in December 1942, and Sabah in January 1943, the conquest of both being completed by March. Those two areas, along with Malaya, remained in Japanese hands until the end of the war. In 1946, Sabah and Sarawak became crown colonies, administered in the same way as the Straits Settlements.

On 10 October 1945, soon after Clement Attlee's Labour government succeeded Winston Churchill's wartime coalition, the new Prime Minister signaled Britain's withdrawal from empire via a statement on the future of Malaya, delivered by the Colonial Secretary in the House of Commons: "His Majesty's Government" had carefully considered the need "to promote the sense of unity and common citizenship which will develop the country's strength and capacity in due course for self-government within the British Commonwealth," which a number of countries in the region took as the green light for seeking their independence.[1] The path to nationhood of all the countries that ultimately formed the Federation of Malaysia was complicated by the high percentage of Chinese in their populations—37 percent in Malaya, 31 percent in Sarawak, 23 percent in Sabah, and 75 percent in Singapore. Because these Chinese provided much of the economic infrastructure and owned much of the commerce, many thought of themselves as Chinese first and as belonging to another nation second; in addition, their possible links to the Chinese Communist Party resulted in their being regarded as a potential source of insurgency. In Malaya—trained, equipped, and supported by the British—the Chinese formed an important part of the resistance against the Japanese, for which, understandably, they felt deserving of a reward. This was the background to the Malayan Communist Party's attempt to seize power in Malaya in 1948, leading the British government immediately to declare an "Emergency."

The Emergency had been brought under control by 1955 and was finally declared ended on 31 July 1960. British countermeasures included the establishment of a unified politico-military command and the introduction of what was called the "fortified kampong" concept, the brainchild of a colonial civil servant, Robert Thompson, then on the staff of the director of operations. Essentially, this involved housing all rubber-estate workers in fortified kampongs, or villages, guarded by the police, from which they went out to work by day. The need to keep them safe justified control of their movements, both at work and at home. A nightly curfew was imposed, with the aim of preventing terrorists from obtaining food and other supplies. Meanwhile, the army operated in the jungle, ambushing tracks used by terrorists and seeking out and attacking their camps. Airpower was used—ineffectively—to bomb camps and—effectively—to deliver supplies to soldiers in the jungle, but the main counterinsurgency efforts were joint, population-centered police-army operations.

Malaya had become an independent federation on 31 October 1957, and Singapore was granted internal self-government on 3 June 1959. It was said that they were "blessed with a good administrative structure, tempered to perfection by successive British Governments," a legacy that "should not suffer inefficiency and loss of integrity in years to come." This administrative structure, practiced throughout the British Empire, consisted of local rulers served by a British hierarchy of officials who spoke the language and lived in the areas for which they were responsible.

Post-war events followed a very different course in the Dutch East Indies. On 17 August 1945, Sukarno, who had been a nationalist leader since 1929, was proclaimed the first president of an Indonesian Republic, triggering a bitter four-year war with the Dutch that ended, in December 1949, with the transfer of all their territories except Western New Guinea (Irian) to Indonesia. In 1959, Sukarno, who was violently anticolonialist rather than communist and who was always faced with internal power struggles between the military and the Indonesian Communist Party, seized full power in order to resolve what he described as "post-revolutionary instability." He also made it clear that he regarded the independence of Malaya as a challenge to Indonesia's interests; he was particularly opposed to Sabah or Sarawak being included in any future Malaysian Federation. Conversely, since communism had just been defeated in the Emergency, Malayan concerns about Indonesia were fueled by suspicion of its growing relationship with Russia, including its receipt of military equipment, and the influence of China, the main promoter of communism in Southeast Asia, which was only too willing to supply modern, sophisticated weapons to would-be dissidents and to train them in their use. Thus, when the 4,000-member North Kalimantan National Army, or TNKU, armed with a few modern weapons and 1,000 shotguns and led by a thirty-four-year-old local politician called Azahari, mounted a revolt in Brunei on 8 December 1962, it was hardly surprising that Indonesia was thought to be behind it.

HOW AND WHY DID BRITAIN BECOME INVOLVED? Throughout the evolution from empire to commonwealth, Britain retained responsibility for the defense of its colonies and protected territories, and also undertook to mount specific operations in emergencies. Following the Suez debacle in 1956, Prime Minister Harold Macmillan developed a new defense policy. National Service was ended in 1962, and the overall size of the British armed forces was reduced from 690,000, including conscripts, to 375,000, the army being reduced to 165,000, plus 13,000 Gurkhas, recruited in Nepal, for service in the Far East. Gurkhas were the mainstay of the ground forces committed to the Malayan Emergency, and they formed a major part of the garrisons in Hong Kong and Singapore. Contingency plans were made to reinforce the Far East by up to three brigades in an emergency, but it would take time for them to arrive from Britain and then to acclimatize.

Following Malaya's independence, Britain promised to provide the country, on request, with "personnel to assist in the staffing, administration and training of the armed forces of the Federation," in return for "the right to maintain . . . such naval, land and air forces[,] including a Commonwealth Strategic Reserve," as might be necessary for the defence of the Federation and "fulfilment of Commonwealth and international obligations," but not for operations outside the Far East area.[2] In addition, the two governments agreed to consult over effective measures for joint action, "in the event of a threat of armed attack against . . . the Federation of Malaya" or the protectorates, "or other threat to the preservation of peace in the Far East."[3]

Therefore Brunei, as a protectorate, was entitled to ask for immediate assistance from Headquarters Far East Command when Azahari's revolt broke out. By ten o'clock on the night of 8 December 1962, two Gurkha companies had been flown from Singapore to Brunei, followed by further Gurkha battalions and a Strategic Reserve battalion, which recovered the main oil refinery. By 12 December, all rebels had been cleared from the immediate area of Brunei, and by the 17th the revolt was over. Azahari fled to the Philippines, and the remains of his TNKU were scattered in the jungles of Sabah or Sarawak and presumed to be trying to make their way back to the Indonesian border.

It was known that the Indonesian Army had been working on plans for organizing pro-Indonesian sentiment in the three territories in North Borneo as well as in Malaya, and that Azahari had visited Jakarta. It was thus inevitable that political and military responses were built around countering Indonesian involvement. On 16 December, Lieutenant General Sir Walter Walker, an experienced Far East soldier who had served in Burma during the war and in Malaya during the Emergency, was appointed unified director of Borneo Operations, with his headquarters on the island of Labuan, off Sabah. In addition, two brigade headquarters were established, one in Kuching, the capital of Sarawak, and one in Sabah, where mopping-up operations continued until May 1963, when the last rebels were captured.

General Walker had only eleven infantry battalions with which to tackle his formidable problems. Politically and militarily, he was tasked with preserving the security and loyalty of the main settled areas of Sabah and Sarawak, which, between them, covered 77,638 square miles (an area about the size of Senegal), and guarding 971 miles of border with Kalimantan, which followed high, jungle-covered ridges for much of its length. There was little, physically, to prevent infiltration, by land or sea, almost anywhere in Sabah. Access to Sarawak was varied: central Sarawak was an area of dense jungle, with no roads and a few large rivers, whereas western Sarawak offered a virtually unrestricted border, the area around Kuching containing little jungle and the coastline being easy to infiltrate.

In addition to mounting an increasingly effective naval blockade, particularly in Sabah, General Walker established a number of semipermanent patrol bases near known border-crossing places, from which platoon-sized patrolling was mounted, and he prepared a number of helicopter landing sites and small grass airstrips into which reinforcements could be flown. In addition, he began recruiting what became a force of 1,500 border scouts, locals who were meant to be the eyes and ears of local people.

On 20 January 1963, the Indonesian Foreign Minister, Subandrio, announced: "We [Indonesia] cannot but adopt a policy of Confrontation against Malaya because at present they present themselves as accomplices of the neo-colonialists and the neo-imperialists pursuing a hostile policy towards Indonesia."[4] While this did not confirm Indonesia's active involvement in the Brunei revolt, it was followed in April by the first recorded infiltration by Indonesian regular

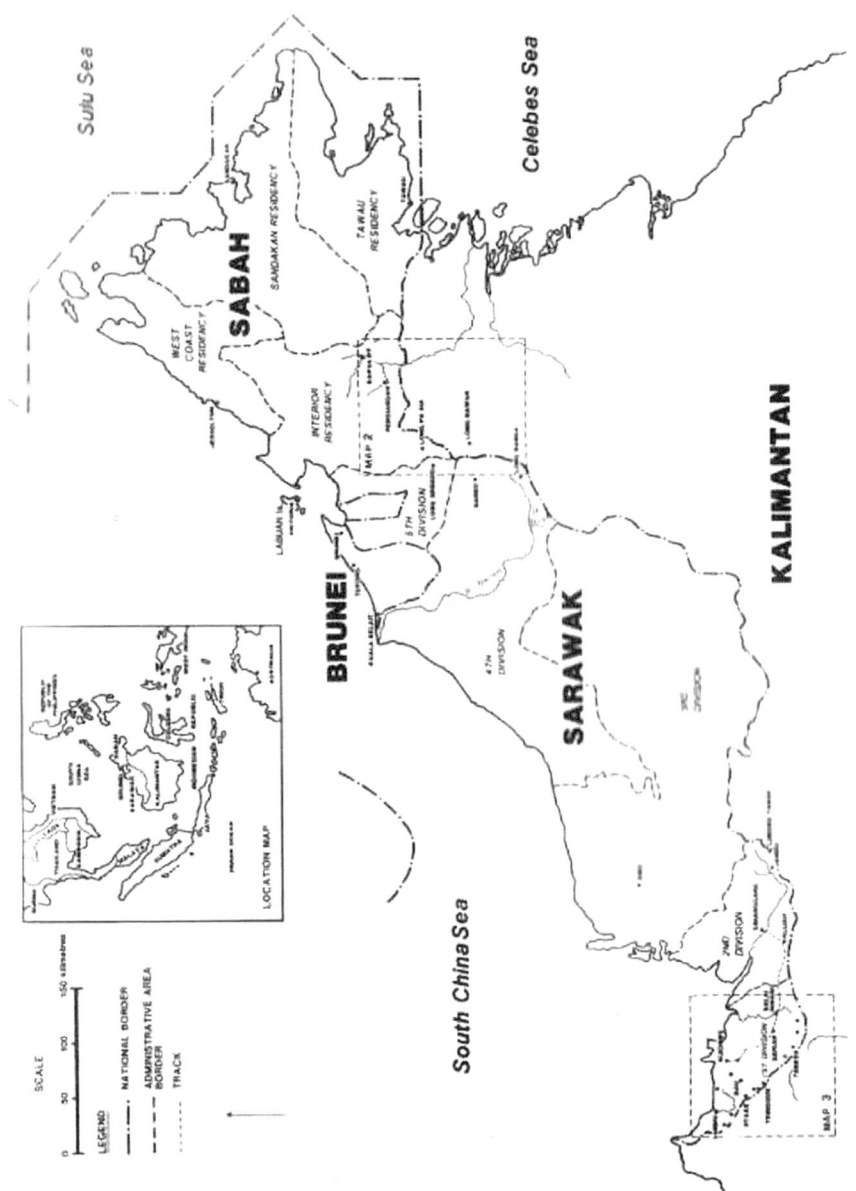

Fig. 25.1. The Borneo campaign, 1963–66

forces, who attacked the police station at Tebedu, forty miles from Kuching, with the presumed aim of encouraging the local communists and other sympathizers to rise up and join them. There followed a number of other attempted infiltrations, which, like the vast majority over the next three years, did not penetrate very far over the border or cause major alarm. What was almost Kafkaesque about this period was that despite Sukarno's pronouncement that he was going to "crush Malaysia," active discussions about the proposed Malaysian Federation were taking place in Manila, during which Indonesia and the Philippines announced their agreement to the proposal, provided it was accepted by a majority in a United Nations–organized referendum in Sabah, Sarawak, and Brunei. In the event, Sabah and Sarawak declared independence before the agreement was confirmed by referendum—which Sukarno regarded as a broken promise and evidence of British imperialism—and Brunei declined to join the federation, which was formally established on 16 September 1963, provoking a furious reaction in Indonesia; the Malaysian ambassador was expelled, and the British and Singaporean embassies in Jakarta were attacked and burned.

The formation of Malaysia made unified politico-military command—the first prerequisite of any counterinsurgency campaign—much easier. All navy, army, and air force elements in the Far East were already under the unified command of the headquarters in Singapore, and those in Borneo under General Walker. Politically, military commanders now had to deal with only a single government, which immediately asked Britain to continue operations in Sabah and Sarawak until it was able to review the situation. It also deployed Malaysian Army units to what was now called East Malaysia, enabling Walker to establish a third brigade area, in central Borneo, and putting a Malaysian brigade in command of operations in Sabah.

Twelve days after federation, on 28 September, occurred what is known as the Battle of Long Jawai, the first major incursion into Sarawak, which was mounted by some 200 guerrillas and directed by a member of the Indonesian Special Forces. Their approach to the village was undetected by the border scouts, a number of whom were captured; the small Gurkha garrison managed to escape into the jungle. Immediate reaction by the parent Gurkha battalion resulted in a number of the insurgents being killed or captured before they could retreat across the border, but not before they had tortured and killed their border scout prisoners. The favorable reaction of the locals to the speed of the Gurkha response, and their revulsion at the Indonesian treatment of the captured scouts, reinforced the importance of winning over and maintaining local hearts and minds. The failure of the scouts resulted in their role being changed to information gathering only.

In early 1964, British tactics changed, and what had been a platoon commander's war became a company commander's one. Gone were the days of having to combat haphazard incursions motivated by wildly ambitious aims and objectives, because the insurgents' aim now seemed to be to penetrate for forty to sixty miles, set up a guerrilla base, and make contact with local communists and other dissidents. Furthermore some 30,000 Indonesian regular troops were deployed on the border, in addition to many irregulars. Dispersed patrol bases were replaced by a number of heavily protected, permanent company bases a short distance from the border and mostly adjacent to a kampong. General Walker ordered that these were to be properly dug in, with overhead cover, and to be defendable overnight by not more than a third of any garrison, against any opposition, including direct infantry assault. The remaining two-thirds of the garrison was always to be out in an offensive role, dominating the jungle and countering any penetrations by the enemy, who, never knowing where their opponents were, always knew that they were liable to be attacked. Conversely, company base commanders, although responsible for very large areas, knew that reinforcements could quickly be made available.

Gunan Gajak, or Bunan Gega, to give it its correct Land Dyak name, in far western Sarawak, was my home from June 1965 to early January 1966. It was about 4,000 yards through the jungle to the fifteen miles of high, jungle-ridged border—as you walked—for which I was responsible, my company area being some twenty miles deep (i.e., 300 square miles), much larger than the 81–144 square miles for which brigades were responsible in western Europe.

Built in 1964, the base was on a small hill above a kampong, approached by a log bridge over a small river and then up 120 steep steps cut into the hillside. Entirely surrounded by a deep trench, from which enough bunkers were dug to enable everyone to sleep underground, the base could accommodate over 200 men. A number of corrugated-iron-roofed huts housed my daytime command post, the cookhouse, a medical center, the main stores, and a canteen, and provided places under which soldiers could shelter from the sun during the heat of the day. You were always wet in the jungle, and I wanted my soldiers to expose their skin to as much fresh air as possible while they were in base, which amounted to about one week in three. Otherwise they were on patrol, usually for five days at a time, mainly in the border area but also regularly carrying out what were called (showing the) flag patrols in the remainder of the company area.

In front of and below the trench, in which everyone had an allocated firing position, were two barbed-wire fences, one put up by us, and its rusty predecessor, which we pushed down the hill. Between the fences were three rows of sharpened bamboo spikes, known as panjis (punji sticks), which could penetrate any jungle boot and cause a nasty wound that would inevitably turn septic because of the dust on the bamboo. In addition, we had a section of mortars, which could bring down fire onto the wire, and also cover from a 105 mm gun in the next-door base, some three and a half miles away as a shell flies, and for which our gun provided similar cover. I reckoned we could have withstood any Indonesian attack.

Because there were no roads or navigable rivers in the area, everyone and everything had to be brought in by air—people and mail by helicopter, everything else by parachute—the weekly and other airdrops directed toward the kampong football field. Our predecessors used a platoon, after every airdrop, to carry all supplies, including gun ammunition and forty-gallon drums of aviation fuel for helicopters, to a wire, which they used to haul goods into the base. This terrible waste of patrolling manpower was solved when someone had the bright idea of asking for a vehicle, which, by reversing, could pull stores up more efficiently than a platoon. One day, to the great excitement of everyone in the kampong, who, although used to aircraft and helicopters, had never seen a motor vehicle, one arrived underslung from a helicopter, and the handling of airdrops was transformed.

Every day, a number of locals turned up for treatment by my medical orderly, who had been given extra training in the hospital in Singapore before the tour. As we left, he told me that he had delivered 99 babies and extracted 999 teeth during our tour, and had handed out goodness knows how many thousands of pills. Twice we called in a helicopter to take a local to hospital in Kuching, where their lives were saved.

As Indonesian military activity across the region increased in 1964, General Walker asked for reinforcements; two additional battalions, including my own, were flown out in early 1965, bringing the total number of forces deployed in Borneo to 17,000, and a further 10,000 were available in Malaya and Singapore, allowing him to add a fourth brigade headquarters. The increase soon appeared justified. In April, the company base west of Gunan Gajak, less than

2,000 yards from the border, was attacked, the only attack on a base during Confrontation. Despite being beaten back and sustaining heavy losses, the Indonesians claimed victory, and the surviving attackers led the August independence parade in Jakarta.

Most significantly as far as Britain's method of operating was concerned, the Labour government in mid-1964 approved Operation Claret, the mounting of top-secret company-sized offensive actions across the Kalimantan border, designed to keep the Indonesians off balance rather than to inflict significant casualties. No one was allowed to cross the border until he had been in theatre for a month, and every operation had to be authorized by the Cabinet in London; incursion distances were initially limited to a depth of 5,000 yards, later increased to 10,000. Curiously, the Indonesians never publicized any of our attacks, even when we suffered casualties—all of whom we had to bring back—following which we announced that a named soldier had been killed or wounded in the follow-up to an Indonesian incursion, allowing Indonesia to claim credit for offensive action that had never taken place. After its first month, every battalion conducted as many Claret operations as it could, some reconnaissance but many aggressive, such as ambushes on rivers used as logistic supply routes. During one of the latter, a Gurkha corporal won the only Victoria Cross awarded during the campaign. There is no doubt that, judged by the reduced number of incursions, Claret operations frightened the Indonesians, proving that offense is often the best form of defense.

One of the nine missions that I led had a most surprising outcome. Previous Claret reconnaissance having confirmed that there were Indonesian troops in two kampongs within our allowed zone, I got approval to mount a platoon-sized ambush on the track along which they moved between the two. As with all Claret operations, so as not to give away the place where we had crossed, we walked rather than helicoptered to the border, which took most of a day, and the following morning I went across with two platoons, leaving a third on the border, responsible for maintaining communications both forward to me and back to base.

Near the bottom of the border ridge, I set up a forward base, from which I could command the whole operation. I stayed there with my signaler and one of the two platoons, the other going forward a further 2,000 yards to establish the ambush. All the time we were covered by our 105 mm gun, ranged some 800 yards in front of us; if required, it could fire a round as reference, from which further fire support could be adjusted. Strict radio silence was observed except at a specified time in the evening, when microphone clicks were used to signal that all was well. Casualty evacuation was another reason for having an extra platoon. Because of the steepness of the jungle-covered border ridge, it took almost all day for a platoon to carry a man on a stretcher to the border. Bearing in mind that a seriously injured man should be on an operating table within six hours of being wounded, we had a contingency plan for calling in cross-border helicopter evacuation, with fighter aircraft support, which we had to use only once, when a rifleman lost a leg to an antipersonnel mine.

On the third morning, the forward platoon commander suddenly broke radio silence, telling me that the ambush had just been compromised by a local, whom he was holding. I decided to abandon the ambush and take the man back to base so that we could question him through interpreters. He turned out to be middle aged, with a prominent goiter on his neck. He did not appear to be mentally all there, but neither did he appear to be frightened of being with us. We took him back to the border, where helicopters picked us up and flew us to Gunan Gajak before dark. As soon as he saw our "guest," my head border scout greeted him warmly, telling me that he was a character whom everyone in the kampong knew, but had not seen since Confrontation started. It seemed more sensible to let him stay overnight in the kampong, rather than our base, and let him talk with and be questioned by people who knew him.

The following morning, the headman, or *tua*, of the kampong came to see me, saying that they had had a wonderful night with their old friend, who had told them a lot about what life was like on the other side of the border, where they were treated very badly by the local police force. Most importantly for those who lived in Gunan Gajak, the man had said that he could perform a vital service for them with my help. The longhouses in the kampong were roofed with tiles made from ironwood trees, which grew only on the Indonesian side of the border. Confrontation had cut off their supply, and many roofs were now in need of repair. Our guest said that he could arrange for replacement tiles to be brought over, provided that we guaranteed the safety of the carriers on our side of the border. I readily agreed, and true to his word, four weeks later he reappeared with a tile-carrying party; as far as Gunan Gajak was concerned, Confrontation was over.

It was political rather than military events that brought Confrontation to an end. On 9 August 1965, Singapore seceded from the Malaysian Federation for internal political reasons. More significantly, on 30 September there was a failed coup in Jakarta, allegedly carried out by the Indonesian Communist Party and left-wing sympathizers in the armed forces. President Sukarno, who was reported to be seriously ill, allowed General Suharto, the commander of the army, to assume emergency command and control. A marked reduction in the level of Confrontation-related military activity followed, although infiltrations continued to be mounted until May. Suharto steadily consolidated his power base until, on 11 March 1966, he was able to form a cabinet that excluded President Sukarno, whose economic and foreign policies he immediately began to reverse while restoring Indonesian relations with the West. On 28 May, at a conference in Bangkok, the Malaysian and Indonesian governments declared the conflict over, and a formal peace treaty, ending hostilities and normalizing relations, was signed on 11 August 1966.

Writing later, General Walker listed six ingredients of successful counterinsurgency operations, all of which were practiced during Confrontation.

1. Unified, people-centered operations, which means that they are conducted under combined politico-military command. In addition, higher-ranking commanders must be prepared to empower subordinates to use their initiative and judgment in making immediate decisions, in line with an overall concept of operations.
2. Timely and accurate intelligence.
3. Speed, mobility, and flexibility.
4. Security of bases.
5. Domination of the jungle or whatever terrain is being operated in. The jungle has to belong to you—you must own it and you must control it. On the assumption that the enemy understood the jungle because it was native to their part of the world, they had to be played at their own game. We had to be prepared to live out in the jungle for days or weeks on end, which we did. So that they smelled no differently from the jungle, soldiers were allowed to cook, wash, or smoke only on flag patrols in the rear areas.
6. Winning the hearts and minds of the people, and especially the indigenous people. Our killing of one civilian would do more harm than the enemy's killing of ten, which was one of the reasons why bombing from the air, because of its indiscriminate nature, was never considered.

Looking back, there was one aspect of Confrontation from which it is easy to draw false lessons. Never once in my six and a half months was I visited by a journalist. Personally, because it would have been impossible to maintain their secrecy, I do not think that we could have conducted the battle-winning Claret operations had the press known about them. When all is said and done, each was a violation of international law, because it amounted to the invasion of another country. When we returned home, we were disappointed that neither our armed forces friends nor the ill-informed British public appeared to have the slightest idea of what we had been doing, other than that it had taken some time. The British press rarely reported on what was clearly regarded as Malaysia's problem. It is now impossible to think of any kind of war not being subjected to media attention.

How to sum up Confrontation? For its military cost-effectiveness, I cannot better the words of Denis Healey, Defence Secretary in 1964: "Our victory in Borneo is too little known . . . I describe our operations in Confrontation—our struggle against the Indonesian invaders—as the most successful use of armed force in the twentieth century. After nearly four years of fighting, the toll of British casualties was no larger than that on the roads of Britain on a single Bank Holiday weekend." Casualty figures are not the only indicator of the intensity of any conflict. Confrontation was fought "by brains and on foot," mainly in jungle, in which weapons of mass destruction would have been of little use. Compared with the dreadful loss of life in the two world wars, and the number whose names are recorded on the walls of the dramatic Vietnam Memorial in Washington, the fatality figures were paltry: 114 servicemen—19 British troops, 43 Gurkhas, 16 Australians, 7 New Zealanders, and 29 Malays. Indonesian casualties were estimated at 590 killed, 222 wounded, and 771 captured. For me, the most important outcome was not the limited loss of life, but that two former colonies, Malaysia and Indonesia, after gaining independence from their imperial masters, have remained at peace ever since Confrontation ended, and peace must be the primary aim of all those involved in counterinsurgency operations.

Fall Semester 2014

1. George Hall, statement in the House of Commons, 10 Oct. 1945, *Parliamentary Debates,* Commons, 5th ser., vol. 414, col. 255.

2. Treaty Series no. 28 (1968), "Exchange of letters between the government of the United Kingdom of Great Britain and Northern Ireland and the government of Malaysia to provide personnel to assist in the staffing, administration and training of the armed forces of Malaysia," Cmnd. 3578; signed 5 Dec. 1967, Kuala Lumpur.

3. Anglo-Malayan Defence Agreement, Cmnd. 263, Sept. 1957; signed in Oct. 1957.

4. Quoted in J. A. C. Mackie, *Konfrontasi: The Indonesia-Malaysia Dispute, 1963–1966* (London, 1974), p. 125.

Tony Blair and George W. Bush at the White House, 2004

26

Bush and Blair

MICHAEL BRENNER

George W. Bush and Tony Blair were contemporaries in more than their service as heads of government. For it was a historically auspicious period, a time of transformation with long-term implications for the place of the United States and of Britain in world affairs as well as for their bilateral relationship. The rise of "terrorism" to the top of the security agenda reshaped the international landscape's features. Gone were the verities and confidence that followed the end of the Cold War and the collapse of the Soviet Union. A new threat was perceived to carry with it a new set of demands and challenges. The events of 9/11 ushered in a novel era in international affairs, one shaped by the invasion and occupation of Iraq, which was conceived and led by the Bush presidency and had Britain's Tony Blair as its loyal deputy. It warrants a close examination that pays due attention to the factor of personality, structural features of the Anglo-American bond, and the ways in which they reinforce each other.

The much-ballyhooed "special relationship" since the Second World War has always been exaggerated—on a number of counts. One, it was far more salient for Britain and the British people that it was for their counterparts across the Atlantic. Britain needed America—strategically and as escort into the circle of great powers; the obverse never has been the case. Two, it is facile to confuse affinities of language, culture, and public philosophy with political partnership. Although the two countries are mutually reinforcing to some degree, each has its own dynamic. That divergence has become increasingly evident over time with the end of the Cold War, the relative eclipse of Europe by the rising prominence of Asian powers, and widening disparities in the global reach of the United States and all its European allies, including Britain. Yet British imagery retains a special place in the minds and sentiments of most Americans even as its practical value to Washington fades. That phenomenon is a counterpart to the British admiration for and instinctive emulation of things American.

Oddly, the Bush-Blair bond was cemented despite both men's distinct lack of interest in history, Bush's ignorance of all things foreign—including Britannia—and Blair's calculated campaign to replace "antique" British imagery with something sleeker and more "with it." Blair's model quite naturally was present-day America: high-tech, forward-looking, global minded, enterprising, and compounded of the materialistic and the moralizing, on both the home front and internationally, in a manner he admired. Bush welcomed an acolyte and courtier, someone who could provide cover for American unilateralism abroad. It was very much a dominant-subordinate relationship, psychologically as well as politically. "Yo, Bush!" is unimaginable. A natural match—perhaps blessed by Providence.

The long saga of the "war on terror" has been marked by an American-instigated series of costly misadventures that roped in its Western partners—some reluctantly and belatedly, others enthusiastically. Iraq was the most mindless and counterproductive of them. Britain has been America's most faithful and devoted junior partner in each chapter of this tragic drama. Tony Blair epitomizes this reflexive response to American magnetism and might. He did so as head of the British government; he did so in his personal capacity as self-designed sidekick to George Bush. Besides serving what Blair thought to be British interests, that relationship aggrandized his individual role on the international stage at a turning point in history. Blair's self-absorbed egoism, bordering on the narcissistic, craved the admiration and special treatment that he received in Washington. His address to the U.S. Congress on the eve of Iraq invasion was an exhilarating tonic—one that served both political ambition and personal esteem.

Tony Blair, like George Bush, had minimal capacity for critical self-reflection. They judged and decided on the basis of instinct and impulse (Bush's famous "gut" feelings) rather than deliberation. Nor were they inclined to review their actions or admit mistakes. Playing Robin to Bush's Batman, Blair further insulated himself from any second-guessing and doubt, since such an indulgence could jeopardize his asymmetrical bond with the President, on whom he was critically dependent. Both sought praise and adulation. Blair was far needier, though, when it came to what the tie provided in the way of enhanced status. Unlike Bush, he did not have his country's establishment and popular sentiment strongly behind him. Moreover, the President's sense of righteousness was more pronounced, drawing as it did on the deep sources of American exceptionalism, American superiority, and American moralism.

Blair's imagined grandiosity came to the fore on the eve of the invasion of Iraq. He conceived of himself as a "war Prime Minister" and was exhilarated at his "first blooding." Blair never saw military service. Blair's evangelical fervor in seconding the opinions and policies of the President carried imitation, including walk and body language, far beyond anything that could be explained in practical, pragmatic terms. His aping of Bush led the former British ambassador Roderic Braithwaite to deride Britain's obedient foreign policy this way: "Why should anyone seek to speak with the monkey when they can go straight to the organ-grinder." That role troubled Blair little. His two foci were his standing in the opinion polls, and prosecuting a war that he genuinely believed was necessary. On the modalities, he deferred to Bush and his officials. Moreover, Blair believed deep down that Britain and the West needed a roughhouse America to fight their corner in an existential battle against the dark forces of Islamic fundamentalism.

Bush and Blair shared another cardinal trait. They were drawn to and used religion; some would say "religiosity." Bush's religiosity is dissected by Jacob Weisberg in his superb character portrait *The Bush Tragedy* (2008). Weisberg tells us that "by the time he heard the call," Bush already had a public career on his mind, a notion put there by Republican politicians on the lookout for a fresh persona. "Jesus talk" became part of the discourse around him, even though there was scant evidence of any serious reflection on matters Christian. This was spiritual atmospherics dressed up as religion. The faith narrative, according to Weisberg, "was a conscious autobiographical construction." There was no sign whatsoever that Bush ever experienced a spiritual self-transformation. The propagation of a "salvation through faith" message proved useful after 9/11. It offered Americans a unified field theory of faith that melded the kingdom of heaven with a divinely inspired America. That was the holy alliance needed to defeat the Satan of international terrorism.

Tony Blair as well cast himself as a man of deep religious faith. A vague High Anglican, he evolved into a believing and practicing Catholic, clandestinely while in office, thereby taking the faith of his wife. Although he did not officially convert until leaving 10 Downing Street, he was in fact a Catholic for some years before, although he took pains never to be photographed while receiving communion. Blair's religious convictions were so private a matter that Alistair Campbell, his close confidant and alter ego, could proclaim early on that "we don't do God," and not hear any dissent from the Prime Minister. Blair's expansive self-identity grew progressively more inflated over time. The heady combination of successive electoral victories, his bonding with fellow apostle George Bush, and mounting concern for his "legacy" led to outsize visions of his place in history. Blair later offered a course at the Yale School of Divinity. Playing Caesar for ten years while engaged in a supposedly spiritual struggle to reconcile the ethic of ultimate ends with the ethic of responsibility evidently qualified him to provide instruction on both, and to earn himself a rightful place among the faithful on the Yale faculty.

How big a role did personalities play in Britain's subservience to Washington during the Bush-Blair years? Did objective, incontrovertible structural factors allow for another kind of relationship? On issue after issue, there is little doubt that the felt imperative not to alienate the United States weighs heavily on the thinking of all British leaders. The inclination to defer or mollify Washington is pervasive. "A British leader does not dare spit in the Atlantic" is the pithy axiom observed by Downing Street. Tony Blair surely conformed his behavior to this admonition. To date, no leader of a major British political party has given public signs that he might reject it. David Cameron's comments in 2010 about the government's overly close embrace of the White House have been belied by his action since assuming the premiership. He has been as staunch and unquestioning a lieutenant of Obama as Tony Blair was of Bush.

Spring Semester 2015

Bert Williams, goalkeeper for the Wolverhampton Wanderers, during a match with Arsenal at Molineux Stadium, November 1950. © Getty Images

27

Well Played!
An Architectural View of Sports

RICHARD CLEARY

The British Empire's legacy of organized sports imposes an enduring burden of high expectations on the fans of teams and individual athletes representing the Home Nations. How exasperating it was for the country that invented soccer (to use the American term) to fall out of the running for the 2014 World Cup before the conclusion of the first round. Thank goodness for the women of England, who crossed the Channel to France six weeks later and returned triumphant with the 2014 Women's Rugby World Cup. And while no citizen of the United Kingdom rose to the final rounds of tennis competition at Wimbledon that year, Rory McIlroy of Northern Ireland set things right in the world of golf by winning the British Open, and he and his British teammates played well in the Ryder Cup.

Alongside the fans who invest their souls in the fortunes of their teams, and the scribes who chronicle the competitions, are scholars who find in sports the opportunities for study through disciplinary lenses as diverse as kinesiology, history, sociology, economics, psychology, geography, literature, and, when called upon to explain exactly how Beckham did "bend it," physics. I would like to add my own discipline of architectural history to the mix. While there is much that we might consider regarding the stadiums and other structures housing sporting events, my interest here pertains to fields of play and the contests they frame. The proposition I offer is that a source of the enjoyment many of us find in sports is our aesthetic response to bodies moving through the bounded space of the playing field.

In the 112th minute of the World Cup final played in Maracanã Stadium, Rio de Janeiro, in July 2014, Germany's André Schürrle broke free with the ball along his left wing into Argentina's side of the pitch (see fig. 27.1). Racing ahead of him downfield, his teammate Mario Götze cut inside toward the goal, drawing the attention of two defenders. Two other defenders converged on Schürrle, but before they could isolate him, he passed to Götze, who neatly controlled the ball from his chest to his foot and fired a shot past goalkeeper Agustín Orión into the far corner of the net for the winning goal. The shot is the iconic moment of the sequence, but it was made possible by Götze's prior moves that created the gaps between opponents in which he could receive Schürrle's perfectly timed pass.

Goals are the measure of victory in soccer, but the heart of the game is the contest to create and control space at the expense of one's opponent. This struggle underlies many other sports. In fencing, for example, the dramatic flurry of lunge and riposte is set up by subtler sequences of threats and feints by which each player seeks to establish the optimal distance from which to strike, cause his or her opponent to inadvertently create an unprotected opening, and maintain a safe distance from a counterattack. In golf, another kind of spatial game, the contest hinges more on the players' individual mastery of the course than on their dynamic interaction with each other. The spatial challenges pertain to determining the most efficient route from tee to hole and then responding to circumstances along the way, such as a misplayed shot into a hazard.

For each of these sports, soccer, fencing, and golf, we can examine its frame (the boundary separating the game from other activities), the physical properties of the field of play, and the movement of players with respect to these features. The specialized vocabularies that athletes, sportswriters, and fans employ usually are directed to achieving tactical advantage over an opponent, but we can address frame, field, and movement in terms that link the locker-room chalkboard to the realms of theater, architecture, and landscape architecture. In dance performances, for example, the stage frames a field that focuses our perception of the dancers' moving bodies. In architecture and landscape architecture, the demarcation of frames establishes relationships of inside and outside, of here and there, that reinforce one's sense of self in relationship to one's surroundings. As in the theater, a frame in architecture can focus our attention on the movement of others within a field, but it also can establish a reference for our own movement, one of the most important ways by which we experience a building. Golf courses, soccer pitches, and fencing strips allow us to explore frame, field, and movement across a range of scales and modes of play.

Historians traditionally situate the origins of golf in Scotland, where the first documented mention of the game appears in an act of Parliament in 1457 banning it as frivolous, the first of a number of futile efforts. Three centuries later, in 1744, the Company of Gentlemen Golfers in Edinburgh drew up the oldest surviving rules of the game. The sport's popularity increased dramatically in the mid-nineteenth century, contemporaneous with the growth of many other modern sports, including soccer and fencing, and golf courses were built throughout the United Kingdom and abroad.

The sandy, rolling linksland of Scotland's eastern coast, which drains well and did not have high agricultural value, offered suitable sites for early golf courses such as St. Andrews, where the game has been played for hundreds of years, and the notion of the course as an appropriation of the natural landscape continues to

Fig. 27.1. Setting up the winning goal at the World Cup final, 2014. Courtesy of the website Outside of the Boot.

inspire design today. In this spirit, the edges of courses may merge seamlessly with their surroundings, the boundary markings stipulated by the rules of the game appearing as an overlay on the natural setting. Inside the course boundaries, the inventory of familiar features, including tee boxes, fairways, roughs, hazards, and greens, was complete by the 1880s, but their precise forms and the overall dimensions of the course were then, and still are today, determined by the designer's subjective assessment of the degree of challenge they offer players possessing an anticipated level of skill.

Golf course design differs from the planning of soccer pitches and fencing strips in the attention devoted to aesthetic qualities, including the variety of views, colors, and textures of vegetation and landforms that players encounter along the way. A course may have a single designer, but its character can change over time according to the practices of the groundskeepers, the life cycles of plantings, and adjustments to changing modes of play, such as the longer drives of modern golfers. Golf course architecture has become a specialized profession, but its aesthetic dimension has its roots in the picturesque tradition of landscape architecture. Ongoing points of debate, such as favoring high drama or subtlety in the design of features, echo those of picturesque landscape design in Britain in the late eighteenth and nineteenth centuries.

While golf course designers generally seek to create a distinctive character for each course, planners of soccer pitches and fencing strips seek uniformity. Soccer as we know it took shape in the second half of the nineteenth century. A rich literature traces its parallel developmental strands among elite and working social classes as it spread throughout the world along the commercial and military corridors of the British Empire. Its popularity owes much to its character as a game that can be adapted to improvised fields of play, requires no specialized equipment other than a ball, and has simple rules codified as the seventeen Laws of the Game.

The regulation pitch took shape between the 1860s and 1937, and its history is characterized by increasing segmentation. The Football Association rules of the 1870s did not specify dimensions other than requiring the length of the pitch to exceed its width and for the corners to be marked by flags. Some fields at the time were 200 yards long by 100 yards wide. Goalposts were set, as they are today, twenty-four feet apart and had tape strung between them at a height of eight feet, introducing a critical third dimension, the height of the goal opening, to the otherwise planar character of the pitch. The first ground markings were introduced in 1882 with the delineation of the touch and end lines defining the perimeter. The center circle, the

Fig. 27.2. Hitting out of a bunker on the Old Course at St. Andrews. From *A History of the Royal & Ancient Golf Club St. Andrews from 1754–1900*, by H. S. C. Everard (1907). Courtesy of the Stark Center for Physical Culture and Sports, University of Texas at Austin.

halfway line, and the goal and penalty areas were demarked by the early twentieth century, and the penalty arcs were added in 1937. Their locations are precisely fixed, but the Laws of the Game still allow the overall dimensions of the pitch to vary within a minimum and maximum range, provided the length exceeds the width.

Compared to soccer pitches, the fields of play for union rugby, league ruby, and American football are considerably more segmented. The dimensions of American football fields have been fixed at 100 yards by 160 feet (53.33 yards) since 1881. As befitting a game based on the measured conquest of territory, the field, or gridiron, is marked by lines at five-yard intervals numbered in descending order on each side of the fifty-yard line at the center of the field. Dashed lines known as hash marks running the length of the field on each side provide a frame within which the ball is placed for each play. Football officials are called upon to make precise measurements of the ball's position. Doing so requires a supporting crew of sideline assistants. Like old-fashioned land surveyors, the members of the chain gang carry a measuring chain and sticks defining the ten-yard distance a team must cover to retain possession of the ball. In contrast, the most common measurement that soccer referees make is the ten-yard pace-off setting the position of defenders at the start of a free kick.

The modern sport of fencing developed from eighteenth-century training practices related to gentlemanly deportment, including preparedness for duels of honor. Its history is more closely tied to the Continent than to Britain, but a mid-eighteenth-century exception was the academy in London of the Italian master Domenico Angelo, who published an internationally influential training manual, *The School of Fencing* (1763). The inclusion of fencing in the modern Olympic games beginning in 1896 spurred the popularity of British fencing clubs, and the sport continues to attract participants.

Most commonly held indoors, a fencing match is conducted on a narrow strip, or *piste*, 14 meters long by 1.5 to 2 meters wide. It may be simply outlined on a floor or consist of a special surface

Fig. 27.3. Illustration of defensive and attacking positions in fencing. From *The School of Fencing, with a General Explanation of the Principal Attitudes and Positions Peculiar to the Art*, by Domenico Angelo (1763).

integrated with an electronic scoring system. It is marked by a center line, starting lines, and shaded warning areas at the ends.

DESPITE THEIR DIFFERENCES, THERE are ways in which we might consider these and the fields of play of other sports collectively. One is through the notion of "magic circles," which the Dutch historian Johan Huizinga postulated in his study of play, *Homo Ludens* (1938). For Huizinga, the act of play transforms its setting from a pragmatic location into a temporary social space, the magic circle, governed by the rules of the game. In sport, the transformation begins by the marking of the field of play, whether improvised, as a game of soccer on a patch of playground, or precisely drawn, as on a professional soccer pitch. It may include rituals that symbolically invoke the spell of the game before the competition begins, such as fencers' salutes or the playing of national anthems, and then release the spell at its conclusion, such as the post-game handshakes customary in many sports.

Some settings for sport retain the aura of magic circles even when no game is being played. They exist as sites of collective memory, which can transcend changes to the physical surroundings. Wembley Stadium in London, for example, the site of major soccer and rugby competitions, as well as concerts and other events, was long identified by the towers built as part of the original stadium in 1923. They and the rest of the structure were demolished in 2003 to make way for the present stadium, designed by the architectural firms Foster + Partners and Populous. Although the old towers are missed, the Wembley aura survives as fans and players pass along their memories from one generation to the next.

The notion of the magic circle and its meaning for those who participate in it as players and spectators correspond closely to theories of place in architecture. Informed by strands of phenomenology shaped by Maurice Merleau-Ponty, Martin Heidegger, and Mircea Eliade, among others, place theory addresses the nature of our experience with the built environment. Boundaries and frames demark a place. Movement is fundamental to our experience of it. The settings and patterns of movement in sport manifest these themes in distilled forms.

In fencing, the competition flows linearly. It is bounded by the long, narrow dimensions of the strip and reinforced by the sideways positioning of the fencers' bodies, which minimizes their own exposure while maintaining their ability to powerfully extend their reach and strike. While some fencers may attempt to force their opponents to the end of the strip in the hope that the position will become a distraction and cause a lapse of concentration, fencing matches do not have a directional object beyond establishing the critical distance for scoring a touch, which can happen anywhere along the strip. Beyond good technique in footwork and sword handling, success depends on the ability to read and disrupt the opponent's tactics while making him or her react to one's own actions. As the fencers move up and down the length of the strip, the distance between them usually remains close, and the advantage each seeks to gain can be a matter of inches. The openings for attack are subtle—a change of angle in the wrist, a slight rotation of the torso, or a shift of weight from one foot to the other—making this game of cat and mouse a difficult sport for spectators to follow.

Golf is a directional game with two types of movement from tee box to hole: the flight of the ball, which matters, and the player's earthbound path, which is incidental, unless one is hunting for a ball that has landed out of sight. Each path requires a different form of visualization by the player. Course designers have taken many approaches to structuring the technical and aesthetic experiences that players encounter in a round of nine or eighteen holes. Holes may be designed for maximum clarity, with plantings and landforms indicating the optimal route to the green, or the paths may be obscured. A classic instance of the latter is the fifth hole of the Old Course at Lahinch Golf Club in Ireland. Created in the 1890s by the early master course designer Old Tom Morris, the green is hidden between two thirty-foot-high sand dunes, and one must gauge one's initial shot from the tee with reference to a marker on a hill behind it. At the other extreme, golfers newly introduced to links courses, such as St. Andrews, can become disoriented by the openness of the landscape, which overwhelms directional cues.

Like golf, the object of soccer is to direct the ball to a specific point—a goal 24 feet wide rather than a hole 4.25 inches in diameter—but while the field of play in golf is a fundamental challenge of the game, the soccer pitch is conceived of as a neutral surface, like the fencing strip. In soccer and fencing, spatial relationships are defined by the dynamic interactions of the players. While the pitch, the object of the game, and the fundamental rules have remained relatively consistent throughout most of soccer's history as a modern sport, the way that coaches and players regard the field of play spatially has changed dramatically.

From the 1860s to the 1880s, English teams played an attacking game. Front lines of six or more players of the eleven-man side would dribble the ball straight to the goal or chase after long kicks into the opponent's territory. The point of attack would be contested by the opposing team's front line. The tactic emphasized the individual ball handler and focused the active field of play around him. Passing was viewed unfavorably. In a match played by England and Scotland in 1877, a member of the England team, Alfred Lyttelton, challenged by a teammate on his failure to pass the ball, reportedly replied, "I am playing for my own pleasure, Sir!"[1]

Scottish teams of the time approached the game differently, by advancing the ball with short passes along the ground as well as dribbling it. Such "combination play," as it was known, allowed players to spread out over more of the field, and as passing techniques expanded to include lofting the ball in the air, players developed techniques for trapping the ball with their chests, directing it with their heads, and receiving passes on the run. Passing made it possible to expand the area of active play to encompass the entire field and to direct rapid attacks against points of weakness.

A glimpse of the future of the passing game was seen in 1872 at soccer's first international match when Scotland, despite fielding smaller players, held favored England to a draw by passing the ball around the opposition rather than trying to run through it. A decade later, in the FA (Football Association) Cup final of 1883, blue-collar Blackburn Olympic shocked the Old Etonians with a winning goal in extra time set up by a cross-field pass. Another factor in Olympic's victory was the team's then-unusual notion of training before important matches, unlike the Old Etonians' confidence in the innate talent of their social class. By 1900, teams had adopted new alignments that reduced the number of players in the front line in order to provide greater coverage over more of the field. The resulting formation of two deep-sitting defensive players, three midfield players, and five attackers on the front line is known in soccer parlance as the 2-3-5, or pyramid, and was widely used in the early twentieth century.

Perhaps the most significant rule change after soccer's formative years was the 1925 revision to the offside rule that made it easier for offenses to initiate attacks deep in their opponents' territory. Among the responses that teams devised, that of Herbert Chapman, the manager of London's Arsenal club, became particularly influential. He strengthened the defensive line and expanded the distribution of midfield players in a formation described as 3-2-2-3, or the W-M, which refers to the diagrammatic pattern of the players on the field. The alignment facilitated a mode of play characterized by quickly falling back and regaining possession of the ball on defense and then transitioning to a counterattack with speed and precise passing.

As the game evolved from the 1930s through the remainder of the twentieth century, the history of tactical innovation takes one from Britain to the Continent and Latin America. One significant trend was the introduction of defensive schemes in which one or more players might be assigned responsibility for defending particular areas of the field (zone defense) rather than a specific opponent (man-to-man coverage).

Alongside the notion of envisioning the field of play as a set of predetermined zones, tactical innovators developed an elastic approach that viewed the field as a frame in which players' perceptions of space could be manipulated. Writing of the parallel innovations of Valeriy Lobanovskyi in Ukraine and Rinus Michels in Holland in the late 1960s and early 1970s, Jonathan Wilson, in his history of soccer tactics, *Inverting the Pyramid* (2008), observes, "The game as they saw it was about space and how you controlled it: make the pitch big when you have the ball and it is easy to retain it; make it small when you do not and it becomes far more difficult for the opposition to keep it."[2] In applied terms, players on offense should position themselves to be able to move the ball around the entire field in order to probe the opposition closely for points of weakness. On defense, they should pressure the ball handler and potential receivers by limiting passing opportunities and stripping the ball from dribblers. This notion of spatial constriction and expansion is analogous to the way that architects employ dimensional changes of room width, floor level, and ceiling height to elicit feelings of constriction and release as one moves through a building. In soccer, the players shape the space.

Rinus Michels's teams of the early 1970s, Ajax of Amsterdam and the Dutch national team led on the field by Johann Cruyff, have achieved mythic stature in European soccer lore for their mode of play, known as Total Football. Barry Hulshoff, who played on both teams, described Total Football this way: "It was all about making space and coming into space. It is a kind of architecture on the field. It is about movement but still it is about space, about organizing space."[3] This architectural structure refers to players envisioning the movement of the ball via networks of triangles or squares that provide multiple options for passing. These principles are fundamental to players and coaches today, whether one favors the *tiki-taka* possession game of FC Barcelona or the counterattacking strategy of Chelsea FC.

Space in soccer is a matter of perception as well as a physical property. Finding and making space requires awareness of the flow of play and creative imagination for directing it in one's favor. The phrase "playing to space," beloved by sportscasters, doesn't mean taking a Hail Mary shot and hoping for the best, but refers to the transformation of an undifferentiated portion of the field of play into a place made meaningful by the realization of an anticipated action, such as the arrival of a teammate to receive a pass. It is a joy for players to achieve that state of focus and heightened awareness commonly described as being "in the zone," in which the flow of the game is clear and time seems to slow, allowing one to assess the situation and make the play. It can be a joy for spectators as well.

THERE ARE MANY THINGS THAT DRAW ONE TO WATCH a sporting event. Familiar attractions are the potential for mayhem, the dramatic tension of a well-played competition, and the camaraderie of fans willing their team to victory. Another one, more commonly associated with arts venues than sports arenas, is aesthetic appreciation.

Although a soccer player's elegant crossover step, a fencer's perfectly timed lunge, or a golfer's precisely measured chip to the green usually is more circumstantial than deliberately artful, the magic circle that frames the game and separates the athletes' movements from the realm of the ordinary creates an opportunity for players and spectators alike to experience aesthetic empathy. As in a dance performance, the focused presentation of bodies in motion (or the potential of motion) on the sports field can inspire a resonance, fleeting or sustained, with our personal sense of bodily movement, and transcend it. I subscribe to the view of the philosopher Arnold Berleant that this connection, which he terms aesthetic engagement, is not a matter of disinterested analysis but an immediate and active interaction of our senses and memories with the properties and context of the act of play. Similar experiences can happen with architecture.

Most buildings and structures don't move, but they are made for people to move through. Berleant and others approaching architecture from a phenomenological perspective ground our aesthetic experience with buildings and landscapes in the full range of sensory perception and argue that buildings and landscapes become meaningful to us when we feel aware and present as we move through them.

Some of the most vivid writing on aesthetic engagement in architecture appeared a hundred years ago in 1914 when a thirty-year-old English scholar named Geoffrey Scott (1884–1929) published *The Architecture of Humanism*, a slender book on architectural aesthetics that remains in print today. Appropriately for my theme, he attended Rugby and even played the eponymous game there, albeit with little pleasure, before going on to New College, Oxford. An aesthete, he acquired interests in architecture, garden design, and art, which he cultivated in Florence in the circle of the American art historians Bernard and Mary Berenson. *The Architecture of Humanism* affirmed the enduring beauty of Greco-Roman and Renaissance classicism at a time when the Italian Futurists were shouting "death to the fathers." Present-day classicists still find his assertions compelling, and modernists, too, have been attracted to the book's broader implications.

Scott was the first writer in English to treat space as an aesthetic category in architecture, and he declared it to be at the center of architectural art. "Space," he explained, "is liberty of movement. That is its value to us, and as such it enters our physical consciousness." Following the German philosopher Theodor Lipps, whom he acknowledged, he went on to assert, "We adapt ourselves instinctively to the spaces in which we stand, project ourselves into them, fill them ideally with our movements."[4] He summarized his position with the statement:

> *We have transcribed ourselves into terms of architecture . . . We transcribe architecture into terms of ourselves . . .* This is the humanism of architecture. The tendency to project the image of our functions into concrete forms is the basis, for architecture, of creative design. The tendency to recognize, in concrete forms, the image of those functions is the true basis, in its turn, of critical appreciation.[5]

Scott found these mutual transcriptions while walking beneath the encompassing shapes of Renaissance domes and regarding the expressions of load and support in their structural systems. His descriptions of empathetic response anticipate Berleant's notion of aesthetic engagement.

Scott focused his analysis on our bodily and psychological engagement with architecture's immutable qualities of mass, order, and proportion. A more recent author, the architect Bernard Tschumi, has considered, over the past forty years, more ephemeral aspects of aesthetic engagement from the perspective of events, his term for the moments when the occupant of a building feels aware and engaged. An architect may not be able to script events, but can imagine them and strive to make settings facilitating their occurrence. In this sense, an event may be a chance encounter with a colleague on a stair landing designed to accommodate a conversation while allowing others to pass by, or it may be the smile inspired by the appearance of a warming ray of sunlight raking a floor, a moment of serendipity made possible by the architect's thoughtful placement of windows. For Tschumi, the notion of event precedes the physical realization of its architectural setting, and he famously asserted, "The greatest architecture of all is the fireworker's," because it inspires a moment of pure aesthetic pleasure that occurs in a burst, lingers briefly as an after image, and then becomes a memory.[6] I find this similar to the aesthetic appreciation of a brilliant split-second play on the sports field.

Aesthetic engagement is not mandatory, and not everyone responds in the same way to the same effects. Sporting events and buildings barrage us with sensory inputs that we process differently from one day to the next in light of many contexts bearing on our experience. The sports fan need not feel guilty about failing to "get" architecture, and the architecture buff need not embrace soccer, but in their enthusiasms, they have more in common than they might admit.

Fall Semester 2014

1. David Goldblatt, *The Ball Is Round: A Global History of Football* (New York, 2008), p. 36.

2. Jonathan Wilson, *Inverting the Pyramid: A History of Football Tactics* (London, 2008), p. 218.

3. David Winner, *Brilliant Orange: The Neurotic Genius of Dutch Soccer* (Woodstock, N.Y., 2002), pp. 46–47.

4. Geoffrey Scott, *The Architecture of Humanism: A Study in the History of Taste* (London, 1914), pp. 168–69.

5. Ibid., p. 159.

6. Bernard Tschumi, "Fireworks," 1974, in Tschumi and Roselee Goldberg, *A Space: A Thousand Words* (London, 1975); quoted in Tschumi, "The Architectural Paradox," *Studio International*, Sept.–Oct. 1975, p. 26.

Logo of the Scottish National Party

28

The Scottish Question in British Politics

ARCHIE BROWN

From Spain to Ukraine, Europe is witnessing governments struggling to hold a multinational state together. Even within that context, the breakup of Britain, which has been one of the most stable and successful countries for more than three centuries, would be quite something. With the dissolution of the Soviet Union, which was in a sense a Greater Russia, the state governed from Moscow lost 20 percent of its territory. It parted with half its population, but it remained physically the largest country in the world. If Scotland becomes a separate state, the UK will lose less than 10 percent of its population but a third of its territory. It will be a Little Britain, not a Great Britain. In geopolitical terms, this divorce would be less consequential than the disintegration of the Soviet Union, but historically more extraordinary. The political union of England and Scotland has lasted for centuries longer than did the Soviet Union and many decades longer than has the United States of America.

The Scottish question has become one of colossal importance in British politics. It has raised much higher up the political agenda an English question, and it could in due course reignite the Irish question. It has called into question the nature of Britishness. Will there be a British state within its present boundaries ten or fifteen years from now? There might be, but only if there is further major constitutional change involving a federal redesign of the British system of government. That is very difficult to achieve for all sorts of reasons, although the biggest single obstacle is the disparity in size of population of the nations that make up the United Kingdom. My own view is that a federal UK would be greatly preferable to breakup, and that it could satisfy the aspirations of many who voted in Scotland for independence in the 2014 referendum (when a federal alternative was not on offer) and who voted for the Scottish National Party in the May 2015 general election.

It would, however, have to be a highly asymmetrical federation in one way or another, and each asymmetry poses problems of acceptability for one or more of the parties involved. The variant probably most acceptable to Scots would be a federation of the four nations living in their historic homelands of England, Scotland, Wales, and Northern Ireland. (The last of these should more precisely be considered two nations, with a majority of the population strongly identifying as British, albeit with distinctive Northern Ireland characteristics, but a very substantial minority seeing themselves primarily as Irish.) Such a federation, with most powers other than foreign and defense policy devolved to the constituent nations, raises the question whether the English, who form 85 percent of the population of the UK, would be content with a 25 percent share in the federal government. Conversely, if England's population size were to be reflected in an overwhelming dominance of the federal government, that would scarcely be acceptable to Scottish opinion. Equally, a federal design that made large regions of England component parts of the federation would be controversial in England itself, and it is inconceivable that the other nations, and Scots in particular, would accept the same powers and status as an English region.

However difficult it would be to achieve, *if* there is to be a federation, it would have to asymmetrical in certain respects. That in itself would make it far from unique in international experience. Spain is both constitutionally (Andalusia, Basque Country, Catalonia, Galicia) and fiscally (Basque Country, Navarre) asymmetrical. The U.S. federal system is far from symmetrical. With each state having two senators in the powerful upper chamber of the U.S. legislature, a vote for the Senate in Wyoming is worth almost seventy times as much as a vote for a senator in the far more populous California. It has been somewhat easier, however, for Americans to accept this as the price of union in a political entity perceived by its citizens to be a nation-state, albeit one of an unusual kind. Britain is *not* a nation-state, but a multinational state. When Westminster politicians use "One Nation" rhetoric, it is well-meaning nonsense. Intended to convey vague "all in this together" sentiments, it might work for England if England stood alone. It bizarrely overlooks, however, the stubborn reality that the UK has several territorially based nations whose long-established national consciousness has been strengthened in recent decades. If that reality is not recognized, the chances of preserving the British state within its present boundaries are slim indeed.

Recent developments, and the immediate challenges that the strength of the Scottish independence movement poses for Britain, must be put in broader context. For a democracy to be viable, it doesn't need consensus on policy or even on values. Indeed, it would be a very peculiar democracy—almost certainly a sham democracy—if that appeared to be the case. But it does need a large measure of agreement on the boundaries of the state, on the legitimacy of the state, and on the means by which change will be brought about. In a democracy, the people supposedly decide, but there has to be some kind of consensus on who constitutes the people.

The post–Second World War era has seen both a coming together of different countries in new unions, of which, in spite of its recent and current difficulties, the most successful example is the European Union. Yet there has been an apparently paradoxical trend in the opposite direction toward ever more nations claiming and often achieving separate statehood. Thus, on the territory of what was formerly a single, powerful state, the Soviet Union, there now stand fifteen countries, each with a seat at the United Nations.

When people with a sense of nationhood are living in their historic homelands within a multinational state or empire, there is always a possibility of this turning into political nationalism—the demand for separate statehood. It happened with the Austro-Hungarian Empire at the end of the First World War, and it happened in the Soviet Union, Czechoslovakia, and Yugoslavia with the end of the Cold War. The risk of political nationalism turning into violent conflict is greatest when different nationalities have reasons for regarding the same territory as their own homeland. Examples are not hard to find. Palestinians and Israelis contest the same land in the Middle East. The large Catholic minority in Northern Ireland, most of whom think of themselves as Irish and aspire to a united Ireland, have only within the past two decades reached a power-sharing agreement (brokered by the British government, with significant help from the Irish government and also from the United States), with the Protestant majority who have put down roots in Northern Ireland over hundreds of years. Armenians and Azeris each see Nagorno-Karabakh as constituting an integral part of their national homeland. Similar conflicting interpretations of history and geography underlay some of the violent conflict in the 1990s in the former Yugoslavia—especially between Serbs and Bosniaks and Serbs and Kosovans.

Compared with such turmoil, the rise of Scottish nationalism has been peaceful but precipitous. The creation and consolidation of the British state was the work of several centuries. Its loosening, and the decline of Britishness, has been a development of the final decades of the twentieth century and the first decade and a half of the twenty-first. As recently as the middle of the last century, the whole of Britain was united in the war against Nazi Germany. In the early post-war elections, the country was sharply divided between support for the Labour and Conservative parties (with other parties getting scarcely a look-in), but the people were overwhelmingly at one in believing that this clash of political values and of ideologically differentiated parties was what mattered in politics. The salient issue was what kind of society Britain should become. The continuity and longevity of the British state were taken for granted.

Scotland poses new challenges for British governments and for all UK-wide political parties, but tensions between England and Scotland have a long history. As Hugh Seton-Watson observed, "The doctrine of nationalism dates from the age of the French Revolution, but nations existed before the doctrine was formulated." In 1789, the Scots—and, of course, the English—were already among "the old nations of Europe."[1] Prior to the early eighteenth-century Union, the Scots were often a source of acute concern for English monarchs, since there was a constant risk, which at times became a reality, of the Scots allying themselves with England's principal enemy, the French. Attempts, however, to keep Scotland loyal by force were never successful for long.

When James VI of Scotland became James I of England on the death of Elizabeth I in 1603, the Scottish and English crowns were helpfully united, but British statehood came a century later, in 1707, with the Union of Parliaments. The Scottish legislature in Edinburgh ceased to exist, and Scotland was accorded seats in the Westminster parliament. Whether the Union was to be or not to be was, ultimately, in the hands of members of the Scottish parliament, and financial inducements were offered to a number of them to help ensure that the members would accept the winding-up of their own legislature. Historians disagree on the extent to which these payments should be regarded as decisive, for they were made mainly to parliamentarians who were already disposed to vote for the Union. There is, though, much more consensus that popular opinion in Scotland at the time of the Union was predominantly against it. The merger was celebrated with great fanfare in London, but Edinburgh was quiet. When bells were finally rung in the Scottish capital, the first tune played was "Why should I be sad on my wedding day?"[2] There was widespread suspicion of skulduggery, and later in the eighteenth century, Robert Burns expressed his view of the Scots parliamentarians of 1707 in the poem that begins:

> Fareweel to a' our Scottish fame,
> Fareweel our ancient glory!
> Fareweel ev'n to the Scottish name
> Sae famed in martial story!

and ends:

> We're bought and sold for English gold—
> Such a parcel of rogues in a nation![3]

Yet whatever the misgivings in Scotland at a time when the country was at least as far away from being a democracy as was England, this was a genuine treaty, not a takeover. Moreover, the Union delivered a much-needed blow to the feudal powers and privileges of the Scottish nobility. Within a few decades, it became clear that both England and Scotland had benefited from the Union. The English believed that they no longer had to worry about an insecure northern border and a Scotland in alliance with France, and from the second half of the eighteenth century that was true, although Jacobite risings in 1715 and 1745 (with many Scots fighting on the Hanoverian side) were early intrusions on the new harmony. Scotland clearly benefited from the widening of the market for its products and the employment opportunities for its people, especially the best-educated Scots. Literacy levels were substantially higher in Scotland than in England and Wales, and there were four universities in Scotland from the sixteenth century. England, in contrast, had only two universities before the nineteenth century. They were far more expensive than the Scottish higher educational institutions and attended by a significantly lower proportion of the population. Educated Scots took advantage of the new opportunities for qualified people in London, arousing a good deal of English resentment in the process.[4]

Scots also made a contribution to the British army greater than their proportion in the population would warrant. This did not make them immune from anti-Scottish feeling. Even James Boswell, who could be obsequious in English company and was deferential to English institutions, was roused to patriotic fury when he went to a comic opera in Covent Garden on 8 December 1762 and witnessed the way two Highland officers were greeted when they came in just before the overture began:

> The mob in the upper gallery roared out, "No Scots! No Scots! Out with them!", hissed and pelted them with apples. My heart warmed to my countrymen, my Scotch blood boiled with indignation. I jumped up on the benches, roared out, "Damn you, you rascals!", hissed and was in the greatest rage. I am very sure at that time I should have been the most distinguished of heroes. I hated the English; I wished from my soul that the Union was broke and that we might give them another Bannockburn.[5]

Boswell, of course, soon calmed down, made himself very much at home in London, and less than half a year later had his first meeting with the Englishman he came to hero-worship and whom he made the subject of one of the greatest biographies in the English language. At that first meeting with Samuel Johnson, Boswell's demeanor was less than heroic. Embarrassed at being introduced as a Scot (since "I knew of his mortal antipathy at the Scotch"), he said that "indeed I come from Scotland, but I cannot help it," and met with the famous Johnsonian response: "Sir, that I find is what a very great many of your countrymen cannot help."[6]

The idea of Britishness became increasingly popular over time. It was promoted more by Scots, wishing to make clear that their country had not become part of England, than by any other of the nations inhabiting the British Isles. People in England, even after the creation of a British state, generally preferred to think of themselves as English (rather than British) and had trouble getting their heads round the idea that Britain was not just another name for England. When I took up an Oxford University teaching post in 1971, having taught in my native Scotland for the previous seven years, I was a bit surprised to find that many supposedly well-educated people still seemed to think that the entire island in which they were living was called England. It is no accident of history that the words of the rousing anthem "Rule, Britannia!"—now, it must be acknowledged, more popular in England than in Scotland—were written in 1740 by a Scot, James Thomson, who was born in a Scottish manse in 1700. The song was to become linked with British imperialism, and the empire offered great opportunities to Scots, who were not slow to take advantage of them. An English historian friend of mine remarked in the summer of 2014, "When we had an empire, the Scots got a lot of the best jobs. Now we don't have an empire, the bastards want to leave us." (Since he was speaking to me, he prefaced the remark with "People will say.")

LACK OF A BRITISH EMPIRE may be one reason why fewer Scots feel British today than they did a hundred years ago, but there are other—and more important—reasons. Memories of the Second World War, which united the whole of the UK, are receding. Every Scottish family in the first six decades of the twentieth century had members who served in the British armed forces. That has changed. There are also very important socioeconomic factors. Scotland had a disproportionately large share of British heavy industry, and so it suffered correspondingly from the industrial decline that was largely a product of global economic forces—the same products could be bought more cheaply elsewhere—but which was accelerated (rather than ameliorated) by the policies of the Conservative government led by Margaret Thatcher. At one time the Protestant religion was an important ingredient in the glue that kept the British state together. Although the Catholic Church has also flourished in Scotland (and was given a boost by Irish immigration from the nineteenth century), the Church of Scotland, which is Presbyterian, has had a pivotal place at the center of national life from long before, and ever since, the establishment of the Union. There has been a drop in religious affiliation and in church attendance in a majority of countries, even the United States, but the decline in religious affiliation has gone further and faster in Scotland, where church membership is now less than a quarter of what it was in the 1950s.

So former prime minister Gordon Brown, who more persuasively than anyone else made a positive intellectual and emotional case for the Union in the run-up to the September 2014 independence referendum, was surely right when he observed: "It is unlikely to be an accident that the rise of political nationalism has coincided with the decline of our traditional industries, our traditional civic institutions and our traditional view of Britain in the world and that political nationalism was not on the rise in the eighteenth, nineteenth or for most of the twentieth century when none of those forces were present."[7] Another big factor underlying the rise of Scottish nationalism was the discovery of North Sea oil. The Scottish National Party got its first significant breakthrough in the 1970s, campaigning under the slogan, "It's Scotland's oil." More crudely, voters were asked whether they would rather be "Rich Scots or Poor Britons."[8] Much of the debate leading up to the independence referendum was on a higher level. The two years between Prime Minister David Cameron and Scotland's First Minister, Alex Salmond, agreeing in October 2012 on the terms of the referendum and the choice itself produced serious political argument, and they were enormously important for the rise of the SNP. In particular, the extension of voting rights to sixteen- and seventeen-year-olds engaged young people in the political process as never before.

The longer-term advance of political nationalism in Scotland has also an international context. The emergence of many new post-communist states within the past quarter of a century has already been touched on. There is not one among the recent additions to the countries with seats at the United Nations that has as long a history of national consciousness or as lengthy a continuity of civic and national institutions as has Scotland. The creation of the European Union is also an important part of the international framework. Before its founding, independent statehood would have been still more a leap in the dark than it would be now. For pro-Union Scots it remains a puzzle, nevertheless, why a Union of which (as part of the UK) Scotland has been a member for less than half a century should be valued more than a Union in which they have generally flourished for more than three centuries. Yet the existence of the European Union, to which Scotland would continue to belong despite some EU members' fear of the separatist example, makes independence a less drastic rupture, both politically and psychologically.[9]

The most important single factor in winning the support of a large majority of Scots for devolution—and subsequently of close to a majority for independent statehood—has been the disparity between voting behavior in Scotland and England. The last time most MPs from Scotland in the House of Commons were Conservatives was following the general election of 1955. From that time on, Labour's dominance in Scotland in general elections grew—until it was rudely interrupted by the SNP in May 2015. At a time when Scotland still had seventy-two members in the House of Commons—following the passing of the Scotland Act of 1998, devolving many powers to the new Scottish parliament, the number of constituencies was reduced to fifty-nine—the Conservatives did not win a single seat in Scotland in 1997. In the two most recent general elections (in 2010 and 2015), they managed to win one seat in each. A favorite quip of former SNP leader Alex Salmond was that there were more pandas in Edinburgh Zoo than Tory MPs in Scotland. In 2015 the political world was so drastically turned upside down that the same could now be said of Scottish Labour MPs. Yet well before that SNP landslide there was growing discontent in Scotland about the extent to which the country voted one way and got a government of a different complexion in London.

The Scottish Labour politicians in the 1990s who formulated policy on devolution believed in a devolved Edinburgh parliament and executive for its own sake. They also, however, "shared the view that . . . a consequence would be the marginalisation of the SNP."[10] This turned out to be wishful thinking. That does not mean that John Major was right in thinking that all would have been well with the Union had the Scottish clamor for its own parliament been resisted. The Conservatives have never recovered in Scotland from opposing devolution both in the 1970s and the 1990s. Had a Labour government similarly ignored the overwhelmingly strong sentiments in favor of "home rule," the meltdown of Labour in Scotland would have occurred much sooner than it did. In fact, however, such a negative response to Scottish aspirations was never likely to happen, because Scotland had heavyweight ministers occupying leading positions in the government headed by Tony Blair, who, though not himself especially enthusiastic about Scottish devolution, had no option but to go along with it.

One consequence of the election result in Scotland in May 2015 is that the Labour Party in Westminster looks more like an overwhelmingly English party than ever before, and that is liable to be damaging to it in Scotland, just as a similar perception of the Conservatives has been detrimental to their hopes of seats north of the border. The SNP benefited greatly from British Prime Minister David Cameron's immediate response to the result of the September 2014 referendum, when he snatched defeat from the jaws of victory by stating that more powers for the Edinburgh parliament would be conditional on there being fewer powers for Scottish MPs at Westminster. On a high turnout of almost 85 percent of the electorate, Scots had rejected the independence on offer by 55 percent to 45 percent. In the later stages of the campaign, the pro-Union parties, at the urging of Gordon Brown, offered powers to the Scottish parliament additional to those they already wielded. By reviving the notion of "English votes for English laws" within twenty-four hours of the referendum result, the Prime Minister put party management ahead of the future of the Union. The announcement was regarded in Scotland as an act of bad faith, and it meant that the Scottish Labour Party, already damaged by having been in temporary alliance with the Conservatives on the overriding issue of winning the referendum, suffered a further erosion of support among hitherto reliably Labour voters.

The rhetoric of "English votes for English laws" could become compatible with the preservation of the Union, but only if it becomes part of a new federal political settlement. As things currently stand, there are few laws passed by the British Parliament that do not have implications for the parts of the UK with a devolved parliament or assembly. Thus, for example, if income tax and health expenditure are both reduced in England, the Barnett formula governing Scottish funding (whose preservation was part of the deal offered Scotland in the run-up to the referendum) means that the block grant to Scotland that is related to UK revenue would be diluted, thus forcing the Scottish government either to cut its own health spending or to increase taxation.[11] To prevent Members of Parliament representing Scottish constituencies from voting on such matters would strain the Union to breaking point. David Cameron subsequently rowed back somewhat from his initial announcement, but if the MPs from Scotland in Westminster were ever to be deprived of voting rights on a wide swath of economic issues, it would be but a short step to saying that no Scottish MP could ever again be Prime Minister or Chancellor of the Exchequer. Since even pro-Union Scots would not accept second-class citizenship, Scotland would very speedily cease to be part of the UK. As the pursuit of independent statehood is the raison d'être of fifty-six out of the fifty-nine MPs now representing Scotland in Westminster, every attempt to downgrade the role of Scottish members of the House of Commons would be greeted with public outrage and private celebration.

The Scottish National Party had a huge impact in the 2015 general election, and not only in Scotland. Apart from taking forty of the forty-one seats that Labour had won there in 2010, their message that a Labour minority government would have to depend on SNP votes was used to great effect by the Conservative Party and by UKIP in England. Since the opinion polls misled the entire country into thinking that no one party would have an overall majority, the leverage the Scottish National Party (whose enormous advance the polls did accurately predict) would supposedly have over a minority Labour government became a major issue in the campaign. The SNP leader Nicola Sturgeon had told her party members, "The SNP will never, ever, put the Tories into government. But I ask you to think about this. Think about how much more we could win for Scotland from a Westminster Labour government if they had to depend on SNP votes."[12] English voters thought about that, too, and they were, moreover, daily reminded by Labour's main opponents south of the border. In words and pictures (including an electronic blitz), they portrayed Ed Miliband in thrall to Nicola Sturgeon and Alex Salmond. It is fairly certain that this cost Labour seats in

England, adding to the damage inflicted on them by the SNP in Scotland.

The SNP has now, through electoral legitimacy, become the voice of Scotland in both London and Edinburgh. It not only has all but three of the MPs sent to Westminster from Scottish constituencies, but is also by a wide margin the third-largest party in the House of Commons after the Conservative and Labour parties. This is combined with an overall majority, as the governing party, in the Holyrood parliament, in spite of the highly proportional voting system for that Edinburgh legislature, which makes majorities hard to achieve. The next election for the Scottish parliament is due in May 2016, but if the Scottish Labour Party, from its current abyss, were to rise to power in Edinburgh within a year, that would be at least as remarkable a turnaround as the SNP triumph in the recent general election. Given that the SNP's dominance of the Scottish political scene seems reasonably secure for the next five years, there will be many opportunities for a clash between Scotland's representatives and the British government to acquire major constitutional proportions.

One such issue is the referendum on UK membership of the European Union, which the Conservative government has promised. The SNP, in line with majority opinion in Scotland (including, of course, that of the Labour Party), is firmly in favor of continuing membership. It seems probable that the UK as a whole will vote the same way, but this cannot be taken for granted, and Nicola Sturgeon has already said that there should be separate votes in England, Scotland, Wales, and Northern Ireland, with exit occurring only if all four component parts of the UK vote for it. Such a demand is clearly unacceptable to the Conservative party and government, and it puts the fate of two Unions at stake in the EU referendum. In the 1975 referendum on European Community membership, there was a two-thirds majority for staying in. What may now make such a comfortable victory less certain is that EU membership is currently much more closely linked to widespread popular concern about excessive immigration and the understanding that UK governments are powerless to do anything to counter the principle of freedom of movement within the EU.

No party in a democracy can expect to be electorally popular forever. The Scottish National Party is no exception. It will wish to hold a second referendum on independence only at a time when it has a realistic prospect of achieving its cherished objective. That might mean sooner rather than later, while it is riding the crest of a wave. The British government may, of course, refuse to give its official sanction to such a referendum. If, however, the Edinburgh government were then to initiate an indicative poll to test opinion on independence, accompanying that with the complaint that the UK government was denying the Scottish people the right to choose their own destiny, this could have great political resonance. For those who are not afraid of further radical constitutional change and who also value Scottish membership of the Union, the time to start thinking seriously about federation is now.

Fall Semester 2014

1. Hugh Seton-Watson, *Nations and States: An Enquiry into the Origins of Nations and the Politics of Nationalism* (London, 1977), pp. 6–7. See also Anthony D. Smith, *The Antiquity of Nations* (Cambridge, 2004).
2. Christopher A. Whatley, *The Scots and the Union: Then and Now* (Edinburgh, 2014), p. 13.
3. Robert Burns, "Such a Parcel of Rogues in a Nation," in *The Poetry of Robert Burns: Centenary Edition*, ed. W. E. Henley and Thomas F. Henderson (London, 1896), vol. 3, pp. 127–28.
4. See especially Paul Langford, "South Britons' Reception of North Britons, 1707–1820," in T. C. Smout, ed., *Anglo-Scottish Relations from 1603 to 1900* (Oxford, 2005), pp. 143–69.
5. James Boswell, *Boswell's London Journal, 1762–1763*, ed. Frederick A. Pottle (London, 1950), pp. 71–72.
6. Ibid., p. 260.
7. Gordon Brown, *My Scotland, Our Britain: A Future Worth Sharing* (London, 2014), p. 48.
8. Richard Finlay, "The Turbulent Century," in Jenny Wormald, ed., *Scotland: A History* (Oxford, 2005), p. 266.
9. Against some contrary assertions, Oxford Professor of European and Human Rights Law, Sinaidh Douglas-Scott, has persuasively argued that Scotland's transition from EU membership as part of the UK to EU membership as an independent state would be relatively straightforward: Douglas-Scott, "How Easily Could an Independent Scotland Join the EU?," Oxford Legal Studies Research Paper No. 46/2014, July 2014.
10. Derry Irvine, "A Skilful Advocate," in Wendy Alexander, ed., *Donald Dewar: Scotland's First First Minister* (Edinburgh, 2005), pp. 125–29, at p. 127.
11. John Kay, "English votes for English laws' Is Easier Said than Done," *Financial Times*, 11 Feb. 2015.
12. "SNP Conference: Nicola Sturgeon Says Party Could Hold Balance of Power," http://www.bbc.co.uk/news/uk-scotland-politics-30061564, 15 Nov. 2014.

Oxford Dictionary of National Biography

29

British National Identity

LAWRENCE GOLDMAN

The *Oxford Dictionary of National Biography* was published in 2004 in print and also online. It then comprised essays on the lives of approximately 55,000 people, covering more than two millennia, in more than 50,000 articles written by some 10,000 contributors and extending to more than 65 million words, making it by far the longest single work in the history of the English language. In a decade it has added a further 5,000 articles. Since it is now established as one of the key sources for the study of British history, it is fitting to consider how, if at all, the publication of the *Oxford DNB* has helped us define the nation: who are the British and how are they presented in this biographical dictionary?

Immediately, one confronts an interesting recent historiographical development: the *Oxford DNB* is not the only major national biographical dictionary to have been published or to have started research in this period. Everybody's doing it, in the words of the British song. The *American National Biography* was published in 1999, the *Australian Dictionary of Biography* went online in 2006. The Germans are close to completing the *Neue Deutsche Biographie* and are also linking together their different regional biographical compilations. The Italians, who began planning in 1925 and who published the first volume of their biographical dictionary in 1960 on the centenary of their nationhood, have got as far as names beginning with the letter *P* in the subsequent fifty-four years. The Spanish succeeded in publishing their dictionary in 2011, but its inclusion of living subjects, the relative absence of women in its pages, and its failure to deal adequately with figures from the Franco era, were met with derision. The Irish published their first biographical dictionary, *The Dictionary of Irish Biography*, in 2009 in nine print volumes as well as online, and it met with the opposite reaction—widespread praise for a mature and scholarly view of Irish history, shorn of national myth and historic grievance. Why should national biographical dictionaries suddenly be in vogue?

At one level, the answer to this question is easy: we have the technology. The rapid development of the Internet, digital technology, and electronic publishing have all made it possible (though at a considerable price) to initiate or republish large reference works on the Web, where they are more easily accessed and, crucially, searched, than as volumes on shelves. A century and more of historical scholarship in most developed countries has also added tremendously to our knowledge of who was who, and of who did what to whom. We know much more about figures from the past than did our great-grandparents.

The major biographical dictionaries of the nineteenth century were, in most cases, the self-conscious products of an age of nationalism. Are we going through a comparable upsurge of nationalism, which might explain the energy and resources devoted to national biography around the world? In fact, much of the motivation is scholarly rather than political, for like the *Dictionary of National Biography* under its first editor, the man of letters Leslie Stephen, the aim is still to provide readers and writers with works of reference of the highest standard that can be regularly updated to keep them accurate and current. Indeed, the creative force behind all these projects may not be nationalism or technology but the maturation of discrete national historiographies: now that the terrains of British, American, and Irish history have been mapped and their contours are clear, they can be peopled. The development of a critical mass of scholars and students in a national culture makes it possible to sustain both the production and the consumption of biographical scholarship.

Nevertheless, it is curious that against the grain of academic fashion, which has been dominated for decades by the study of the past though methodologies and ideologies from Marxism and structuralism to feminism and postmodernism, there is such an appetite for history as the record of individual lives. Of course, the ordinary reader has never given up on biography: open the book pages of any decent Sunday newspaper and there is plenty of history being reviewed, though most of it is in the form of biography. Indeed the enthusiasm for these many biographical dictionaries—and one of the key reasons why scholars have been so keen to write for them—is the thought that by penning a sharp and witty sketch of a life based on the latest archival research, the author may bridge the gap between the academic and popular, laying down a source that will be quarried in university libraries by the professional researcher but that may also be accessed in public libraries by the simply curious. For the professional scholar there may be another motivation as well: to present a biography, and hence an aspect of the nation's history, warts and all, shorn of national legend or glorification. These contemporaneous and simultaneous biographical projects in Europe and across the English-speaking world mark a transition in national historiography from biographical celebration and accusation to the sober, careful, and well-documented presentation of lives as they were actually lived. The attempt is being made to give a view of the nation's history without mischief, embodying the fruits of the latest research. Whatever the motivation, the initiation and publication of so many national biographical dictionaries in the present generation is an event in historiography to be savored.

THE PUBLICATION OF THE ORIGINAL *Dictionary of National Biography* between 1885 and 1901 was celebrated as a national achievement both at the time and since. That the first *DNB* was an evocation of national triumphs and a characteristic product of the age of empire is almost axiomatic among modern historical writers and commentators. But they are all wrong, at least if we consider the intent of the founding editor of the *DNB*, Leslie Stephen. Stephen was always clear that he was editing a biographical work of reference with a scholarly rationale alone: the *DNB* was to be a source of reliable information on national history, an authoritative work, at a stage when the professionalization of history was just beginning. It is difficult to find evidence of national celebration in any of its articles; the tone is businesslike, sober, unsentimental, factual. As Stephen wrote in 1882, "We should aim at giving the greatest possible amount of information in a thoroughly business-like form."[1] As one of its authors, Alfred Ainger, once wrote, the *DNB*'s motto was "no flowers, by request."[2] But there was a difference between Stephen's original intent and the way the first *DNB* was received; press and public inevitably focused on it as a collection of the nation's most worthy sons (there were relatively few daughters in the first *DNB*) and hence as a record of national achievement. And Stephen's successor as editor, his former assistant, Sidney Lee, was more given than Stephen to making comparisons with other national biographical projects then in progress and assessing the relative significance of worthies in different national cultures—comparisons that always seemed to favor the British over Germans or Spaniards or the French. But as originally projected, the first *DNB* was more a product of cultural uncertainty than of imperial self-confidence. Stephen came from a long line of evangelical opponents of slavery; he experienced religious doubt in the 1860s and gave up his Cambridge fellowship; like many of the late-Victorian intellectual elite, he lacked both religious faith—belief in God—and secular faith, the belief in progress.

In addition, Stephen quite deliberately left vague the identity of the nation itself. The *Dictionary of National Biography* was not so called out of any national arrogance or insouciance on the assumption that everyone would know automatically which nation its pages embodied. Rather, Stephen recognized that Britain and the British nation were both difficult to define and had emerged only in the eighteenth century. For most of the recorded history of the islands, people have adopted other national and regional identities and been fiercely hostile to their neighbors rather than citizens of a single, peaceable kingdom. It would have been anachronistic, not to say excessively self-limiting, to focus on the British only.

When Leslie Stephen advertised for assistance in an article in the *Athenaeum* in December 1882 for what became the *DNB*, he referred to the project as a new "Biographia Britannica," which was an eighteenth-century compilation of British worthies and a rather unpropitious comparator, since the second edition of the *Biographia Britannica* only got as far as surnames beginning with the letter F. Nevertheless, a century after Stephen, the *Oxford DNB* has taken what might be called a "Britannic" approach as well, if by "Britannic" we understand a purely geographic principle of definition rather than an historic or political one. The *DNB* is concerned with the lives of noteworthy people who have lived in, or had some substantive connection with, the British Isles. It includes people from all four component nations: there are well over 5,000 Scots, and just under that number of Irish, along with more than 2,000 Welsh in its pages. In all three cases there has been a very considerable expansion in coverage with the addition of more "Celtic" lives in all periods. In adding new lives to the *Dictionary,* we were conscious of the need to break down stereotypes—to break through the perception of eighteenth-century Wales, for example, as the habitation of bardic scholars and pioneering Methodists—and to find influential personalities who had not yet received biographical attention. Whether the inclusion of Marged ferch Ifan, a Welsh "harpist and wrestler" as the *ODNB* describes her, who lived a remarkably long life in the eighteenth century, has achieved this may be debatable: the article describes her as "a great weightlifter who could wrestle any man to the ground, so that even when she was seventy years old the young men of the district treated her with respect."[3]

Many of the subjects in the *Dictionary*, from all four national groupings, acknowledged a regional or a county identity before a national one. On the other hand, some lives, for instance the entry on Edward Bruce (c. 1280–1318), Earl of Carrick and the brother of the Scottish king Robert, who tried to conquer Ireland in the early fourteenth century, had to be set in a context embracing the whole of the British Isles. The *Dictionary* reflects the consensus that Scottish history should be studied as a discrete subject, not just as a distorting mirror of events further south. That said, it must be observed that much Scottish history in the *Oxford DNB* is contained in articles on subjects from other nations—first Roman, then Irish, finally English. The role of monks from Iona in the early ecclesiastical development of Scotland was vital. Archbishops of York and bishops of Carlisle and Durham were often involved in, and affected by, events in Scotland, and the same is true of many English aristocrats who owned substantial estates north of the border. Thus, the articles on the Umfraville family start with them when they were a northern English family c. 1100, cross to Scotland with them c. 1250, and return to Northumberland for their last members in the early fifteenth century.

The same point can be made for the Welsh and Irish. Throughout the Middle Ages, some of the most powerful English noble families owned great estates in Wales and often involved themselves in Welsh politics. There is much about Wales in articles on members of the Bohun family, Earls of Hereford in the twelfth, thirteenth, and fourteenth centuries; the Clare family, Earls of Gloucester in the same period; the Fitzalans, Earls of Arundel in the thirteenth and fourteenth centuries; and the Mortimers, Earls of March at this time. The same is true of landowners, soldiers, and administrators who were active on the Welsh march in the later Middle Ages. Similarly, the *Dictionary* contains few politicians in the Hanoverian period who can be labeled specifically Welsh, an effect of the local gentry and aristocracy detaching themselves from Welsh culture and identifying more strongly with London society. The territorial feuds between families within Wales that had dominated seventeenth-century politics gave way to a pattern more familiar from England, where county and borough representation were carved up with Westminster as well as local politics in mind.

There are also thousands of subjects in the *Dictionary* whose lives are associated with places much further afield than the British Isles: approximately 950 are linked with Australia; 850 with Canada; and more than 2,000 with India. Beyond the empire, the *Dictionary* has 35 subjects linked with Chile, 16 with Finland, more than 100 with Japan, and 18 with Madagascar. Many subjects in the *Dictionary* came to Britain from elsewhere and made it their permanent home or stayed for only a short time but made an impact nonetheless. Karl Marx, who came in 1848 and remained until his death in 1883, is in the first category; Sigmund Freud, Jimi Hendrix, and Forrest Mars are in the second category. Freud lived in London for a matter of months at the very end of his life as a refugee from Vienna, but his very presence stimulated the institutionalization of British psychoanalysis; Hendrix became a guitar hero only after he swapped Seattle for London in the mid-1960s; and Forrest Mars invented the Mars Bar during a three-year sojourn at Slough in the 1930s, and then returned to the United States to build the confectionary empire of the Mars corporation. There are thousands in the *Oxford DNB* who were born in the British Isles but who lived most of their lives overseas, usually as servants of empire from the seventeenth century onward. The *Dictionary* also includes people who never set foot in the British Isles or who came only for very short periods, but who influenced British history nonetheless: for example, the many twentieth-century leaders of indigenous anticolonial protest movements around the empire and Commonwealth, including, for example, Mahatma Gandhi, Jomo Kenyatta, and Idi Amin. As we sometimes point out (with tongue in cheek), this is how the empire strikes back: we include in the *Oxford DNB* many figures who fervently hoped to break the link with Britain but have now been subsumed into British history.

We can see how these different categories break down in the *Dictionary*'s coverage of subjects associated with Australia and New Zealand. Thus, among those who were born in Britain but lived in Australia and New Zealand are Caroline Chisholm (1808–1877), who provided support for female emigrants to Australia, and Liverpool-born Kate Sheppard (1847–1934), who successfully promoted women's suffrage in New Zealand. Among those who were born in Australia and New Zealand but made their careers in Britain, we number the artist Roy de Maistre (1894–1968), the fashion designer Leigh Bowery (1961–1994), and the pioneers of plastic surgery Sir Harold Gillies (1882–1960) and Sir Archibald McIndoe (1900–1960). Included in our third category, meanwhile, is the aborigine Pemulwoy (c. 1760–1802), a leader of resistance to European settlement in Australia. In the case of Australia, we may discern a fourth category as well: those who were transported but who returned to Britain after their sentence. These include the Scottish radicals Maurice Margarot (1745–1815) and William Skirving (d. 1796); the trade unionists the Tolpuddle Martyrs (who are the subject of a group article); and the Young Irelander Kevin O Doherty (1823–1905).

The same exercise can be accomplished from among the 700 colonial Americans included in the *Oxford DNB* on the principle that until 1776 they were subjects of the British crown. Thus the most notable initial settlers from Britain who founded the colonies in Virginia and Massachusetts are included in the *Dictionary*. So too are those born in the Americas who came to Britain, comprising a collection as varied as Pocahontas, Benjamin Franklin, and a group article on sixteenth-century Native American who came to Britain by a variety of means and routes. The *Oxford DNB* also finds room for American colonists who never came to Britain but are part of British as well as American history, such as George Washington and several signatories of the Declaration of Independence, including Thomas Jefferson.

One of my favorite lives in the *Oxford DNB* shows very well its pluralism and scope: that of Josiah Henson. He began life as a slave in Maryland; he escaped to Canada; he became an antislavery orator and author there, and was said to have been the model for Harriet Beecher Stowe's Uncle Tom; he was an exhibitor at the Great Exhibition in the Crystal Palace in 1851; he preached across the length and breadth of Britain on several occasions; toward the end of his life he enjoyed a private audience with Queen Victoria in Windsor.

As this demonstrates, the ethos and policy of the *Oxford DNB*, as set down by its founding editor, the late Colin Matthew, has been inclusive rather than exclusive. This is in accordance with contemporary political trends and historical interests: the *Dictionary* reflects the commitment to diversity and pluralism in British society over the past generation. If it was to be an accurate reflection of our present view of national history, it had to be inclusive. But it is also a symptom of a growing understanding among historians and many others that the history of the British Isles is an essentially international one, made up of waves of inward and outward migration; and that British culture, like so many other national cultures, has amalgamated many external traditions and strains in its history. It may also be a function of the difficulty of deciding who, exactly, were or are the British? If we cannot be precise on this point—and I hope my initial examples show the difficulty—the *Dictionary*'s policy has been to err on the side of caution and include all those with a claim to the national identity.

The *Oxford DNB* set out to redress the underrepresentation of several notable groups in Leslie Stephen's *Dictionary*—women, most obviously, whose numbers have trebled in the *Oxford DNB*, but also entrepreneurs and businessmen; engineers and technologists; labor leaders and radicals; and figures from the worlds of popular entertainment and culture, an area of national life that has expanded greatly since the late nineteenth century. The original, relative exclusion of these groups had a social rather than a national explanation; they were not thought to have made a sufficient contribution to the making of national history to merit a place. In including many more from these categories, we have responded to new concepts of historical significance—indeed to the very broadening of history itself to include women's history, the history of technology, social history, the history of leisure, and so forth.

These social and economic categories are not difficult to define; in expanding the *Dictionary* to include more subjects from them, we have encountered little controversy. But some cultural, ethnic, and religious identities present, in microcosm, difficulties similar to those found with national identities. Following the changes and about-turns in the religious life of many of our subjects is often problematic, for example, especially in more recent decades, during which religion has become an increasingly private aspect of national and personal life. In many cases it has not been clear whether figures being added to the *Dictionary* had a religious conviction or affiliation, because of their reticence on the matter. In other cases, the very complexity of religious identity can be baffling for authors and editors alike. Jewish identity is familial, religious, ethnic, and cultural simultaneously. Some figures who do not meet the strict criteria of familial descent have been considered Jewish through their lives; some who do meet those criteria have overtly rejected their identity. Defining individuals in a situation in which group identity is so vague and also contested has not been easy. In the case of the Anglo-Jewish community, which now numbers about 250,000 only, there is an intense pride in their contributions to British public life in the past century, and also anxiety about their future in British society. Both factors explain why they have taken such an interest in the *Oxford DNB* and lobbied to ensure that it represents their community and their achievements to the full. No other minority has taken such an interest.

Is the inclusion of more Welsh, Scottish, and Irish subjects a response to recent political developments, notably the upsurge since the 1960s of Celtic nationalism in all these nations? This is certainly the case, but then the British state and British culture generally have had to adapt to changing relations between the component nationalities since the construction of Britain itself in the early modern period. It was no different for Leslie Stephen. The first number of the *DNB* was published in 1885, a matter of months before Gladstone's first Home Rule Bill for Ireland, and Stephen, like many members of the late-Victorian intelligentsia, was a Liberal Unionist, committed to the maintenance of the Union and hostile to Gladstone's project. The Oxford historian Paul Langford reported soon after the inception of the *Oxford DNB* project that the first *Dictionary* had overrepresented Irish subjects of the late eighteenth century, particularly the Irish rebels of 1798, and Colin Matthew interpreted this as an attempt by Stephen, as a Liberal Unionist, to demonstrate the place of the Irish in British, or "national," history. In other words, problems of national definition and the relation of these to contemporary political events are not peculiar to the present generation.

GIVEN THESE DIFFICULTIES OF CONTEXT and definition, does this make the British, as Benedict Anderson might have put it, an "imagined community"? And was it the purpose of the original *DNB* to give spurious shape and form to the nation in a nationalistic age? Several nineteenth-century projects of national biography were explicitly designed to help construct a new sense of nationhood, such as the dictionaries composed by the Belgians, the Danes, the Americans, and, most notably, the Germans.

But if the original *DNB* had sought to do this as well, its understated and distinctly rational rather than celebratory tone would have subverted the intention—though, in truth, the intention was never there. And in the case of the *Oxford DNB*, its wide scope and catholicity are at odds with any desire to capture the essence of British identity. Had we worked with any clear criteria of what it is to be British, or who might properly describe themselves as such, the *Oxford DNB* would have been shorter, less varied, and less interesting.

There are figures in the *Dictionary* who have been taken to represent supposed national characteristics. When we published, there was—and still remains—a great interest in eccentricity in the pages of the *Oxford DNB*. Notorious misers, cross-dressers, women who claimed to have given birth to cats or to rabbits, men who went out with mad dogs in the midday sun—these were the sort of lives that attracted press attention and that were easily subsumed under the national category "English eccentrics." But it is impossible to discern a set of clear national characteristics that define the British (or the English, for that matter) among the teeming thousands in the *Dictionary*. Indeed, many of the most notable people in its pages seem to have been entirely at odds with supposed national characteristics, including among them pragmatism, empiricism, understatement, and self-control—"stiff upper lip," in short. Churchill, regularly voted the greatest of Britons, was loquacious, impetuous, romantic, sentimental, emotional, depressive. And the stereotype would not fit those who have been depicted in recent times on our banknotes. Was Isaac Newton, who spent more than twenty years of his life in devotion to alchemy, an empiricist? Was Charles Dickens ever understated? Was Florence Nightingale, driven herself and a driver of those around her, just a pragmatist? Perhaps the most notable figures in our history were such precisely because they were quite different from our supposed national character—though, as is widely agreed, historical arguments premised on national character have fallen into disuse, not to say disrepute.

If the construction of a British national character is so hazardous, it follows that an assumption that the *Dictionary* somehow mirrors British qualities and British identity is hazardous also. Indeed, in the difficulty encountered in defining the British nation through the *Dictionary*, we have an example of the widespread problem of defining nationhood in general, particularly in old European societies, which have gone through many different stages and formations in their history. We may contrast this with a national identity premised on certain ideas, institutions, and political procedures, as in the case of the United States. The essence of American identity is embodied in the documents—in the Declaration of Independence, the Constitution, perhaps also the Gettysburg Address—and in the modes of self-government that they have given birth to. This is lacking in the British case, where an organic system of government is without such fundamental expressions of national purpose, national unity, and national procedure. Without doubt, Americans make more out of the Magna Carta as the foundation of the rule of law than the British themselves, who are at pains to explain its proximate origins and precise, limited context.

Colin Matthew, the first editor of the *Oxford DNB*, who planned the *Dictionary*, whose triumph it was, and who died in 1999, midway through its preparation, was acutely aware of the timing of his new British biographical dictionary. As a Lowland Scot, he was conscious of the fragility of the Union in a manner that often surprised the largely English-born historians with whom he collaborated in Oxford and who took the Union for granted. As the biographer of Mr. Gladstone, he was intensely interested in the historical development of British political and constitutional institutions, and aware at every turn of the Victorian traditions that underpin so much of

British public life. He thus saw the *ODNB* as marking an epoch in British history. It was compiled and published during a generation when centuries of self-government and global reach were giving way to a new identity and constitutional reality within the European Union. Those who knew Matthew appreciated his ambivalence toward these changes—an ambivalence that may be reflected in the breadth and catholicity of the *Oxford DNB*. At this point of profound political uncertainty—surely the most uncertain phase in Britain's history since the Second World War—in which Britain's place in Europe is not yet settled and the United Kingdom itself may very well fracture in the coming period, the *Dictionary* may be read, in political terms, and as Matthew intended, as indeterminate and undecided: an interim statement giving due weight to all of Britain's international relations and history—regional, national, imperial, transatlantic and European—without choosing and defining. That is how Matthew wanted it, because it is a fair reflection of Britain's current historical position: a work in rapid progress. In time, the *Oxford DNB* may come to represent the last view of British history before Britain itself took on a new meaning, or perhaps ceased to exist in a recognizable form.

My suggestion, therefore, is that we should jettison the idea of the *Oxford DNB* being reflective of British identity and think instead of it as something rather different, as helping constitute the nation, though a different sort of nation from the concept that word usually conjures. The *Dictionary* is a record of human endeavor *in* the British Isles and thus is itself among the most useful tools that we possess for defining what I will call the British presence and British influence.

This is not some sort of postmodern argument that there is no history outside the text, or that the text can be written and interpreted as one pleases. I am not arguing that British identity lives only in the pages of the *Oxford DNB* or in some other "book of the British." Nor is it a species of arrogance: I am not saying that whatever the nature of British identity, the *Dictionary* has captured it. In spirit, the best example of my point is probably the famous preface that Edward Thompson wrote to his classic study *The Making of the English Working Class* (1963), in which, when faced with the obligation to define the working class—and social classes as entities in general—Thompson contended that they could be understood only in and through their history: that, in some sense, the working class was what the working class experienced and did over decades of its history. In other words, class is not a construct that can be defined at any moment in time, but is an evolving category that can define itself only through experience. Class is not a thing: it is a series of happenings in history.

Perhaps it is not fanciful to see the *Oxford DNB* like this: it gives us no definition of "the British," either in the past or in the present. It is a record of what people who lived in the British Isles and spoke English (as well as other languages) did for more than two millennia. But insofar as it provides a vast record of the experiences, thoughts, material productions, orations, and writings of these people in and through time, it allows us to form an impression of the British as defined by their historical experience. And perhaps there is no other way of defining nations except through the shared experience of their history. This is what the *Oxford DNB* has attempted to do: to set many different lives in their contexts and to present the record of what they achieved in such a way that their deeds and thoughts define who they were, collectively as well as individually.

In its scale and scope, the *Dictionary* makes generalization impossible; in its variety and plurality, it demands that we accept that we live in a messy world where firm definitions of identity—identity of any sort, be it social, religious, or national—cannot be made with security or certainty. In truth, my conclusion is that the *Oxford DNB* doesn't solve the problem of national identity but restates it in another and more complex form. And I am content to live with that.

Spring Semester 2015

1. Leslie Stephen, "A New 'Biographia Britannica,'" *Athenaeum*, 2878, 23 Dec. 1882, p. 850.
2. Noel Annan, *Leslie Stephen: The Godless Victorian* (London, 1984), p. 84.
3. Ceridwen Lloyd-Morgan, "Marged ferch Ifan (*bap.* 1696, *d.* 1793)," *Oxford Dictionary of National Biography* (Oxford, 2004).

U 1016/36

BRITISH EMBASSY,
WASHINGTON, D.C.

CONFIDENTIAL
GUARD

21st September, 1950.

Dear Michael,

    I am sending you a paper on the people of the United States of America. It has been written by Duckham, the Agricultural Attaché. He wrote this paper not with any idea of circulation but to clear his own mind just before his return to England after five years in the U.S.A. During this time he has visited every State of the Union at least once, By the nature of his work it is with rural America that he has concerned himself. He has produced this paper as a collection of his ideas and comments and in no way as a definitive work.

    I have found Duckham's ideas of real interest and his thought at times has originality. I have therefore decided to send the paper to you with the suggestion that it be considered for Foreign Office print.

    This analysis of some of the components of the American character is written with understanding and appreciation of its good qualities, but the paper also contains some frank criticisms and remarks which could hardly be considered flattering. Therefore the paper is marked "Guard". If it is not considered advisable to circulate this paper in print, I hope it may have a wide circulation amongst officials who concern themselves with a study of the U.S.A.

Yours ever

Oliver Franks.

M. Wright Esq., C.M.G.,
   Foreign Office,
     London S.W.1.

Letter from Oliver Franks, 31 September 1950, transmitting the memorandum by A. N. Duckham

30

Some Notes on the Americans

A. N. DUCKHAM

(Confidential Guard)

The enclosed notes have been compiled by Mr. A. N. Duckham when Agricultural Attaché at His Majesty's Embassy, Washington.

American Department,
 Foreign Office,
  27th October, 1950

* * *

Enclosure

In the past five years I have travelled some 100,000 miles in North America and been at least once in every State of the Union and in every province of Canada. In the course of my work as Agricultural Attaché I have met literally hundreds of farmers (their wives, children and employees), officials, professors and small business men, and several scores of industrialists and trade union leaders. My contacts with industry are, of course, mainly limited to the technical sides of food processing, farm machinery and agricultural chemicals. I cannot pretend to know anything about the United States factory worker. I realise that many others have written about the Americans in the last fifty years and that an Agricultural Attaché has no right to dabble in sociology—other than rural sociology—and still less to attempt to forecast the effect of current trends on American foreign policy. Nevertheless, because I have been privileged to see so much of the United States, because my approach to the American scene has been *inwards* from the land rather than *outwards* from Washington, New York or Chicago, and because rural America is not only a strong force in domestic politics but is still a potent source of population for the towns, the attached notes may be of interest and possibly of some use.

2. These notes are essentially a somewhat hurried assembly of comments and ideas which I have jotted down at odd moments and which I have not had time to organise or edit properly.

3. It will be seen that no reference is made below to the American Constitution, the structure of Congress, to the fact that the United States is a Federation, or to the influence of any of these political institutions on the Americans. This is intentional, because it seems to me that they have and have had little influence on, but rather reflect, the American character.

* * *

Enclosure in Enclosure

1. There are two dangerously deceptive facts about the United States. The first is its apparent similarity to Europe and the Commonwealth and particularly to the United Kingdom in language, in historical origins, in democratic institutions, and culture. The second is the apparent diversity of its geography, ethnic groups, economic development and range of personal incomes. In fact, both its similarity to external cultures and its internal diversity mask a synthetic but now indigenous pseudo-culture which has an astounding and increasing uniformity and which differs fundamentally from the ways of living found in most of Europe and the "white" countries of the Commonwealth.

National characteristics are the product of the interaction between genetic, cultural and geographical environments. The diverse genetic and cultural origins of the Americans, and the wide range of climatic and other geographical factors found in the States would lead one to, first, expect economic and social diversity; second, emotional stability; third, the frugal husbandry of the peasant; fourth, physical and intellectual vigour. In practice, however, the Americans do not conform with these expectations.

The Americans and the way they live are surprisingly uniform. They are more emotional than the peoples of the countries which most influenced their culture. They are very hospitable, friendly and profligate in their use of natural resources. Their undoubted physical vigour does not seem to be matched by an equal intellectual vigour. In brief, though of the same racial stock, they differ very substantially from their European cousins. Why are the Americans unlike their ancestors?

GENETIC INFLUENCES

2. In the British Commonwealth, there has been relatively little national or racial interbreeding, *e.g.,* between the Boers and the British in South Africa, the French and the British in Canada, the Welsh and the Scots in Britain. In the United States, on the other hand, (with relatively minor exceptions, *e.g.,* the Kentucky hill-billies, the Pennsylvania "Dutch," the French Acadians of Louisiana) there has been very considerable *interbreeding* not only amongst the immigrants from the many nations of Europe but also between Europeans and Negroes and to a lesser extent, with the Indians and Mexicans. Biologically, this interbreeding appears (as one would expect) to have had two major effects. First, some losses of original phenotypic characters; secondly, considerable signs of hybrid vigour (heterosis). Thus, though it is still possible to identify the Latin type in *e.g.,* New York and the Nordic type in say Minnesota, over large parts of the country speculations about the genetic origin of the people one meets are idle exercises, but their vigour is quite noticeable.

There are, moreover, still some marked "colonies" of predominantly Scandinavian, German, Irish or Italian origin. As these disintergrate, they will tend to bring "new blood" into the mass of the population and thus maintain *hybrid vigour.*

In a livestock breeder's terms, however, the American Herd Book was practically closed when mass immigration ceased in the early twenties of this century, and over the long pull any contribution which heterosis may make to American vigour will probably tend to decline.

But whilst this loss of ancestral "national" appearance (phenotypical characters) and the gradual emergence of a rather nondescript "typical American" is, like their apparent hybrid vigour, easy for a biologist to understand and explain, their mental attributes are not. In logic, two negatives make a positive, but in genetics they frequently make another negative. Why, therefore, are the Americans—the descendants of some of the most stolid nations of the world—so unreserved? Why, in fact, in America, is the progeny of two introvert immigrants usually an extrovert? Apart from the obvious answer that the laws of genetics do not govern the affairs of nations, it seems that, as discussed below, their boisterous lack of restraint may be partly a "front" to hid [sic] a basic *psychological insecurity*.

This insecurity may spring, in part, from what one may perhaps call a "sense of racial illegitimacy." One is sometimes inclined to think, when one hears interminable discussion, about the overcrowding on the *Mayflower* and about "where my folks came from," that the Americans are 150 million people in search of an ancestry. Their professed antipathy to the heriditary [sic] principle and their overt resentment against and secret envy of anyone from an English peer or an old Boston family to an Indian warrior who can lay claims to a long pedigree, may be devices to hide a feeling that they are mongrels. This feeling may partly account for those who, like Henry Ford, maintain that "History is Bunk"; for their admirable absence of class consciousness; for their malicious delight in robbing prominent people of their dignity; for their strong desire to conform to the phenotypical American (*i.e.*, the cult of the average) and to criticise those who do not; for their rather somatic way of living; and for their habit of a judging a man by what he is and even though this often means that an individual is judged by what he can make himself appear to be, *i.e.*, a man is judged by the size and year of his car, not his social class.

GEOGRAPHICAL ENVIRONMENT

3. In a country where, for instance, the types of farming are as varied as those of a Kentish fruit grower, a North African olive producer, an Australian wheat producer, a South African wool grower or a Jamaican sugar planter, one would expect to find marked regional characteristics in the human population, whether rural or urban. In fact, *regional differences* are surprisingly small. It is true that the Vermont dairy farmer or the Colorado wheat grower differ in manner and outlook from the New York Italian or Hollywood Hebrew, but these differences are little, if any, more than those between a Welsh hill farmer and a Cockney, even though the latter are less than 300 miles apart and the former may be 3,000 miles from each other.

The relatively short time the country has been settled, and the occupational and geographical mobility of its population both play their part in minimising potential regional differences. Cultural factors, such as the strenuous indoctrination of Americanism and the influence of the cult of the average are also, no doubt, at work. But one additional and important factor, *viz.*, the country's richness in natural resources, should not be overlooked. Thus, cheap fuel and power enable the people of North Dakota to enjoy, in winter, many of the amenities of the Southern Californian. In summer, air conditioning stimulates [*sic*], for the Washingtonian, at least some of the coolness of Maine. A high standard of living promotes uniformity because ways of living do not have to be so closely tied to the local economic habitat as they tend to be in districts or amongst groups which live on the poverty line (*e.g.,* the Eastern Kentucky hill people, the Mexicans of the South West). In the United States, as elsewhere, regional characters are most marked amongst the "underprivileged." Ecological differences are minimised by high living standards.

Thus some of the more obvious regional differences are being increasingly smoothed out by modern technology. At first sight, however, they leave a substantial residuum of differences. How else can one account for the briskness of the New Yorker and the lazy easy-going life of the Southern gentleman? This particular difference, however, is partly explained, I think, by the traditions of the South and by the general poverty of the Southern population. For in South-Eastern Texas, where the summer is almost as trying as that of the Mississippi Delta, one finds a very vigorous economy which has not fallen into easy-going, slow "Southern ways."

The prevalence of artificial controls of temperature and humidity probably affect American *physical vigour and mental capacity.* Huntingdon and Williams (Business Geography, London, 1926) maintain that an average temperature somewhat over 60°F. is the optimum for physical work, but that mental vigour is higher at lower temperatures. Though to most foreigners, summer and indoor winter temperatures may be too high for comfort, general observation would, I thing [*sic*], tend to support the view that these higher temperatures do favour high physical output per man if only because under cold conditions more of one's food intake is used in maintaining body temperatures and less is available for productive effort.

The good diet (partly a reflection of huge natural resources) also, no doubt, helps to stimulate output whilst over most of the United States the frequency of sunny days (both in summer and winter) and the absence of damp chilly fogs may favourably influence industrial morale. The same factors, viz., temperature, good diet, &c. plus posibly [*sic*] the shorter summer and longer winter day lengths (which through the pituitary glands are known to influence reproductive activity in most mammals) may, in the absence of social restraints, help to account for those amatory activities and reproductive precocity which are, at least to an agricultural physiologist, more noticeable in the United States than in the United Kingdom. New York and Naples have (geographically) the same latitude.

Further, monotonous climates are, it is generally accepted,

unfavourable to physical vigour and high output per man, even when the temperature and humidity cause little or no discomfort (*e.g.,* Lake Victoria in Uganda). Though we think that the United Kingdom weather is changeable, its variance is small compared to the big differences in temperature found in most parts of the United States. For instance, only the Gulf Coast and Florida have less than one day of snow cover per annum, although even northerly Maine may have summer-day temperatures in the 90's. The greater weather variance of the United States does not necessarily mean that this factor favours higher output than in the United Kingdom. It is merely listed as one of the factors which may favourably influence United States productivity.

Conversely, however, this United States weather variance may have *emotional effects.* It is not difficult to feel that the contrast of sunshine, punctured at intervals by violent rainstorms of tropical intensity, creates an air charged, both literally and metaphorically, with electricity. The occasional irrational irritability of Congress and the apparent emotional instability of a nation drawn in large part from stolid Western European sources, may therefore be, in part, attributable to the climate of the United States, including the latitude.

The effect of the country's vast *natural resources* of fuel and food on uniform living has already been mentioned. This richness, however, also encourages a profligacy in the use of raw materials and land which appals the European or Asiatic. Many immigrants were driven to the United States by land hunger, yet their sons do not love the soil. This is, presumably, partly a reaction against the poverty in which many Americans or their ancestors lived before they emigrated and partly because the philosophy of economic individualism and the absence of roots (see below) encourages them to "eat, drink and be merry for to-morrow we die." The future, therefore, can look after itself. The very richness of the country permits Americans the luxury of unrestrained emotion (which we sometimes misinterpret as the irresponsible petulance of a spoilt child) and fosters that characteristic hospitality and somewhat wayward generosity which many of us find so attractive.

Whereas in our crowded island, we are forced to husband our resources, the American finds a certain virtue in using up resources in consumption for its own sake and in what Veblen called "the theory of conspicuous waste." Their vast resources stimulate the industrial production of quantity for expendable consumption rather than for durable quality, and make the new car each year or two years acceptable to the psychology of the consumer. We are inclined to use labour to conserve material things; the Americans to use materials to save labour.

Further, the immense and widespread natural resources permit that *geographical mobility* of labour and capital which is so characteristically American. The frontier was largely pushed to the West Coast by Eastern farmers who had exhausted one farm and found it cheaper and easier to go West and start to ruin another than to rebuild their native soil. When cotton spinning became less profitable in New England, much of the industry abandoned its buildings and equipment and moved South. In brief, the American tendency to overcome obsolescence by abandonment is attributable both to a plenitude of natural resources and to ample geographical "elbow room."

HISTORICAL INFLUENCES

> When Daniel Boone goes by, at night,
> The phantom deer arise
> And all lost wild America
> Is shining in their eyes.
>   (*Stephen Vincent Benet*)

4. Alexander Hamilton, the oligarch, Thomas Jefferson, the cultured exponent of Arcadian democracy, and Daniel Boone, the prototype of the frontiersman—would probably be dismayed—each in his own way—at modern America. The existing American cultural pattern was largely produced by the Anglo-Americans of the original thirteen colonies and the British, German, Scandinavian and Irish immigrants of the nineteenth century. It is essentially a North-Western European product, though this is sometimes very difficult to believe.

In the past 170 years the Americans have, therefore, done a first-class job first in making a nation out of the thirteen colonies and, second in *absorbing onto* rather than *absorbing into* this structure the millions of immigrants from North-West and finally from South and East Europe. This they did, consciously or unconsciously, by "detribalising" the immigrants, by destroying, in large part, the ancestral cultures (rooted in the manorial system) of the newcomers, and replacing it by Americanism. In doing so they have, however, largely destroyed the relatively staple [stable] agrarian cultures of the original thirteen colonies. The dreams of Jefferson have been swamped by successive waves of immigrants and engulfed by big business and industrialism. "Americanism" was initially based on liberal 18th-century and particularly French revolutionary political thinking; on Jefferson's tenet that the best government is the least government; and on cheap or free land with "no strings attached." This not only attracted down-trodden peasants to the States but it was probably the only way in which such a motley immigration could be handled with the administrative machinery then available and without catastrophic social unrest. One cannot help but feel, however, that "Americanism" has taken the bit between its teeth and galloped the population in directions of which the founding fathers would disapprove and about which some contemporary Americans are profoundly unhappy.

Thus, firstly, a comparison of the United States with Canada shows that the detribalisation and destruction of culture helped to create serious psychological problems which are discussed below and which partly account for the emotional instability of the American who largely derived from stolid North-Western European sources.

Secondly, the emphasis on economic freedom encouraged an individualism which was probably the only way to open up the country and build industries, railways, &c. The emphasis on social equality, which was fostered on the frontier, left millions without natural social leaders and encouraged that absence of class consciousness which is, to some of us, a most attractive feature of the American character. But this individualism and equality largely destroyed the Hellenic culture of the 18th century, which the founding fathers bequeathed to the new Republic, and left behind an intellectual vacuum. This vacuum unfortunately substantially persists to this day; it has not been fully replaced by Americanism, which is a religion and not a culture in the anthropological sense. This fact contributes to the American intolerance and ignorance of other ways of life, to the distrust of intellectualism and the dislike of classical and literary allusions in speech and on paper. It thus affects American contemporary foreign policy and, it may be added, limits her ability to behave like a great Power.

The American educational system is only slowly remedying this defect. It still concentrates, although emigration has long ceased, on turning the descendants of immigrants into American citizens and on teaching them how to earn a living rather than how to live. Advertisers in the press and radio also endlessly indoctrinate Americanism.

THE INADEQUACY OF AMERICANISM

5. Americanism is the end product of genetic, geographical and historical influences. There are, of course, many "good Americans"

who realise that "Americanism is not enough." Their experience in the depression of the thirties and with Father Coughlin (the "Fascist" Priest of that era) has convinced them that the combination of schools, press and radio could, in the wrong hands, be more effective in the United States than in say Canada and the United Kingdom. With this view I would concur. The labile American population could be twisted to another ideology more rapidly than their almost blind devotion to Americanism might suggest. Americanism and the American way of life is not, like the British way of life, firmly secured on a culture with strong biological roots. It is more of a necessary but synthetic pseudo-religion or cult built by political engineers and maintained by a propaganda machine which is at present, whatever its other defects, not operated by a monopoly. Much of the United States antagonism for socialism and criticism of contemporary Britain seems to spring more from a fear that nationalisation or extensive social services would somehow give the Federal Government control of this machine than from a specific belief in the virtues of private enterprise. Hence partly for this reason and partly for obvious historical reasons, some anti-British propaganda is an inevitable corollary of Americanism. Realisation that Americanism has an underlying fragility also accounts, in part, for what may appear to us to be the American's obsessional fear of communism. They are more afraid of the ideological than of the military powers of the Russians.

6. This underlying fragility of Americanism, if real, calls for further analysis. It is not enough merely to describe its genetic, geographical and historical origins. There is, it seems, a fundamental dichotomy in American life. On the one hand, the individual desires to achieve security and, as the anthropologists would say, "to belong," or in laymen's language, to have roots. On the other hand, he desires to forward his own selfish interests, to express himself and to acquire prestige amongst his fellows by making money—partly because apart from becoming a Senator or a Hollywood film star, making a fortune is the easiest way to achieve prestige.

This emphasis on material incentives is exaggerated by the educational system and by its persistent indoctrination by the press, radio and commercial advertisers. "Keeping up with the Joneses" means that the individual must make enough money to conform with the ever-rising material standard of living and to buy himself physical comfort and economic security through home-ownership, life insurance, &c. The individual is thus superficially persuaded that the American way of life can resolve this inner conflict between self and security. In practice, however, though he may achieve physical and material security he lacks psychological security. And it is this absence of psychological security—of a real ability to stand on his feet—that is at the bottom of much of the emotionalism, the bombast, and lack of self-confidence which Americans individually and collectively display in their domestic and political life and, to some extent, in their foreign affairs. This desire to achieve self-advancement through money, prestige or power without sacrificing psychological security is, of course, found in every nation or tribe from the primitive Masai or Kikuyu of East Africa to the advanced countries of Western Europe and in new countries like Canada, Australia and the Argentine. But unlike the Americans, all these people have roots. They have some feeling of "belonging" which is based on historical, religious or other group associations or traditions stretching back hundreds of years. If one lives among the Americans but crosses the United States–Canadian border frequently or visits the United Kingdom from time to time, one cannot avoid noticing that, though the Americans try hard to grow or to pretend they have "roots," Americans feel deep down that they do "not belong." Perhaps this is why a well-known French medical biologist once described psychoanalysis to me as "La maladie Americaine."

The American is in fact often a pathetically lonely rebel. It is true that, after the War of Independence, they continued or adopted many of our legal, parliamentary and social institutions and that, through the United Kingdom, they are in the Hellenic line of historical descent. But, in the nineteenth century, the post-revolutionary influence of the Anglo-American was, as pointed out above, in part swamped by the flood of immigrants, most of whom were urban or rural peasants escaping from real or imagined tyranny, oppression or poverty. In their "old countries" they had been denied or were below the level of Hellenic culture; their roots were in the earth not in classical education. When they exiled themselves they cut off these roots; they have found that they cannot rebuild them and are in too much of a hurry to grow them. They are still "exiles from our fathers' shores" though, publicly, they hotly deny it. The Canadians or Australians, however, admit it and probably thereby gain some stability.

The lonely rootless rebel seeks consolation through what appears to us as an artificial gregariousness, as a too obvious fraternity, as loud and hearty assurance and, sometimes, when he is abroad, in an arrogance which some people find trying. The American passion for joining service and women's clubs, college fraternities, veteran's organisations, his thirst for knowledge, and his capacity to enjoy organised picnics, square dance festivals and the like are signs of his rootless loneliness. He is a church "member" who "belongs" to the .... Church; whereas, at home, he would be a chapel "goer" just "C. of E." Many Americans

> ".... have lost
> The power of being alone with
>   earth and skies,
> Of going about a task with
>   quietude...."

Thus, on the one hand, his overconfident assurance and belief in the infallibility of the American system, and his pride in his high standard of living are perhaps symptoms of his desire to convince himself that he (or his ancestors) were right to be rebels and to cut himself off from the cultural womb which bore him or his ancestors. In such a context, it is understandable that he attributes the material succes [sic] of his country more to his personal qualities and to the American way of life rather than to its immense natural resources.

On the other hand, the persistent and high-powered indoctrination of Americanism by the schools, the press, radio &c., his overt antipathy to but private envy of European traditions and culture, his sensitivity to criticism of American institutions or culture, his distrust of intellectualism and his feeling of injured innocence if he is outsmarted by the British are some of the indications of inferiority and insecurity which peep out from under the crust of assurance.

Anything which divides this gregariousness or punctures this assurance ultimately breeds resentment. Imports may be good in theory, but as America is the best, richest and most efficient country in the world, it is an insult to be undercut by foreigners on your domestic market. Conversely, charity to the unfortunate or oppressed, giving away United States products or know-how to other countries feeds this self-assurance and bolsters national morale.

Similarly the enthusiasm with which the Americans have embraced United Nations and its agencies (despite their earlier failure to join the League and their traditional isolationism) is not entirely explicable in terms of strategic necessity or international security. The facts that the United Nations started with a large charitable organisation (U.N.R.R.A.) and that the United States could this time "belong" to the society of nations as a leading member both bolstered their need for self-assurance and met their need "to belong." Any events which seriously deflate this self-assurance are likely to end either in war or isolationism.

7. The fact that the Americans lack a well-rooted culture with a small "c"—*i.e.,* in the anthropological sense, does not, of course mean that there are not many millions of "cultured" Americans. Some Europeans are still prone to class them as intellectual barbarians because they were not brought up on Shakespeare or Plutarch's *Lives.*

However, whilst the Americans are distrustful of intellectuals and obvious æsthetes their artistic interests are deeper and more widespread than most Europeans seem willing to admit. Their recreations are, however, biased more heavily towards the emotional arts than to the pleasures of the mind. Few Americans can truly say, "My mind to me a Kingdom is." But in the upper middle classes (especially in the German and Hebrew sectors) the interest in music is genuine; there is a vigorous indigenous interest in the plastic arts (as witness the skyscrapers, modern United States domestic architecture, the craze for amateur painting and interior decoration); folk songs and folk arts, as one would expect amongst a nation of predominantly peasant origins, are strongly developed, craft hobbies (*e.g.,* wood carving) are probably more common than in the United Kingdom. The strongly developed indigenous literature, like the movies, is centred on people—rather than ideas. They are more interested in "folks" than in "Man." One may perhaps summarise Arts and Letters in the United States by saying that they are somatic rather than psychic. The emphasis is on "gracious living" rather than on "high thinking." A symphony orchestra doing the Brahms 4th is *de rigeur,* but a string quartet playing Benjamin Britten is suspect. American civilisation tastes more of Rome than of Greece.

8. To sum up, the Americans are a surprisingly uniform nation of successful, friendly and now highly industrialised "kulaks." They are detribalised peasants who have made good in a country abounding in natural resources. They are out to share what they regard as the secret of their success (*viz.,* "the American way of life") with those whom they consider to be less fortunate. But underlying their success is a feeling of insecurity, of "not belonging." They try to overcome this by conforming to a uniform social pattern, by gregariousness and by various devices to boost their morale including self-assurance, hospitality and genuine generosity. Thus, this insecurity and certain genetic and geographical factors help to account for their unexpected emotionalism in both domestic and foreign affairs and for many of their most likeable charcteristics—their enthusiasm, their friendliness and lack of class consciousness.

Will these characters—most of which have been recorded by

other observers of the American scene over the past hundred years or so—persist? Or, if they change, in what direction will they move?

POSSIBLE FUTURE TRENDS

9.— (*a*) *Uniformity*.—With the virtual cessation of immigration we may expect the gradual disappearance of the national groups, and the foreign language newspapers and the complete Americanisation of these and other unassimilated groups. Under the impact of the education system, the radio, the press, the films and the spread of industrialisation and social mobility, such cultural "pockets" as the Southern aristocracy, the Acadians of Louisiana, the French hierachy [*sic*] of New Orleans, the "Ivy League" of Boston and the Eastern Seaboard are slowly but surely becoming Americanised. Last year, for instance, the President of the National Association of Manufacturers was a practising Mormon with a factory in Utah. Industry is moving into the South and West. The monocultured farming areas are slowly moving towards mixed farming.

This increasing uniformity of an already surprisingly uniform nation will add to the political power of the United States in world affairs. At present the residual diversity of economic interest and national origins hampers the formulation and execution of United States foreign policy. One of our strengths in international affairs is that, despite our varied social pattern and our controversies about domestic economic policy, our external economic interests are well defined.

(*b*) Secondly, this increasing uniformity, the slow trend to the left and growing intervention of the Federal Government in economic life will strengthen the internal power of the Central Executive.

By the same token, however, the increasing intervention of the Central Government should increase the stability of the economy. The growth of trade unions, of farm price supports and the like will also add their quota of rigidity. This stability should indirectly add to the emotional stability and quieten down those psychological excesses which tend to coincide with periods of prosperity and depression in the United States.

This strengthening of internal political power and more stabilised economy combined with a tendency towards the less profligate use of national resources will still further increase the political and economic power of the United States in the world.

(*c*) One form in which this power might be expressed may well be further attempts to sell Americanism to the world, in part as a counter measure to Communism, in part to bolster their own morale and in part because many Americans genuinely believe that one has only to persuade less enlightened countries to embrace the American "way of life" and American "know-how" for all the latter's troubles to disappear. This may be Imperialism. But it is at least as sincere as our own feeling that we had a duty to the world to bear the "White Man's Burden."

(*d*) It is sometimes argued that, as the Americans gain experience as a world power, so will they "sober up" and take their international responsibilities more seriously. This may well be so. But it would perhaps be unwise to assume that it will be so. The growth of internal uniformity, of internal economic stability and of the power of the Federal Government may enable them to pursue a more consistent foreign policy, but there is no guarantee that it would be a positive one. Historically, American isolationism was, it seems, at least partly an attempt to disown their brawling European ancestors. It was an essential step if the United States were to weld millions of European immigrants into the semblance of a unified nation. But in this process, as pointed out above, the Americans developed an underlying sense of insecurity which they try to overcome by a somewhat synthetic self-assurance. A major failure of United States foreign policy might deflate this self-assurance and make way for a resurgence of isolationism.

On the other hand, they may, of course, continue to pursue an active, positive foreign policy. This, however, though it would probably tend to become more sustained, is still, it seems to me, likely to have strong emotional tinges for many years to come. Experience may teach sobriety, but the mixture of genetic, geographic and psychological influences discussed earlier in these notes makes a "powerful strong" brew. We must, therefore, expect the Americans to continue to be more prone to go on an occasional "international bender."

(*e*) Finally, the undercurrent of insecurity, to which reference was made above, is likely to evaporate slowly. We must, therefore, continue to expect the Americans to be sensitive to outside criticism, particularly from the United Kingdom. A son who has disowned his father and has gone out and very successfully made his own way in the world is, nevertheless, particularly thin skinned when it comes to grandparental comments on his children's defects.

British Studies at the University of Texas, 1975–2015

Fall Semester 1975

Paul Scott (Novelist, London), 'The *Raj Quartet*'
Ian Donaldson (Australian National University), 'Humanistic Studies in Australia'
Fritz Fellner (Salzburg University), 'Britain and the Origins of the First World War'
Wm. Roger Louis (History), 'Churchill, Roosevelt, and the Future of Dependent Peoples during the Second World War'
Michael Holroyd (Biographer, Dublin), 'Two Biographies: Lytton Strachey and Augustus John'
Max Beloff (Buckingham College), 'Imperial Sunset'
Robin Winks (Yale University), 'British Empire-Commonwealth Studies'
Warren Roberts (HRHRC) and David Farmer (HRHRC), 'The D. H. Lawrence Editorial Project'
Harvey C. Webster (University of Louisville), 'C. P. Snow as Novelist and Philosopher'
Anthony Kirk-Greene (Oxford University), 'The Origins and Aftermath of the Nigerian Civil War'

Spring Semester 1976

Joseph Jones (English), 'World English'
William S. Livingston (Government), 'The British Legacy in Contemporary Indian Politics'
John Higley (Sociology), 'The Recent Political Crisis in Australia'
Round Table Discussion, 'Reassessments of Evelyn Waugh': Elspeth Rostow (Dean, General and Comparative Studies), Standish Meacham (History), and Alain Blayac (University of Paris)
Jo Grimond (former Leader of the Liberal Party), 'Liberal Democracy in Britain'

Round Table Discussion, 'The Impact of Hitler on British Politics': Gaines Post (History), Malcolm Macdonald (Government), and Wm. Roger Louis (History)
Round Table Discussion, 'Kipling and India': Robert Hardgrave (Government), Gail Minault (History), and Chihiro Hosoya (University of Tokyo)
Kenneth Kirkwood (Oxford University), 'The Future of Southern Africa'
C. P. Snow, 'Elite Education in England'
Hans-Peter Schwarz (Cologne University), 'The Impact of Britain on German Politics and Society since the Second World War'
B. K. Nehru (Indian High Commissioner, London), 'The Political Crisis in India'
Round Table Discussion, 'Declassification of Secret Documents: The British and American Experiences Compared': Robert A. Divine (History), Harry J. Middleton (LBJ Library), and Wm. Roger Louis (History)

Fall Semester 1976

John Farrell (English), 'Revolution and Tragedy in Victorian England'
Anthony Honoré (Oxford University), 'British Attitudes to Legal Regulation of Sex'
Alan Hill (English), 'Wordsworth and America'
Ian Nish (London School of Economics), 'Anglo-American Naval Rivalry and the End of the Anglo-Japanese Alliance'
Norman Sherry (University of Lancaster), 'Joseph Conrad and the British Empire'
Peter Edwards (Australian National University), 'Australia through American Eyes: The Second World War and the Rise of Australia as a Regional Power'
Round Table Discussion, 'Britain and the Future of Europe': David Edwards (Government), Steven Baker (Government), Malcolm Macdonald (Government), William S. Livingston (Government), and Wm. Roger Louis (History)
Michael Hurst (Oxford University), 'The British Empire in Historical Perspective: The Case of Joseph Chamberlain'
Ronald Grierson (English Banker and former Public Official), 'The Evolution of the British Economy since 1945'
Marian Kent (University of New South Wales), 'British Oil Policy between the World Wars'
Constance Babington-Smith (Cambridge University), 'The World of Rose Macaulay'
Round Table Discussion, 'Adam Smith after 200 Years': William Todd (History), Walt Rostow (History and Economics), and James McKie (Dean, Social and Behavioral Sciences)

Spring Semester 1977

Carin Green (Novelist) and Elspeth Rostow (American Studies), 'The Achievement of Virginia Woolf'
Samuel H. Beer (Professor of Government, Harvard University), 'Reflections on British Politics'
David Fieldhouse (Oxford University), 'Decolonization and the Multinational Corporations'
Gordon Craig (Stanford University), 'England and Europe on the Eve of the Second World War'

John Lehmann (British Publisher and Writer), 'Publishing under the Bombs—The Hogarth Press during World War II'
Round Table Discussion, 'The Author, His Editor, and Publisher': Philip Jones (University of Texas Press), William S. Livingston (Government), Michael Mewshaw (English), David Farmer (HRC), Roger Louis (History), and William Todd (History)
Dick Taverne (former Member of Parliament), 'The Mood of Britain: Misplaced Gloom or Blind Complacency?'
Round Table Discussion, 'The Origins of World War II in the Pacific': James B. Crowley (Yale University), Lloyd C. Gardner (Rutgers University), Akira Iriye (University of Chicago), and Wm. Roger Louis (History)
Rosemary Murray (Cambridge University), 'Higher Education in England'
Burke Judd (Zoology) and Robert Wagner (Zoology), 'Sir Cyril Burt and the Controversy over the Heritability of IQ'
Round Table Discussion, 'The Wartime Reputations of Churchill and Roosevelt: Overrated or Underrated?': Alessandra Lippucci (Government), Roger Louis (History), William S. Livingston (Government), and Walt Rostow (Economics)

Fall Semester 1977

Donald L. Weismann (Art and Art History), 'British Art in the Nineteenth Century: Turner and Constable—Precursors of French Impressionism'
Standish Meacham (History), 'Social Reform in England'
Joseph Jones, 'Recent Commonwealth Literature'
Lewis Hoffacker (former US Ambassador), 'The Katanga Crisis: British and Other Connections'
Round Table Discussion, 'The Copyright Law of 1976': James M. Treece (Law), Wm. Roger Louis (History), Warren Roberts, and Bill Todd (History)
Round Table Discussion, 'Freedom at Midnight: A Reassessment of Britain and the Partition of India Thirty Years After': Charles Heimsath (Visiting Professor of Indian History), Bob Hardgrave (Government), Thomasson Jannuzi, (Center for Asian Studies), C. P. Andrade (Comparative Studies), and William S. Livingston (Government),
Lord Fraser of Kilmorack (Conservative Party Organization), 'The Tory Tradition of British Politics'
Bernth Lindfors (English), 'Charles Dickens and the Hottentots and Zulus'
Albert Hourani (Oxford University), 'The Myth of T. E. Lawrence'
Mark Kinkead-Weekes (University of Kent) and Mara Kalnins (British Writer), 'D. H. Lawrence: Censorship and the Expression of Ideas'
J. D. B. Miller (Australian National University), 'The Collapse of the British Empire'
Round Table Discussion, 'The Best and Worst Books of 1977': Peter Green (Classics), Robert King (Dean, Social and Behavioral Sciences), William S. Livingston (Government), Bob Hardgrave (Government), Wm. Roger Louis (History), and Warren Roberts (HRHRC)

Spring Semester 1978

Round Table Discussion, 'British Decadence in the Interwar Years': Peter Green (Classics), Malcolm Macdonald (Government), and Robert Crunden (American Studies),

Round Table Discussion, 'R. Emmet Tyrrell's *Social Democracy's Failure in Britain*': Terry Quist (UT Undergraduate), Steve Baker (Government), and Wm. Roger Louis (History),
Stephen Koss (Columbia University), 'The British Press: Press Lords, Politicians, and Principles'
John House (Oxford University), 'The Rhodesian Crisis'
T. S. Dorsch (Durham University), 'Oxford in the 1930s'
Stephen Spender (English Poet and Writer), 'Britain and the Spanish Civil War'
Okot p'Bitek (Ugandan Poet), 'Idi Amin's Uganda'
David C. Goss (Australian Consul General), 'Wombats and Wivveroos'
Leon Epstein (University of Wisconsin), 'Britain and the Suez Crisis of 1956'
David Schoonover (Library Science), 'British and American Expatriates in Paris in the 1920s'
Peter Stansky (Stanford University), 'George Orwell and the Spanish Civil War'
Alexander Parker (Spanish and Portuguese), 'Reflections on the Spanish Civil War'
Norman Sherry (Lancaster University), 'Graham Greene and Latin America'
Martin Blumenson (Department of the Army), 'The Ultra Secret'

Fall Semester 1978

W. H. Morris-Jones (University of London), 'Power and Inequality in Southeast Asia'
Round Table Discussion, 'The British and the Shaping of the American Critical Mind: Edmund Wilson's *Letters on Literature and Politics*': Hartley Grattan (History), Gilbert Chase (American Studies), Bob Crunden (American Studies), and Wm. Roger Louis (History)
James Roach (Government), 'The Indian Emergency and its Aftermath'
Bill Todd (History), 'The Lives of Samuel Johnson'
Lord Hatch (British Labour Politician), 'The Labour Party and Africa'
John Kirkpatrick (HRHRC), 'Max Beerbohm'
Brian Levack (History), 'Witchcraft in England and Scotland'
M. R. Masani (Indian Writer), 'Gandhi and Gandhism'
A. W. Coates (Economics), 'The Professionalization of the British Civil Service'
John Clive (Harvard University), 'Great Historians of the Nineteenth Century'
Geoffrey Best (University of Sussex), 'Flight Path to Dresden: British Strategic Bombing in the Second World War'
Kurth Sprague (English), 'T. H. White's *Once and Future King*'
Gilbert Chase (American Studies), 'The British Musical Invasion of America'

Spring Semester 1979

Round Table Discussion, 'P. N. Furbanks's Biography of E. M. Forster': Peter Green (Classics), Alessandra Lippucci (Government), and Elspeth Rostow (LBJ School)
Round Table Discussion, 'E. M. Forster and India': Wm. Roger Louis (History), Bob Hardgrave (Government), Gail Minault (Professor of History), Peter Gran (History), and Bob King (Dean of Liberal Arts)
Paul M. Kennedy (University of East Anglia), 'The Contradiction between British Strategic Policy and Economic Policy in the Twentieth Century'
Richard Rive (Visiting Fulbright Research Fellow from South Africa), 'Olive Schreiner and the South African Nation'

Charles P. Kindleberger (Massachusetts Institute of Technology), 'Lord Zuckerman and the Second World War'
John Press (English Poet), 'English Poets and Postwar Society'
Richard Ellmann (Oxford University), 'Writing a Biography of Joyce'
Michael Finlayson (Scottish Dramatist), 'Contemporary British Theater'
Lawrence Stone (Institute for Advanced Study, Princeton), 'Family, Sex, and Marriage in England'
C. P. Snow, 'Reflections on the Two Cultures'
Theodore Zeldin (Oxford University), 'Are the British More or Less European than the French?'
David Edwards (Government), 'How United the Kingdom: Greater or Lesser Britain?'
Michael Holroyd (British Biographer), 'George Bernard Shaw'
John Wickman (Eisenhower Library), 'Eisenhower and the British'

Fall Semester 1979

Robert Palter (Philosophy), 'Reflections on British Philosophers: Locke, Hume, and the Utilitarians'
Alfred Gollin (University of California, Santa Barbara), 'Political Biography as Political History: Garvin, Milner, and Balfour'
Edward Steinhart (History), 'The Consequences of British Rule in Uganda'
Paul Sturges (Loughborough University, UK), and Dolores Donnelly (Toronto University), 'History of the National Library of Canada'
Sir Michael Tippett (British Composer), 'Moving into Aquarius'
Steven Baker (Government), 'Britain and United Nations Emergency Operations'
Maria Okila Dias (University of São Paulo), 'Intellectual Roots of Informal Imperialism: Britain and Brazil'
Alexander Parker (Spanish and Portuguese), 'Reflections on *Brideshead Revisited*'
Barry C. Higman (University of the West Indies), 'West Indian Emigrés and the British Empire'
Gaines Post (History), 'Britain and the Outbreak of the Second World War'
Karen Gould (Art and Art History), 'Medieval Manuscript Fragments and English Seventeenth-Century Collections: New Perspectives from *Fragmenta Manuscripta*'
Round Table Discussion, 'Jeanne MacKenzie's *Dickens: A Life*': John Farrell (English), Eric Poole (HRHRC) and James Bieri (English):
Joseph O. Baylen (Georgia State University), 'British Journalism in the Late Victorian and Edwardian Eras'
Peter T. Flawn (President, University of Texas), 'An Appreciation of Charles Dickens'

Spring Semester 1980

Annette Weiner (Anthropology), 'Anthropologists in New Guinea: British Interpretations and Cultural Relativism'
Bernard Richards (Oxford University), 'Conservation in the Nineteenth Century'
Thomas McGann (History), 'Britain and Argentina: An Informal Dominion?'
Mohammad Ali Jazayery (Center for Middle Eastern Studies), 'The Persian Tradition in English Literature'
C. Hartley Grattan (History) 'Twentieth-Century British Novels and the American Critical Mind'

Katherine Whitehorn (London *Observer*), 'An Insider's View of the *Observer*'
Guy Lytle (History), 'The Oxford University Press's *History of Oxford*'
C. P. Snow, 'Reflections on *The Masters*'
Harvey Webster, '*The Masters* and the Two Cultures'
Brian Blakeley (Texas Tech University), 'Women and the British Empire'
Stephen Koss (Columbia University), 'Asquith, Balfour, Milner, and the First World War'
Tony Smith (Tufts University), 'The Expansion of England: New Ideas on Controversial Themes in British Imperialism'
Stanley Ross (History), 'Britain and the Mexican Revolution'
Rowland Smith (Dalhousie University), 'The British Intellectual Left and the War, 1939–1945'
Richard Ellmann (Oxford University), 'Oscar Wilde: A Reconsideration and Problems of the Literary Biographer'
James Bill (Government), 'The United States, Britain, and the Iranian Crisis of 1953'

Fall Semester 1980

Decherd Turner (HRHRC), 'The First 1000 Days'
Wm. Roger Louis (History), 'Britain and Egypt after the Second World War'
Alistair Horne (Woodrow Wilson Center), 'Britain and the Fall of France'
Round Table Discussion, 'Literary Fraud: H. R. Trevor-Roper and the Hermit of Peking': Edward Rhodes (History), Peter Green (Classics), William Todd (History), and Wm. Roger Louis (History),
Mark Kinkead-Weekes (Kent University), 'D. H. Lawrence's *Rainbow:* Its Sense of History'
Sir John Crawford (Australian National University), 'Hartley Grattan: In Memoriam'
John Stubbs (University of Waterloo), 'The Tory View of Politics and Journalism in the Interwar Years'
Donald L. Weismann (Art and Art History), 'British Art in the Nineteenth Century'
Fran Hill (Government), 'The Legacy of British Colonialism in Tanzania'
R. W. B. Lewis (Yale University), 'What's Wrong with the Teaching of English?'
Charlene Gerry (British Publisher), 'The Revival of Fine Printing in Britain'
Peter Gran (History), 'The Islamic Response to British Capitalism'
Tina Poole (HRHRC) 'Gilbert and Sullivan's Christmas'

Spring Semester 1981

Bernard N. Darbyshire (Visiting Professor of Government and Economics), 'North Sea Oil and the British Future'
Christopher Hill (Oxford University), 'The English Civil War'
Elizabeth Heine (UT San Antonio), and Wm. Roger Louis (History), 'A Reassessment of Leonard Woolf'
Bernard Richards (Oxford University), 'D. H. Lawrence and Painting'
Miguel Gonzalez-Gerth (Spanish and Portuguese), 'Poetry Once Removed: The Resonance of English as a Second Language'
John Putnam Chalmers (HRHRC), 'English Bookbinding from Caedmon to Le Carré'
Peter Coltman (Architecture), 'The Cultural Landscapes of Britain: 2,000 Years of Blood, Sweat, Toil & Tears to Wrest a Living from this Bloody Mud'

Thomas H. Law (former Regent, University of Texas), 'The Gold Coins of the English Sovereigns'
Round Table Discussion, 'Canadian-American Economic Relations': Sidney Weintraub (LBJ School), James W. McKie (Economics), and Mary Williams (Canadian Consulate, Dallas)
Amedée Turner (European Parliament), 'Integrating Britain into the European Community'
Muriel C. Bradbrook (Cambridge University), 'Two Poets: Kathleen Raine and Seamus Heaney'
Ronald Sampson (Industrial Development Department, Aberdeen), 'Scotland—Somewhat of a British Texas?'

Fall Semester 1981

Jerome Bump (English), 'From Texas to England: The Ancestry of Our Victorian Architecture'
Lord Fraser of Kilmorack, 'Leadership Styles of Tory Prime Ministers since the Second World War'
William Carr (University of Sheffield), 'A British Interpretation of American, German, and Japanese Foreign Policy 1936–1941'
Iqbal Narain (Rajasthan University, Jaipur), 'The Ups and Downs of Indian Academic Life'
Don Etherington (HRHRC), 'The Florence Flood, 1966: The British Effort—or: Up to our Necks in Mud and Books'
E. V. K. Fitzgerald (Visiting Professor of Economics), 'The British University: Crisis, Confusion, and Stagnation'
Robert Crunden (American Studies), 'A Joshua for Historians: Mordecai Richter and Canadian Cultural Identity'
Bernth Lindfors (English), 'The Hottentot Venus and Other African Attractions in Nineteenth-Century England'
Chris Brookeman (London Polytechnic), 'The British Arts and Society'
Nicholas Pickwoad (Freelance Book Conservator), 'The Libraries of the National Trust'
Kurth Sprague (English), 'John Steinbeck, Chase Horton, and the Matter of Britain'
Martin J. Wiener (Rice University), 'Cultural Values and Socio-Economic Behavior in Britain'
Werner Habicht (University of Würzburg), 'Shakespeare in Nineteenth-Century Germany'

Spring Semester 1982

Stevie Bezencenet (London College of Printing), 'Contemporary Photography in Britain'
Jane Marcus (English), 'Shakespeare's Sister, Beethoven's Brother: Dame Ethel Smyth and Virginia Woolf'
Wilson Harris (English) and Raja Rao (Philosophy), 'The Quest for Form: Britain and Commonwealth Perspectives'
Al Crosby (American Studies), 'The British Empire as a Product of Continental Drift'
Lord St. Brides (Visiting Scholar), 'The White House and Whitehall: Washington and Westminster'

Elizabeth Fernea (English and Middle East Studies), 'British Colonial Literature of the Middle East'
Maurice Evans (Actor and Producer), 'My Early Years in the Theater'
Joan Bassin (Kansas City Art Institute), 'Art and Industry in Nineteenth-Century England'
Eugene N. Borza (Pennsylvania State University), 'Sentimental British Philhellenism: Images of Greece'
Ralph Willett (University of Hull), 'The Style and Structure of British Television News'
Wm. Roger Louis (History), 'Britain and the Creation of the State of Israel'
Peter Russell (Oxford University), 'A British Historian Looks at Portuguese Historiography of the Fifteenth Century'
Rory Coker (Physics), 'Frauds, Hoaxes and Blunders in Science—a British Tradition?'
Ellen DuBois (State University of New York, Buffalo), 'Anglo-American Perspectives on the Suffragette Movement'
Donald G. Davis, Jr. (Library Science), 'Great Expectations—and a Few Illusions: Reflections on an Exchange Teaching Year in England'
Anthony Rota (Bertram Rota Ltd.), 'The Changing World of the Bookdealer'
Eisig Silberschlag (Visiting Professor of Judaic Studies), 'The Bible as the Most Popular Book in English'

Fall Semester 1982

Woodruff Smith (UT San Antonio), 'British Overseas Expansion'
The Rt. Hon. George Thomas (Speaker of the House of Commons), 'Parliamentary Democracy'
Nigel Nicolson (English Historian and Biographer), 'The English Country House as an Historical Document'
Lord St. Brides (Visiting Scholar), 'A Late Leaf of Laurel for Evelyn Waugh'
Lt. Col. Jack McNamara, USMC (Ret.), 'The Libel of Evelyn Waugh by the *Daily Express*'
James Wimsatt (English), 'Chaucer and Medieval French Manuscripts'
Christopher Whelan (Visiting Professor, UT Law School), 'Recent Developments in British Labour Law'
Brian Wearing (University of Canterbury, Christchurch), 'New Zealand: In the Pacific, but of It?'
Robert Hardgrave (Government), 'The United States and India'
James McBath (University of Southern California), 'The Evolution of *Hansard*'
Paul Fromm (University of Toronto), 'Canadian–United States Relations: Two Solitudes'
John Velz (English), 'When in Disgrace: Ganzel's Attempt to Exculpate John Payne Collier'
Wm. Roger Louis (History), 'British Origins of the Iranian Revolution'

Spring Semester 1983

Sir Ellis Waterhouse (Oxford University), 'A Comparison of British and French Painting in the Late Eighteenth Century'
E. J. L. Ride (Australian Consul General), 'Australia's Place in the World and Her Relationship with the United States'
Edward Bell (Royal Botanic Gardens, Kew), 'Kew Gardens in World History'

The Very Rev. Oliver Fiennes (Dean of Lincoln), 'The Care and Feeding of Magna Carta'
C. V. Narasimhan (former Under-Secretary of the United Nations), 'Last Days of the British Raj: A Civil Servant's View'
Warren G. Osmond, 'Sir Frederic Eggleston and the Development of Pacific Consciousness'
Richard Ellmann (Oxford University), 'Henry James among the Aesthetes'
Janet Caulkins (University of Wisconsin–Madison), 'The Poor Reputation of Cornish Knights in Medieval Literature'
Werner Habicht (University of Würzburg), 'Shakespeare and the Third Reich'
Gillian Peele (Oxford University), 'The Changing British Party System'
John Farrell (English), 'Scarlet Ribbons: Memories of Youth and Childhood in Victorian Authors'
Peter Russell (Oxford University), 'A Not So Bashful Stranger: *Don Quixote* in England, 1612–1781'
Sir Zelman Cowen (Oxford University), 'Contemporary Problems in Medicine, Law, and Ethics'
Dennis V. Lindley (Visiting Professor of Mathematics), 'Scientific Thinking in an Unscientific World'
Martin Blumenson (Department of the Army), 'General Mark Clark and the British in the Italian Campaign of World War II'

Fall Semester 1983

Anthony King (University of Essex), 'Margaret Thatcher and the Future of British Politics'
Alistair Gillespie (Canadian Minister of Energy, Mines, and Resources), 'Canadian-British Relations: Best and Worst'
Charles A. Owen, Jr. (University of Connecticut), 'The Pre-1400 Manuscripts of the *Canterbury Tales*'
Major-General (Ret.) Richard Clutterbuck (University of Exeter), 'Terrorism in Malaya'
Wayne A. Wiegand (University of Kentucky), 'British Propaganda in American Public Libraries during World War I'
Stuart Macintyre (Australian National University, Canberra), 'Australian Trade Unionism between the Wars'
Ram Joshi (Visiting Professor of History), 'Is Gandhi Relevant Today?'
Sir Denis Wright (former British Ambassador to Iran), 'Britain and the Iranian Revolution'
Andrew Horn (University of Lesotho), 'Theater and Politics in South Africa'
Philip Davies (University of Manchester), 'British Reaction to American Politics: Overt Rejection, Covert Assimilation'
H. K. Singh (Embassy of India), 'United States-Indian Relations'
Round Table Discussion, 'Two Cheers for Mountbatten: A Reassessment of Lord and Lady Mountbatten and the Partition of India': Wm. Roger Louis (History), Ram Joshi (Visiting Professor of History), and J. S. Mehta (LBJ School)

Spring Semester 1984

M. S. Venkataramani (Jawaharlal Nehru University), 'Winston Churchill and Indian Freedom'

Sir John Thompson (British Ambassador to the United Nations), 'The Falklands and Grenada in the United Nations'
Robert Farrell (Cornell University), 'Medieval Archaeology'
Allon White (University of Sussex), 'The Fiction of Early Modernism'
Round Table Discussion, 'Orwell's *Nineteen Eighty-Four*': Peter Green (Classics), Wm. Roger Louis (History), Miguel Gonzalez-Gerth (Spanish and Portuguese), Standish Meacham (History), and Sid Monas (Slavic Languages and History)
Uriel Dann (University of Tel Aviv), 'Hanover and Britain in the Time of George II'
José Ferrater-Mora (Bryn Mawr College), 'A. M. Turing and his "Universal Turing Machine"'
Rüdiger Ahrens (University of Würzburg), 'Teaching Shakespeare in German Universities'
Michael Brock (Oxford University), 'H. H. Asquith and Venetia Stanley'
Herbert Spiro (Free University of Berlin), 'What Makes the British and Americans Different from Everybody Else: The Adversary Process of the Common Law'
Nigel Bowles (University of Edinburgh), 'Reflections on Recent Developments in British Politics'
Harold Perkin (Rice University), 'The Evolution of Citizenship in Modern Britain'
Christopher Heywood (Sheffield University), '*Jane Eyre* and *Wuthering Heights*'
Dave Powers (Kennedy Library), 'JFK's Trip to Ireland, 1963'
R. W. Coats (Visiting Professor of Economics), 'John Maynard Keynes: The Man and the Economist'
David Evans (Astronomy), 'Astronomy as a British Cultural Export'

Fall Semester 1984

John Henry Faulk, 'Reflections on My Sojourns in the British Middle East'
Lord Fraser of Kilmorack, 'The Thatcher Years—and Beyond'
Michael Phillips (University of Edinburgh), 'William Blake and the Rise of the Hot Air Balloon'
Erik Stocker (HRHRC), 'A Bibliographical Detective Story: Reconstructing James Joyce's Library'
Amedée Turner (European Parliament), 'Recent Developments in the European Parliament'
Michael Hurst (Oxford University), 'Scholars versus Journalists on the English Social Classes'
Charles Alan Wright (Law), 'Reflections on Cambridge'
J. M. Winter (Cambridge University), 'Fear of Decline in Population in Britain after World War I'
Henk Wesseling (University of Leiden), 'Dutch Colonialism and the Impact on British Imperialism'
Celia Morris Eckhardt (Biographer and author of *Fannie Wright*), 'Frances Wright and *England as the Civilizer*'
Sir Oliver Wright (British Ambassador to the United States), 'British Foreign Policy—1984'
Leonard Thompson (Yale University), 'Political Mythology and the Racial Order in South Africa'

Flora Nwapa (Nigerian Novelist), 'Women in Civilian and Military Rule in Nigeria'
Richard Rose (University of Strathclyde), 'The Capacity of the Presidency in Comparative Perspective'

Spring Semester 1985

Bernard Hickey (University of Venice), 'Australian Literary Culture: Short Stories, Novels, and "Literary Journalism"'
Kenneth Hafertepe (American Studies), 'The British Foundations of the Smithsonian Castle: The Gothic Revival in Britain and America'
Rajeev Dhavan (Visiting Professor, LBJ School and Center for Asian Studies), 'Race Relations in England: Trapped Minorities and their Future'
Sir John Thompson (British Ambassador to the United Nations), 'British Techniques of Statecraft'
Philip Bobbitt (Law), 'Britain, the United States, and Reduction in Strategic Arms'
David Bevington (Drama Critic and Theater Historian), 'Maimed Rites: Interrupted Ceremony in *Hamlet*'
Standish Meacham (History), 'The Impact of the New Left History on British and American Historiography'
Iris Murdoch (Novelist and Philosopher), and John O. Bayley (Oxford University), 'Themes in English Literature and Philosophy'
John P. Chalmers (HRHRC), 'Malory Illustrated'
Thomas Metcalf (University of California, Berkeley), 'The Architecture of Empire: The British Raj in India'
Robert H. Wilson (English), 'Malory and His Readers'
Lord St. Brides, '*A Passage to India:* Better Film than Novel?'
Derek Pearsall (York University), 'Fire, Flood, and Slaughter: The Tribulations of the Medieval City of York'
E. S. Atieno Odhiambo (University of Nairobi), 'Britain and Kenya: The Mau Mau, the "Colonial State," and Dependency'
Francis Robinson (University of London), 'Indian Muslim Religious Leadership and Colonial Rule'
Charles B. MacDonald (U.S. Army), 'The British in the Battle of the Bulge'
Brian Levack (History), 'The Battle of Bosworth Field'
Kurth Sprague (English), 'The Mirrors of Malory'

Fall Semester 1985

A. P. Thornton (University of Toronto), 'Whatever Happened to the British Commonwealth?'
Michael Garibaldi Hall (History), and Elizabeth Hall (LBJ School), 'Views of Pakistan'
Ronald Steel (Visiting Professor of History), 'Walter Lippmann and the British'
Douglas H. M. Branion (Canadian Consul General), 'Political Controversy and Economic Development in Canada'
Decherd Turner and Dave Oliphant (HRHRC), 'The History of the Publications of the HRHRC'
Robert Fernea (Anthropology), 'The Controversy over Sex and Orientalism: Charles Doughty's *Arabia Deserta*'

Desley Deacon (Government), 'Her Brilliant Career: The Context of Nineteenth-Century Australian Feminism'
John Lamphear (History), 'The British Colonial "Pacification" of Kenya: A View from the Other Side'
Kingsley de Silva (University of Peradeniya, Sri Lanka), 'British Colonialism and Sri Lankan Independence'
Thomas Hatfield (Continuing Education), 'Colorado on the Cam, 1986: From "Ultra" to Archaeology, from Mr. Micawber to Mrs. Thatcher'
Carol Hanbery MacKay (English), 'The Dickens Theater'
Round Table Discussion, 'The Art of Biography: Philip Ziegler's *Mountbatten*': Ronald Brown, Jo Anne Christian, Wm. Roger Louis (History), Harry Middleton (LBJ Library), and Ronald Steel

Spring Semester 1986

Round Table Discussion, '*Out of Africa:* The Book, the Biography, and the Movie': B. J. Fernea (English and Middle Eastern Studies), Bernth Lindfors (English), and Wm. Roger Louis (History)
Robert Litwak (Woodrow Wilson Center), 'The Great Game: Russian, British, and American Strategies in Asia'
Gillian Adams Barnes (English), and Jane Manaster (Geography), 'Humphrey Carpenter's *Secret Gardens* and the Golden Age of Children's Literature'
Laurie Hergenhan (University of Queensland), 'A Yankee in Australia: The Literary and Historical Adventures of C. Hartley Grattan'
Brian Matthews (Flinders University, Adelaide), 'Australian Utopianism of the 1880s'
Richard Langhorne (Cambridge University), 'Apostles and Spies: The Generation of Treason at Cambridge between the Wars'
Ronald Robinson (Oxford University), 'The Decline and Fall of the British Empire'
William Rodgers (Social Democratic Party), 'Britain's New Three-Party System: A Permanent or Passing Phenomenon?'
John Coetzee (University of Cape Town), 'The Farm Novel in South Africa'
Ayesha Jalal, (Cambridge University), 'Jinnah and the Partition of India'
Andrew Blane (City College of New York), 'Amnesty International: From a British to an International Movement'
Anthony Rota (Antiquarian Bookseller and Publisher), 'London Pride: 1986'
Elspeth Rostow (LBJ School), 'The Withering Away of Whose State? Colonel Qaddafi's? Reflections on Nationalism at Home and Abroad, in Britain and in the Middle East'
Ray Daum (HRHRC), 'Broadway—Piccadilly!'

Fall Semester 1986

Round Table Discussion: Dean Robert King and Members of the '"Unrequired Reading List" Committee—The British Component'
Paul Sturges (Loughborough University, UK), 'Popular Libraries in Eighteenth-Century Britain'
Ian Bickerton (University of Missouri), 'Eisenhower's Middle East Policy and the End of the British Empire'
Marc Ferro (Visiting Professor of History), 'Churchill and Pétain'

David Fitzpatrick (Visiting Professor of History, Queen's University, Ontario), 'Religion and Politics in Ireland'
Adam Watson (University of Virginia), 'Our Man in Havana—or: Britain, Cuba, and the Caribbean'
Norman Rose (Hebrew University), 'Chaim Weizmann, the British, and the Creation of the State of Israel'
Elaine Thompson (American University), 'Legislatures in Canberra and Washington'
Wm. Roger Louis (History), 'Suez Thirty Years After'
Antonia Gransden (University of Nottingham), 'The Writing of Chronicles in Medieval England'
Hilary Spurling (British Biographer and Critic), 'Paul Scott's *Raj Quartet:* The Novelist as Historian'
J. D. B. Miller (Australian National University), 'A Special and Puzzling Relationship: Australia and the United States'
Janet Meisel (History), 'The Domesday Book'

Spring Semester 1987

Round Table Discussion, 'Contemporary Perspectives on Evolution': Miguel Gonzalez-Gerth (Spanish and Portuguese), Robert Fernea (Anthropology), Joe Horn (Psychology), Bruce Hunt (History), and Delbert Thiessen (Psychology)
Alistair Campbell-Dick (Strategic Technology), 'Scottish Nationalism'
Anthony Mockler (British Freelance Historian and Biographer), 'Graham Greene: The Interweaving of His Life and Fiction'
Michael Crowder (Visiting Professor of African History, Amherst College), 'The Legacy of British Colonialism in Africa'
Carin Green (Classics), 'Lovers and Defectors: Autobiography and *The Perfect Spy*'
Lord St. Brides, 'The Modern British Monarchy'
Victor Szebehely (Aerospace Engineering), 'Sir Isaac Newton'
Patrick McCaughey (National Gallery of Victoria, Melbourne), 'The Persistence of Landscape in Australian Art'
Adolf Wood (*Times Literary Supplement*), 'An Informal History of the *TLS*'
Nissan Oren (Hebrew University), 'Churchill, Truman, and Stalin: The End of the Second World War'
Sir Michael Howard (Oxford University), 'Britain and the First World War'
Sir John Graham (former British Ambassador to NATO), 'NATO: British Origins, American Security, and the Future Outlook'
Daniel Mosser (Virginia Polytechnic Institute and State University), 'The Chaucer Cardigan Manuscript'
Sir Raymond Carr (Oxford University), 'British Intellectuals and the Spanish Civil War'
Michael Wilding (University of Sydney), 'The Fatal Shore? The Convict Period in Australian Literature'

Fall Semester 1987

Round Table Discussion, 'Anthony Burgess: The Autobiography': Peter Green (Classics), Winfred Lehmann (Linguistics), Wm. Roger Louis (History), and Paul Woodruff (Philosophy)

Robert Crunden (History and American Studies), 'Ezra Pound in London'
Carol MacKay (English), and John Henry Faulk (Austin), 'J. Frank Dobie and Thackeray's Great-Granddaughter: Another Side of *A Texan in England*'
Sarvepalli Gopal (Jawaharlal Nehru University and Oxford University), 'Nehru and the British'
Robert D. King (Dean of Liberal Arts), 'T. S. Eliot'
Lord Blake (Visiting Professor of English History and Literature), 'Disraeli: Problems of the Biographer'
Alain Blayac (University of Montpellier), 'Art as Revelation: Gerard Manley Hopkins's Poetry and James Joyce's *Portrait of the Artist*'
Mary Bull (Oxford University), 'Margery Perham and Africa'
R. J. Moore (Flinders University, Adelaide), 'Paul Scott: The Novelist as Historian, and the *Raj Quartet* as History'
Ian Willison (British Library), 'New Trends in Humanities Research: The *History of the Book in Britain* Project'
The Duke of Norfolk, 'The Lion and the Unicorn: Ceremonial and the Crown'
Hans Mark (Chancellor, UT System), 'The Royal Society, the Royal Observatory, and the Development of Modern Research Laboratories'
Henry Dietz (Government), 'Sherlock Holmes: A Centennial Celebration'

Spring Semester 1988

Lord Jenkins (Oxford University), 'Changing Patterns of British Government from Asquith via Baldwin and Attlee to Mrs. Thatcher'
Lord Thomas (author of *The Spanish Civil War* and *Cuba, or the Pursuit of Freedom*), 'Britain, Spain, and Latin America'
Round Table Discussion, 'Chinua Achebe: The Man and His Works': Barbara Harlow (English), Bernth Lindfors (English), Wahneema Lubiano (English), and Robert Wren (University of Houston)
Charles Townshend (Keele University, UK), 'Britain, Ireland, and Palestine, 1918–1947'
Richard Morse (Woodrow Wilson Center), 'T. S. Eliot and Latin America'
Chinua Achebe (Nigerian Novelist), 'Anthills of the Savannah'
Tapan Raychaudhuri (Oxford University), 'The English in Bengali Eyes in the Nineteenth Century'
Lord Chitnis (Rowntree Trust and the British Refugee Council), 'British Perceptions of U.S. Policy in Central America'
Kurth Sprague (English), 'Constance White: Sex, Womanhood, and Marriage in British India'
George McGhee (former US Ambassador to Turkey and Germany), 'The Turning Point in the Cold War: Britain, the United States, and Turkey's Entry into NATO'
Robert Palter (Trinity College), 'New Light on Newton's Natural Philosophy'
J. Kenneth McDonald (CIA), 'The Decline of British Naval Power, 1918–1922'
Yvonne Cripps (Visiting Professor of Law), '"Peter and the Boys Who Cry Wolf": *Spycatcher*'
Emmanuel Ngara (University of Zimbabwe), 'African Poetry: Nationalism and Cultural Domination'
Kate Frost (English), 'Frat Rats of the Invisible College: The Wizard Earl of Northumberland and His Pre-Rosicrucian Pals'
B. Ramesh Babu (Visiting Professor of Government), 'American Foreign Policy: An Indian Dissent'

Sir Antony Ackland (British Ambassador to the United States), 'From Dubai to Madrid: Adventures in the British Foreign Service'
In the Spring Semester 1988, British Studies helped sponsor four lectures by Sir Brian Urquhart (former Under-Secretary of the United Nations) under the general title 'World Order in the Era of Decolonization.'

Fall Semester 1988

Round Table Discussion, 'Richard Ellman's *Oscar Wilde*': Peter Green (Classics), Diana Hobby (Rice University), Wm. Roger Louis (History), and Elspeth Rostow (American Studies),
Hugh Cecil (University of Leeds), 'The British First World War Novel of Experience'
Alan Knight (History), 'Britain and the Mexican Revolution'
Prosser Gifford (Former Deputy Director, Woodrow Wilson Center, Washington, DC), and Robert Frykenberg (University of Wisconsin–Madison), 'Stability in Post-Colonial British Africa: The Indian Perspective'
Joseph Dobrinski (Université Paul-Valéry), 'The Symbolism of the Artist Theme in *Lord Jim*'
Martin Stannard (University of Leicester), 'Evelyn Waugh and North America'
Lawrence Cranberg (Fellow, American Physical Society), 'The Engels-Marx Relationship and the Origins of Marxism'
N. G. L. Hammond (Bristol University), 'The British Military Mission to Greece, 1943–1944'
Barbara Harlow (English), 'A Legacy of the British Era in Egypt: Women, Writing, and Political Detention'
Sidney Monas (Slavic Languages and History), 'Thanks for the Mummery: *Finnegans Wake*, Rabelais, Bakhtin, and Verbal Carnival'
Robert Bowie (Central Intelligence Agency), 'Britain's Decision to Join the European Community'
Shirley Williams (Social Democratic Party), 'Labour Weakness and Tory Strength—or, The Strange Death of Labour England'
Bernard Richards (Oxford University), 'Ruskin's View of Turner'
John R. Clarke (Art History), 'Australian Art of the 1960s'
Round Table Discussion, 'Paul Kennedy's *The Rise and Fall of the Great Powers*': Alessandra Lipucci (Government), Wm. Roger Louis (History), Jagat Mehta (LBJ School), Sidney Monas (Slavic Languages and History), and Walt Rostow (Economics and History)

Spring Semester 1989

Brian Levack (History), 'The English Bill of Rights, 1689'
Hilary Spurling (Critic and Biographer), 'Paul Scott as Novelist: His Sense of History and the British Era in India'
Larry Carver (Humanities Program), 'Lord Rochester: The Profane Wit and the Restoration's Major Minor Poet'
Atieno Odhiambo (Rice University), 'Re-Interpreting Mau Mau'
Trevor Hartley (London School of Economics), 'The British Constitution and the European Community'
Archie Brown (Oxford University), 'Political Leadership in Britain, the Soviet Union, and the United States'
Lord Blake (Editor, *Dictionary of National Biography*), 'Churchill as Historian'

Weirui Hou (Shanghai University), 'British Literature in China'
Norman Daniel (British Council), 'Britain and the Iraqi Revolution of 1958'
Alistair Horne (Oxford University), 'The Writing of the Biography of Harold Macmillan'
M. R. D. Foot (Editor, *Gladstone Diaries*), 'The Open and Secret War, 1939–1945'
Ian Willison (former Head of the Rare Books Division, British Library), 'Editorial Theory and Practice in The History of the Book'
Neville Meaney (University of Sydney), 'The "Yellow Peril": Invasion, Scare Novels, and Australian Political Culture'
Round Table Discussion, '*The Satanic Verses*': Kurth Sprague (American Studies), Peter Green (Classics), Robert A. Fernea (Anthropology), Wm. Roger Louis (History), and Gail Minault (History and Asian Studies)
Kate Frost (English), 'John Donne, Sunspots, and the British Empire'
Lee Patterson (Duke University), 'Chaucerian Commerce'
Edmund Weiner and John Simpson (Editors of the new *OED*), 'Return to the Web of Words'
Ray Daum (HRHRC), 'Noel Coward and Cole Porter'
William B. Todd (History), 'Edmund Burke on the French Revolution'

Fall Semester 1989

D. Cameron Watt (London School of Economics), 'Britain and the Origins of the Second World War: Personalities and Politics of Appeasement'
Gary Freeman (Government), 'On the Awfulness of the English: The View from Comparative Studies'
Hans Mark (Chancellor, UT System), 'British Naval Tactics in the Second World War: The Japanese Lessons'
T. B. Millar (Menzies Centre for Australian Studies, London), 'Australia, Britain, and the United States in Historical Perspective'
Dudley Fishburn (Member of Parliament and former Editor of *The Economist*), '*The Economist*'
Lord Franks (former Ambassador in Washington), 'The "Special Relationship"'
Herbert L. Jacobson (Drama Critic and friend of Orson Welles), 'Three Score Years of Transatlantic Acting and Staging of Shakespeare'
Roy Macleod (University of Sydney) 'The "Practical Man": Myth and Metaphor in Anglo-Australian Science'
David Murray (Open University), 'Hong Kong: The Historical Context for the Transfer of Power'
Susan Napier (UT Assistant Professor of Japanese Language and Literature), 'Japanese Intellectuals Discover the British'
Dr. Karan Singh (Ambassador of India to the United States), 'Four Decades of Indian Democracy'
Paul Woodruff (Philosophy), 'George Grote and the Radical Tradition in British Scholarship'
Herbert J. Spiro (Government), 'Britain, the United States, and the Future of Germany'
Robert Lowe (*Austin American-Statesman*), '"God Rest You Merry, Gentlemen": The Curious British Cult of Sherry'

Spring Semester 1990

Thomas F. Staley (HRHRC), 'Harry Ransom, the Humanities Research Center, and the Development of Twentieth-Century Literary Research Collections'

Thomas Cable (English), 'The Rise and Decline of the English Language'
D. J. Wenden (Oxford University), 'Sir Alexander Korda and the British Film Industry'
Roger Owen (Oxford University), 'Reflections on the First Ten Years of Thatcherism'
Robert Hardgrave (Government), 'Celebrating Calcutta: The Solvyns Portraits'
Donatus Nwoga (University of Nigeria, Nsukka), 'The Intellectual Legacy of British Decolonization in Africa'
Francis Sitwell (Etonian, Seaman, and Literary Executor), 'Edith Sitwell: A Reappraisal'
Robert Vitalis (Government), 'The "New Deal" in Egypt: Britain, the United States, and the Egyptian Economy during World War II'
James Coote (Architecture), 'Prince Charles and Architecture'
Harry Eckstein (University of California, Irvine), 'British Politics and the National Health Service'
Alfred David (Indiana University), 'Chaucer and King Arthur'
Ola Rotimi (African Playwright and Theater Director), 'African Literature and the British Tongue'
Derek Brewer (Cambridge University), 'An Anthropological Study of Literature'
Neil MacCormick (University of Edinburgh), 'Stands Scotland Where She Should?'
Janice Rossen (Senior Research Fellow, HRHRC), 'Toads and Melancholy: The Poetry of Philip Larkin'
Ronald Robinson (Oxford University), 'The Decolonization of British Imperialism'

Fall Semester 1990

Round Table Discussion, 'The Crisis in the Persian Gulf': Hafez Farmayan (History), Robert Fernea (Anthropology), Wm. Roger Louis (History), and Robert Stookey (Center for Middle Eastern Studies)
John Velz (English), 'Shakespeare and Some Surrogates: An Account of the Anti-Stratfordian Heresy'
Michael H. Codd (Department of the Prime Minister and Cabinet, Government of Australia), 'The Future of the Commonwealth: An Australian View'
John Dawick (Massey University, New Zealand), 'The Perils of Paula: Young Women and Older Men in Pinero's Plays'
Gloria Fromm (University of Illinios, Chicago), 'New Windows on Modernism: The Letters of Dorothy Richardson'
David Braybrooke (Government), 'The Canadian Constitutional Crisis'
Sidney Monas (Slavic Languages and History), 'Paul Fussell and World War II'
James Fishkin (Government), 'Thought Experiments in Recent Oxford Philosophy'
Joseph Hamburger (Yale University), 'How Liberal Was John Stuart Mill?'
Richard W. Clement (University of Kansas), 'Thomas James and the Bodleian Library: The Foundations of Scholarship'
Michael Yeats (Former Chairman of the Irish Senate and only son of the poet William Butler Yeats), 'Ireland and Europe'
Round Table Discussion, 'William H. McNeill's *Arnold J. Toynbee: A Life*': Standish Meacham (Dean, Liberal Arts), Peter Green (Classics), Wm. Roger Louis (History), and Sidney Monas (Slavic Languages and History)
Jeffrey Meyers (Biographer and Professor of English, University of Colorado), 'Conrad and Jane Anderson'

Alan Frost (La Trobe University, Melbourne), 'The Explorations of Captain Cook'

Sarvepalli Gopal (Jawaharlal Nehru University), 'The First Ten Years of Indian Independence'

Round Table Discussion, 'The Best and Worst Books of 1990': Alessandra Lippucci (Government), Wm. Roger Louis (History), Tom Staley (HRHRC), Steve Weinberg (Physics), and Paul Woodruff (Philosophy)

Spring Semester 1991

David Hollway (Prime Minister's Office, Government of Australia), 'Australia and the Gulf Crisis'

Diane Kunz (Yale University), 'British Post-War Sterling Crises'

Miguel Gonzalez-Gerth (Spanish Literature and the HRHRC), 'T. E. Lawrence, Richard Aldington, and the Death of Heroes'

Robert Twombly (English), 'Religious Encounters with the Flesh in English Literature'

Alan Ryan (Princeton University), 'Bertrand Russell's Politics'

Hugh Kenner (Johns Hopkins University), 'The State of English Poetry'

Patricia Burnham (American Studies), 'Anglo-American Art and the Struggle for Artistic Independence'

Round Table Discussion, 'The Churchill Tradition': Lord Blake (former Provost of Queen's College, Oxford), Lord Jenkins (Chancellor, Oxford University), Field Marshal Lord Carver (former Chief of the Defence Staff), Sir Michael Howard (former Regius Professor, Oxford, present Lovett Professor of Military and Naval History, Yale University), with a concluding comment by Winston S. Churchill, M.P.

Woodruff Smith (UT San Antonio), 'Why Do the British Put Sugar in Their Tea?'

Peter Firchow (University of Minnesota), 'Aldous Huxley: The Poet as Centaur'

Irene Gendzier (Boston University), 'British and American Middle Eastern Policies in the 1950s: Lebanon and Kuwait; Reflections on Past Experience and the Post-War Crisis in the Gulf'

John Train (*Harvard* Magazine and *Wall Street Journal*), 'Remarkable Catchwords in the City of London and on Wall Street'

Adam Sisman (Independent Writer, London), 'A. J. P. Taylor'

Wm. Roger Louis (History), 'The Young Winston'

Adrian Mitchell (Melbourne University), 'Claiming a Voice: Recent Non-Fiction Writing in Australia'

Bruce Hevly (University of Washington), 'Stretching Things Out versus Letting Them Slide: The Natural Philosophy of Ice in Edinburgh and Cambridge in the Nineteenth Century'

Henry Dietz (Government), 'Foibles and Follies in Sherlock's Great Game: Some Excesses of Holmesian Research'

Summer 1991

Wm. Roger Louis (History), and Ronald Robinson (Oxford University), 'Harold Macmillan and the Dissolution of the British Empire'

Robert Treu (University of Wisconsin–Lacrosse), 'D. H. Lawrence and Graham Greene in Mexico'

Thomas Pinney (Pomona College), 'Kipling, India, and Imperialism'

Ronald Heiferman (Quinnipiac College), 'The Odd Couple: Winston Churchill and Chiang Kai-shek'

John Harty (Alice Lloyd College, Kentucky), 'The Movie and the Book: J. G. Ballard's *Empire of the Sun*'
A. B. Assensoh (Southern University, Baton Rouge), 'Nkrumah'
Victoria Carchidi (Emory and Henry College), 'Lawrence of Arabia on a Camel, Thank God!'
James Gump (University of California, San Diego), 'The Zulu and the Sioux: The British and American Comparative Experience with the "Noble Savage"'

Fall Semester 1991

Round Table Discussion, 'Noel Annan's *Our Age*': Peter Green (Classics), Robert D. King (Dean, Liberal Arts), Wm. Roger Louis (History), and Thomas F. Staley (HRHRC)
Christopher Heywood (Okayama University), 'Slavery, Imagination, and the Brontës'
Harold L. Smith (University of Houston, Victoria), 'Winston Churchill and Women'
Krystyna Kujawinska-Courtney (University of Lodz), 'Shakespeare and Poland'
Ewell E. Murphy, Jr. (Baker Botts, Houston), 'Cecil Rhodes and the Rhodes Scholarships'
I. N. Kimambo (University of Dar es Salaam), 'The District Officer in Tanganyika'
Hans Mark (Chancellor, UT System), 'The Pax Britannica and the Inevitable Comparison: Is There a Pax Americana? Conclusions from the Gulf War'
Richard Clutterbuck (Major-General, British Army, Ret.), 'British and American Hostages in the Middle East: Negotiating with Terrorists'
Elizabeth Hedrick (English), 'Samuel Johnson and Linguistic Propriety'
The Hon. Denis McLean (New Zealand Ambassador to the United States), 'Australia and New Zealand: The Nuisance of Nationalism'
Elizabeth Richmond (English), 'Submitting a Trifle for a Degree: Dramatic Productions at Oxford and Cambridge in the Age of Shakespeare'
Kenneth Warren, M.D. (Director for Science, Maxwell Macmillan), 'Tropical Medicine: A British Invention'
Adolf Wood (*Times Literary Supplement*), 'The Golden Age of the *Times Literary Supplement*'
Eugene Walter (Poet and Novelist), 'Unofficial Poetry: Literary London in the 1940s and 1950s'
Sidney Monas (Slavic Languages and History), 'Images of Britain in the Poetry of World War II'
St. Stephen's Madrigal Choir, 'Celebrating an English Christmas'

Spring Semester 1992

Jeremy Treglown (Critic and Author), 'Wartime Censorship and the Novel'
Toyin Falola (History), 'Nigerian Independence, 1960'
Donald S. Lamm (W.W. Norton and Company), 'Publishing English History in America'
Colin Franklin (Publisher and Historian of the Book), 'The Pleasures of Eighteenth-Century Shakespeare'
Thomas F. Staley (HRHRC), '*Fin de Siècle* Joyce: A Perspective on One Hundred Years'
Sarvepalli Gopal (Jawaharlal Nehru University), '"Drinking Tea with Treason": Halifax and Gandhi'

Michael Winship (English), 'The History of the Book: Britain's Foreign Trade in Books in the Nineteenth Century'
Richard Lariviere (Sanskrit and Asian Studies), 'British Law and Lawyers in India'
Round Table Discussion, 'A. S. Byatt's *Possession*': Janice Rossen (Visiting Scholar, HRHRC), John P. Farrell (English), and Wm. Roger Louis (History)
William H. McNeill (University of Chicago), 'Arnold Toynbee's Vision of World History'
Derek Brewer (Cambridge University), 'The Interpretation of Fairy Tales: The Implications for English Literature, Anthropology, and History'
David Bradshaw (Oxford University), 'Aldous Huxley: Eugenics and the Rational State'
Steven Weinberg (Physics), 'The British Style in Physics'
Sir David Williams (Cambridge University), 'Northern Ireland'

Summer 1992

R. A. C. Parker (Oxford University), 'Neville Chamberlain and Appeasement'
Adrian Wooldridge (Oxford University and *The Economist*), 'Reforming British Education: How It Happened and What America Can Learn'
Chris Wrigley (Nottingham University), 'A. J. P. Taylor: An English Radical and Modern Europe'

Fall Semester 1992

Round Table Discussion, 'E. M. Forster's *Howards End:* The Movie and the Book': Robert D. King (Linguistics), Wm. Roger Louis (History), Alessandra Lippucci (Government), and Thomas F. Staley (HRHRC)
Lord Skidelsky (Warwick University), 'Keynes and the Origins of the "Special Relationship"'
Sir Samuel Falle (former British Ambassador), 'Britain and the Middle East in the 1950s'
Ian MacKillop (University of Sheffield), 'We Were That Cambridge: F. R. Leavis and *Scrutiny*'
Walter Dean Burnham (Government), 'The 1992 British Elections: Four-or-Five-More Tory Years?'
Don Graham (English), 'Modern Australian Literature and the Image of America'
Richard Woolcott (former Secretary of the Australian Department of Foreign Affairs), 'Australia and the Question of Cooperation or Contention in the Pacific'
Ian Willison (1992 Wiggins Lecturer, American Antiquarian Society), 'The History of the Book in Twentieth-Century Britain and America'
Iain Sproat, (Member of Parliament), 'P. G. Wodehouse and the War'
Standish Meacham (History), 'The Crystal Palace'
Field Marshal Lord Carver (former Chief of the British Defence Staff), 'Wavell: A Reassessment'
Lesley Hall (Wellcome Institute for the History of Medicine, London), 'For Fear of Frightening the Horses: Sexology in Britain since William Acton'
Michael Fry (University of Southern California), 'Britain, the United Nations, and the Lebanon Crisis of 1958'
Brian Holden Reid (King's College, London), 'J. F. C. Fuller and the Revolution in British Military Thought'

Neil Parsons (University of London), '"Clicko," or Franz Taaibosch: A Bushman Entertainer in Britain, Jamaica, and the United States c. 1919–40'
John Hargreaves (Aberdeen University), 'God's Advocate: Lewis Namier and the History of Modern Europe'
Round Table Discussion, 'Robert Harris's *Fatherland*': Henry Dietz (Government), Robert D. King (Linguistics), Wm. Roger Louis (History), and Walter Wetzels (Germanic Languages)
Kevin Tierney (University of California), 'Robert Graves: An Outsider Looking In, or An Insider Who Escaped?'

Spring Semester 1993

Round Table Discussion, 'The Trollope Mystique': Janice Rossen (author of *Philip Larkin* and *The University in Modern Fiction*), Louise Weinberg (Law School), and Paul Woodruff (Plan II Honors Program and Philosophy)
Bruce Hunt (History), 'To Rule the Waves: Cable Telegraphy and British Physics in the Nineteenth Century'
Martin Wiener (Rice University), 'The Unloved State: Contemporary Political Attitudes in the Writing of Modern British History'
Elizabeth Dunn (HRHRC), 'Ralph Waldo Emerson and Ireland'
Jason Thompson (Western Kentucky University), 'Edward William Lane's "Description of Egypt"'
Sir Michael Howard (Yale University), 'Strategic Deception in the Second World War'
Gordon A. Craig (Stanford University), 'Churchill'
Round Table Discussion, 'The Indian Mathematician Ramanujan': Robert D. King (Linguistics), James W. Vick (Mathematics), and Steven Weinberg (Physics)
Martha Merritt (Government), 'From Commonwealth to Commonwealth, and from Vauxhall to *Vokzal:* Russian Borrowing from Britain'
Sidney Monas (Slavic Languages and History), 'James Joyce and Russia'
Peter Marshall (King's College, London), 'Imperial Britain and the Question of National Identity'
Michael Wheeler (Lancaster University), 'Ruskin and Gladstone'
Anthony Low (Cambridge University), 'Britain and India in the Early 1930s: The British, American, French, and Dutch Empires Compared'

Summer 1993

Alexander Pettit (University of North Texas), 'Lord Bolingbroke's *Remarks on the History of England*'
Rose Marie Burwell (Northern Illinois University), 'The British Novel and Ernest Hemingway'
Richard Patteson (Mississippi State University), 'New Writing in the West Indies'
Richard Greene (Memorial University, Newfoundland), 'The Moral Authority of Edith Sitwell'

Fall Semester 1993

Round Table Discussion, 'The British and the Shaping of the American Critical Mind—Edmund Wilson, Part II': Wm. Roger Louis (History), Elspeth Rostow (American Studies), Tom Staley (HRHRC), and Robert Crunden (History and American Studies)

Roseanne Camacho (University of Rhode Island), 'Evelyn Scott: Towards an Intellectual Biography'
Christopher Heywood (Okayama University), 'The Brontës and Slavery'
Peter Gay (Yale University), 'The Cultivation of Hatred in England'
Linda Ferreira-Buckley (English) 'England's First English Department: Rhetoric and More Rhetoric'
Janice Rossen (HRHRC), 'British University Novels'
Ian Hancock (O Yanko Le Redzosko) (Linguistics and English), 'The Gypsy Image in British Literature'
James Davies (University College of Swansea), 'Dylan Thomas'
Jeremy Lewis (London Writer and Editor), 'Who Cares about Cyril Connolly?'
Sam Jamot Brown (British Studies) and Robert D. King (Linguistics), 'Scott and the Antarctic'
Martin Trump (University of South Africa), 'Nadine Gordimer's Social and Political Vision'
Richard Clogg (University of London), 'Britain and the Origins of the Greek Civil War'
Herbert J. Spiro (United States Ambassador, Ret.), 'The Warburgs: Anglo-American and German-Jewish Bankers'
Colin Franklin (Publisher and Antiquarian Bookseller), 'Lord Chesterfield: Stylist, Connoisseur of Manners, and Specialist in Worldly Advice'
Jeffrey Segall (Charles University, Prague), 'The Making of James Joyce's Reputation'
Rhodri Jeffreys-Jones (University of Edinburgh), 'The Myth of the Iron Lady: Margaret Thatcher and World Stateswomen'
John Rumrich (English), 'Milton and Science: Gravity and the Fall'
J. D. Alsop (McMaster University), 'British Propaganda, Espionage, and Political Intrigue'
Round Table Discussion, 'The Best and the Worst Books of 1993': David Edwards (Government), Creekmore Fath (Liberal Arts Foundation), Betty Sue Flowers (English), and Sidney Monas (Slavic Languages and History)

Spring Semester 1994

Thomas F. Staley (HRHRC), 'John Rodker: Poet and Publisher of Modernism'
Martha Fehsenfeld, and Lois More Overbeck (Emory University), 'The Correspondence of Samuel Beckett'
M. R. D. Foot (Historian and Editor), 'Lessons of War on War: The Influence of 1914–1918 on 1939–1945'
Round Table Discussion, 'Requiem for Canada?': David Braybrooke (Government), Walter Dean Burnham (Government), and Robert Crunden (American Studies)
Ross Terrill (Harvard University), 'Australia and Asia in Historical Perspective'
Sir Samuel Falle (British Ambassador and High Commissioner), 'The Morning after Independence: The Legacy of the British Empire'
Deborah Lavin (University of Durham), 'Lionel Curtis: Prophet of the British Empire'
Robin W. Doughty (Geography), 'Eucalyptus: And Not a Koala in Sight'
Al Crosby (American Studies and History), 'Captain Cook and the Biological Impact on the Hawaiian Islands'
Gillian Adams (Editor, *Children's Literature Association Quarterly*), 'Beatrix Potter and Her Recent Critics'

Lord Amery, 'Churchill's Legacy'
Christa Jansohn (University of Bonn), and Peter Green (Classics), '*Lady Chatterley's Lover*'
R. A. C. Parker (Oxford University), 'Neville Chamberlain and the Coming of the Second World War'
John Velz (English), 'King Lear in Iowa: Jane Smiley's *A Thousand Acres*'
Jan Schall (University of Florida), 'British Spirit Photography'
Daniel Woolf (Dalhousie University), 'The Revolution in Historical Consciousness in England'

Fall Semester 1994

Kenneth O. Morgan (University of Wales), 'Welsh Nationalism'
Round Table Discussion, 'Michael Shelden's *Graham Greene: The Man Within*': Peter Green (Classics), Wm. Roger Louis (History), and Thomas F. Staley (HRHRC)
Robert D. King (Linguistics), 'The Secret War, 1939–1945'
Brian Boyd (University of Auckland), 'The Evolution of Shakespearean Dramatic Structure'
Lord Weatherill (former Speaker of the House of Commons), 'Thirty Years in Parliament'
Hans Mark (Aerospace Engineering), 'Churchill's Scientists'
Steven Weinberg (Physics), 'The Test of War: British Strengths and Weaknesses in World War II'
Dennis Welland (University of East Anglia), 'Wilfred Owen and the Poetry of War'
Alan Frost (La Trobe University), 'The *Bounty* Mutiny and the British Romantic Poets'
W. O. S. Sutherland (English), 'Sir Walter Scott'
Hazel Rowley (Deakin University, Melbourne), 'Christina Stead's "Other Country"'
Herman Bakvis (Dalhousie University), 'The Future of Democracy in Canada and Australia'
Peter Stansky (Stanford University), 'George Orwell and the Writing of *Nineteen Eighty-Four*'
Henry Dietz (Government), 'Sherlock Homes and Jack the Ripper'
James Coote (Architecture), 'Techniques of Illusion in British Architecture'
Round Table Discussion, 'The Best and Worst Books of 1994': Dean Burnham (Government), Alessandra Lippucci (Government), Roger Louis (History), Sidney Monas (Slavic Languages and History), and Janice Rossen (HRHRC)

Spring Semester 1995

Elizabeth Butler Cullingford (English), 'Anti-Colonial Metaphors in Contemporary Irish Literature'
Thomas M. Hatfield (Continuing Education), 'British and American Deception of the Germans in Normandy'
Gary P. Freeman (Government), 'The Politics of Race and Immigration in Britain'
Donald G. Davis, Jr. (Library and Information Science), 'The Printed Word in Sunday Schools in Nineteenth-Century England and the United States'
Brian Bremen (English), "Healing Words: The Literature of Medicine and the Medicine of Literature'

Frances Karttunen (Linguistic Research Center), and Alfred W. Crosby (American Studies and History), 'British Imperialism and Creole Languages'
Paul Lovejoy (York University, Canada), 'British Rule in Africa: A Reassessment of Nineteenth-Century Colonialism'
Carol MacKay (English), 'Creative Negativity in the Life and Work of Elizabeth Robins'
John Brokaw (Theatre and Dance), 'The Changing Stage in London, 1790–1832'
Linda Colley (Yale University), 'The Frontier in British History'
Iwan Morus (University of California, San Diego), 'Manufacturing Nature: Science, Technology, and Victorian Consumer Culture'
Brian Parker (University of Toronto), 'Jacobean Law: The Dueling Code and "A Faire Quarrel" (1617)'
Kate Frost (English), '"Jack Donne the Rake": Fooling around in the 1590s'
Mark Kinkead-Weekes (University of Kent), 'Beyond Gossip: D. H. Lawrence's Writing Life'

Summer 1995

S. P. Rosenbaum (University of Toronto), 'Leonard and Virginia Woolf at the Hogarth Press'
Maria X. Wells (HRHRC), 'A Delicate Balance: Trieste, 1945'
Kevin Tierney (University of California, Berkeley), 'Personae in Twentieth Century British Autobiography'

Fall Semester 1995

Brian Levack (History), 'Witchcraft, Possession, and the Law in Jacobean England'
Janice Rossen (HRHRC), 'The Home Front: Anglo-American Women Novelists and World War II'
Dorothy Driver (University of Cape Town), 'Olive Schreiner's Novel *From Man to Man*'
Philip Ziegler (London), 'Mountbatten Revisited'
Joanna Hitchcock (Director, University of Texas Press), 'British and American University Presses'
Samuel H. Beer (Harvard University), 'The Rise and Fall of Party Government in Britain and the United States, 1945–1995'
Richard Broinowski (Australian Ambassador to Mexico and Central America), 'Australia and Latin America'
John Grigg (London), 'Myths about the Approach to Indian Independence'
Round Table Discussion, '*Measuring the Mind* by Adrian Wooldridge and *The Bell Curve* by Richard J. Herrnstein and Charles Murray': David Edwards (Government), Sheldon Ekland-Olson (Dean of Liberal Arts), Joseph Horn (Psychology), and Robert D. King (Linguistics)
Paul Addison (University of Edinburgh), 'British Politics in the Second World War'
John Sibley Butler (Sociology), 'Emigrants of the British Empire'
Round Table Discussion, '*Carrington*': Peter Green (Classics), Robin Kilson (History), Wm. Roger Louis (History), Sidney Monas (Slavic Languages and History), and Elizabeth Richmond-Garza (English)

Spring Semester 1996

Kevin Kenny (History), 'Making Sense of the Molly Maguires'
Brigadier Michael Harbottle (British Army), 'British and American Security in the Post-Cold War'

Carol MacKay (English), 'The Singular Double Vision of Photographer Julia Margaret Cameron'
John Ramsden (University of London), '"That Will Depend on Who Writes the History": Winston Churchill as His Own Historian'
Jack P. Greene (Johns Hopkins University), 'The British Revolution in America'
Walter D. Wetzels (German), 'The Ideological Fallout in Germany of Two British Expeditions to Test Einstein's General Theory of Relativity'
Thomas Pinney (Pomona College), 'In Praise of Kipling'
Michael Charlesworth (Art History), 'The English Landscape Garden'
Stephen Gray (South African Novelist), 'The Dilemma of Colonial Writers with Dual Identities'
Jeremy Black (University of Durham), 'Could the British Have Won the War of American Independence?'
Dagmar Hamilton (LBJ School), 'Justice William O. Douglas and British Colonialism'
Gordon Peacock and Laura Worthen (Theatre and Dance), 'Not Always a Green and Pleasant Land: Tom Stoppard's *Arcadia*'
Bernard Crick (University of London), 'Orwell and the Business of Biography'
Geoffrey Hartman (Yale University), 'The Sympathy Paradox: Poetry, Feeling, and Modern Cultural Morality'
Dave Oliphant (HRHRC), 'Jazz and Its British Acolytes'
R. W. B. Lewis (Yale University), 'Henry James: The Victorian Scene'
Alan Spencer (Ford Motor Company), 'Balliol, Big Business, and Mad Cows'
Peter Quinn: A Discussion of His Novel, *Banished Children of Eve*

Summer 1996

Martin Stannard (Leicester University), 'Biography and Textual Criticism'
Diane Kunz (Yale University), 'British Withdrawal East of Suez'
John Cell (Duke University), 'Who Ran the British Empire?'
Mark Jacobsen (U.S. Marine Corps Command and Staff College), 'The North-West Frontier'
Theodore Vestal (Oklahoma State University), 'Britain and Ethiopia'
Warren F. Kimball (Rutgers University), 'A Victorian Tory: Churchill, the Americans, and Self-Determination'
Louise B. Williams (Lehman College, City University of New York), 'British Modernism and Fascism'

Fall Semester 1996

Elizabeth Richmond-Garza (English and Comparative Literature), 'The New Gothic: Decadents for the 1990s'
Robin Kilson (History), 'The Politics of Captivity: The British State and Prisoners of War in World War I'
Sir Brian Fall (Oxford University), 'What Does Britain Expect from the European Community, the United States, and the Commonwealth?'
Wm. Roger Louis (History), 'Harold Macmillan and the Middle East Crisis of 1958'
Ian Willison (Editor, *The Cambridge History of the Book in Britain*), 'The History of the Book and the Cultural and Literary History of the English-Speaking World'
Walter L. Arnstein (University of Illinois), 'Queen Victoria's Other Island'
Noel Annan (London), '*Our Age* Revisited'

Michael Cohen (Bar-Ilan University, Tel Aviv), 'The Middle East and the Cold War: Britain, the United States, and the Soviet Union'
Reba Soffer (California State University, Northridge), 'Catholicism in England: Was it Possible to Be a Good Catholic, a Good Englishman, and a Good Historian?'
Wilson Harris (Poet and Novelist), 'The Mystery of Consciousness: Cross-Cultural Influences in the Caribbean, Britain, and the United States'
H. S. Barlow (Singapore), 'British Malaya in the late Nineteenth Century'
Donald G. Davis, Jr. (Library and Information Science), 'British Destruction of Chinese Books in the Peking Siege of 1900'
Round Table Discussion, *Michael Collins*': Elizabeth Cullingford (English), Kevin Kenny (History), Robin Kilson (History), and Wm. Roger Louis (History)
A. G. Hopkins (Cambridge University), 'From Africa to Empire'
Austin Chapter of the Society for the Preservation and Encouragement of Barber Shop Quartet Singing in America

Spring Semester 1997

Round Table Discussion, 'T. S. Eliot and Anti-Semitism': Robert D. King (Jewish Studies), Sidney Monas (Slavic Languages and History), and Thomas F. Staley (HRHRC)
Phillip Herring (University of Wisconsin–Madison), 'Djuna Barnes and T. S. Eliot: The Story of a Friendship'
Bryan Roberts (Sociology), 'British Sociology and British Society'
Andrew Roberts (London), 'The Captains and the Kings Depart: Lord Salisbury's Skeptical Imperialism'
Colin Franklin (London), 'In a Golden Age of Publishing, 1950–1970'
Susan Pedersen (Harvard University), 'Virginia Woolf, Eleanor Rathbone, and the Problem of Appeasement'
Andrew Seaman (Saint Mary's University, Halifax, Nova Scotia), 'Thomas Raddall: A Novelist's View of Nova Scotia during the American Revolution'
Gordon Peacock (Theatre and Dance), 'Noel Coward: A Master Playwright, a Talented Actor, a Novelist and Diarist: Or a Peter Pan for the Twentieth Century?'
Roland Oliver (University of London), 'The Battle for African History, 1947–1966'
Alistair Horne (Oxford University), 'Harold Macmillan's Fading Reputation'
Richard Begam (University of Wisconsin–Madison), 'Samuel Beckett and the Debate on Humanism'
Christopher Waters (Williams College), 'Delinquents, Perverts, and the State: Psychiatry and the Homosexual Desire in the 1930s'
Sami Zubaida (University of London), 'Ernest Gellner and Islam'
Walter Dean Burnham (Government), 'Britain Votes: The 1997 General Election and Its Implications'

Fall Semester 1997

Judith Brown (Oxford University), 'Gandhi: A Victorian Gentleman'
Thomas Cable (English), 'Hearing and Revising the History of the English Language'
Round Table Discussion, 'The Death of Princess Diana': Judith Brown (Oxford),

David Edwards (Government), Elizabeth Richmond-Garza (English), Anne Baade (British Studies), Alessandra Lippucci (Government), and Kevin Kenny (History)
David Hunter (Music Librarian, Fine Arts Library), 'Handel and His Patrons'
Anne Kane (Sociology), 'The Current Situation in Ireland'
James S. Fishkin (Government), 'Power and the People: The Televised Deliberative Poll in the 1997 British General Election'
Howard D. Weinbrot (University of Wisconsin–Madison), 'Jacobitism in Eighteenth-Century Britain'
J. C. Baldwin, M.D. (Houston), 'The Abdication of King Edward VIII'
Kenneth E. Carpenter (Harvard University), 'Library Revolutions Past and Present'
Akira Iriye (Harvard University), 'Britain, Japan, and the International Order after World War I'
Anthony Hobson (London), 'Reminiscences of British Authors and the Collecting of Contemporary Manuscripts'
David Killingray (University of London), 'The British in the West Indies'
Alan Knight (Oxford University), 'British Imperialism in Latin America'
Round Table Discussion, 'King Lear in Iowa: The Film *A Thousand Acres*': Linda Ferreira-Buckley (English), Elizabeth Richmond-Garza (English), Helena Woodard (English), and John Velz (English)
Timothy Lovelace (Music) and the Talisman Trio

Spring Semester 1998

Richard Ollard (Biographer and Publisher), 'A. L. Rowse: Epitome of the Twentieth Century'
Round Table Discussion, 'Arundhati Roy's *The God of Small Things*': Phillip Herring (HRHRC), Brian Trinque (Economics), Kamala Visweswaran (Anthropology), and Robert Hardgrave (Government)
Jonathan Schneer (Georgia Institute of Technology), 'London in 1900: The Imperial Metropolis'
Trevor Burnard (University of Canterbury, New Zealand), 'Rioting in Goatish Embraces: Marriage and the Failure of White Settlement in British Jamaica'
Felipe Fernández-Armesto (Oxford University), 'British Traditions in Comparative Perspective'
Michael Mann (University of California, Los Angeles), 'The Broader Significance of Labour's Landslide Victory of 1997'
Dane Kennedy (University of Nebraska), 'White Settlers in Colonial Kenya and Rhodesia'
Round Table Discussion, 'Noel Annan, Keynes, and Bloomsbury': Jamie Galbraith (LBJ School), Elspeth Rostow (LBJ School), and Walt Rostow (Economics and History)
Lisa Moore (English), 'British Studies—Lesbian Studies: A Dangerous Intimacy?'
James Gibbs (University of the West of England), 'Wole Soyinka: The Making of a Playwright'
Marilyn Butler (Oxford University), 'About the House: Jane Austen's Anthropological Eye'
R. J. Q. Adams (Texas A&M University), 'Britain and Ireland, 1912–1922'
John M. Carroll (Asian Studies), 'Nationalism and Identity in pre-1949 Hong Kong'

Round Table Discussion, 'The Irish Referendum': Anne Kane (Sociology), Kevin Kenny (History), Wm. Roger Louis (History), and Jennifer O'Conner (History)

Fall Semester 1998

Louise Hodgden Thompson (Government), 'Origins of the First World War: The Anglo-German Naval Armaments Race'
John P. Farrell (English), 'Thomas Hardy in Love'
Carol MacKay (English), 'The Multiple Conversions of Annie Besant'
Roy Foster (Oxford University), 'Yeats and Politics, 1898–1921'
Robert Olwell (History), 'British Magic Kingdoms: Imagination, Speculation, and Empire in Florida'
Sara H. Sohmer (Texas Christian University), 'The British in the South Seas: Exploitation and Trusteeship in Fiji'
Helena Woodard (English), 'Politics of Race in the Eighteenth Century: Pope and the Humanism of the Enlightenment'
D. A. Smith (Grinnell College), 'Impeachment? Parliamentary Government in Britain and France in the Nineteenth Century'
Round Table Discussion, 'The Irish Insurrection of 1798': Robert Olwell (History), Lisa Moore (English), and Kevin Kenny (History)
Robert D. King (Jewish Studies), 'The Accomplishments of Raja Rao: The Triumph of the English Language in India'
Donald G. Davis, Jr. (Library and Information Science and History), 'Religion and Empire'
A. D. Roberts (University of London), 'The Awkward Squad: African Students in American Universities before 1940'
Chaganti Vijayasree (Osmania University, Hyderabad), 'The Empire and Victorian Poetry'
Martha Deatherage (Music), 'Christmas Celebration: Vauxhall Gardens'

Spring Semester 1999

Round Table Discussion, '*Regeneration:* Pat Barker's Trilogy on the First World War': Betty Sue Flowers (English), Wm. Roger Louis (History), and Paul Woodruff (Humanities)
Alistair Campbell-Dick (Cybertime Corporation), 'The Immortal Memory of Robert Burns'
Hugh Macrae Richmond (University of California, Berkeley), 'Why Rebuild Shakespeare's Globe Theatre?'
Ralph Austen (University of Chicago), 'Britain and the Global Economy: A Post-Colonial Perspective'
Jerome Meckier (University of Kentucky), 'Aldous Huxley's American Experience'
Peter Marsh (Syracuse University), 'Joseph Chamberlain as an Entrepreneur in Politics: Writing the Life of a Businessman Turned Statesman'
Roger Adelson (Arizona State University), 'Winston Churchill and the Middle East'
Margot Finn (Emory University), 'Law, Debt, and Empire: The Calcutta Court of Conscience'
Fred M. Leventhal (Boston University), 'The Projection of Britain in America before the Second World War'
Larry Siedentop (Oxford University), 'Reassessing the Life of Isaiah Berlin'
Ross Terrill (Harvard University), 'R. H. Tawney's Vision of Fellowship'
Juliet Fleming (Cambridge University), 'The Ladies' Shakespeare'

Elizabeth Fernea (English and Middle Eastern Studies), 'The Victorian Lady Abroad: In Egypt with Sophia Poole and in Texas with Mrs. E. M. Houstoun'

Richard Schoch (University of London), 'The Respectable and the Vulgar: British Theater in the Mid-Nineteenth Century'

Ferdinand Mount (Editor, *TLS*), 'Politics and the *Times Literary Supplement*'

Fall Semester 1999

Round Table Discussion, 'The Boer War, 1899–1902': Barbara Harlow (English), John Lamphear (History), and Wm. Roger Louis (History)

Sharon Arnoult (Southwest Texas State University), 'Charles I: His Life after Death'

Kenneth O. Morgan (Oxford University), 'Lloyd George, Keir Hardie, and the Importance of the "Pro-Boers"'

Richard Cleary (Architecture), 'Walking the Walk to Talk the Talk: The Promenade in Eighteenth-Century France and England'

Keith Kyle (Journalist and Historian), 'From Suez to Kenya as Journalist and as Historian'

Malcolm Hacksley (National English Literary Museum, Grahamstown, South Africa), 'Planting a Museum, Cultivating a Literature'

Ben Pimlott (University of London), 'The Art of Writing Political Biography'

Geraldine Heng (English), 'Cannibalism, the First Crusade, and the Genesis of Medieval Romance'

A. P. Martinich (Philosophy), 'Thomas Hobbes: Lifelong and Enduring Controversies'

Round Table Discussion, 'Lyndall Gordon's *T. S. Eliot: An Imperfect Life*': Brian Bremen (English), Thomas Cable (English), Elizabeth Richmond-Garza (Comparative Literature), and Thomas F. Staley (HRHRC)

Shula Marks (University of London), 'Smuts, Race, and the Boer War'

Round Table Discussion, 'The Library of the British Museum': William B. Todd (English), Irene Owens (Library and Information Science), and Don Davis (Library and Information Science and Department of History)

Henry Dietz (Government), '*The Hound of the Baskervilles*'

Spring Semester 2000

Susan Napier (Asian Studies), 'The Cultural Phenomenon of the Harry Potter Fantasy Novels'

Round Table Discussion, '*Dutch: A Memoir of Ronald Reagan:* A Chapter in the "Special Relationship"?': Wm. Roger Louis (History), Harry Middleton (LBJ Library), and Elspeth Rostow (LBJ School)

Norman Rose (Hebrew University, Jerusalem), 'Harold Nicolson: A Curious and Colorful Life'

Charlotte Canning (Theatre and Dance), 'Feminists Perform Their Past'

John Ripley (McGill University), 'The Sound of Sociology: H. B. Tree's *Merchant of Venice*'

Sergei Horuji (Russian Academy of Sciences), 'James Joyce in Russia'

Janice Rossen (Biographer and Independent Scholar), 'Philip Toynbee'

Max Egremont (Novelist and Biographer), 'Siegfried Sassoon's War'

Paul Taylor (London School of Economics and Political Science), 'Britain and Europe'

Lord Selborne (Royal Geographical Society), 'The Royal Geographical Society: Exploration since 1830'
Craig MacKenzie (Rand Afrikaans University, Johannesburg), 'The Mythology of the Boer War: Herman Charles Bosman and the Challenge to Afrikaner Romanticism'
Peter Catterall (Institute of Contemporary British History, London), 'Reform of the House of Lords'
Bernard Porter (University of Newcastle), 'Pompous and Circumstantial: Sir Edward Elgar and the British Empire'
Craufurd D. Goodwin (Duke University), 'Roger Fry and the Debate on "Myth" in the Bloomsbury Group'
Jamie Belich (University of Auckland), 'Neo-Britains? The "West" in Nineteenth-Century Australia, New Zealand, and America'
Round Table Discussion, 'Norman Davies's *The Isles*': Sharon Arnoult (Midwestern State University, Wichita Falls), Raymond Douglas (Colgate University), Walter Johnson (Northwestern Oklahoma State University), David Leaver (Raymond Walters College, Cincinnati), and John Cell (Duke University)

Fall Semester 2000

Round Table Discussion, 'Paul Scott, the Raj Quartet, and the Beginning of British Studies at UT': Peter Green (Classics), Robert Hardgrave (Government and Asian Studies), and Wm. Roger Louis (History)
Suman Gupta (Open University), 'T. S. Eliot as Publisher'
Jeffrey Cox (University of Iowa), 'Going Native: Missionaries in India'
Kevin Kenny (Boston College), 'Irish Nationalism: The American Dimension'
Joseph Kestner (University of Tulsa), 'Victorian Battle Art'
James E. Cronin (Boston College), 'From Old to New Labour: Politics and Society in the Forging of the "Third" Way'
Gerald Moore (Mellon Visiting Research Fellow, HRHRC), 'When Caliban Crossed the Atlantic'
Richard Howard (Shakespearean Actor, London), '"Health and Long Life to You": A Program of Irish Poetry and Prose Presented by an Englishman, with Anecdotes'
Stephen Foster (Northern Illinois University), 'Prognosis Guarded: The Probable Decolonization of the British Era in American History'
Frank Prochaska (University of London), 'Of Crowned and Uncrowned Republics: George V and the Socialists'
Robert H. Abzug (History and American Studies), 'Britain, South Africa, and the American Civil Rights Movement'
Paula Bartley (Visiting Research Fellow, HRHRC), 'Emmeline Pankhurst'
Thomas Jesus Garza (Slavic Languages), 'A British Vampire's Christmas'

Spring Semester 2001

Betty Sue Flowers (UT Distinguished Teaching Professor), 'From Robert Browning to James Bond'
Larry Carver (English), 'Feliks Topolski at the Ransom Center'
Oscar Brockett (Theatre and Dance), 'Lilian Baylis and England's National Theatres'
Linda Levy Peck (George Washington University), 'Luxury and War'
R. James Coote (Architecture), 'Architectural Revival in Britain'
Adam Roberts (Oxford University), 'Britain and the Creation of the United Nations'

Mark Southern (Germanic Studies), 'Words over Swords: Language and Tradition in Celtic Civilization'
Round Table Discussion, 'Ben Rogers's *A Life of A. J. Ayer*': David Braybrooke (Government and Philosophy), Al Martinich (History and Philosophy), David Sosa (Philosophy), and Paul Woodruff (Plan II and Philosophy)
Bartholomew Sparrow (Government), 'British and American Expansion: The Political Foundations'
Jose Harris (Oxford University), 'Writing History during the Second World War'
Charles Loft (Westminster College), 'Off the Rails? The Historic Junctions in Britain's Railway Problem'
Dan Jacobson (University of London), 'David Irving and Holocaust Denial'— Special Lecture
Dan Jacobson (University of London), 'Self-Redemption in the Victorian Novel'
George S. Christian (British Studies), 'The Comic Basis of the Victorian Novel'
Paul Taylor (London *Independent*), 'Rediscovering a Master Dramatist: J. B. Priestley'

Fall Semester 2001

Round Table Discussion, 'Ray Monk's Biography of Bertrand Russell, *The Ghost of Madness*': Al Martinich (History and Philosophy), David Sosa (Philosophy and British Studies), and Paul Woodruff (Plan II and Philosophy)
Alex Danchev (Keele University), 'The Alanbrooke Diaries'
Robert M. Worcester (LSE and Market Opinion Research International), 'Britain and the European Union'
Martha Ann Selby (Asian Studies), 'The Cultural Legacy of British Clubs: Manners, Memory, and Identity among the New Club-Wallahs in Madras'
Roger Owen (Harvard University), 'Lord Cromer and Wilfrid Blunt in Egypt'
James Loehlin (English), 'A Midsummer Night's Dream'
Jeffrey Meyers (Biographer), 'Somerset Maugham'
Elspeth Rostow (LBJ School), 'From American Studies to British Studies—And Beyond'
Nicholas Westcott (British Embassy), 'The Groundnut Scheme: Socialist Imperialism at Work in Africa'
Round Table Discussion, 'The Anglo-American Special Relationship': Gary Freeman (Government), Wm. Roger Louis (History), Elspeth Rostow (American Studies), and Michael Stoff (History)
Christopher Heywood (Sheffield University), 'The Brontës: A Personal History of Discovery and Interpretation'
James Bolger (New Zealand Ambassador and former Prime Minister), 'Whither New Zealand? Constitutional, Political, and International Quandaries'
R. J. Q. Adams (Texas A&M), 'Arthur James Balfour and Andrew Bonar Law: A Study in Contrasts'
Ferdinand Mount (Editor, *Times Literary Supplement*), 'British Culture since the Eighteenth Century: An Open Society?'
James Loehlin (English), 'A Child's Christmas in Wales'

Spring Semester 2002

Round Table Discussion, 'Adam Sisman's *Boswell's Presumptuous Task*': Samuel Baker (English), Linda Ferreira-Buckley (English), Julie Hardwick (History), and Helena Woodward (English)
A. G. Hopkins (History), 'Globalization: The British Case'

Susan Napier (Asian Studies), 'J. R. R. Tolkein and *The Lord of the Rings:* Fantasy as Retreat or Fantasy as Engagement?'
Wilfrid Prest (Adelaide University), 'South Australia's Paradise of Dissent'
Tom Palaima (Classics), 'Terence Rattigan's *Browning Version*'
Alan H. Nelson (University of California, Berkeley), 'Thoughts on Elizabethan Authorship'
Penelope Lively (London), 'Changing Perceptions of British and English Identity'
Hans Mark (Aerospace Engineering), 'The Falklands War'
David Butler (Oxford University), 'Psephology—or, the Study of British Elections'
Robert L. Hardgrave (Government), 'From West Texas to South India and British Studies'
Geoffrey Wheatcroft (London), 'The Englishness of English Sport'
Eileen Cleere (Southwestern University), 'Dirty Pictures: John Ruskin and the Victorian Sanitation of Fine Art'
Jamie Belich (Auckland University), 'A Comparison of Empire Cities: New York and London, Chicago and Melbourne'
Churchill Conference: Geoffrey Best (Oxford University), Sir Michael Howard (Oxford University), Warren Kimball (Rutgers University), Philip Ziegler (London), Wm. Roger Louis (History)
Catherine Maxwell (University of London), 'Swinburne's Poetry and Criticism'
Round Table Discussion, 'Churchill and the Churchill Conference': Rodrigo Gutierrez (History), Adrian Howkins (History), Heidi Juel (English), David McCoy (Government), Joe Moser (English), Jeff Rutherford (History), William S. Livingston (UT Senior Vice President), and Wm. Roger Louis (History)

Fall Semester 2002

James K. Galbraith (LBJ School of Public Affairs), 'The Enduring Importance of John Maynard Keynes'
Michael Green (University of Natal), 'Agatha Christie in South Africa'
Sumit Ganguly (Asian Studies), 'Kashmir: Origins and Consequences of Conflict'
Margaret MacMillan (University of Toronto), 'At the Height of His Power: Lloyd George in 1919'
Douglas Bruster (English), 'Why We Fight: *Much Ado About Nothing* and the West'
John Darwin (Oxford University), 'The Decline and Rise of the British Empire: John Gallagher as an Historian of Imperialism'
Kevin Kenny (Boston College), 'The Irish in the British Empire'
David Wallace (University of Pennsylvania), 'A Chaucerian's Tale of Surinam'
Peter Bowler (Queen's University, Belfast), 'Scientists and the Popularization of Science in Early Twentieth-Century Britain'
Bernardine Evaristo (London), 'A Feisty, Funky Girl in Roman England'
Frank Moorhouse (Australia), 'Dark Places and Grand Days'
David Cannadine (University of London), 'C. P. Snow and the Two Cultures'
Round Table Discussion, 'Edmund S. Morgan's Biography of Benjamin Franklin': Carolyn Eastman (History), Bruce Hunt (History), Wm. Roger Louis (History), Alan Tully (History)
Mark Lawrence (History), 'The Strange Silence of Cold War England: Britain and the Vietnam War'
Tom Cable (English), 'The Pleasures of Remembering Poetry'

Spring Semester 2003

Round Table Discussion, 'W. G. Sebald's *Rings of Saturn*': Brigitte Bauer (French and Italian), Sidney Monas (History and Slavic Languages), Elizabeth Richmond-Garza (English and Comparative Literature), Walter Wetzels (Germanic Studies)
Diana Davis (Geography), 'Brutes, Beasts, and Empire: A Comparative Study of the British and French Experience'
Colin Franklin (Publisher), 'Rosalind Franklin—Variously Described as "The Dark Lady of DNA" and "The Sylvia Plath of Molecular Biology"'
Sidney Monas (History and Slavic Languages), 'A Life of Irish Literature and Russian Poetry, Soviet Politics and International History'
Neville Hoad (English), 'Oscar Wilde in America'
Selina Hastings (London), 'Rosamond Lehman: Eternal Exile'
Bernard Wasserstein (Glasgow University), 'The British in Palestine: Reconsiderations'
Anne Chisholm (London), 'Frances Partridge: Last of the Bloomsberries'
Philip Morgan (Johns Hopkins University), 'The Black Experience and the British Empire'
Jeremy duQuesnay Adams (Southern Methodist University), 'Joan of Arc and the English'
Didier Lancien (University of Toulouse), 'Churchill and de Gaulle'
Avi Shlaim (Oxford University), 'The Balfour Declaration and Its Consequences'
Martin J. Wiener (Rice University), 'Murder and the Modern British Historian'
Winthrop Wetherbee (Cornell University), 'The Jewish Impact on Medieval Literature: Chaucer, Boccaccio, and Dante'
Philippa Levine (University of Southern California), 'Sex and the British Empire'

Summer 2003

Donald G. Davis, Jr. (History and the School of Information), 'Life without British Studies Is Like . . . '
Kurth Sprague (English and American Studies), 'Literature, Horses, and Scandal at UT'
David Evans (Astronomy), 'An Astronomer's Life in South Africa and Texas'
Tom Hatfield (Continuing Education), 'Not Long Enough! Half a Century at UT'

Fall Semester 2003

Richard Oram (HRHRC), 'Evelyn Waugh: Collector and Annotator'
Round Table Discussion, 'Booker Prize Winner James Kelman: Adapting a Glasgow Novel for the Texas Stage': James Kelman (Glasgow), Mia Carter (English), Kirk Lynn, and Dikran Utidjian
Simon Green (All Souls College, Oxford University), 'The Strange Death of Puritan England, 1914–1945'
Elizabeth Richmond-Garza (English and Comparative Literature), '*Measure for Measure*'
Lewis Hoffacker (U.S. Ambassador), 'From the Congo to British Studies'
A. P. Thornton (University of Toronto), 'Wars Remembered, Revisited, and Reinvented'
Deryck Schreuder (University of Western Australia), 'The Burden of the British Past in Australia'

Robert Mettlen (Finance), 'From Birmingham to British Studies'
Paul Schroeder (University of Illinois), 'The Pax Britannica and the Pax Americana: Empire, Hegemony, and the International System'
Ferdinand Mount (London), 'A Time to Dance: Anthony Powell's *Dance to the Music of Time* and the Twentieth Century in Britain'
Brian Bond (University of London), '*Oh! What a Lovely War:* History and Popular Myth in Late-Twentieth Century Britain'
Wendy Frith (Bradford College, England), 'The Speckled Monster: Lady Mary Wortley Montagu and the Battle against Smallpox'
Harry Middleton (LBJ Library), 'The Road to the White House'
Jeremy Lewis (London), 'Tobias Smollett'
Christian Smith (Austin, Texas), 'Christmas Readings'

Spring Semester 2004

Round Table Discussion, 'The Pleasures of Reading Thackeray': Carol Mackay (English), Judith Fisher (Trinity University), George Christian (British Studies)
Thomas F. Staley (HRHRC), '"Corso e Recorso:" A Journey through Academe'
Patrick O'Brien (London School of Economics), 'The Pax Britannica, American Hegemony, and the International Order, 1793–2004'
Michael Wheeler (former Director of Chawton House Library), 'England Drawn and Quartered: Cultural Crisis in the Mid-Nineteenth Century'
Walter Wetzels (Germanic Studies), 'Growing Up in Nazi Germany, and later American Adventures'
Kathleen Wilson (State University of New York, Stony Brook), 'The Colonial State and Governance in the Eighteenth Century'
Elizabeth Fernea (English and Middle Eastern Studies), 'Encounters with Imperialism'
Chris Dunton (National University of Lesotho), 'Newspapers and Colonial Rule in Africa'
Miguel Gonzalez-Gerth (Spanish and Portuguese), 'Crossing Geographical and Cultural Borders—and Finally Arriving at British Studies'
Peter Stansky (Stanford University), 'Bloomsbury in Ceylon'
Round Table Discussion, '*The Crimson Petal and the White*': John Farrell (English), Betty Sue Flowers (LBJ Library), Wm. Roger Louis (History), Paul Neimann (English)
Ann Curthoys (Australian National University), 'The Australian History Wars'
Martha Ann Selby (Asian Studies), 'Against the Grain: On Finding My Voice in India'
Steven Isenberg (UT Visiting Professor of Humanities), 'A Life in Our Times'

Summer 2004

Carol Mackay (English), 'My Own Velvet Revolution'
Erez Manela (Harvard University), 'The "Wilsonian Moment" in India and the Crisis of Empire in 1919'
Scott Lucas (Birmingham University), '"A Bright Shining Mecca": British Culture and Political Warfare in the Cold War and Beyond'
Monica Belmonte (U.S. Department of State), 'Before Things Fell Apart: The British Design for the Nigerian State'
Dan Jacobson (London), 'Philip Larkin's "Elements"'

Bernard Porter (University of Newcastle), "'Oo Let 'Em In? Asylum Seekers and Terrorists in Britain, 1850–1914'

Fall Semester 2004

Richard Drayton (Cambridge University), 'Anglo-American "Liberal" Imperialism, British Guiana, 1953–64, and the World Since September 11'
David Washbrook (Oxford University), 'Living on the Edge: Anxiety and Identity in "British" Calcutta, 1780–1930'
Joanna Hitchcock (University of Texas Press), 'An Accidental Publisher'
Alan Friedman (English), '*A Midsummer Night's Dream*'
Antony Best (London School of Economics), 'British Intellectuals and East Asia in the Inter-war Years'
John Farrell (English), 'Beating a Path from Brooklyn to Austin'
Christopher Middleton (Liberal Arts), 'Relevant to England—A Reading of Poems'
Gail Minault (History and Asian Studies), 'Growing Up Bilingual and Other (Mis)adventures in Negotiating Cultures'
Wm. Roger Louis (History), 'Escape from Oklahoma'
John Trimble (English), 'Writing with Style'
Niall Ferguson (Harvard University), 'Origins of the First World War'
James Hopkins (Southern Methodist University), 'George Orwell and the Spanish Civil War: The Case of Nikos Kazantzakis'
James Currey (London), 'Africa Writes Back: Publishing the African Writers Series at Heinemann'
Sidney Monas (History and Slavic Languages), 'A Jew's Christmas'
Geoffrey Wheatcroft (London), '"In the Advance Guard": Evelyn Waugh's Reputation'

Spring Semester 2005

Katharine Whitehorn (London), 'It Didn't *All* Start in the Sixties'
Gertrude Himmelfarb (Graduate School, City University of New York), 'The Whig Interpretation of History'
Kurt Heinzelman (English and HRHRC), 'Lord Byron and the Invention of Celebrity'
Brian Levack (History), 'Jesuits, Lawyers, and Witches'
Richard Cleary (Architecture), 'When Taste Mattered: W. J. Battle and the Architecture of the Forty Acres'
Edward I. Steinhart (Texas Tech University), 'White Hunters in British East Africa, 1895–1914'
Don Graham (English), 'The Drover's Wife: An Australian Archetype'
A. C. H. Smith, (London) 'Literary Friendship: The 40-Year Story of Tom Stoppard, B. S. Johnson, and Zulfikar Ghose'
Paul Woodruff (Philosophy and Plan II), 'A Case of Anglophilia—And Partial Recovery: Being an Account of My Life, with Special Attention to the Influence of England upon My Education'
Toyin Falola (History), 'Footprints of the Ancestors'
Robert Abzug (History) 'Confessions of an Intellectual Omnivore: The Consequences on Scholarship and Career'
Deirdre McMahon (Mary Immaculate College, University of Limerick), 'Ireland and the Empire-Commonwealth, 1918–1972'

James Coote (Architecture), 'Building with Wit: Sir Edwin Lutyens and British Architecture'
Jay Clayton (Vanderbilt University), 'The Dickens Tape: Lost and Found Sound before Recording'
Christopher Ricks (Oxford University), 'The Force of Poetry: Shakespeare and Beckett'

Summer 2005

Blair Worden (Oxford University), 'Poetry and History of the English Renaissance'
Robert Bruce Osborn (British Studies), 'The Four Lives of Robert Osborn'
Alessandra Lippucci (Government), 'Perseverance Furthers: A Self-Consuming Artifact'
William H. Cunningham (former President of the University of Texas), 'Money, Power, Politics, and Ambition'
David V. Edwards (Government), 'Friendly Persuasion in the Academy'
Elizabeth Richmond-Garza (English), 'A Punk Rocker with Eight Languages'
Richard Lariviere (Liberal Arts), 'Confessions of a Sanskritist Dean'

Fall Semester 2005

Celebration of 30th Anniversary and Publication of *Yet More Adventures with Britannia*
Robert D. King (Jewish Studies), 'T.S. Eliot Reconsidered'
Round Table Discussion, 'The London Bombings': James Galbraith (LBJ School), Elizabeth Cullingford (English), Clement Henry (Government), Wm. Roger Louis (History)
Dolora Chapelle Wojciehowski (English), 'The Erotic Uncanny in Shakespeare's *Twelfth Night*'
Karl Hagstrom Miller (History), 'Playing Pensativa: History and Music in Counterpoint'
James D. Garrison (English), 'Translating Gray's *Elegy*'
Miguel Gonzalez-Gerth (Spanish and Portuguese), 'Another Look at Orwell: The Origins of *1984*'
Round Table Discussion, 'The Imperial Closet: Gordon of Khartoum, Hector McDonald of the Boer War, and Roger Casement of Ireland': Barbara Harlow (English), Neville Hoad (English), John Thomas (HRHRC)
Guy Ortolano (Washington University, St. Louis), 'From *The Two Cultures* to *Breaking Ranks:* C.P. Snow and the Interpretation of the 1960s'
Catherine Robson (University of California, Davis), 'Poetry and Memorialization'
Round Table Discussion, 'Britain and the Jewish Century': Lauren Apter (History), Robert D. King (Jewish Studies), Sidney Monas (History and Slavic Languages)
Hans Mark (Aerospace Engineering), 'Churchill, the Anglo-Persian Oil Company, and the Origins of the Energy Crisis: From the Early 20th Century to the Present'
Randall Woods (University of Arkansas), 'LBJ and the British'

Spring Semester 2006

Richard Gray (London), 'Movie Palaces of Britain'
Samuel Baker (English), 'The Lake Poets and the War in the Mediterranean Sea'

Thomas F. Staley (HRHRC), 'Graham Greene and Evelyn Waugh'
Gary Stringer (Texas A&M), 'Love's Long Labors Coming to Fruition: The John Donne Variorum Donne'
Caroline Elkins (Harvard University), 'From Malaya to Kenya: British Colonial Violence and the End of Empire'
Grigory Kaganov (St. Petersburg), 'London in the Mouth of the Neva'
Graham Greene (London), 'A Life in Publishing'
John Davis (Oxford University), 'Evans-Pritchard: Nonetheless A Great Englishman'
Barry Gough (Wilfrid Laurier University), 'Arthur Marder and the Battles over the History of the Royal Navy'
Ivan Kreilkamp (Indiana University), '"Bags of Meat": Pet-Keeping and the Justice to Animals in Thomas Hardy'
James Wilson (History), 'Historical Memory and the Mau Mau Uprising in Colonial Kenya'
Anne Deighton (Oxford University), 'Britain after the Second World War: Losing an Empire and Finding a Place in a World of Superpowers'
Steve Isenberg (Liberal Arts), 'Auden, Forster, Larkin, and Empson'
Harriet Ritvo (MIT), 'Animals on the Edge'
Peter Quinn (New York), 'Eugenics and the Hour of the Cat'
Dan Jacobson (London), 'Kipling and South Africa'

Fall Semester 2006

Michael Charlesworth (Art and Art History) and Kurt Heinzelman (English), 'Tony Harrison's "v."'
Peter Stanley (Australian War Memorial), 'All Imaginable Excuses: Australian Deserters and the Fall of Singapore'
Selina Hastings (London), 'Somerset Maugham and "Englishness"'
James W. Vick (Mathematics), 'A Golden Century of English Mathematics'
John O. Voll (Georgetown University), 'Defining the Middle East and the Clash of Civilizations'
James Loehlin (English), 'The Afterlife of Hamlet'
Daniel Topolski (London), 'The Life and Art of Feliks Topolski'
John Darwin (Oxford University), 'The British Empire and the British World'
David Cannadine (University of London), 'Andrew Mellon and Plutocracy Across the Atlantic'
John Lonsdale (Cambridge University), 'White Settlers and Black Mau Mau in Kenya'
Kate Gartner Frost (English), 'So What's Been Done about John Donne Lately?'
John Summers (Harvard University), 'The Power Elite: C. Wright Mills and the British'
Marrack Goulding (Oxford University), 'Has it been a Success? Britain in the United Nations'
Priya Satia (Stanford University), 'The Defence of Inhumanity: British Military and Cultural Power in the Middle East'
Don Graham (English), 'Burnt Orange Britannia: A Missing Contributor!'

Spring Semester 2007

Bernard Porter (Newcastle University), 'Empire and British Culture'
Paul Sullivan (Liberal Arts Honors Program), 'The Headmaster's Shakespeare: John Garrett and British Education'

Round Table Discussion, '*The Queen*': Elizabeth Cullingford (English), Karen King (American Studies), Wm. Roger Louis (History), Bryan Roberts (Sociology)
Martin Francis (University of Cincinnati), 'Cecil Beaton's Romantic Toryism and the Symbolism of Wartime Britain'
Susan Crane (Columbia University), 'Animal Feelings and Feelings for Animals in Chaucer'
Michael Charlesworth (Art History), 'The Earl of Strafford and Wentworth Castle'
Adam Sisman (London), 'Wordsworth and Coleridge'
Jenny Mann (Cornell University), 'Shakespeare's English Rhetoric: Mingling Heroes and Hobgoblins in *A Midsummer Night's Dream*'
David Atkinson (Member of Parliament), 'Britain and World Peace in the 21st Century'
Bertram Wyatt-Brown (University of Florida), 'T. E. Lawrence, Reputation, and Honor's Decline'
Wm. Roger Louis (History), 'All Souls and Oxford in 1956: Reassessing the Meaning of the Suez Crisis'
Indivar Kamtekar (Jawaharlal Nehru University), 'India and Britain during the Second World War'
Cassandra Pybus (University of Sydney), 'William Wilberforce and the Emancipation of Slaves'
Stephen Howe (University of Bristol), 'Empire in the 21st Century English Imagination'
Geoffrey Wheatcroft (London), 'The Myth of Malicious Partition: The Cases of Ireland, India, and Palestine'
Charles Rossman (English), 'D. H. Lawrence and the "Spirit" of Mexico'
Kenneth O. Morgan (House of Lords), 'Lloyd George, the French, and the Germans'

Fall Semester 2007

R. J. Q. Adams (Texas A&M), 'A. J. Balfour's Achievement and Legacy'
Robin Doughty (Geography), 'Saving Coleridge's Endangered Albatross'
Caroline Williams (University of Texas), 'A Victorian Orientalist: John Frederick Lewis and the Artist's Discovery of Cairo'
Susan Pedersen (Columbia University), 'The Story of Frances Stevenson and David Lloyd George'
Eric S. Mallin (English), 'Macbeth and the Simple Truth'
Mark Oaten, M.P., 'How "Special" Is the Special Relationship?'
Dan Birkholz (English), 'Playboys of the West of England: Medieval Cosmopolitanism and Familial Love'
Jeremy Lewis (London), 'The Secret History of Penguin Books'
Matthew Jones (Nottingham University), 'Britain and the End of Empire in South East Asia in the Era of the Vietnam War'
Martin Wiener (Rice University), '"Who knows the Empire whom only the Empire knows?": Reconnecting British and Empire History'
Book Launch: *Penultimate Adventures with Britannia* (Follett's Intellectual Property)
Hermione Lee and Christopher Ricks (Oxford), 'The Elusive Brian Moore: His Stature in Modern Literature'
Gabriel Gorodetsky (Tel Aviv University), 'The Challenge to Churchill's Wartime Leadership by Sir Stafford Cripps (the "Red Squire")'
Helena Woodard (English), 'Black and White Christmas: The Deep South in the Eighteenth Century'

Spring Semester 2008

Round Table Discussion, 'Tim Jeal's *Stanley: The Impossible Life of Africa's Greatest Explorer*': Diana Davis (Geography), A. G. Hopkins (History), Wm. Roger Louis (History)
Elizabeth Richmond-Garza (English and Comparative Literature), 'New Year's Eve 1900: Oscar Wilde and the Masquerade of Victorian Culture'
Robert Hardgrave (Government), 'The Search for Balthazar Solvyns and an Indian Past: The Anatomy of a Research Project'
Lucy Chester (University of Colorado), 'Zionists, Indian Nationalism, and British Schizophrenia in Palestine'
Michael Brenner (University of Pittsburgh), 'Strategic and Cultural Triangulation: Britain, the United States, and Europe'
Roger Morgan (European University, Florence), 'The British "Establishment" and the Chatham House Version of World Affairs'
Jason Parker (Texas A&M), 'Wilson's Curse: Self-Determination, the Cold War, and the Challenge of Modernity in the "Third World"'
Stephen Foster (Northern Illinois University), 'The American Colonies and the Atlantic World'
A. G. Hopkins (History), 'Comparing British and American "Empires"'
James Turner (Notre Dame University), 'The Emergence of Academic Disciplines'
Dror Wahrman (Indiana University), 'Invisible Hands in the Eighteenth Century'
Narendra Singh Sarila (Prince of Sarila), 'Mountbatten and the Partition of India'
Pillarisetti Sudhir (American Historical Association), 'The Retreat of the Raj: Radicals and Reactionaries in Britain'
Keith Francis (Baylor University), 'What Did Darwin Mean in *On the Origin of Species*? An Englishman and a Frenchman Debate Evolution'

Fall Semester 2008

Round Table Discussion, 'Ted and Sylvia': (UT English), Judith Kroll, Kurt Heinzelman, Betty Sue Flowers, Tom Cable
Roby Barrett (Middle East Institute), 'The Question of Intervention in Iraq, 1958–59'
John Kerr (San Antonio), 'Cardigan Bay'
Sue Onslow (London School of Economics), 'Julian Amery: A Nineteenth-Century Relic in a Twentieth-Century World?'
John Rumrich (English), 'Reconciliation in *The Winter's Tale:* The Literary Friendship of Robert Greene and William Shakespeare'
Richard Jenkyns (Oxford), 'Conan Doyle: An Assessment beyond Sherlock Holmes'
Theresa Kelley (University of Wisconsin), 'Romantic British Culture and Botany in India'
Sir Adam Roberts (Oxford), 'After the Cold War'
Geoffrey Wheatcroft (London), 'Churchill and the Jews'
Sir Brian Harrison (Oxford), 'Prelude to the Sixties'
Eric Kaufmann (London School of Economics), 'The Orange Order in Northern Ireland'
Robert McMahon (Ohio State University), 'Dean Acheson: The Creation of a New World Order and the Problem of the British'
Mark Metzler (History), 'Eye of the Storm: London's Place in the First Great Depression, 1872–96'

James Loehlin (English), Christmas Party at the New Campus Club, reading passages from Charles Dickens, *A Christmas Carol*

Spring Semester 2009

Margaret MacMillan (Oxford University), 'The Jewel in the Crown'
Bernard Wasserstein (University of Chicago), 'Glasgow in the 1950s'
Dominic Sandbrook (London), 'The Swinging Sixties in Britain'
Karl Meyer and Shareen Brysac (New York Times and CBS), 'Inventing Iran, Inventing Iraq: The British and Americans in the Middle East'
Albert Lewis (R. L. Moore Project), 'The Bertrand Russell Collection: The One That Got Away from the HRC'
Sir David Cannadine (Institute of Historical Research, London), 'Colonial Independence'; Linda Colley (CBE, Princeton University), 'Philip Francis and the Challenge to the British Empire'
George Scott Christian (English and History), 'Origins of Scottish Nationalism: The Trial of Thomas Muir'
Discussion led by Brian Levack and Roger Louis (History), 'Trevor-Roper and Scotland'
Warren Kimball (Rutgers University), 'Churchill, Roosevelt, and Ireland'
Ferdinand Mount (London) and R. J. Q. Adams (Texas A&M), 'A. J. Balfour and his Critics'
Dan Jacobson (London), Betty Sue Flowers (LBJ Library), and Tom Staley (HRHRC), Tribute to Betty Sue Flowers—'Hardy and Eliot'
John Darwin (Nuffield College, Oxford), 'Britain's Global Empire'
Saul Dubow (Sussex University), 'Sir Keith Hancock and the Question of Race'
Weslie Janeway (Cambridge), 'Darwin's Cookbook'
Julian Barnes, Barbara Harlow, Miguel Gonzalez-Gerth, 'Such, Such Was Eric Blair'
Cassandra Pybus (Visiting Fellow, UT Institute of Historical Studies), 'If you were regular black . . . ': Slavery, Miscegenation, and Racial Anxiety in Britain'

Fall Semester 2009

Peter Green (Classics), 'The Devil in Kingsley Amis'
John Farrell (English), 'Forgiving Emily Brontë'
Samuel Baker (English), 'Wedgwood Gothic'
Louise Weinberg (Law), 'Gilbert and Sullivan: The Curios Persistence of Savoyards'
Elizabeth Richmond-Garza (English), 'Love in a Time of Terror: King Lear and the Potential for Consolation'
John Rumrich (English), 'John Milton and the Embodied Word'
Round Table Discussion, 'Effective Teaching': Tom Cable (English), David Leal (Government), Lisa Moore (English), Bob Woodberry (Sociology)'
James M. Vaughn (History and British Studies), 'The Decline and Fall of Whig Imperialism, 1756–1783'
Round Table Discussion, 'Bloomsbury': Betty Sue Flowers (English), Wm. Roger Louis (History), Lisa Moore (English), David Sosa (Philosophy)
Sir Harold Evans, 'Murder Most Foul'
Peter Cain (Sheffield Hallam University), 'The Radical Critique of Colonialism'
John Gooch (Leeds University), 'Pyrrhic Victory? England and the Great War'

Maya Jasanoff (Harvard University), 'The British Side of the American Revolution'
Maeve Cooney (British Studies), Christmas Party at the Littlefield Home, reading O. Henry's 'The Gift of the Magi'

Spring Semester 2010

Thomas Jesus Garza (UT Language Center), 'The British Vampire's Slavic Roots'
Marilyn Young (New York University), 'The British and Vietnam'
Daniel Howe (University of California at Los Angeles), 'What Hath God Wrought'
Roberta Rubenstein (American University), 'Virginia Woolf and the Russians'
Samuel R. Williamson (University of the South at Sewanee), 'The Possibility of Civil War over Ireland in 1914'
Steve Pincus (Yale), 'The First Modern Revolution: Reappraising the Glorious Events of 1688'
Selina Hastings (London), 'Somerset Maugham: A Life Under Cover'
Eugene Rogan (Oxford), 'Modern History through Arab Eyes'
T. M. Devine (University of Edinburgh), 'Did Slavery Make Scotland Great?'
Phillip Herring (University of Wisconsin–Madison), 'A Journey through James Joyce's *Ulysses*'
Alison Bashford (Harvard), 'Australia and the World Population Problem, 1918–1954'
Berny Sèbe (Birmingham University), 'French and British Colonial Heroes in Africa'
J. L. Berry (Austin, Texas), 'The Post-Twilight of the British Empire on the Zambian Copper Belt'
Bernard Porter (University of Newcastle), 'The Myth of Goths and Vandals in British Architecture'

Fall Semester 2010

Jonathan Schneer (Georgia Institute of Technology), 'The Balfour Declaration'
Larry Carver (Liberal Arts Honors Program), 'Reacting to the Past: How I Came to Love Teaching Edmund Burke'
Thomas Pinney (Pomona College), 'Kipling and America'
Donna Kornhaber (English), 'Accident and Artistry in *The Third Man*'
Doug Bruster (English), 'Rating *A Midsummer Night's Dream*'
Peter Stansky (Stanford University), 'Julian Bell: From Bloomsbury to Spain'
Crawford Young (University of Wisconsin, Madison), 'The British Empire and Comparative Decolonization'
Jeffrey Cox (University of Iowa), 'From the Kingdom of God to the Third World'
Roberta Rubenstein (American University), 'Approaching the Golden Anniversary: Dorris Lessing's *The Golden Notebook*'
Kenneth O. Morgan (House of Lords), 'Aneurin Bevan: Pragmatist and Prophet of the Old Left'
Robert Vitalis (University of Pennsylvania), 'From the Persian Gulf to the Gulf of Mexico: What We Know About BP'
James Curran (Sydney University), 'The Great Age of Confusion: Australia in the Wake of Empire'
Archie Brown (St Antony's College, Oxford), 'Margaret Thatcher and the End of the Cold War'
Phyllis Lassner (Northwestern University), 'The End of Empire in the Middle East and the Literary Imagination'

Spring Semester 2011

Tillman Nechtman (Skidmore College), 'Nabobs: Empire and the Politics of National Identity in Eighteenth-Century Britain'
Brian Levak (History), 'Demonic Possession in Early Modern Britain'
David Kornhaber (English), 'George Bernard Shaw: Modernist'
Lisa L. Moore (English), 'Sister Arts: The Erotics of Lesbian Landscape'
Bartholomew Sparrow (Government), 'Brent Scowcroft, Mrs. Thatcher, and National Security'
Philip Bobbitt (Law School and LBJ School), 'The Special Relationship'
Deborah Harkness (UCLA), 'Fiction and the Archives: The Art and Craft of the Historian'
Peter Clarke (Trinity Hall, Cambridge), 'The English-Speaking Peoples'
A. G. Hopkins (History), 'The United States, 1783–1861: Britain's Honorary Dominion?'
Reba Soffer (California State University at Northridge), 'Intellectual History, Life, and Fiction'
Joanna Lewis (London School of Economics), 'Harold Macmillan and the Wind of Change'
Andrew Lycett (London), 'Arthur Conan Doyle and Rudyard Kipling'
Geoffrey Wheatcroft (London), 'The Grand Illusion: Britain and the United States'
Priscilla Roberts (University of Hong Kong), 'Henry James and the Erosion of British Power'
John Higley (Government), 'Degeneration of Ruling Elites? Recent American and British Elites'

Fall Semester 2011

Round Table Discussion, 'The Oxford of Maurice Bowra and Hugh Trevor Roper': Paul Woodruff (Philosophy), Wm. Roger Louis (History), and David Leal (Government),
Marian Barber (UT Austin), 'The Scots, Irish, English, and Welsh in the Making of Texas'
Geoffrey Davis (University of Aachen), 'The Territory of My Imagination: Rediscovering Dan Jacobson's South Africa'
Nadja Durbach (University of Utah), 'Poverty, Politics, and Roast Beef: Poor Relief and the Nation in Early Nineteenth-Century Britain'
Leonard Barkan (Princeton University), 'What's for Dinner on a Desert Island: Feast and Famine in *The Tempest*'
Lindsey Schell (University Libraries), 'The Royal Wedding and the Making of a Modern Princess'
Laurence Raw (Baskent University), 'Shakespeare and Home Front during World War II'
Sir Brian Harrison (Oxford University), 'Surprising Resilience: Historians of British Conservatism since 1945'
Troy Bickham (Texas A&M), 'A New Grand Transatlantic Drama: Britain and the Anglo-American War of 1812'
Eli P. Cox III (Marketing), 'The Betrayal of Adam Smith'
Nicholas Rogers (York University), 'Crime, Punishment, and Governance in Eighteenth-Century Britain'

Donald Lamm (WW Norton and Company), 'The History of Oxford University Press'
Al Martinich (History and Government), 'Locke and the Limits of Toleration'

Spring Semester 2012

Philippa Levine (Chair), John Berry (Austin), Donna Kornhaber (English), Wm. Roger Louis (History), Elizabeth Richmond-Garza (English), '*The Iron Lady*'
Brian Cowan (McGill University), 'Henry Sacheverell and the Cult of Eighteenth-Century Personalities'
Ronald Heiferman (Quinnipiac University), 'Churchill, Roosevelt, and China'
Jeremi Suri (History and LBJ School), 'British Imperialism and American Nation-Building'
Susan Napier (Tufts University), 'Harry Potter and the Fantastic Journey'
Andrew Roberts (School of Oriental and African Studies), 'Poetry, Anthology, and Criticism: Michael Roberts and the BBC'
Michael Charlesworth (Art History), 'Derek Jarman and British Films: Paintings, Poetry, and Prose'
John Voll (Georgetown University), 'Britain and Islam in the Twentieth Century'
Sheldon Garon (Princeton University), 'Anglo-Japanese Cultural Relations, 1868–1950'
Anand Yang (University of Washington, Seattle), 'Convicts in British India'
George Bernard (University of Southampton), 'Editing the *English Historical Review*'
Selina Todd (St. Hilda's College, Oxford), 'The Problem Family in Postwar Britain'
Christine Krueger (Marquette University), 'The Victorian Historian Mary Anne Everett Green'
Jeremy Lewis (London), 'David Astor and the Observer'
Michael Winship (English), 'Napoleon Comes to America: The Publishing of Sir Walter Scott's *Life of Napoleon Buonaparte* (1827)'
Adam Sisman (London), 'Writing the Biographies of A. J. P. Taylor and Hugh Trevor-Roper'

Fall Semester 2012

Donna Kornhaber (English), 'Charlie Chaplin's Forgotten Feature: A Countess from Hong Kong'
Tom Palaima (Classics), 'The War Poems of Robert Graves'
Rosemary Hill (All Souls College, Oxford), 'Prince Albert'
Sucheta Mahajan (Jawaharlal Nehru University), 'Independence and Partition of India Reassessed'
Richard Davenport-Hines (London), 'Ivy Compton-Burnett'
Albert Beveridge III (Johns Hopkins), 'The Rise, Fall, and Revival of Anthony Trollope'
Philip Stern (Duke University), 'The Evolution of the City of Bombay'
Betty Smocovitis (University of Florida), 'Rhapsody on a Darwinian Theme'
Jad Adams (University of London), 'Tony Benn: The Making of a British Radical'
Steve Isenberg (Quondam Executive Director of PEN), 'Fathers and Sons: Edmund Gosse and J. R. Ackerley'
Paul Levy (*Wall Street Journal*), 'Lytton Strachey'

William Janeway (New York), 'Beyond Keynesianism: Maynard Keynes and the Good Life'
Dan Raff (Wharton School of Business), 'The Ancient University Presses Make Up Their Minds'
David Leal (Government), 'Method and Irrationality in the Traditions of Sherlock Holmes'

Spring Semester 2013

Kariann Yokata (University of Colorado, Denver), 'Unbecoming British? The Place of Post-Colonial Americans in the British Empire'
Brian Levack (History), 'The British Imperial State in the Eighteenth Century'
Anne Chisholm (London), 'Dora Carrington and the Bloomsbury Circle'
James Banner (Washington, D.C.), 'Academics, Intellectuals, and Popular History'
Selina Hastings (London), 'The Red Earl'
John Spurling (London), 'Sir Edmund Gibson and the British Raj'
Hilary Spurling (London), 'Pearl Buck and China'
Janine Barchas (English), 'Jane Austen between the Covers'
Wm. Roger Louis (History and British Studies), 'The History of Oxford University Press, 1896–1970'
Sir Christopher Bayly (Cambridge), 'Distant Connections: India and Australia in the Colonial Era'
Philip Waller (Oxford),'Writers, Readers, and Reputations'
Jordanna Bailkin (University of Washington), 'Unsettled: Refugee Camps in Britain'
Geoffrey Wheatcroft (London), 'Assessing Margaret Thatcher'
Daniel Baugh (Cornell University), 'France and the British State and Empire, 1680–1940'
Richard Carwardine (Oxford), 'Lincoln and Emancipation: the British and International Consequences'

Fall Semester 2013

Henry Dietz (Government) 'British Sea Power and Napoleon in the Novels of Patrick O'Brian'
Christopher Benfey (Mount Holyoke College), 'The Myth of Tarzan'
Stephen Brooke (York University, Toronto), 'Photography and the Working Class in the 1950s'
Aram Bakshian (Washington, D.C.), '*The Economist*'
David Cressy (George III Professor of History, Ohio State), 'Gypsies and Cultural Tradition'
Stephen Weinberg (Josey Regental Chair of Science), 'The Last Magician: Isaac Newton'
James Scott (UT Statistics), 'Isaac Newton and the Birth of Money'
Lara Kriegel (Indiana University), 'Who Blew the Bugle? The Charge of the Light Brigade and the Legacy of the Crimean War'
Benjamin Gregg (Government), 'The Stasi and Secret Files'
Douglas Bruster (English), 'Shakespeare and Othello'
Miguel Gonzalez-Gerth (Founding Member of British Studies), 'Ian McEwan's Novels: Sex, Espionage, and Literature'
Allen MacDuffie, 'Dickens and Energy'

Walter Wetzels (Founding Member of British Studies), 'The Bombing of German Cities during the Second World War'

Spring Semester 2014

William S. Cunningham (UT Past President), 'Money, Power, Politics—and British Studies—at UT'
Michael Anderson (Government), 'Britain's Pacific Relations'
Rosemary Hill (London), 'Bloomsbury's Memoir Club'
Benjamin Brower (History), 'The Muslim Pilgrimage'
Margaret Jacobs (University of Nebraska), 'White Mother to a Dark Race'
Diana Solomon (Simon Fraser University), 'Seduction and Rape in Shakespeare'
Michael Stoff (History), 'Wilfred Burchett's "Warning to the World": An Australian War Correspondent Rewrites the Atomic Bomb Narrative"
Peter Green (Classics), 'Paul Scott'
Arthur Nicholson (San Antonio), 'Former Naval Person: Winston Churchill and the Royal Navy'
John Fair (UT Kinesiology), 'The Diverse Roots of Physical Culture'
Ian Hancock (UT Romani Studies), 'The Historical Identity of "Gypsies"'
Roy Ritchie (Huntington Library), 'The Advent of Beach Culture in Britain'
Bernard Wasserstein (University of Chicago), 'The Men Who Ruled Palestine'
James Vaughn (History), 'The Ideological Origins of the American Revolution Revisited'
Steven Isenberg (Visiting Professor of the Humanities), 'The Literary Legacy of the Great War'
William Whyte (Oxford), 'A Hotbed of Cold Feet? Architecture in Oxford Since 1950'
George Christian (History), 'Scotland's Independence?'

Fall Semester 2014

Stephen Enniss (Harry Ransom Center), 'The Ransom Center Looks Ahead'
John Gurney (Oxford), 'Nancy Lambton and Iran'
James D. Garrison (English), 'Gray, Johnson, and Elegy'
General David Ramsbotham (House of Lords), 'The Last Colonial War'
Elena Schneider (University of California, Berkeley), 'Perspectives on Revolution'
Roger Billis (London), 'The Reform Club: Its Creation and Traditions'
Max Egremont (London), 'Siegfried Sassoon: A Reassessment'
Joseph Epstein (Essayist and Critic, Chicago), 'Philip Larkin'
William Meier (Texas Christian University), 'Drugs in Twentieth-Century Britain'
Richard Davenport-Hines (London), 'The Death of General Gordon in Khartoum'
Leah S. Marcus (Vanderbilt), '*Much Ado about Nothing* and *The Taming of the Shrew*'
Kenneth O. Morgan (House of Lords), 'Wales, Lloyd George, and the First World War'
Round Table Discussion, 'The Link between Psychology and History': Robert Abzug (Jewish Studies), Randy Diehl (Dean of Liberal Arts), Wm. Roger Louis (British Studies)
Jane Ridley (Buckingham University), 'George V, the Tsar, and the British Monarchy'
Richard Cleary (Architecture), 'Well Played! Sports Settings and the Perspective of Architecture'

Sir Keith Thomas (Oxford), 'Army Life in Jamaica'
Archie Brown (Oxford), 'The Scottish Referendum'
Miranda Seymour (Brown), 'Germany and England: Romantic Connections'

Spring Semester 2015

Kurt Heinzelman (English), 'The Disappearance of Dylan Thomas'
Michael Brenner (University of Pittsburgh), 'Blair and Bush: Partners in Reaction'
Bartholomew Sparrow (Government), 'Legacy of Colonialism: America's Forgotten Class'
Bain Attwood (Harvard), 'Indigenous Rights in Australia and New Zealand'
Bernard Porter (Newcastle), 'Genocide in Tasmania?'
Ingrid Norton (Harvard Divinity School), 'The Poetry of Valentine's Day'
Perry Anderson (UCLA), 'Gandhi'
Ferdinand Mount (London), 'Harold Macmillan'
Thomas Meaney (Columbia University), 'The United Nations and Colonial Independence'
Lawrence S. Graham (Government), 'Northern Ireland's Continuing Troubles: Reflections on the Belfast Agreement of 1998'
Gabriel Paquette (Johns Hopkins University), 'Allies yet Adversaries? Portugal and Britain in the Age of Empire'
Molly McCullers (University of West Georgia), 'South Africa and the Question of African Independence: The Case of South-West Africa (Namibia)'
Robert D. King (Liberal Arts), 'British Studies and Liberal Arts at UT'
Jane Ohlmeyer (Trinity College, Dublin), 'Making Ireland English'
Dane Kennedy (George Washington University), 'Lost Expeditions, Lost Histories'
Round Table Discussion, 'Racial and Social Prejudice in British and American Universities': Holly McCarthy (British Studies), Wm. Roger Louis (British Studies), and Tom Palaima (Classics)
Andrew O'Shaughnessy (University of Virginia), 'The Men Who Lost America'
John Milton Cooper (University of Wisconsin), 'Colonel House and the British'
Lawrence Goldman (Institute of Historical Research, London), 'The Oxford Dictionary of National Biography and National Identity'